INFORMAL MARKET WORLDS – READER

PETER MÖRTENBÖCK, HELGE MOOSHAMMER,
TEDDY CRUZ, FONNA FORMAN

INFORMAL MARKET WORLDS

READER

THE ARCHITECTURE OF ECONOMIC PRESSURE

NAI010 PUBLISHERS

INTRODUCTION

The world's centres of gravity are shifting. Former peripheries are moving to centre stage, challenging not only the economic dominance of the Western powers but the very system on which the established global order has been operating. Informal activities are a crucial factor in this transformation, extending the reach of novel business and commercial formations into ever new areas. Once understood as a marginal phenomenon, informal economies are rapidly becoming a primary focus of efforts to direct future developments, and the attempts of competing politi-co-economic power constellations to integrate these emerging markets are now a significant source of conflict. But informality is not just an economic issue. Informal markets are also places of intense social interaction, fostering cultures of different values and alternate relations. They are not only sites of the circulation of mone-tary values but also places where questions of resource sustainability, cooperative decision making, and social cohesion come into play — issues that acquire critical importance in times of crisis.

This reader forms part of a two-volume publication: While the objective of its sister volume, the *Informal Market Worlds* atlas, is to put informal markets on the map[1] — rendering visible the fault lines within global economic governance — this collection of essays written by leading scholars in the fields of architecture, sociology, spatial culture, urban anthropology and globalization studies aims to address what is at stake in the politics of informality in the age of global markets. What connects the chapters of this book is their quest to identify, analyze and engage with the competing interests that are directing today's political framing and application of the concept of informality in different parts of the world.

When the anthropologist Keith Hart, one of the contributors to this volume, coined the term "informal economy" in his article on "Informal Income Opportunities and Urban Employment in Ghana" in 1973, he was motivated in part by a dissatisfaction with the ignorance of hegemonic economic discourses and the conceptual failure of "western categories" to grasp a significant share of the world's economic goings-on.[2] Since then, among the many things that have changed in global economic politics is a surging interest in informality, its varying conditions, ramifications and poten-tials. Numerous conferences have been held on issues across multiple dimensions of informality, from informal labour and informal finance to informal dwelling and the informal city to informal governance and informal power. International and de-velopment studies programmes at major world institutions and leading universities are now investigating the informal sector in a range of different contexts. And in the area of architectural education, field trips to developing countries that include working on improvement schemes for informal marketplaces and designing low-cost infrastructure have almost become a staple of curriculums.

While estimates of the size of the informal economy vary — in some accounts encom-passing more than half of all economic activities in certain regions[3], in others affecting up to two thirds of their working populations[4] — it represents a huge potential market.

Initially the notion of informality was primarily embraced by institutions such as the International Labour Organization (ILO), which sought to promote highly regulated economies, equating informality with a passive suffering of underemployment (i.e. lack of employment opportunities) that needed to be overcome. There are increasing signs now that this framing has shifted toward an awareness of the appeal of a "culture of informality" and its influence on the interaction between state and society. A 2007 regional flagship publication by the World Bank approached the steady rise of the informal economy in Latin America and the Caribbean in terms of a dialectic of "exclusion and exit".[5] Besides the often-cited mechanisms of exclusion, the tackling of which is commonly understood to fall within the reach of policy intervention, the report emphasized the impact of exit strategies — conscious decisions not to participate in the regulated economy — by large parts of the continent's population. Apart from problems of tax evasion and lack of social security, from the perspective of the World Bank, this withdrawal from officially recognized economic institutions poses a wider problem in the sense that it entails an evasion of paradigms of constant growth based on increasing production and efficiency.

This notion of independence — of making the organization of daily life contingent on a set of values that have more to do with the quality of social relations than the accumulation of wealth — has been at the core of many activist-led projects aiming to utilize informal arrangements as catalysts for alternative economies. Conceiving of the informal sphere as a habitat in its own right, these initiatives often draw on the spatial realities of informal organization in which relations revolve around structures of community and cooperation. Spurred by a sense of crisis regarding the limitations of delineable socio-economic models, these contrasting interests in informality are underpinned by a host of speculations and desires that are projected onto this other economy.

The aim of this volume is thus twofold. First, it seeks to sketch out the dynamics animating these multiple demands on informality and, second, it seeks to explore ways of breaking through dominant ways of framing these activities by engaging perspectives from within informal marketplaces as key elements in the forging of new economic protocols. While covering a wide selection of sites and diverse forms of engagement, a common thread that runs through the three sections of this volume is the way they probe the political mentality that shapes our understanding of and ways of dealing with informality: from discussing the operative capital generated by positing informal economies as the "other market" to analyzing the geopolitical conditions shaping the quest for a new political economy and from investigating the multiplicity of bottom-up realignments to examining the potential of informality to contribute to the architecture and spatial organization of our environments.

The essays included in Part I of this book provide an analysis of the growing interest among a wide range of stakeholders in informality's agency in the organization of human coexistence, both in terms of social relations in concrete, local contexts and, increasingly, at the level of global interaction. This shift in focus reflects the capacity of informal arrangements to mitigate the crisis-ridden logic of the capitalist system. An important point of departure for the chapters in this section is thus the perceived need to critically reflect on the reasons behind informality's increased relevance as well as to speculate about dispositions that lend themselves to the emergence of an alternative political economy.

This discussion is opened up by Helge Mooshammer's introductory essay, which examines the power structures and instruments involved in the politics of informality. He argues that the parameters of informality are not a given but a matter of definition, that the value systems attached to the informal are thus an issue of framing and perspective, of interest and intention. As a consequence, the rise of informal markets as a global phenomenon needs to be understood as situated in a complex web of economic, territorial and ideological interests: the struggle between bottom-up responses to the polymorphic geographies of globalization and persistent top-down attempts to control the main capital of informal markets — collectively created trade environments.

A seminal voice in the debate about the operational value and political currency of informality is the economist Keith Hart, whose work has been ground-breaking in recognizing the significance of economic activities outside the radar of Western institutions. Drawing on a historical delineation of the close intertwinement between formal institutions and informal realities in economic interaction, Hart outlines the necessity of a much more pluralistic and inclusive approach to the relationship between formal and informal and the tension between controlled societal co-ordination (bureaucracy as "the power of public office") and the diversity of social life in a democratic system ("the power of the people"). Observing an informal take-over of the world by equally informalized finance industries — capital transactions outside the reach of national government policies — he alerts us to the urgent need to conceive new political instruments and establish new social contracts in order to overcome the destructive legacy of three decades of neoliberal deregulation.

Saskia Sassen's account of the dialectic frenzy between shrinking economies and growing expulsions echoes the sentiment that we are not simply witnessing a particularly difficult phase in the cyclical development of free markets. Sassen points out that we are facing a systemic edge in which the associated acceleration of global inequality is not merely an expression of prevailing economic conditions but has become the guiding principle of the global business of debt-mongering and profit-making. The process of counteracting this negation, Sassen insists, has to begin with making the expelled conceptually visible, with conceiving of an informal jurisdiction. What are the spaces of the expelled? They are not simply dark holes; they are complex sites that are present everywhere.

In her analysis of the global rise of microfinance and the visual politics surrounding it, Ananya Roy shows how aesthetic recognition has been employed in reframing the plight of the world's poor, transforming them from a dead "non-contributing" residue into a laboratory for creative capitalism. Key to this integrative orientation of "bottom billion capitalism" is a combination of informally orchestrated micro-creditor/debtor relations and a discursive readjustment of informality along economic benchmarks and imperatives of heroic self-entrepreneurship. As Roy argues, affective capital (community coercion, emotional appeal to distant customers, etc.) plays a strategic role in opening up these new market worlds.

The historical consistency of this logic is elaborated in detail in Ignacio Valero's genealogy of the naturalization of capitalism in Western societies and the ongoing transition in the exploitation and alienation of the masses from the proletariat to the cognitariat and "emotariat", the precarious workers of our times whose main assets targeted by speculative markets are their hearts and minds. Contrasting the prevailing chrematistics — the obsession with short-term accumulation of monetary value — with his *EcoDomics* concept, Valero proposes an ecological practice of human and non-human interaction, one in which a triangulated interconnection between *Oikos* (hearth, home, household), *Aisthesis* (matter, senses) and *Koinos* (sociality, community) may lead us to an art of living and making (in) common(s).

Examining the conditions for intervening in the incessant marketization of global relations, the first section of the book concludes with Gayatri Chakravorty Spivak's response to the occupiers of Wall Street in 2011. In her exploration of the conditions informing a contemporary "What is to be Done?", Spivak warns against mistaking the creativity of informal markets for a sign of liberation and against separating engagement with the economic realities of the Global South from scrutinization of the manoeuvres of the financial complex of the Global North. She argues that in order to ensure a consistent and comprehensive perspective all instances of democratic intervention will have to be oriented toward educating an undeterred will to social justice and building the public institutions required to cultivate it.

Sharing a focus on the global enmeshment of informal markets and the increasing pressure at the bottom of the economic pyramid, the chapters in Part II turn toward examining informality not as a phenomenon born solely out of local circumstances but as embedded in global politico-economic logics. The reference points for these critical analyses and engagements thus include not only specific places and regions but also distant sites of decision-making, such as multi-national trade associations, global nodes of the financial industries and elite forums of international politics.

The opening essay by Peter Mörtenböck traces these multifarious strata of interference in informal traders' everyday lives. It locates informal markets as paradigmatic sites of territorial and conceptual mobilizations that unfold by means of transient land use, flexibilized citizenships, and transnational networks of "grey" production. Here, spatial organization is accorded a signifying role in the continuous processes of global political restructuring. Pivotal to the success of emerging attempts to counter-balance this situation (international street trader associations, new civic institutions, etc.), Mörtenböck argues, are thus steps that go beyond the reduction of informal markets to a concept of space and instead embrace them as spheres of a counter-public, as an expression of social praxis.

AbdouMaliq Simone and Rika Febriyani's study of informal produce markets in Jakarta that have nested themselves into the spatial and temporal voids of urban infrastructures and official governance demonstrates how formal and informal arrangements are not opposing features but complimentary practices of life in a twenty-first-century mega-city that exist *within* each other and are supported by a web of mutual aspirations and diffusions. Their observations reveal that this interdependency should not be equated with a kind of stable equilibrium. Instead, we need to take into account the fluid transitions between an upheld indeterminacy as a prerequisite of informal trade and the deteriorating livelihoods of the urban poor in the wake of macro-changes in urban economies.

Moving on to the media markets of Bangalore, Lawrence Liang takes us on a tour through the intricate labyrinth of cultural references and transnational trade relations unfolding in the deals of global stakeholders. Teasing out how corporate decisions have shaped the availability of technological resources in Southeast Asia and how these outcomes have in turn been appropriated through the acquisition of cross-cultural knowledge helps to challenge dominant narratives about the informal being inescapably subordinate. Yet Liang's essay also highlights how moments of economic self-determination are consistently met with violent policing by the state as a proxy for vested interests.

In the majority of disputes about pirated goods and copyright infringements, China is presented as the main culprit. In "Informal China" Jiang Jun embarks on an epic journey through the historical evolution of the country's political, economic and cultural mindset. Beginning in the eight century B.C.E. and exploring the divergent interests of agriculturally based, centralized rule on the one hand and trade-oriented port cities on the other, the rise and fall of China as a maritime power during the Yuan and Ming dynasties, Communist rule and the evolution of "socialism with Chinese characteristics", in which development is the only absolute principle, Jun sketches the overarching tensions in governance between the cultivation of an "economic" spirit as expressed in peripheral, informal, bottom-up activities and territorially exercised control. In the past decades, the maxim of "seeking common ground while allowing for minor differences" has become spatially imprinted in the country's development of Special Economic Zones, in-between spaces straddling the inside and outside of liberalized markets, geographically, ideologically and socially.

Urban transformation is also at the core of Vyjayanthi Rao and Vineet Diwadkar's essay about the displacement of informal trade in the cities of Ahmedabad and Mumbai. Their documentation of emerging patterns of spatio-political intervention in marginalized economies shows how informality is conceived of foremost as a problem of governance in the formalization of markets in post-colonial contexts. The ensuing patterns of intervention not only dispossess people. Indifferent to the spatial logics of informal economies, the disciplinary matrix of enforced boundaries and regulations violates and destroys the complex foundations of informal social ecologies based on the flux of collective resource adaptations and situational absorption.

The task at hand is thus not a reconciliation between the formal and the informal. Indeed, what emerges from these analyses is the insight that an integration of informality exclusively geared to hegemonic economic and political paradigms raises the dual threat of augmenting the exploitative dimensions of informality while eroding the social and cultural wealth of informal relations. In "Speculative Futures", the last chapter of the second section of this book, Matias Viegener opens up the discussion of how to think differently about our implicatedness in these processes through an experimental engagement in the aesthetics of informality. Unravelling the relations between social practice and cognitive capitalism, Viegener revisits emblematic sites of artistic engagement with informality. Highlighting the precariousness of symbolic intervention in an environment of naturalized markets, he insists that we must focus precisely on the changing nature of capital when searching for alternative ways of exchange.

Employing dialogic formats in its analysis of informal spatial production, Part III of this book discusses the possibilities for a changing practice of engagement with informality. In their introductory chapter, Teddy Cruz and Fonna Forman continue the search for critical as well as productive ways of intervening in the politics of informality. They seek to determine how structural improvements in the informal city can contribute to developing a more sustainable economic environment rather than propelling the privatization of the urban realm through formalization: How can we foster ways of encroachment that interrupt the logics of solely profit-oriented markets without themselves emulating capitalist entrepreneurship? As Cruz and Forman's concluding conversation with the architects Alejandro Echeverri and Jean-Philippe Vassal — which is complemented by a set of responses from activists, artists, curators, and theorists, including atelier d'architecture autogérée [Constantin Petcou and Doina Petrescu], Marty Chen, Mauricio Corbalan, Emiliano Gandolfi, Hou Hanru, MAP Office [Laurent Gutierrez and Valérie Portefaix], Rahul Mehrotra, Alejandro Meitin, William Morrish, Henry Murraín, Robert Neuwirth, Kyong Park, Alessandro Petti, Marjetica Potrč, Lorenzo Romito, Lloyd and Susanne Rudolph, Saskia Sassen, Richard Sennett, STEALTH.ultd [Ana Džokić and Marc Neelen] and Jeanne van Heeswijk — makes clear, this implies taking into account a multitude of different perspectives well beyond the narrow framework put in place by official state and industry actors. Emphasizing the spatial performance of informality, this polyphonic analysis shows how such an endeavour requires an understanding of the informal that conceives of it less as an aesthetic category than as a set of everyday practices and processes while clearly recognizing the politics of aesthetics that are at stake.

Informal markets have emerged as a vital part of cities around the world. From the new mega-cities of the Global South to the old centres of political and economic power, they form complex sites of negotiation between multiple political demands, social actors and environmental constraints. Spurred by deregulation and accelerating global flows, they are in many instances tolerated as shock-absorbers of widening social divisions. Yet, whenever these markets show signs of establishing realms of their own, official rhetoric paints them as a threat to social and economic order, a response often followed by government-directed demolition, relocation or privatization. Examining the spatial, cultural and political trajectories of informal economies, the essays assembled in the *Informal Market Worlds* reader — together with the case studies in the atlas — open up an important arena for thinking about alternative approaches and how the practices and mechanisms that sustain informal milieus can contribute to the articulation of policies better adapted to the transnational realities of today's populations.

***

The making of this two-volume publication has been embedded in a multi-year and multi-sited research project based at the Institute of Art and Design at Vienna University of Technology and conducted in collaboration with the Visual Cultures Department at Goldsmiths College, University of London as well as the Center for Urban Ecologies and the Center on Global Justice at the University of California

San Diego (UCSD) and Hong Kong University's Shanghai Study Centre. The latter two institutions have been actively involved in hosting a series of onsite research forums that have been instrumental in shaping the direction and outcomes of this project. For the meeting in San Diego in February 2012 we would like to thank Misael Diaz and Amy Sanchez for organizing visits for the forum participants to marketplaces in the San Diego/Tijuana area and Geovanni Zamudio for providing assistance during our research in Tijuana. For the forum in Shanghai in November 2012 we owe sincere thanks to the then academic director of HKU's Shanghai Study Center, Pascal Berger, and to Jonathan D Solomon, who as dean of HKU's School of Architecture initiated the first steps that led to this gathering. Steven Chen, Daan Roggeveen and Bert de Muynck played important roles in programming the three-day workshop in Shanghai and we are grateful to them for facilitating a number of field trips in the Shanghai area.

Many of the authors represented in this publication have also contributed to these research forums and we would like to take this opportunity to thank them for their continuous support and commitment. We would also like to express our gratitude to Raul Cardenas, Cognate Collective, Julian D'Angiolillo, Alfonso Hernandez, Rick Lowe, Alfonso Morales, Gerald Murray, Fernando Rabossi and Brechtje Spreeuwers for their substantive contributions to the meetings in San Diego and Shanghai.

The research for and the production of this book would not have been possible without the financial support provided by the Austrian Science Fund (FWF), the International Research Centre for Cultural Studies Vienna, the School of Architecture and Planning at the Vienna University of Technology and the Department of Visual Arts at the University of California San Diego.

We are indebted to numerous colleagues and friends for reviewing and publishing earlier outcomes of this research and for hosting related talks and seminars at universities, conferences, museums and other venues. Among many others, we wish to thank Jorella Andrews, Gulsen Bal, Anette Baldauf, Andrew Ballantyne, Mabe Bethônico, Adrian Blackwell, Adam Bobbette, Brigitta Busch, Jonathan Darling, Cordula Gdaniec, Simon Harvey, Lydia Matthews, Mick O'Kelly, Irene Nierhaus, Doina Petrescu, Lee Rodney, Irit Rogoff, Caroline Schmitt, the late Werner Sewing, Chris Smith, Jilly Traganou, Renata Tyszczuk, Asta Vonderau, Aleksandra Wasilkowska, Richard Weston and Helen Wilson. Their generous invitations and comments have helped us to advance the public and pedagogical relevance of this research and have been indispensable to the process of refining the editorial framing of this publication.

The production of this book has further benefited from research assistance provided by several students at the Vienna University of Technology and the University of California San Diego, among them Jose Escamilla, who assisted with translation, and Aaron Cotkin, who served as our project coordinator and editorial assistant throughout the process. Many more students in studio and seminar courses have contributed with their work to mapping out the global landscape of informal markets. We also owe a debt of gratitude to Andreas Kofler and Mario Pruner for their assistance with the preparation of cartographic material for the *Informal Market Worlds* atlas volume and to Andreas Barnet for his invaluable help with setting up a website to present part of the research (www.othermarkets.org).

Sincere thanks are also due to Studio Grootens for their skilful design of both *Informal Market Worlds* volumes and to Joseph O'Donnell, who copy-edited the manuscript with great care and precision. Eelco van Welie, director of nai010 Publishers and committed mentor of our project, deserves special acknowledgment for his enduring and enthusiastic support during the realization of this publication.

Peter Mörtenböck, Helge Mooshammer, Teddy Cruz, Fonna Forman
January 2015

1   The accompanying atlas brings together more than 70 case studies on the spatial and visual culture of informal markets from around the world. Sites range from street vending in Bangkok's "red zones" and remittance trade on the Polynesian island of Tonga to Vietnamese markets on the Czech border and the 7th Kilometre container market outside Odessa, from Tijuana's sprawling *mercados sobreruedas* and the cross-border trade between Haiti and the Dominican Republic to Guangzhou's counterfeit markets and micro-retailing in Lima. Together, these portraits produce a comprehensive picture of newly emerging spatio-economic typologies of informal exchange and the ways they are adapted to the use of territorial, social and legal resources. Introductory cartographic analyses of the transnational trajectories characterizing these irregular economic and social forces provide multi-angle perspectives on these intersections of local particularities and global dynamics.
2   Keith Hart, "Informal Income Opportunities and Urban Employment in Ghana," *The Journal of Modern African Studies* 11, no. 1 (March 1973), 61–89. See also his chapter "How the Informal Economy Took Over the World" in this volume on pages 33–44.
3   Colin C. Williams and Friedrich Schneider, *The Shadow Economy* (London: Institute of Economic Affairs, 2013), 45–61.
4   Jacques Charmes, "Concepts, Measurements and Trends," in *Is Informal Normal? Towards More and Better Jobs in Developing Countries*, ed. Johannes P. Jütting and Juan R. de Laiglesia (Paris: OECD, 2009), 27–62.
5   Guillermo E. Perry et al., eds., *Informality: Exit and Exclusion* (World Bank: Latin American and Caribbean Studies, 2007).

PART I OTHER MARKETS

OTHER MARKETS: SITES AND PROCESSES OF ECONOMIC PRESSURE

Helge Mooshammer

In his posthumously published lecture "Of Other Spaces" (*Des espaces autres*), which he originally held in March 1967, Michel Foucault famously addresses the ways in which space in our epoch takes the form of relations among sites. He explains how during the twentieth century the paradoxical form of relations between different sites — simultaneities, entanglements and intersections — increasingly began to define our experience of the world and ultimately to determine which forms of circulation, exchange, emplacement and classification were perceived as suitable. Continuity and duration were replaced by processes of connection-making between different fields of action, which, depending on the status of their development and decay curves, present themselves as differently valued structures of opportunity.[1] While not explicitly mentioned among his line-up of gardens, cemeteries, brothels and ships, informal marketplaces are rich embodiments of such Foucauldian heterotopias, both in the sense of "heterotopias of crisis" providing shelter for the excluded as well as in the sense of "deviant heterotopias" harbouring all kinds of non-conformity.

A critical moment of rupture often lies at the root of informal markets' genesis, and as a consequence they are often located in territories marked by war, disaster and migration, where distinct groups of people are regarded as different and undesirable. One well-known example is the Arizona Market near Brčko in Bosnia-Herzegovina, which emerged at one of the most violently embattled intersections of ethnic frontlines during the disintegration of the Socialist Federal Republic of Yugoslavia. Similarly internationally entwined yet locally unfolding crises also triggered the temporary phenomenon of the Iranian Bazar in the Turkish city of Gaziantep, which emerged in response to the diversion of routes taken by pilgrims trying to circumnavigate the Middle East's many pockets of sectarian violence. As spaces of exception, informal markets simultaneously uphold systems of power while concentrating their negation in a particular locale where they engender encounters between otherwise incompatible trajectories. In this way, sites of alternative exchange in dropout communities like Quartzsite in southeastern California's Mojave Desert and the new wave of creative entrepreneurship at hipster markets around the world become places of both resistance and commodification.[2]

The role and function of these contemporary heterotopias are shaped by the ongoing mutations in the production of space from emplaced and extended spaces into sites of relations structured through proximity and distance, "simultaneity" and "juxtaposition".[3] In this sense, "other markets" refer to the multiplicity of economic and non-economic events that are brought together and relayed through informal markets.

This rise of informal sites and processes thrives on a new intensity of spatial relations boosted by technological progress and infrastructural advances. Laying the ground for recent decades of globalization and incessant economic integration, the accompanying boom in global wealth — worldwide GDP tripled from US$ 25 to 75 trillion between 1993 and 2013 — has not been followed by a corresponding demise of the informal economy. On the contrary, in many regions of the world, such as Latin America and the Caribbean, informal employment numbers have been steadily rising and continue to involve the majority of the working population.[4]

Foucault's relational model of spatial production reverberates in the dynamics of market transactions. Every exchange at a market takes place in relation to many other exchanges. Its conduct is thereby determined not only by the references of the particular site where it occurs but also by those of numerous others, near and far, involved in the intricate fabric of trade relations. Indeed, a key characteristic of market protocols is their capacity to enable contact and transmission between otherwise often incompatible spheres, either through regimes of externalization or the employment of boundary objects[5] that can move between different realms of meaning.

In the case of informal markets, externalization is key to how they operate. Social capital and family or community ties often form the crucial support structures that compensate for a lack of monetary means, insufficient equipment and supply shortages. Interacting with global chains of production, the microscale nature of informal markets depends on a mobile network of intermediaries that shuttle goods across hundreds of miles, relying on relations of kinship and trust to successfully carry out their business. The distribution centres for these atomized channels of commerce, such as the 7th Kilometre Market in Odessa, the now dismantled Cherkizovsky Market in Moscow or the Feirinha Madrugada in São Paulo, form the mega-nodes of informal trade. Employing hundreds of thousands of people, these intermediary markets constitute cities within cities. Politically induced periodic crackdowns on these transnational economic hubs by government officials ripple through to millions of livelihoods around the world.

In a seemingly paradoxical twist of economic logics, the relentless branding of consumer goods, which constitutes one of the key marketing strategies deployed by big corporations, prepares the ground for one of the most successful kinds of boundary objects in informal market transactions: Through the back door of counterfeit production and informal trade, the visual language of brands leverages the economic and social participation of a diverse set of actors on multiple levels. From the migrant workers doing "night run" shifts in Chinese factories and selling spill-overs at their local street markets to the African and Arab traders attending the big commodity fairs in newly emerging trade hubs such as Yiwu to the shops in Dubai's Karama Centre selling fake bags to foreign tourists, and the ostensibly vernacular artisan markets in Latin American cities, the heterotopias of informal markets fuse disparate times and spaces into a mutually aspired to climate of exchange by means of deception and compensation.

The rapid advance in information technologies has played an important role in the mushrooming of these transactions, ushering in a new quality of interconnectedness and thereby giving new meaning to the co-implicatedness of other spaces. Opening up new channels in the sourcing of producers, traders and buyers rearranges the directions and conventions of informal trade, and we are seeing a conspicuous proliferation of trade relations that substitute established trading strata and bypass the traditional choke points of reigning economic powers. Places like Yiwu in China, the self-styled small commodities capital of the world, or the Asian trade centres in Dubai are powerful manifestations of these developments. Undermining the intentions of major global economic institutions, increased levels of connectivity and the diversification of supply thus need not necessarily entail stronger market integration along the lines initially envisaged.

Tactics of Economic Diplomacy

Although the multiplication of informal economies proceeding parallel to formal global economic growth is creating an ever denser network of connections between individual marketplaces and dynamics at other locations, this interdependency cannot be equated with the possibility of exercising direct influence. At the same time, these developments show how new trading spaces are being opened up by improved transport and communication possibilities. As a result, attempts are being made via numerous channels to bring these substantial future markets of informal trading into the sphere of influence of established trading blocks. These include, on the one hand, direct attempts to undermine or dissolve the operational level of informal markets and, on the other, various strategies geared to influence the boundary conditions of informal economies in order to gradually divert the flow of these activities and ultimately absorb them into the interests of larger trading blocks. Rather than destroying informal trading networks, interventions of this kind often aim to achieve a far more fundamental reshaping of the economic landscape, one that not only targets informal commercial activities but is envisioned as reorientating entire national economies.

The annually published list of "notorious markets" — which is now a regular part of the Special 301 Reports released by the Office of the U.S. Trade Representative (USTR) — has developed into a particularly effective instrument which combines these two processes. Building on data supplied by organizations representing the interests of individual industries on the infringement of their copyrights and trademarks in particular marketplaces, the reports pillory a selection of countries and the regulatory arms of their state apparatuses. The core of these reports comprises lists of countries in which cases of economic piracy and counterfitting enterprises have been identified as well as recommendations as to how the protection of copyright can be improved, sanctions can be implemented and the barriers to free market access can be eliminated.[6] These lists play an important role in foreign trade policies because, backed by the threat of sanctions, they exercise a form of diplomatic pressure on other states geared to compelling national authorities to intervene in concrete marketplaces and thereby to secure access for foreign investors, producers and suppliers. Faced with this consequential linkage of the workings of local markets with their scope for action in the international diplomatic arena, governments throughout the world take careful note of their status in these reports and particularly of whether their countries appear on the annual "watch list" or "priority watch list".[7] Indicative of the orientation of current trading interests, these reports draw a global map of good and evil, with the latter exhibiting a conspicuous concentration on China, Southeast Asia and Latin America. In spite of the fact that, according to most assessments, the highest concentration of informal economies is found in North and Sub-Saharan Africa, this continent still seems to be a USTR blind spot.

The extensive influence of the Special 301 Reports is based on the openness of the parameters governing the way in which they are compiled. Apart from data provided by hundreds of interest groups, NGOs and individuals that specifically investigate rights infringements in informal markets throughout the world, most of the contributions come from businesses and associations such as Oxfam, Time Warner, the Motion Picture Association and the Washington-based International AntiCounterfeiting Coalition (IAAC). The annual reports are thus centrally organized compilations of facts, but the investigations on which the reports are based are conducted within a network of informal channels, where information is collected and inquiries are commissioned by commercial enterprises. The result of these ever more comprehensive investigations is an expanding body of factual information and reports that are becoming more extensive by the year. In the process, the Special 301 Reports have not only extended their range in terms of the quantity of information and the number of countries on the "watch list" but have also developed into a flexible instrument that mixes the application of law with the formulation of trade policy. While the original idea behind the report was to provide a legal basis for possible economic sanctions, it has now become more of an instrument of surveillance and admonition. The report has thus become a steering instrument that combines judicial power with political strategy. Although these two components are nominally kept separate, they are also "economically" coordinated: states targeted in the report are effectively being advised to step in as substitute regulatory instances to "rectify" the situation.[8]

These annual reports contain highly detailed descriptions of physical marketplaces deemed "notorious" because they infringe the rights of U.S. companies or citizens to protection of their intellectual property. Since 2005 these descriptions have no longer been part of the country reports but are instead included in a dedicated document titled "Notorious Markets". This change has been accompanied by a great flexibility of the criteria qualifying a market for inclusion in the annual report. The label "notorious" is now already attached to markets in regions where local authorities are neglecting to review their own approach to the theft of intellectual property.[9] Since 2011, selected cases have been presented to the public in a media-friendly "out-of-cycle review of notorious markets" shortly before the release of the more comprehensive Special 301 Report. This "hit parade" of informal markets lists marketplaces as diverse as La Salada in Buenos Aires, Tepito in Mexico City, Beijing's Silk Market, the Urdu Bazaars in Karachi and Lahore, the Petrivka Market in Kiev, the Harco Glodok shopping centre in Jakarta and the Lo Wu shopping centre in Shenzhen. Without having to back up the claims and demands associated with them, these lists have in the meantime become a worldwide reference for Twitter feeds and television news flashes about illegal economic activities — the ideal governance instrument for state and commercial actors aiming to give the public the right signal at the right time and to prepare the ground for intervention in marketplaces outside the USA.

What emerges from mapping the delinquencies of informal markets is not only a cartography of trademark violations and copyright infringements but a map of the world that renders the frontlines of late capitalism visible. As the urban theorist Ananya Roy has demonstrated in her extensive study of the struggles around policy agendas in microfinance, an engagement with the informal sector on behalf of centres of power is always also a question of managing the truth about our economic and social system.[10] The professionalization of microfinance investments indicates the tensions around the appropriation of the microcredit model — once conceived as an attempt to alleviate poverty by NGOs in developing countries — into the capital markets of the West. It is one of the key theatres for effectively integrating the productivity of the poor into global economic circuits.[11] Where microcredit operations once aimed, for instance, to improve the livelihoods of women in patriarchal societies, criteria of human development such as access to education, child mortality and self-sustainability in crisis situations are now being replaced by benchmarks based on operational costs, investment returns and transferability.

The establishment of such codes of best practice shifts the focus of engagement with the bottom of the economic pyramid. In this context, social capital is less valued as an intrinsic capacity of informal communities; rather it is framed as a potential asset for financial speculation. Simultaneously, these measures shape public opinion of the motivations, potentials and prospects of the economic activities of the poorest billion. While hard financial facts and parameters are given precedence when it comes to assessing and calculating engagement with the world's poor, this approach establishes the moral and ethical imperatives of a "natural" market economy. In a combination of allegedly unquestionable financial fact and ethical legitimization, the emerging narrative of microfinance's expertise provides justification for intervention by external actors in informal economies and for turning the social capital of the world's poor into the finance capital of global investors.

Roy's work on the transformation of microfinance from a development initiative into a speculative market has highlighted how politically administered excursions into new economic domains rely on a simultanous preparation of an accompanying discourse. These motives are clearly discernible, for example, in the way in which a recent flagship report by the World Bank on Latin America and the Caribbean presents the paradigms and triggers of informal economies in its introductory paragraphs.[12] Rather than proceeding from far more fundamental questions regarding inquality as a principle and motor of the capitalist market economy, the report, which draws on dominant literature in the field such as the theses of Hernando de Soto, refers in the first place to "burdensome entry regulations" as the reason for the exclusion of small firms and traders from what is euphemistically termed the "circuits of the modern economy". Moreover, the fact that informal working conditions are not only found among the self-employed and those working in small firms but that large enterprises also make informal arrangements with their workers is attributed above all to "excessive tax and regulatory burdens". Framed as decisions not to participate in formal institutions, these phenomena are interpreted as blunt social indictments of failures of states' enforcement capabilities, the rectification of which is high on the agenda of instruments such as the Special 301 Reports.

These statements are followed by the converse argument that the most urgent econom-ic-policy steps required to curtail informal economies and reduce the correspondingly low level of engagement of people with the institutions of the state are the reduction of taxes and charges as well as a general deregulation and disencumbering of the economies in these countries. Measures to achieve "more enabling investment cli-mates" suggested in the World Bank publication on informality in Latin America and the Caribbean range from reforming labour markets and reducing "excessive labor costs, whether arising through labor legislation or unrealistic union demands (such as exaggerated minimum wages, severance costs, or labor taxes and contributions)" to reforming welfare programmes so that free social protection services do not un-dermine contribution-based formal systems, and from simplifying tax laws in order to increase access to markets, services and bank credit to strengthening enforcement by the state.[13] Favouring such measures is in line with the conventional ideas of inter-national economic associations regarding the harmonization and opening of global markets and the promotion of similar principles in other spheres of socio-economic organization (provision of education, housing and pensions or the governance of the digital sector, information technologies and other public domains).

With this orientation to government failures, the discourse on informality acquires two tasks: first, the identification of informal economies as a negative condition and, second, the reinforcement of the call to tackle informality. For instance, the Cluster for Research on the Informal Sector and Policy (CRISP) based at Sheffield University in the UK, which brings together some of the most influential academic opinions in the field of international policy formulation, sees its mission as one of seeking "un-derstanding of the characteristics of the informal sector and the motives for people working in the informal sector so that policies can be formulated for tackling this issue", and draws its rationale from the fact that "across the world, what needs to be done about this informal sector is becoming a priority issue for many governments."[14] One of the main features of this attitude is its tendency to present the phenomenon of informality as an effect of external circumstances and thereby to generate the causal foundation for the necessity and possibility of interventions. Whether informality is described as a residue accompanying economic advances or as a complimentary by-product of fast-paced market cycles, it is above all posited as an inferior condition marked by poverty, failing states, irresponsibility, illegality and criminality.[15]

Rather than engaging in a disciplinary dispute about the rights and wrongs of each position, it seems more productive to consider the dynamics behind these ma-noeuvres to define and apply distinct conceptualizations of informality, its causes and consequences. What kind of power struggle is implemented through a rhetoric that ties the formal and informal economy into a dichotomy grounded on a normative notion of form? The diversity of the informal markets we have studied in the framework of the Other Markets project notwithstanding, what emerges as a key pattern when looking at the contradictory histories of government interventions in these places is the deployment of politico-juridical instruments to allocate properties and rights to particular economic endeavours. Through framing certain informal activities as illegal and inducing policing actions, these realignments clear the ground for privi-leged groups of actors. Strikingly, these interventions often occur at moments when the operations of informal marketplaces are deemed to have become too successful. While these measures are ostensibly carried out through judicial channels, in many instances the overall picture is one of political arbitrariness and discrimination against particular social or ethnic groups — whether in the case of the closures of Moscow's gigantic Eurasian markets in Izmailovo and the Vietnamese-run Four Tigers Market in Budapest, the U.S.-aided transformation of the Arizona Market in Bosnia Herzegovina into a privately owned shopping mall or the struggle of São Paulo street vendors against the corrosion of their organizational strength by a spatio-adminis-trative splintering of license regulations.

Informality is thus a matter of definition. Defining the characteristics of infor-mality becomes pivotal in paving the way to, first, identifying informal economies in specific areas and, consequently, initiating state actions to counteract the alleged threats posed by them. In this way, informality is used as an umbrella term for all sorts of activities that could constitute a "drag on growth", as the World Bank flagship report on Latin America and the Caribbean puts it. In other words, rather than sim-ply capturing a quasi-inevitable by-product or intrinsic component of the capitalist economy, the concept of informality engenders a set of actions attuned to particular hegemonic beliefs and strategic interests in market expansion. The definition of concrete processes as informal is part of a long-term strategy of opening up new markets, geographically as well as in terms of different population segments. This is not to say that the situations addressed by the term informality do not entail adverse conditions of poverty, exploitation and abuse. Yet the way the concept of informality has been appropriated by international economic institutions since its emergence in the 1970s has resulted in its transformation into an instrument for orchestrating top-down change along specific lines of socio-economic organization.

This instrumentalization of informality, which is orientated less to the development of an understanding of its implications than to the pros and cons of external inter-vention, also raises questions regarding the widespread preoccupation of academic discourse with the "correct" conception of informality, one that dominates the majority of informality studies.[16] Indeed, the very conflict about the deficiencies in defining and covering all forms of informal activities manifests how the concept of informality in these discourses is less a question of acknowledging the diversity of everyday realities than one of establishing referential frameworks attuned to the ideologies of competing actors and institutions. It follows that the fact that informality is both up for debate and at the same time on trial is an expression of targeted economic-political interven-tion. In this context, informality as such serves not so much as an instrument in its own right as does the introduction of formality as a new measure in order to discredit certain markets and privilege others. However, the duality of formal economies and their supposedly inferior informal counterpart effectively shifts attention to the latter even though the source of conflict is actually to be found in the demands of interest groups whose operations are legitimized as formal. Cases in point are the Special 301 Reports discussed above as well as the numerous measures introduced to coordinate and integrate markets in the course of establishing trade agreements. Informal thus denotes not simply that which happens "outside state regulation"[17] but in particular that which does not allow for access by the capitalist market circuits of the Global North.

Struggles over Registering Informality

Capitalism relies on state intervention to prepare economies for wealth accumulation and to safeguard investments. Global finance, in particular, has conjured up numerous techniques and strategies for employing the state and its institutions to manage and intervene in economies according to its fluctuating interests. The build-up and subsequent fall-out of the international debt crisis from 2007 onwards has brought to the fore a vociferous campaign to cultivate a political climate conducive to the creation of new investment opportunities coupled with the demand for a redirection of the associated risks. While keeping profits private, countless governments worldwide have been coerced into assuming liability for speculation that has gone wrong and covering accumulated debt with recources from state budgets. The ensuing meltdown of the so-called "real economy" that led to widespread unemployment and the destruction of the wealth of the masses has, on the one hand, paved the way for demanding further "adjustments" of national economies (privatization of public enterprises and property, deregulation of markets) and, on the other, pushed large segments of populations into the realm of informality, which may as a consequence be subject to demands for regulatory intervention.[18]

In the case of policies around informality we are also being confronted with the bundling of complex problems, which are taken as a basis for calling for appropriate interventions by national authorities and international bodies. It remains questionable, though, to what degree these problems should be confined to issues of economic regulation and enforcement. Given the microscale and subsistence character of many of these activities, many of the social challenges associated with informality could be addressed through re-thinking the relationship between societies and their institutions in the light of global inequality rather than through the integration of informality into top-down controlled global markets. Tax regimes, for instance, could well be arranged differently, targeting areas of significant profit generation rather than whole populations as a default measure. The charge of tax evasion would then not apply to the majority of what are essentially economies of survival. Similarly, social protection could be tied to programmes of general rights and provisions based on schemes of redistribution rather than individually financed insurance requiring a controlled labour market. When it comes to securing standards and protecting consumers, on a local level at least, community controls and cooperative arrangements have managed to meet these needs without state bureaucracies in many places for a long time. What remains then as the core of incentive programmes to reduce informality are issues of intellectual property rights (IPRS) and market integration.

The development and dividing up of markets in accordance with IPRS and their enforcement has become a major structuring instrument in increasingly knowledge-based economies. The accompanying interplay of political moves fuelled by the lobbying of powerful economic players conjures up a nexus of the informal and the illegal, which becomes popularized by mass media and high-profile legal actions. The process leading up to Morocco becoming the first developing country to sign the Anti-Counterfeiting Trade Agreement (ACTA) in October 2011, for instance, was facilitated by diplomatic pressure based on reports by U.S. political and economic sections abroad on the infringement of copyright at Casablanca's "infamous black market" of Derb Ghallef.[19] The exercise of definitional sovereignty over Moroccan governmental offices was channelled into bringing the country into line with the requirements of "liberalized" markets by demanding an improvement of economic administration and enforcement operations as well as access for foreign investors and corporations, particularly to the new markets of services and information technologies. The correlation between growing state intervention and a rise of informal activities, as Portes and Haller have observed in their account of the paradox of state control,[20] becomes apparent in these manoeuvres by the state, which involve applying measures to selected economic sectors on behalf of influential sets of interests.

In this sense, informality is a relational concept. The critical role questions of perspective play in the politics of informality becomes evident in the plurality of approaches toward framing what constitutes informality. That the question of measuring informality has come to dominate the debate ties into a logic whose aim is to steer particular developments within labour markets, capital flows and trade relations. Indeed, the differentiation of multiple subcategories and aspects specifically addressing the situation of migrants, women or selected economic activities and the ways in which these are targeting concrete regions such as developing countries, the former Eastern Bloc or migrant quarters in Western metropolises highlight above all the currently increasing appetite of major economic powers for access to these areas.

Informality is an effect of capitalism. Capitalism produces informality — not merely in the direct sense of keeping part of the world's population in inferior conditions but by means of political definitions that render certain segments of economic life informal in order to allow for outside intervention. Yet the major obstacle facing these ambitions is that activities divided into formal and informal in this way are often complexly intertwined. Moreover, informal economies are often capable of functioning independently through elaborate forms of organization that they develop on their own. The shadow economies of migrant and marginalized communities and countries kept in a state of dependence frequently interact with the circuits of "formal" capital but in many cases also maintain other networks of exchange and communication, which escape direct control and are only partly susceptible to outside manipulation.

Even if selected marketplaces are routinely portrayed as violating the norm and thereby transformed into sites of exception, closer inspection reveals that the majority of them are in fact variations on regional norms and form part of a historic sequence of related phenomena. The container markets in Eastern Europe followed a longstanding fashion of modular spatial production instantiated by the kiosk trade, which had come to service serially erected mass residential quarters. Many street and open-air markets in African and Asian countries that have been singled out as hotbeds of illegal trade also represent developments within a long tradition of market relations. What marks them as objects of contestation over formal and informal attributes is often their exposure to assimilation attempts by national or international powers. The conflicting intentions involved range from the nationalist agenda in 1940s Thailand promoting one flea market per village to secure economic independence from its neighbouring powers to the colonial spread of modernist planning objectives favouring functionalist cities that saw the prohibition of street trade in many Latin American countries and the revival of such policies in many places in Africa and Asia in recent years to prepare the way for Western style shopping malls and entertainment districts.[21]

What becomes evident in the proliferation of policies targeting informal markets is a significant shift in ways of exercising power. If twentieth-century power was founded on managing populations in discrete spaces, the control of markets has become a key priority in today's environment of transnational capital flows. The battle for profit and power unfolds around the hunt for identifying, occupying, expanding and creating new investment opportunities. These speculations bank on a solidifying allegiance of the political classes to paradigms of neoliberal economics. The intensifying stranglehold of a capitalist mentality on the business of politics has turned governance into a matter of economic performance. Policies around informality are thus shaped by a myriad of deferred motifs far outweighing more immediate issues relating to the well-being of people involved in the day-to-day operations of informal economies. The arbitrary mix of media power and wealth grabbing, of populism and corruption at work here is epitomized by a globally circulating anecdote about the reasons behind the closure of Cherkizovsky Market in Moscow, one of the major nodes of Eurasian informal trade that sheltered a large number of displaced communities: the sudden action was allegedly triggered by annoyance among Russian politicians about the ostentatious birthday celebrations of one of the oligarch owners at a Turkish luxury resort.

The merger between formal and informal played out through the phalanx of market liberalization, de-regulation and harmonization points towards the prevailing rationale that underpins this race for economic supremacy. The primary aim of newly appropriated frontiers is not to be integrated on an equal level but to accommodate externalized risks and costs associated with speculative markets. In this sense, the role of informal markets (as the "other" markets) is already implemented in the establishment of formal trading operations. In order to protect their investments, individual actors constantly seek to appoint and create subordinate sites to mitigate elements of crisis. Informal markets thus emerge at and become attached to a variety of critical points in the neoliberal market economy, beginning with leveraging the volatility of supply and demand in the case of the gigantic intermediate markets with their shuttle traders and networks of small scale sweatshops[22] and ending with absorbing the wastefulness of throw-away consumerism and the crisis of environmental degradation in the global hubs of recycling markets.[23]

However, this strategy of outsourcing is far from an easily manageable process and is marked by numerous contradictions and conflictual movements. In fact, it is precisely this modality of deferral that also opens up a space for deviations and resistance. Even if power, and the market economy for that matter, is prone to increasing abstraction, it still relies on its actual performance to become effective. Power, again following a Foucauldian perspective, is not simply imposed on subjects but instilled through orchestrating their actions.[24] In that power has to pass through their bodies and be performed accordingly, subjects become relays in the flows of power. Whether intentionally or not, each one of these power-affirming acts entails an element of divergence from prescribed protocols and norms. Constituting sites of intense concentrations of people, informal markets embody particularly high risks of deviation. The most prevalent expression of the diversion of power is the production of counterfeit goods. While off-shoring production and, increasingly, services constitutes a staple measure of post-industrialist economies aimed at securing high profit margins for investors in their home countries, this measure cannot simply be achieved through commanding supply networks but requires a deferral of production know-how as well. With the shift to higher-skilled lines of production and high-tech products, exposure to rights infringements (i.e. the redirection of power in the form of knowledge appropriation) increases.

The umbrella concept of informality in international policies thus often covers the focal points of these undesired activities by groups of people otherwise attributed a subordinate position. The expanding scope of knowledge transfer that propels the global economy lends power an inconvenient degree of precariousness and explains the rise in efforts to combat the spread of informal knowledge distribution (Special 301 programme, TRIPS agreement, ACTA, etc.). The annual changes in markets listed by the Special 301 Reports as well as the highly selective focus on certain marketplaces, featuring book markets in India or the distribution of software and media products in China and Latin America, indicate current critical intersections in the flows of power and looming economic confrontations. Yet the procurement of information for Special 301 Reports via filings from industry lobbyists might itself be deemed informal. Indeed, as Portes and Haller have pointed out, the more state officials are enlisted to service particular interests, "as de facto employees of outside entrepreneurs", the more "informal" the interaction of free market forces becomes, essentially erasing the demarcations of the formal market these interventions are supposedly meant to protect.[25]

The Commoning of Markets

While recognizing that informal economies are established through projections, through the deferral of future options and as theatres of global interest, the emerging tissue of knowledge societies that spreads through these sites also poses the question whether and in what ways these marketplaces yield instances amenable to appropriating resources, redirecting power relations and allowing other interests to surface. In other words, what forms of other markets can be engendered through the workings of the informal economy beyond the neoliberal paradigm of unfettered growth and wealth accumulation? If the potentiality of change is envisaged as bound to a shift in power relations, then interventions in dominant systems of reference and the establishment of alternative registers to the top-down framing of formal/ legal and informal/illegal become key. Sidestepping folkloristic conceptions of an indigenous exchange economy, changing technological capacities provide the clue to emergent landscapes of re-distributed creativity and the proliferation of novel forms of capital. Changing access to information, in particular, can fundamentally disempower the operational force of the scarcity paradigm as an overriding market regulative. The ability of Kenyan market women to check the availability of and demand for certain commodities or compare prices at different markets via mobile phones not only liberates them from a dependency on manipulative middlemen but also subverts conventional notions of centre and periphery, of whose capital counts and of what is deemed superfluous.

The concomitant dissolution of structures of control is contributing to a steady atomization of economic activities. Widely perceived through the lens of casualization, the intrusion of economic considerations into ever more aspects of life facilitated by new technologies and social media brings with it a hitherto unknown convertibility and ease in switching between different roles. The spread of apps advertising microjobs and services — tasks that can be undertaken flexibly and in a short time without further obligations or requiring special equipment — form part of the wider crowd-sourcing movement, the consequences of which for conventional systems of capital circulation have yet to be fully comprehended. The paradoxical question is whether this all-encompassing invasiveness of economic operations and their infinite disintegration into tradable units in effect causes the normative power of established economic forces to evaporate. If through the simultaneous engagement with multiple platforms of microtrade, one is constantly switching between being a trader at one moment and someone else at another, the descriptive power of being confined to one role and position also diminishes.

What is at stake in these experiments is thus the question of who and what bestow meaning on particular economic activities. In much of the literature on informality, social ties, variously affirmed through rites of solidarity, ethnic communities and family relations, are cited as essential frameworks for operations in informal markets.[26] In the case of the recent phenomenon of hipster markets, though, the logics of this relation are reversed. Rather than being employed as a tool for concluding economic transactions, the creation and affirmation of social ties becomes an equally relevant reason for participating in these markets. Notwithstanding many other aspects involved in the promotion of hipster markets, such as their role as harbingers of gentrification or the glorification of commodified subject formation, the onset of economic decisions becoming directed by social desires heralds a tipping point in the global economic power balance. What makes these developments so decisive is their global spread in the wake of the establishment of new creative classes, establishing their own realms in many pockets of the world and multiplying centres of activity from New York to Bangkok.[27]

A technology-induced atomization of decisions brings with it a distinct uncontrollability as well as a potential for bottom-up value generation. When informality becomes a permanent condition, this situation can no longer be relegated by mechanisms of exclusion administered through agents of the formal state. Erecting networks of informal exchange facilitated by new technologies provides the first steps toward counteracting the de-territorialization strategies of late capitalism. Not unlike the demands of many indigenous communities for the "right to antenna" as they embark on strategies of territorialization on their path to recognition, the claiming of space which is enacted through informal markets becomes a decisive step in objecting to the ongoing privatization of the public sphere. The widely imitated response by authorities entailing the displacement of public marketplaces to privately run facilities ties in with the corporate de-politicization of urban encounters by substituting street life with the consumption of prescribed entertainment. In this context, the campaigns of street vendors against the wholesale criminalization of their existence and for their right to operate in public space are fostering crucial catalytic communities that are forming the vanguard of contemporary civic movements. Contesting the capacities of public space is a vital part of claiming one's role in the political sphere, of reclaiming *res publica*.

Attributing a state of informality has come to serve as a convenient vehicle for top-down intervention — describing something as the other for a particular purpose — and it is high time we engaged with these assemblages from the perspective of those who are implicated in them. One of the most important avenues of inquiry that presents itself here has to do with the ways in which informal markets engage in practices of commoning — whether in the form of young peer groups congregating around the exchange of lifestyle accessories or of street vendors joining forces in their legal battles. Besides providing livelihoods for themselves, the biggest achievement of informal traders as a whole lies in the creation of a unique common good, the establishment of a market environment. Informal markets are not a naturally given occurrence but only come into being through collective action and contribution. It is precisely this scope and value of informal markets as an economic resource that triggers the interest of outside parties. Similar to the contestations around the control of and profit extraction from other common, pooled resources, questions concerning the people involved in informal markets are overshadowed by struggles over how to best appropriate the capital flows generated by this trade.

Much of the discussion about dealing with informal markets therefore echoes the arguments around the best management of commons. "What is common to the greatest number has the least care bestowed upon it. Everyone thinks chiefly of its own, hardly at all of the common interest"[28]: Aristotle is quoted by Elinor Ostrom in the introduction to her seminal 1990 book *Governing the Commons* to underline how the so-called "tragedy of the commons" has come to dominate Western thinking about the individual use of common-pool resources. For centuries, the all-pervasive conclusion has been that "where a number of users have access to a common-pool resource, the total of resource units withdrawn from the resource will" — inevitably it appears — "be greater than the optimal economic level of withdrawal"[29]. As Ostrom points out, the two most commonly recommended solutions to this problem derive from an intervention by an external agent that places the management of a common-pool resource in the hands of private enterprises or a centrally organized state authority, the latter being based on the reasoning that if "private interests cannot be expected to protect the public domain then external regulation by public agencies, governments, or international authorities is needed"[30]. Most of the "solutions" applied to the frictions around informal markets follow this template and combine both privatization and state-interventist measures.

These policies draw in particular on arguments around the resource of space as a vital resource of society itself, one that determines how we co-exist and interact with one another. This has become a key plane of contestation in the conflicts around informal markets, which are routinely accused of irresponsibly blocking and congesting public space. The presence of a monitoring and controlling authority is repeatedly claimed to be crucial to ensuring if not a fair then at least a safe way of co-existing. The aim of planning with regard to the common resource of space is thus predominantly directed toward maintaining order vis-à-vis otherwise chaotic and anarchic instances of urban conduct. Hence, every spatial activity that falls outside the reach of the planning authority and evades its regulations, such as the spatial arrangements of informal markets, is considered a failure of planning, of its institutional mandate to provide for a governed usage of space. However, as Ostrom has pointed out, one of the main difficulties for any centrally controlled agency of resource management lies in the sheer impossibility of always having all relevant information at hand to substantiate its regulations and decisions in a way that is appropriate to the actual demands and situations on the ground. Particularly in a globalized world, where not only are local situations being increasingly implicated in global developments but the macro constellations themselves are subject to rapid and constant change, the sufficient development and successful application of up-to-date and appropriate regulations seem to become an insurmountable challenge.

The main question that emerges in the light of this problematic is thus whether recognizing informal markets as a form of commons can provide beneficial inspiration for future global co-existence. Investigating this issue requires an engagement with the capacities of informal markets beyond strictly economic categories. First, as an instance of self-organization, can informality provide an environment conducive to the development of alternative responses to the "tragedy of the commons" that neither advocate total individualization in the form of private enterprises nor rely indispensably on top-down governance? Approaches to such modes of cooperative organization are already evident in the work of many street vendor associations and alliances between trade unions and neighbourhood assemblies to develop urban infrastructures from the bottom up. The key point here is how intelligence on the ground can be utilized to organize collective action for the general good. Framing the general good in both the longer as well as the short term leads to the second point, which again mirrors many contemporary discussions of the commons, namely whether the elasticity and social groundedness of informal economies might provide the foundation for a more responsible and sustainable way of dealing with resources, both natural and social. Over the past 35 years, global resource extraction has grown steadily, and, if it continues at it current rate, will reach the 100-billion-tonne mark by 2030, almost double the amount extracted in 2005. Much of this incessant resource exploitation is propelled by a parallel acceleration in urbanization. It is predicted that by 2025, two thirds of the world's population will be living in urban agglomerations. In many parts of the world, informal systems play a vital role in the socio-economic fabric supporting these processes of urban expansion. Given this intricate involvement in structuring contemporary urban life, informality is predestined to occupy a central position in developing more resourceful urban economic modes.

Rather than portraying informality as a "drag on growth", we could conceive of it as encouraging alternative moments of growth and vigour. Much in the way that Arjun Appadurai or Paul Gilroy have described contemporary forms of social organization that depart from the dominant Western model of modernity as imagining and creating "alternative modernities",[31] we can think of informal marketplaces not as a force opposing prosperity but as an alternative social and spatial rendering of contemporarity — "marketscapes" that are imbued with complex cultural meanings, spreading out in various directions and offering a plethora of amorphous shapes and sizes. In contrast to the hegemonic understanding of growth, informal trade does not necessarily entail unfettered expansion and augmented resource consumption. This alternative perspective rests partly on informal markets' microscale operations, which allow for differentiations in trade more attuned to the actual needs of populations, and partly on opportunities opening up through online trading platforms, which might allow for more complex circuits of usage and recycling. As materials and relations move along these trajectories, entering legal and illegal domains, and are put to use in many different ways, they generate an increasingly inextricable interweaving of economic and social values, which may ultimately undermine the supremacy of purely economically enforced power. The capacity of informal markets to appropriate different realms enables an exchange of much more than goods and money. Responding to more than economic imperatives, informal market relations can create a world of "being-in-common"[32]. However, as long as informality is imposed as a mode of discrimination whereby a lack of capital funds constitutes a criterion of deficiency justifying external intervention and "readjustment", exploitation of the informal will prevail.

1   Michel Foucault, "Of Other Spaces," trans. J. Miskowiec, *Diacritics* 16, (1986 [1967]): 22–27.

2   For detailed descriptions and analyses of the markets mentioned in this chapter see the sister volume of this publication: Peter Mörtenböck and Helge Mooshammer, eds., *Informal Market Worlds Atlas* (Rotterdam: naio1o Publishers, 2015).

3   Foucault, "Of Other Spaces," 22.

4   See Leonardo Gasparini and Leopoldo Tornarolli, "Labor Informality in Latin America and the Carribean: Patterns and Trends of Household Survey Microdata," *Desarrollo y Sociedad* 63 (2009): 13–80.

5   I am referring here to the use of this term by Susan Leigh Star and James R. Griesemer, who describe boundary objects as elements that embody a stable core meaning but can be appropriated by different groups for very different ends. First published in: Susan Leigh Star and James R. Griesemer, "Institutional Ecology, 'Translations' and Boundary Objects: Amateurs and Professionals in Berkeley's Museum of Vertebrate Zoology, 1907–39," *Social Studies of Science* 19, no.4 (1989): 387–420.

6   For further analysis of the operational matrix of the Special 301 Reports, see also the introductory text to the section "'Notorious' Markets" in Mörtenböck and Mooshammer, *Informal Market Worlds Atlas*, 24–27.

7   For a full version of the 2014 Special 301 Report, released in April 2014, see: http://www.ustr.gov/about-us/press-office/reports-and-publications/2014/2014-special-301-report

8   Detailed analyses of the Special 301 process can be found in Kim Newby, "The Effectiveness of Special 301 in Creating Long Term Copyright Protection for U.S. Companies Overseas," *Syracuse Journal of International Law* 21 (1995): 29–62; Joe Karaganis and Sean Flynn, "Networked Governance and the USTR," in *Media Piracy in Emerging Economies*, ed. Joe Karaganis (Social Science Research Council, March 2011), 75–98, http://piracy.ssrc.org; Sean Flynn, "What is Special 301? A Historical Primer," infojustice.org blog (American University Washington College of Law, 1 May 2013), http://infojustice.org/archives/29465

9   Neil Turkewitz, Executive Vice President of the Recording Industry Association of America, letter to the USTR, 4 November 2010: "[Many sites] fail to address their own conduct in facilitating the theft of intellectual property and therefore deserve to be identified as notorious pirate markets."

10 Ananya Roy, *Poverty Capital. Microfinance and the Making of Development* (London and New York: Routledge, 2010).

11 David Harvey, *Rebel Cities: From the Right to the City to the Urban Revolution* (London and New York: Verso, 2012), 20–21; Robert Neuwirth, *Stealth of Nations: The Global Rise of the Informal Economy* (New York: Pantheon Books, 2011), 130–144.

12 Guillermo E. Perry et al., eds., *Informality: Exit and Exclusion* (World Bank: Latin American and Caribbean studies, 2007).

13 Ibid., 13–19. See also Friedrich Schneider, Andreas Bühn and Claudio E. Montenegro, "Shadow Economies All over the World. New Estimates for 162 Countries from 1999 to 2007," World Bank Policy Research Working Paper 5356 (July 2010).

14 Cluster for Research on the Informal Sector and Policy (CRISP), based at the Centre for Regional Economic and Enterprise Development (CREED), University of Sheffield, UK.

15 For an overview of scholarly approaches to informal economies see, for instance, Jan L. Losby et al., „Informal Economy Literature Review" (Newark, DE: ISED Research and Consulting & Washington, DC: The Aspen Institute, December 2002); Lalesh Nand, "A Theoretical Review of the Urban Informal Sector or Informal Economy in Developing Countries and Its Future Directions in an Era of Globalisation," research paper (Sydney: Western Sydney Institute, 2006). For an overview of research on markets see Yolande Pottie-Sherman, "Markets and Diversity — Annotated Bilbiography," MMG Working Paper 12–15 (Göttingen: Max Planck Institute for the Studies of Religious and Ethnic Diversity, 2012).

16 See, for instance, Colin C. Williams and John Round, "Re-thinking the Nature of the Informal Economy: Some Lessons from Ukraine," *International Journal of Urban and Regional Research* 31, no.2 (June 2007), 425–441; Jens Beckert and Frank Wehinger, "In the Shadow: Illegal Markets and Economic Sociology," *Socio-Economic Review* 11, no.1 (2013): 5–30.

17 See Manuel Castells and Alejandro Portes, "World Underneath: The Origins, Dynamics, and Effects of the Informal Economy," in *The Informal Economy: Studies in Advanced and Less Developed Countries*, ed. Alejandro Portes, Manuel Castells and Lauren A. Benton (Baltimore, MD: John Hopkins University Press, 1989), 11–37.

18 Prominent examples are the southern European countries on the edge of the Mediterranean that have been forced into severe restructuring programmes under the aegis of the EU and the IMF and burdened by unemployment rates of 25 per cent and higher (unemployment rates for under 25s widely hover around the 50 per cent mark). See eurostat: http://epp. eurostat.ec.europa.eu/cache/ITY_PUBLIC/3-02052014-AP/ EN/3-02052014-AP-EN.PDF

19 See Peter Mörtenböck and Helge Mooshammer, "Derb Ghallef Valley," in *Informal Market Worlds Atlas*, ed. Mörtenböck and Mooshamer, 62–67.

20 As Portes and Haller state: "The paradox of state control is that official efforts to obliterate unregulated activities through the proliferation of rules and controls often expand the very conditions that give rise to these activities." Alejandro Portes and William Haller, "The Informal Economy," in *Handbook of Economic Sociology*, second edition, ed. Neil J. Smelser and Richard Swedberg (New York: Russell Sage Foundation, 2005), 409.

21 See, for instance, the case studies on Jarmark Europa (Warsaw), Oshodi Market (Lagos), Moran Market (Songnam) and Rot Fai Market (Bangkok) in Mörtenböck and Mooshammer, *Informal Market Worlds Atlas*.

22 See, for instance, the case studies on 7th Kilometre Market (Odessa) and Cherkizovsky Market (Moscow) for the impact on Eastern Europe or La Salada (Buenos Aires) and Feirinha da Madrugada (Saõ Paulo) for Latin America in ibid.

23 See, for instance, the case studies on Alaba International Market (Lagos) or Nairobi markets in ibid.

24 Michel Foucault, *Society Must Be Defended — Lectures at the Collège de France 1975–76* (London: Penguin Books, 2004 [1975]), 29–30.

25 Portes and Haller, "The Informal Economy," 405.

26 Ibid., 408; see also Mark S. Granovetter, "The Strength of Weak Ties," *American Journal of Sociology* 78, no.6 (1973): 1360–1380.

27 See, for instance, the case studies on Brooklyn Night Market (New York) and Rot Fai Market (Bangkok) in Mörtenböck and Mooshammer, *Informal Market Worlds Atlas*.

28 Aristotle, *Politics*, Book II, chapter 3, as quoted in Elinor Ostrom, *Governing the Commons: The Evolutions of Institutions for Collective Actions* (Cambridge and New York: Cambridge University Press, 1990), 2.

29 Ostrom, *Governing the Commons*, 3.

30 David W. Ehrenfield, *Conserving Life on Earth* (Oxford and New York: Oxford University Press, 1972), 322; quoted in Ostrom, *Governing the Commons*, 9.

31 Arjun Appadurai, *Modernity at Large: Cultural Dimensions of Globalization* (Minneapolis, MN: University of Minnesota Press, 1996); Paul Gilroy, *The Black Atlantic: Modernity and Double Consciousness* (Cambridge, MA: Harvard University Press, 1993).

32 Jean-Luc Nancy, *The Creation of the World or Globalization* (Albany,

NY: SUNY Press, 2007).

HOW THE INFORMAL ECONOMY TOOK OVER THE WORLD

Keith Hart

A la recherche du temps perdu

The idea of an informal economy was born at the moment when the post-war era of developmental states was drawing to a close. The 1970s were a watershed between three decades of state management of the economy and the free market decades of one-world capitalism that culminated in the financial crisis of 2008. It seems now that the economy has escaped from all attempts to make it publicly accountable. What are the forms of state that can regulate a world of money that is now essentially lawless? The informal economy started off forty years ago as a way of talking about the Third World urban poor living in the cracks of a rule system that could not reach down to their level. Now the rule system itself is in question. Everyone ignores the rules, especially the people at the top — the politicians and bureaucrats, the corporations, the banks — and they routinely escape being held responsible for their illegal actions. Privatization of public interests is probably universal, but what is new about neoliberalism is that, whereas the alliance between money and power used to be covert, now it is celebrated as a virtue, wrapped up in liberal ideology. This is the context for what follows. The informal economy seems to have taken over the world, while cloaking itself in the rhetoric of free markets. We are witnessing the world-historic collapse of the twentieth-century attempt to impose national controls on the economy. Inevitably, when witnessing this collapse, we dream of restoring the era of social democracy, developmental states and even Stalinism. The rules operated then with some degree of success. This nostalgia for the heyday of what I call "national capitalism"[1] will not serve us well today. We need to analyze the contemporary world economic crisis at a number of levels. Above all, we should acknowledge that the core problem is not narrowly economic, but one of political failure, both national and international. Money and markets have escaped from public control and cannot be put back in that straitjacket. The question then concerns what democratically accountable structures might be capable of regulating the world economy and under what social conditions? I will try to answer that question by reflecting initially on the history of a concept with which I have been closely associated.

Origins and Critique of the Informal Economy

Before the First World War no-one believed that the state, a hangover from pre-industrial society, could manage the turbulence of urban commerce. Industrial capitalists and the military landlord class formed an alliance in the 1860s and afterwards to keep in check the proliferating working class spawned by the machine revolution.[2]

Germany and Japan took cooperation between these classes within new state structures to an unprecedented level. But the Great War revealed hitherto unimagined government powers: to raise and kill off huge armies, organize industrial production, control market prices and monopolize propaganda. After the war, the issue was which kind of state — welfare democracy, fascist or communist — would win the race to organize world society. The whole period, 1914–1945, was a nightmare: two world wars, the Great Depression, a succession of ugly conflicts such as the Spanish civil war, the Japanese invasion of Manchuria, the Italian attack on Abyssinia. Writing just before the end of all this, Karl Polanyi blamed it all on the nineteenth-century experiment to make society conform to market principles.[3]

No wonder then that, in the late 1940s, the world turned to post-war governments of various kinds to build an alternative system. Their mission, for the first and only time in world history, was to reduce the gap between rich and poor, to increase the purchasing power of working people and to expand public services. The European empires were dismantled, beginning in Asia; a new world order was inaugurated under U.S. hegemony, implementing the accords of Bretton Woods; the United Nations was formed and "development" — a post-colonial compact between rich and poor nations — was the order of the day. All of this took large amounts of state intervention and it generated the longest boom in global economic history. This boom began to come unstuck around 1970. By the end of that decade, neoliberal conservatives were installed in power throughout the West. Their slogan was the free market and in the 1980s, with the active support of the IMF and World Bank, they set about dismantling state restrictions on the international flow of money in the name of "structural adjustment", at first in the developing countries. This was the context in which the "informal economy" emerged, first as a description of the Third World urban poor, then as a universal feature of modern economies.

In the early 1990s, not long after the fall of the Berlin Wall, I wrote a critique of my own concept.[4] I made the obvious point that the formal/informal pair, representing bureaucracy and popular self-organization as they did, mirrored the poles of the Cold War, "state socialism" vs. "the free market". I had earlier argued, in a published lecture on money, that the habit of contrasting market and state theories of money as alternatives — at that time Milton Friedman's monetarism vs. Keynesian macroeconomics — was ruinous since currency was both a token of political authority ("heads") and a commodity ("tails").[5] After three decades of welfare-state democracy, the neoliberal counter-revolution was well under way by the 1980s; and we may now be witnessing the start of another long swing back from over-reliance on the market to increased state intervention in some form or another. So the state/market pair has not faded away. In the immediate aftermath of the Cold War, however, I was optimistic that new paradigms could emerge; and I questioned the usefulness of the informal economy as a concept, given its origins in the ideological poles of twentieth-century society's nuclear nightmare.

The formal/informal pair first saw light in the context of development debates during the world crisis of the early 1970s — a sequence of events that included America's losing war in Vietnam, the dollar being detached from gold in 1971, the invention of money market futures the next year and the dismantling of the Bretton

Woods regime of fixed parity exchange rates. This was soon followed by a world depression induced by the energy crisis of 1973 and then by a glut of euro-dollar loans that ended up as the Third World debt crisis of the 1980s. "Stagflation" in the West (high unemployment and inflation) prepared the ground for Reagan, Thatcher and their imitators from 1979–80 onwards. After the "modernization" boom of the 1960s, the notion that poor countries could become rich by emulating "us" gave way to gloomier scenarios around 1970, fed by zero-sum theories of "underdevelopment", "dependency" and "the world system" advanced by the other side in the Cold War.

In development policy-making circles, this trend manifested itself as fear of "Third World urban unemployment". It had been noted that cities there were growing rapidly, but without comparable growth in "jobs", conceived of as regular employment by government and businesses. At this time, Keynesians and Marxists alike held that only the state could lead an economy towards development and growth. Richard Nixon reflected this consensus shortly before his fall when he said, "We are all Keynesians now". There were a few liberal economists around, but none of them influenced policy. The question was, how are "we" (the bureaucracy and its academic advisors) going to provide the people with the jobs, health, education, housing and transport that they need? And what will happen if we don't? The spectre of urban riots and even revolution raised its head. The word "unemployment" evoked images of the Great Depression.

This whole story didn't square with my fieldwork experience in the slums of Ghana's capital, Accra. It took me some time to work out why, but the result was a paper for a 1971 conference on "Urban unemployment in Africa". It eventually appeared,[6] after an International Labour Office report influenced by my paper had launched the idea of an "informal sector" in Kenya.[7] I wanted to persuade development economists to abandon the "unemployment" idea and to accept that there was more going on in the grassroots economy than their bureaucratic imagination allowed for. To that end, I had two sections: the first was a vivid ethnographic description ("I have been there and you haven't"); the second tried to engage their interest in the consequences for development theory, using what I call "economese" — how to sound like an economist without formal training in the discipline — something I had learned by moonlighting as a writer for *The Economist*.

I had no ambition to coin a concept, just to insert a vision of irregular economic activity into the debates of development professionals. This was a classic move in the genre of "realism".[8] The ILO Kenya report, on the other hand, did want to coin a concept and that is what it subsequently became, a keyword helping to organize a segment of the academic and policy-making bureaucracy. The idea of an "informal economy" thus has a double provenance reflecting its two sides, suspended between bureaucracy (the ILO) and the people (my ethnography). Drawing attention to activities that had previously been invisible to the bureaucratic gaze had a clear value, but I was struck later by how *static* my analysis had been. My aim had been to show that no single idea ("the state") can ever capture the complexity of real life. But I conceived of informal income opportunities as at best a minor appendage to the state-made economy, perhaps a bit more than "taking in each other's washing", but essentially going nowhere.

No-one could have anticipated what happened next: under a neoliberal imperative to reduce the state's grip on "the free market", manifested in Africa as "structural adjustment policies" (SAPs), national economies and the world economy itself became radically informal. Not only did the management of money go offshore, but corporations outsourced, downsized and casualized their labour forces, public functions were privatized, often corruptly, the illicit drugs and arms trades took off, the global war over "intellectual property" dominated capitalism's contradictions and whole countries, such as Mobutu's Zaire, abandoned any pretence of formality in their economic affairs. Here was no "hole-in-the-wall" operation living between the cracks of the law. The market frenzy led to the "commanding heights" of the informal economy taking over the state-made bureaucracy. Just as the Cold War ended in confusion between the poles that launched it, "negative dialectic"[9] — "state capitalism", "market socialism", the Pentagon fighting for the free market as the largest non-market collective in world history — so too the formal/informal pair, inspired by the state/market opposition, leaked into each other to the point of becoming often indistinguishable. What is the difference between a Wall Street bank laundering gangsters' money through the Cayman Islands and the mafias running opium out of Afghanistan with the support of several national governments?[10]

I concluded then that the informal economy concept was insufficiently dynamic. I thought this might be partly a consequence of living under the threat of nuclear holocaust. We did not want the opposed sides and their symbols to move, since the result could be the annihilation of all life on the planet. In any case, they did move eventually — at several levels. Another criticism was that "informal" says what these activities are not, but not what they are. We need to know more about what is going on under the rubric of "informal" when it has expanded to include activities of bewildering variety. The urgent task is to expose the positive principles organizing the informal economy and to place these investigations within an adequately broad historical framework.

The Dialectics of Form
"General Forms have their vitality in Particulars, and every Particular is a Man" (*William Blake*).

Most readers of this book live substantially inside what we may call the formal economy. This is a world of salaries or fees paid on time, regular mortgage payments, clean credit ratings, fear of the tax authorities, regular meals, moderate use of stimulants, good health cover, pension contributions, school fees, driving the car to the commuter station, summer holidays by the sea. Of course, middle class households suffer economic crises from time to time and some people feel permanently vulnerable, not least many students. But what makes this lifestyle "formal" is the regularity of its order, a predictable rhythm and sense of control that we often take for granted. I only discovered how much of this had become natural to me when I went to live in a West African city slum almost 50 years ago.

I would ask people questions that just did not make sense to them, like, how much do you spend on food a week? Most households were in any case unbounded and transient. Assuming that someone had a regular wage (which many did not), it was pitifully small; the wage earner might live it up for a day or two and then was broke, relying on credit, help from family and friends or not eating at all. A married man might use his wage to buy a sack of rice and pay the rent, knowing that he would have to hustle until the next pay check. In the street people moved everything from marijuana to refrigerators in deals marked more by flux than stable incomes. After completing my doctorate, I went to work in a development studies institute. There I saw my main task as trying to get this ethnographic experience across to development economists. My use of the conceptual pair formal/informal came out of those conversations. The formal and informal aspects of society are already linked, since the idea of an "informal economy" is entailed in the institutional effort to organize society along formal lines. "Form" is *the rule*, an idea of what ought to be universal in social life; and for most of the twentieth century the dominant forms have been those of bureaucracy, particularly of national bureaucracy, since society was identified to a large extent with nation-states. This identity is now ending as a result of neoliberal policies, the digital revolution in communications and the global economic crisis.

Formal and informal appear to be separate entities because of the use of the term "sector". This gives the impression that the two exist in different places, like agriculture and manufacturing, whereas both the bureaucracy and its antithesis contain the dialectic within themselves, as well as between them. There is a widespread perception that together they constitute a class war between the bureaucracy and the people. It was not supposed to be like this. Modern bureaucracy was invented by the Italian city-states of the *quattrocento* as part of a democratic political project to give citizens equal access to what was theirs as a right. It still has the ability to co-ordinate public services on a scale that is beyond the reach of individuals and most groups. So it is disheartening that bureaucracy ("the power of public office") should normally be seen now as the negation of democracy ("the power of the people") rather than as its natural ally.

Forms are necessarily abstract and a lot of social life is left out as a result. The gap may be reduced by naming a variety of practices as an "informal sector". They appear to be informal because their forms are largely invisible to the bureaucratic gaze. Mobilizing the informal economy will require a pluralistic approach based on at least acknowledgement of those forms. Equally, the formal sphere of society is not just abstract, but consists of the people who staff bureaucracies and their informal practices. Somehow, the human potential of both has to be unlocked together.

"Form" is an idea whose origin lies in the mind. Form is the rule, the invariant in the variable. It is predictable and easily recognized. Idealist philosophers from Plato onwards thought the general idea of something was more real than the thing itself. Words are forms, of course. In his *Science of Logic*, Hegel shows the error of taking the idea for reality. We all know the word "house" and might think there is nothing more to owning one than saying "my house". But before long the roof leaks, the paint peels and we are forced to acknowledge that the house is a material thing, a process that requires attention. The "formal sector" is likewise an idea, a collection of people, things and activities; but we should not mistake the category for the reality it identifies.

What makes something "formal" is its conformity with such an idea or rule. Thus, formal dress often means that the men are supposed to look the same, so they adopt a "uniform" that cancels out their individuality. Formality endows a class of people with universal qualities, with being the same and equal. What makes dress "informal" is the absence of such a shared code. But anyone can see that clothing styles in an informally dressed crowd are not random. We might ask what these informal forms are and how to account for them. The dialectic is infinitely recursive. No wonder that most economists find the conceptual dichotomy confusing and impossible to measure.

There is a hierarchy of forms and this hierarchy is not fixed forever. The twentieth century saw a general experiment in impersonal society whose forms were anchored in national bureaucracy, in centralized states and laws carrying the threat of punishment. The dominant economic forms were also bureaucratic and closely linked to the state as the source of universal law. Conventionally these were divided according to principles of ownership into "public" and "private" sectors. This uneasy alliance of governments and corporations is now sometimes classified as "the formal sector". On the surface they share being subject to regulation, conformity to the rule of law. How then might unregulated economic activities, "the informal economy", relate to this formal order? They may be related in any of four ways: as *division*, *content*, *negation* and *residue*. The moral economy of capitalist societies is based on an attempt to keep separate impersonal and personal spheres of social life. The establishment of a formal public sphere entailed another based on domestic privacy. The pair was meant to constitute complementary halves of a single whole. Most people, once men more than women, divide themselves every day between production and consumption, paid and unpaid work, submission to impersonal rules in the office and the free play of personality at home. Money is the means whereby the two sides are brought together, so that their interaction is an endless process of separation and integration or *division*. The division of the populations into males and females is the master metaphor for this dialectic of complementary unity. When the lines between the paired categories become blurred, we enter a phase of "negative dialectic", from which a new idea may eventually emerge. Identifying the informal practices that constitute a bureaucracy implies such a blurring of the ideal.

For any rule to be translated into human action, something else must be brought into play, such as personal judgment. So informality is built into bureaucratic forms as unspecified *content*. This is no trivial matter. Workable solutions to problems of administration invariably contain processes that are invisible to the formal order. For example, workers sometimes "work to rule". They follow their job descriptions to the letter without any of the informal practices that allow these abstractions to function. Everything grinds to a halt. Or take a commodity chain from production by a transnational corporation to final consumption in an African city. At various points, invisible actors fill the gaps that the bureaucracy cannot handle directly, from the factories to the docks to the supermarkets and street traders. Informal processes are indispensable to commerce, as variable content to the form.

Of course, some of these activities break the law, through a breach of safety regulations, tax evasion, smuggling, the use of child labour, selling without a licence etc. The third way that informal activities relate to formal organization is thus as its *negation*. Rule-breaking takes place both within bureaucracy and outside it; and so the informal is often illegal. It is hard to draw a line between colourful women selling oranges on the street and the gangsters who exact tribute from them.

When the rule of law is weak, the forms that emerge in its place are often criminal in character. Modern civilization protects the public image of bureaucratic processes from a hybrid reality that mixes formal order with corruption and criminality. We enjoy watching movies about cops and gangsters, but we insulate these fictions from belief in the rule of law that helps us to sleep at night.

The fourth category is not so obviously related to the formal order. Some "informal" activities exist in parallel, as *residue*. They are just separate from the bureaucracy. It would be stretching the logic of the formal/informal pair to include peasant economy, traditional institutions and domestic life as somehow "informal". Yet the social forms characteristic of these domains often shape informal economic practices and *vice versa*. Is society just one thing — one state with its rule of law — or can it tolerate institutional pluralism, leaving some spheres to their own devices? Communities depend on members understanding each other for practical purposes; and so they operate through culture. They use implicit rules (customs) rather than state-made laws and regulate their members informally, through the sanction of exclusion rather than punishment. European empires, faced with a shortage of administrative resources, turned to "indirect rule" as a way of governing semi-autonomous subject peoples. Anthropologists played their part in making this work. Any serious attempt to combine the formal and the informal anew requires similar openness to plurality of form.

The Demise of National Capitalism

To talk of the world economy being "informalized" suggests that there is a global rule-system, whereas effective rules are now absent at all levels of society, from the top to the bottom. We need to be clear about the different dimensions of this crisis. It is not merely financial, a moment in the historical cycle of credit and debt. I prefer to approach our times as a formative episode in the history of money. The removal of political controls over money in recent decades has led to a situation where politics is still mainly national, but the money circuit is global and lawless. We are witnessing the collapse of the money system that the world lived by in the twentieth century. This system has been unravelling since the U.S. dollar went off gold in 1971 and its chief symbol today is the crisis for the single currency that was meant to protect European countries from their individual vulnerability. As the need for international cooperation grows, the disconnection between economy and political institutions makes effective solutions unattainable.

The informal economy's improbable rise to global dominance is the result of the mania for deregulation during the last three decades, linked to the wholesale privatization of public goods and services and to the capture of politics by high finance. Deregulation provided a fig leaf for corruption, rentier accumulation, tax evasion and public irresponsibility. Nowhere was this more evident than in the culture of the Wall Street banks from the 1980s. This was no secret at the time. Each major bank spawned a tell-all book written by undercover reporters or disillusioned employees — from *Liar's Poker* (Salomon Bros)[11] to *F.I.A.S.C.O.* (Morgan Stanley)[12]. The removal of official restraints on financial practices generated a culture of personal excess from the trading floor to boardroom politics; moral responsibility towards clients was replaced by an ethos of predation. Yet, while the credit boom lasted, criticism was drowned by celebrations of unending prosperity. Even after the bust, the political ascendancy of finance has hardly been challenged. And we wonder why our leaders routinely refuse to take responsibility for their own failures.

Apart from the main financial houses, the shadow banking system — hedge funds, money market funds and structured investment vehicles that lie beyond state regulation — is literally out of control. Tax evasion is an international industry that dwarfs national budgets.[13] The Cambridge economist, Sir James Mirlees, won a Nobel Prize for proving that you cannot force the rich to pay more than they are willing to. Mitt Romney's non-disclosure of his tax returns has inscribed this principle at the heart of the U.S. presidential elections! None of this touches on the outright criminal behaviour of transnational corporations who now outnumber countries by two to one in the top 100 economic entities on the planet.[14] Where to stop? The drug cartels from Mexico and Colombia to Russia, the illegal armaments industry, the global war over intellectual property ("piracy"), fake luxury goods, the invasion and looting of Iraq, four million dead in the Congo scramble for minerals. In 2006, the Japanese electronics firm NEC discovered a criminal counterpart of itself, operating on a similar scale under the same name and more profitably because it was wholly outside the law.[15] The informal economy was always a way of labelling the unknowable, but the scale of all this goes beyond comprehension.

2011 saw the first political consequences of the financial crisis of 2008. We still tend to talk about the encroaching disaster we are living through in economic rather than political terms. Even neoliberalism's detractors reproduce the free market ideology they claim to oppose. The euro is by no means the only symptom of this crisis, but it may come to be seen as the decisive nail in the coffin of the world economy today.[16] We seem to be at the end of something. What is ending is "national capitalism", the synthesis of nation-states and industrial capitalism. Its main symbol has been national monopoly currency (legal tender). It was the institutional attempt to manage money, markets and accumulation through central bureaucracy within a cultural community of national citizens. National capitalism was never the only active principle in world political economy: regional federations, empires and globalization are at least as old or much older.

National capitalism's origins lay in a series of linked revolutions of the 1860s and early 1970s based on a new alliance between capitalists and the military landlord class.[17] These ranged from the American civil war and Japan's Meiji restoration to Italian and German unification, Russia's abolition of serfdom, the French Third Republic and Britain's second Reform Act. In all this, Marx published *Capital*[18] and a revolution in transport and communications (steamships, continental railways and the telegraph) took place. These new national governments launched a bureaucratic revolution in the late nineteenth century and then sponsored large business corporations in a drive towards mass production. The national system became generalized after the First World War when states turned inward to manage their economies in war and depression. Its apogee was the social democracy built after 1945, what the French call *les trente glorieuses*.

Money expands the capacity of individuals to stabilize their own personal identity by holding something durable that embodies the desires and wealth of all the other members of society. People learn to understand each other as members of communities and money is an important vehicle for this. Nation-states have been so successful in a relatively short time that it is hard for us to imagine society in any other way. Five different types of community come together in the nation-state form:

Political community: a link to the world and a source of law at home
Community of place: territorial boundaries of land and sea
Imagined or virtual community: the constructed cultural identity of citizens
Community of interest: subjectively and objectively shared purposes in trade and war
Monetary community: common use of a national monopoly currency

The rise and fall of single currencies is therefore one way of approaching national capitalism's historical trajectory.

Money is the principal means for us all to bridge the gap between everyday personal experience and a society whose wider reaches are impersonal. According to Georg Simmel, it is the concrete symbol of our human potential to make universal society.[19] At present national politics and media frame economic questions in such relentlessly parochial terms that we find it hard to think about the human predicament as a whole. But money is already global in scope and the need to overcome these limitations is urgent. My fear is that only a major war and all the losses it would bring will concentrate our minds once more on fixing the world we live in.

Karl Polanyi is enjoying a major revival today for the good reason that our crisis is strongly reminiscent of the disaster he sought to explain then, namely the collapse of the Victorian free market ideal, resulting in world war and depression.[20] He listed money, along with land and labour, as a "fictitious commodity" whose unregulated exchange came close to buying and selling society itself. He held that money and markets originate in the extension of society beyond its local core; society has to become more inclusive since none was ever self-sufficient. But conflict between the internal and external dimensions of an economy is often highly disruptive. This is why societies have traditionally held markets at arm's length and why acceptance of market principles at the core of modern societies invites disaster.

Mainstream economics says more about what money does than what it is. Its main function is held to be as a *medium of exchange*, a more efficient lubricant of markets than barter. Another school emphasizes money's function as a *means of payment*, especially of taxes to the government and hence on "purchasing power". It is also a *standard of value* or unit of account, with the focus again on government's role in establishing the legal conditions for trade; while John Locke conceived of money as a *store of wealth*, a new form of property that allowed the accumulation of riches to escape from the limitations of natural economy.[21]

In a little-known article, Polanyi later approached money as a semantic system, like writing. He argued that only modern money combines the four functions (payment, standard, store and exchange) in a few "all-purpose" symbols, national currency.[22] By contrast, primitive and archaic forms of money attached the separate uses to different symbolic objects or "special-purpose" monies. Polanyi argued against the primacy of money as a medium of exchange and for a multi-stranded model of its evolution. For him and for Keynes, it was above all a *means of payment* or the "purchasing power" of citizens, which drives modern economies, not so much a *medium of exchange* for buying and selling as such.

Although this analysis was intended only to illuminate the history of money, Polanyi's approach offers profound insight into the causes of today's global economic crisis. Our challenge is to conceive of society once more as something plural rather than singular, as a federated network rather than as a centralized hierarchy, the nation-state. The era of national monopoly currencies is very recent (from the 1850s); it took the United States, for example, half a century to secure an uncontested monopoly for "greenbacks"; and "all-purpose money" has been breaking up for four decades now, since the U.S. dollar was de-pegged from gold.

Since the break-up of the Bretton Woods system of fixed parity exchange rates, the world economy has reverted to the plural pattern of competing currencies that was normal before central banks learned how to control national economies in the second half of the nineteenth century through the bank rate, for example. One aspect of the crisis is that the international rule system imposed after the Second World War was systematically subverted by the creation of an offshore banking system, which brought the informal economy to the heart of global finance. Nick Shaxson provides an astonishing account of how the City of London replaced the colonial empire it lost with another based on tax havens.[23] The separation of functions between different types of monetary instruments was also crucial to money's great escape from the rules of the Keynesian consensus that was institutionalized in the Bretton Woods system. Central bank control was eroded by a shift to money being issued in multiple forms by a global distributed network of corporations, not just governments and banks.

Some brief examples must serve to indicate the momentous changes that have overtaken money in the last few decades. In Switzerland today, euros are commonly accepted in shops alongside the national currency. If you pay with a card, you can often choose the unit of account (Swiss franc, euro, pound sterling, U.S. dollar). But only francs are acceptable for payment of local taxes. Are national currencies a store of wealth? Hardly — they have all been radically depreciated and may even disappear; hence the flight to gold. But gold could turn out to be the biggest asset bubble of them all. As for real estate, the collapse of subprime mortgages got us into the present mess. And we have not even touched on what credit default swaps and collateral debt obligations are used for or who issues them.

Simmel considered money's twin anchors to be its physical substance (coins, paper, etc.) and the social institutions supporting the community of its users. He predicted that the first would wither away, making the second more visible. Radical cheapening of the cost of transferring information as a result of the digital revolution in communications has been transforming money and exchange for two decades now, confirming Simmel's prophecy. But globalization has made national society seem a lot less self-sufficient than it did a century ago. This process whereby markets, money and telecommunications have extended society rapidly beyond national boundaries, even as they have invaded the core institutions of domestic society, is fraught with danger. We need to extend systems of social rights to the global level before the contradictions of the market system collapse again into world war.

But local political organization resists such a move. After centuries of a unipolar divergent world economy ruled by the West, ours is a multi-polar world whose plurality of associations and convergent income distribution resembles the medieval period more than any since.

The Euro Crisis: An Episode in the History of Money

The monetary crisis that has overwhelmed the Eurozone of late needs to be seen in this context. The apparent triumph of the free market at the end of the Cold War in 1989/90 induced two huge political blunders, both of them based on the premise that society should be shaped by market economy rather than the other way round. Radical privatization of Soviet bloc public economies ignored the common history of politics, law and social custom that shored up market economies in the West, thereby delivering the economy into the hands of gangsters and oligarchs. And the European single currency was supposed to provide the social glue for political union without first developing effective fiscal institutions or economic convergence between North and South.

The big mistake was to *replace* national currencies with the euro. An alternative proposal, the *hard ECU,* would have floated politically managed national currencies alongside a low-inflation European central bank currency. Countries that did not join the euro, like Britain and Switzerland, have in practice enjoyed the privilege of this plural option. Eurozone countries cannot devalue and so must reduce their debts through deflation or default. Argentina's example of default after the peso crashed is directly relevant to countries like Greece and Spain today. The euro was invented *after* money was already breaking up into multiple forms and functions. The Americans centralized their currency after a civil war; the Europeans centralized theirs as a means of achieving political union.

The infrastructure of money has already become decentralized and global. A return to the national solutions of the 1930s or to a Keynesian regime of managed exchange rates and capital flows is bound to fail. Where are the levers of democratic power to be located, now that globalization has exposed the limitations of national economic management? The cultural logic of national capitalism leads the political classes who got us into this mess to repeat the same mistakes. Politics is a dialogue of the deaf, between those who deny the need for any political regulation of markets and others who remain trapped in the outmoded model of central bank money.

The idea of world society is still perceived by most people as at best a utopian fantasy or at worst a threat to us all.[24] We need to build an infrastructure of money adequate to humanity's common needs. "Economy" has multiple meanings, but the idea of putting ones house in order in a world shaped increasingly by markets combines several of them. In this conception, economy is pulled inwards to secure local guarantees of a community's rights and interests; and outwards to make good local supply by engaging with outsiders through the medium of money and markets of various sorts, not just our own. The trick is to manage this dialectic of internal and external forces effectively.

Our societies are becoming increasingly emancipated from their territorial base. Three things count above all in these societies — people, machines and money, in that order. But money buys the machines that control the people. Our political task — and

I believe it was Marx's too — is to reverse that order of priority, not to help people escape from machines and money, but to encourage them to develop themselves through machines and money. To the idea of economic crisis and its antidotes, we must add in 2011-12 the possibility of political revolution. Europe has become the main focus once more of a world revolution. Meanwhile, the EU persists with purely monetary measures such as the European Central Bank's latest commitment to underwrite sovereign debt, when the issue is the political union itself and its current democratic deficit. National capitalism was based on a class compromise that reached its peak in the post-war decades. In the absence of a replacement with some prospect of offering economic democracy to the masses, informality and extreme inequality will continue to be the norm, until the next world war, that is.

Appendix on Periodization

As an antidote to the daily news, I attempt a historical periodization of the last two centuries or more, mainly to indicate that the present rupture in history opens up the prospect of several decades of turbulence. It is commonplace to compare the current crisis with the 1930s, but this is misleading, since the Great Depression was part of a sequence launched after three decades of financial globalization by the outbreak of war in 1914.

1776-1815	Age of war and revolutions
1815-1848	The industrial revolution
1848-1873	Origins of national capitalism
1873-1914	First age of financial globalization
1914-1945	The second thirty years war
1945-1979	The golden age of national capitalism
1979-2008	Second age of financial globalization
2008-	Another age of war and revolutions?

1 Keith Hart, "Money in the Making of World Society," in *Market and Society. The Great Transformation Today*, ed. Chris Hann and Keith Hart (Cambridge: Cambridge University Press, 2009).

2 Ibid.

3 Karl Polanyi, *The Great Transformation: The Political and Economic Origins of Our Time* (Boston, MA: Beacon, 2001 [1944]).

4 Keith Hart, "Market and State After the Cold War: The Informal Economy Reconsidered", in *Contesting Markets*, ed. Roy Dilley (Edinburgh: Edinburgh University Press,1992), 214-227.

5 Keith Hart, "Heads or Tails? Two Sides of the Coin," *Man* 21, no. 4 (1986): 637-656.

6 Keith Hart, "Informal Income Opportunities and Urban Employment in Ghana," *Journal of Modern African Studies* 11, no. 3 (1973): 61-89.

7 International Labour Office, *Incomes, Employment and Equality in Kenya* (Geneva: ILO, 1972).

8 Raymond Williams, "Realism and the Contemporary Novel," in *The Long Revolution*, idem (Swansea: Parthian Books, 2011 [1961]).

9 G.W.F. Hegel, *Science of Logic* (New York: Prometheus, 1998 [1817]).

10 Keith Hart, *The Hit Man's Dilemma: Or Business, Personal and Impersonal* (Chicago, IL: Prickly Paradigm, 2005).

11 Michael Lewis, *Liar's Poker* (New York: Norton, 1989).

12 Frank Partnoy, *F.I.A.S.C.O.: The Inside Story of a Wall Street Trader* (New York: Penguin, 1999).

13 Nicholas Shaxson, *Treasure Islands: Tax Havens and the Men Who Stole the World* (London: Bodley Head, 2011).

14 John Perkins, *Confessions of an Economic Hit Man* (New York: Plume, 2004).

15 Adrian Johns, *Piracy: The Intellectual Property Wars from Gutenberg to Gates* (Chicago, IL: University of Chicago Press, 2009).

16 Keith Hart, "Why the Euro Crisis Matters to us All," *Scapegoat* 4 (2013): 36-46.

17 Hart, "Money in the Making of World Society."

18 Karl Marx, *Capital: The Critique of Political Economy* (London: Lawrence and Wishart, 1970 [1867]).

19 Georg Simmel, *The Philosophy of Money* (London: Routledge, 1978 [1900]).

20 Polanyi, *The Great Transformation.*

21 John Locke, *Two Treatises on Government* (Cambridge: Cambridge University Press, 1960 [1690]).

22 Karl Polanyi, "Money Objects and Money Uses," *The Livelihood of Man* (New York: Academic Press, 1977 [1964]): 97-121.

23 Shaxson, *Treasure Islands.*

24 Hart, "Money in the Making of World Society."

SHRINKING ECONOMIES, GROWING EXPULSIONS[1]

Saskia Sassen

The aim of this chapter is to put some flesh on the idea that we may have entered a new phase of advanced capitalism in the 1980s, one with reinvented mechanisms for primitive accumulation. Today's is a form of primitive accumulation executed through complex operations and much specialized innovation, ranging from the logistics of outsourcing to the algorithms of finance. After 30 years of these types of development, we face shrinking economies in much of the world, escalating destructions of the biosphere all over the globe, and the re-emergence of extreme forms of poverty and brutalization where we thought they had been eliminated or were on their way out.

What is usually referred to as economic development has long depended on extracting goods from one part of the world and shipping them to another. Over the past few decades this geography of extraction has expanded rapidly, in good part through complex new technologies, and is now marked by even sharper imbalances in its relation to, and use of, natural resources. The mix of innovations that expands our capacities for extraction now threatens core components of the biosphere, leaving us also with expanded stretches of dead land and dead water.

Some of this is old history. Economic growth has never been benign. But the escalations of the past three decades mark a new epoch in that they threaten a growing number of people and places throughout the world. Such growth still takes on distinctive formats and contents in the mix of diversely developed countries we refer to as the Global North versus the mix of less or differently developed countries we refer to as the Global South. For instance, predatory elites have long been associated with poor countries that have rich natural resources, not with developed countries. Yet increasingly we see some of this capture at the top also in the latter, albeit typically in far more intermediated forms.

My thesis is that we are seeing the making not so much of predatory elites but of predatory "formations", a mix of elites and systemic capacities with finance a key enabler, that push toward acute concentration.[2] Concentration at the top is nothing new. What concerns me is the extreme forms it takes today in more and more domains across a good part of the world. I see the capacity for generating extreme concentration in some of the following trends, to mention just a few. There has been a 60 per cent increase in the wealth of the top 1 per cent globally in the past 20 years; at the top of that 1 per cent, the richest "100 billionaires added US$240 billion to their wealth in 2012 — enough to end world poverty four times over".[3] Bank assets grew by 160 per cent between 2002, well before the full crisis, and 2011, when financial recovery had started — from US$40 trillion to US$105 trillion, which is over one and a half times the value of global GDP. In 2010, still a period of crisis, the profits of the

5.8 million corporations in the United States rose 53 per cent over 2009, but despite skyrocketing profits, their United States corporate income tax bills actually shrank by US$1.9 billion, or 2.6 per cent.

Rich individuals and global firms by themselves could not have achieved such extreme concentration of the world's wealth. They need what we might think of as systemic help: a complex interaction of these actors with systems regeared toward enabling extreme concentration. Such systemic capacities are a variable mix of technical, market, and financial innovations plus government enablement. They constitute a partly global condition, though one that often functions through the specifics of countries, their political economies, their laws, and their governments.[4] They include enormous capacities for intermediation that function as a kind of haze, impairing our ability to see what is happening — but unlike a century ago, we would not find cigar-smoking moguls in this haze. Today, the structures through which concentration happens are complex assemblages of multiple elements, rather than the fiefdoms of a few robber barons.

Part of my argument is that a system with the capacity to concentrate wealth at this scale is distinctive. It is different, for instance, from a system with the capacity to generate the expansion of prosperous working and middle classes, as happened during most of the twentieth century in the Global North, in much of Latin America, and in several African countries, notably Somalia. This earlier system was far from perfect: there were inequality, concentration of wealth, poverty, racism, and more. But it was a system with a capacity to generate a growing middle sector that kept expanding for several generations, with children mostly doing better than their parents. Also, these distributive outcomes were not simply a function of the people involved. It took specific systemic capacities. By the 1980s, these earlier capacities had weakened, and we saw the emergence of capacities that push toward concentration at the top rather than toward the development of a broad middle. Thus the fact, for example, that the top 10 per cent of the income ladder in the United States got 90 per cent of the income growth of the decade beginning in 2000 signals more than individual capacity — it was enabled by that complex mix I conceive of as a predatory formation.

In this chapter I elaborate on how economic growth can get constituted in diverse ways with diverse distributive effects. I find that in our global modernity, we are seeing a surge of what are often referred to as primitive forms of accumulation, usually associated with earlier economies. The format is no longer something like the enclosure of farmers' fields so that wool-bearing sheep can be raised there, as was done in England to satisfy textile manufacturers' demands during the industrial revolution. Today, enormous technical and legal complexities are needed to execute what are ultimately elementary extractions. It is, to cite a few cases, the enclosure by financial firms of a country's resources and citizens' taxes, the repositioning of expanding stretches of the world as sites for extraction of resources, and the regearing of government budgets in liberal democracies away from social and workers' needs.

Unsustainable Contradictions? From Incorporation to Expulsion

The ways in which economic growth takes place matter. A given growth rate can describe a variety of economies, from one with little inequality and a thriving middle class to one with extreme inequality and concentration of most of the growth in a small upper tier. These differences exist across and within countries. Germany and Angola had the same rate of GDP growth in 2000 but clearly had very different economies and saw very different distributive effects. Although Germany is reducing the level, it still puts a good share of government resources into countrywide infrastructure and offers a wide array of services to its people, from health care to trains and buses. Angola's government does neither, choosing to support a small elite seeking to satisfy its own desires, including luxury developments in its capital city, Luanda, now ranked as the most expensive city in the world. These differences can also be seen in a single country across time, such as the United States just within the past 50 years. In the decades after World War II, growth was widely distributed and generated a strong middle class, while the decade beginning in 2000 saw the beginnings of an impoverished middle class, with 80 per cent of the growth in income going to the top 1 per cent of earners.

In the post–World War II era, the critical components of Western market economies were fixed-capital intensity, standardized production, and the building of new housing in cities, suburbs, and new towns. Such patterns were evident in a variety of countries in North and South America, Europe, Africa, and Asia, most prominently Japan and Asia's so-called Tiger economies. These forms of economic growth contributed to the vast expansion of a middle class. They did not eliminate inequality, discrimination, or racism. But they reduced systemic tendencies toward extreme inequality by constituting an economic regime centred on mass production and mass consumption, with strong labour unions at least in some sectors, and diverse government supports. Further deterrents to inequality were the cultural forms accompanying these processes, particularly through their shaping of the structures of everyday life. For instance, the culture of the large suburban middle class evident in the United States and Japan contributed to mass consumption and thus to standardization in production, which in turn facilitated unionization in manufacturing and distribution.[5]

Manufacturing, in tandem with state policies, played a particularly strong role in this conjunction of trends. As the leading sector in market-based economies for much of the twentieth century, mass manufacturing created the economic conditions for the expansion of the middle class because (1) it facilitated worker organizing, with unionization the most familiar format; (2) it was based in good part on household consumption, and hence wage levels mattered in that they created an effective demand in economies that were for the most part fairly closed; and (3) the relatively high wage levels and social benefits typical of the leading manufacturing sectors became a model for broader sectors of the economy, even those not unionized nor in manufacturing. Manufacturing played this role in non-Western-style industrial economies as well, notably in Taiwan and South Korea, and, in its own way, in parts of the Soviet Union. It has also played a significant part in the growth of a middle class in China since the 1990s, though not as consequential a role as it did in the West in the twentieth century.

By the 1990s, these economic histories and geographies had been partly destroyed. The end of the Cold War launched one of the most brutal economic phases of the modern era. It led to a radical reshuffling of capitalism. The effect was to open global ground for new or sharply expanded modes of profit extraction even in unlikely domains, such as subprime mortgages on modest residences, or through unlikely instruments, such as credit default swaps, which were a key component of the shadow banking system. Thus I see China's rapid manufacturing growth as part of this new phase of global capitalism that takes off in the 1980s;[6] this also helps explain why that growth did not lead to the vast expansion of a prosperous working and middle class in China. Such a difference also marks manufacturing growth in other countries that have become part of the outsourcing map of the West.

Two logics run through this reshuffling. One is systemic and gets wired into most countries' economic and (de)regulatory policies — of which the most important are privatization and the lifting of tariffs on imports. In capitalist economies we can see this in the unsettling and de-bordering of existing fiscal and monetary arrangements, albeit with variable degrees of intensity in different countries.

The second logic is the transformation of growing areas of the world into extreme zones for these new or sharply expanded modes of profit extraction. The most familiar are global cities and the spaces for outsourced work. Each is a type of thick *local* setting that contains the diverse conditions *global* firms need, though each does so at very different stages of the global economic process, for instance, computers for high-finance versus manufacturing components for those computers. Other such local settings in today's global economy are plantations and places for resource extraction, both producing mostly for export. The global city is a space for producing some of the most advanced inputs global firms need. In contrast, outsourcing is about spaces for routinized production of components, mass call centres, standardized clerical work, and more, all of it massive and standardized. Both these types of spaces are among the most strategic factors in the making of today's global economy, besides intermediate sectors such as transport. They concentrate the diverse labour markets, particular infrastructures, and built environments critical to the global economy. And they are the sites that make visible, and have benefited from, the multiple de-regulations and guarantees of contract developed and implemented by governments across the world and by major international bodies — in both cases, work mostly paid for by the taxpayers in much of the world.

Inequality in the profit-making capacities of different sectors of the economy and in the earning capacities of different types of workers has long been a feature of advanced market economies. But the orders of magnitude today across much of the developed world distinguish current developments from those of the post-war decades. The United States is probably among the most extreme cases, so it makes the pattern brutally clear.

Figures 1 and 2 show the extraordinary rise in corporate profits and assets over the past ten years, and this in a country that has long had extraordinary corporate results.

The decade of the 2000s helps illuminate this relentless rise in corporate profits and reduction of corporate taxes as a share of federal tax revenues. The crisis late in the decade brought a sharp but momentary dip in corporate profits, but overall these kept growing. The extent of inequality and the systems in which inequality is embedded and through which these outcomes are produced have generated massive distortions in the operations of diverse markets, from investment to housing and labour. For instance, using Internal Revenue Service data on corporate tax returns, David Cay Johnston finds that in 2010 the 2,772 companies that own 81 per cent of all business assets in the United States, with an average of US$23 billion in assets per firm, paid an average of 16.7 per cent of their profits in taxes (down from 21.1 per cent in 2009), even though their combined profits rose 45.2 per cent, a new record.[7] Profits growing three times faster than taxes means their effective tax rates fell.[8] The effects are visible in the composition of federal tax revenues: a growing share of individual taxes and a declining share of corporate taxes. The share of individual taxes is estimated to rise from 41.5 per cent of federal revenues in fiscal 2010 to 49.8 per cent in fiscal 2018. In contrast, corporate income taxes — assuming current rates — are expected to grow by only 2.4 percentage points over the same period, from 8.9 per cent of federal revenues in 2010 to 11.3 per cent in 2018.[9]

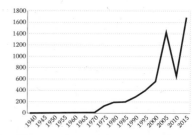

Fig. 1: Corporate profits after tax in the United States, 1940s–2010s (in US$ billions). *Data source: Federal Reserve Bank of St. Louis, 2013.*

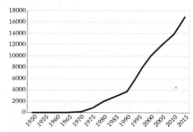

Fig. 2: Corporate assets in the United States, 1950s–2010s (in US$ billions). *Data source: Federal Reserve Bank of St. Louis, 2013.*

The trajectory of governments in this same period is one of growing indebtedness. Today, most of the developed-country governments could not engage in the large-scale infrastructure projects common in the post-war decades. Using International Monetary Fund (IMF) data, the Organisation for Economic Co-operation and Development (OECD) finds widespread growth of central government debt as a percentage of GDP. Table 1 presents numbers for several, mostly developed countries. The trend holds for very different types of governments: Germany saw its central government debt increase from 13 per cent of GDP in 1980 to 44 per cent in 2010; U.S. government debt increased from 25.7 per cent of GDP in 1980 to 61 per cent in 2010; and China's rose from 1 per cent of GDP in 1984 to 33.5 per cent in 2010.

The rise of government deficits has also been fed by the increase in tax evasion, partly facilitated by the development of complex accounting, financial, and legal instruments. In a 2012 research project for the Tax Justice Network, accountant Richard Murphy estimates tax evasion globally at US$3 trillion in 2010, which represents 5 per cent of the global economy and 18 per cent of global tax collections in 2010.[10] The study covered 145 countries with US$61.7 trillion of gross product, or 98.2 per cent of the world total. The estimated tax evasion is based on a juxtaposition of World Bank data on the estimated size of shadow economies with a Heritage Foundation analysis of average tax burdens by country.[11] Figure 3 presents tax evasion estimates for several developed countries, including those generally seen as well governed and well functioning, such as Germany, France, and the United Kingdom. It ranges from 8.6 per cent of GDP in the United States to 43.8 per cent in Russia. Murphy finds that a key reason for this tax evasion is the combination of weak rules on accounting and disclosure combined with inadequate budgets to enforce tax laws. The United States has the largest amount of absolute tax evasion, clearly a function partly of the size of its economy. Murphy estimates U.S. tax evasion at US$337.3 billion, which is 10.7 per

COUNTRY	YEAR			
	1980	1990	2000	2010
Australia	8.0	6.1	11.4	11.0
Canada	26.1	46.6	40.9	36.1
China	1.0[a]	6.9	16.4	33.5
Germany	13.0	19.7	38.4	44.4
Greece	n/a	97.6[b]	108.9	147.8
Italy	52.7	92.8	103.6	109.0
Japan	37.1	47.0	106.1	183.5[c]
Portugal	29.2	51.7	52.1	88.0
Spain	14.3	36.5	49.9	51.7
Sweden	38.2	39.6	56.9	33.8
United States	25.7	41.5	33.9	61.3

Table 1: Central government debt (% of GDP) in eleven countries, 1980–2010. *Data source: OECD, 2014.*
Notes:
a. Data for 1984
b. Data for 1993
c. Data for 2009

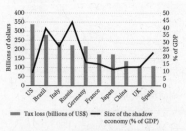

— Tax loss (billions of US$)   — Size of the shadow economy (% of GDP)

Fig. 3: Countries with the largest absolute levels of tax evasion, 2011. *Data source: Johnston, 2011.*

cent of global evasion; this is not too different from the official U.S. Internal Revenue Service tax gap estimates. Given the measures used in the report, it excludes "lawful" tax evasion, which we know has increased sharply over the last decade thanks to extremely creative accounting, including the use of private contractual arrangements that can bypass state regulations *lawfully,* so to speak.[12]

The losers in much of this are the majority of citizens and their governments. Governments become poorer, partly as a result of tax evasion and partly because more of their citizens are impoverished and therefore less capable of meeting their social obligations. The Genuine Progress Indicator (GPI) is a comprehensive measure that includes social conditions and environmental costs; it adjusts expenditure using 26 variables so as to account both for costs such as pollution, crime, and inequality and for beneficial activities where no money changes hands, such as housework and volunteering. An international team led by Ida Kubiszewski from Australian National University collected GPI estimates for 17 countries, which together account for over half the world's population and GDP, to generate a global overview of GPI changes over the last five decades. They found that GPI per person peaked in 1978 and has been declining slowly but steadily ever since.[13] In contrast, GDP per capita has been rising steadily since 1978. The research team argues that this signals that social and environmental negatives have outpaced the growth of monetary wealth. Clearly, an additional factor is the distribution of that monetary wealth, which, as we know from other data examined in this chapter, has become increasingly concentrated at the top.

Using IMF data on public expenditures and adjustment measures in 181 countries, Isabel Ortiz and Matthew Cummins examine the impact of the crisis, from 2007 through the forecasts for 2013–2015. The authors find that the IMF data used in 314 studies show that a quarter of the countries are undergoing excessive contraction. "Excessive contraction" is defined as a cut in government expenditures as a percentage of GDP in the 2013–2015 post-crisis period compared to the equivalent measure in the pre-crisis levels of 2005–2007. Fiscal contraction is found to be most severe in the developing world. Overall, 68 developing countries are projected to cut public spending by 3.7 per cent of GDP on average in 2013–2015, compared to 2.2 per cent in 26 high-income countries. In terms of population, austerity will affect 5.8 billion people, or 80 per cent of the global population, in 2013; this is expected to increase to 6.3 billion, or 90 per cent of people worldwide, by 2015. This leads the authors to question the desirability of fiscal contraction as the way out of the crisis. They argue that the worldwide propensity toward fiscal consolidation is likely to aggravate unemployment, produce higher food and fuel costs, and reduce access to essential services for many households in all these countries. These households are bearing the costs of a "recovery" that has passed them by.[14]

Some of the major processes feeding the increased inequality in profit-making and earnings capacities are an integral part of the advanced information economy; thus this growing inequality is not an anomaly nor, in the case of earnings, the result of low-wage immigrant labour, as is often asserted. One such process is the ascendance and transformation of finance, particularly through securitization, globalization, and the development of new telecommunications and computer networking technologies. Another source of inequalities in profit making and earnings is the growing service intensity in the organization of the economy generally, that is to say, the increased demand for services by firms and households.[15] Insofar as there is a strong tendency in the service sector toward polarization in the levels of technical expertise that workers need, and in their wages and salaries, the growth in the demand for services reproduces these inequalities in the broader society.

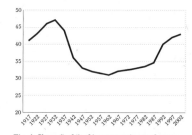

Fig. 4: Share (in %) of income going to the top 10 per cent of U.S. households, 1917–2002.
Data source: Mishel, 2004.[18]
Note: Income is defined as market income but excludes capital gains.

The exceptionally high profit-making capacity of many of the leading service industries is embedded in a complex combination of new trends. Among the most significant over the past 20 years are technologies that make possible the hypermobility of capital at a global scale; market deregulation, which maximizes the implementation of that hypermobility; and financial inventions such as securitization, which liquefy hitherto illiquid capital and allow it to circulate faster, hence generating additional profits (or losses).

Globalization adds to the complexity of these service industries, their strategic character, and their glamour. This in turn has contributed to their valorization and often overvalorization, as illustrated in the unusually high salary increases for top-level professionals that began in the 1980s, a trend that has now become normalized in many advanced economies.[16]

Of all the highly developed countries, it is the United States where these deep structural trends are most legible. National-level data for the United States show a sharp growth in inequality. For instance, earnings growth during the pre-crisis level for 2001 to 2005 was high but very unequally distributed. Most of it went to the upper 10 per cent and, especially, the upper 1 per cent of households. The remaining 90 per cent of households saw a 4.2 per cent decline in their market-based incomes.[17] Figure 4 traces a longer-term pattern from the boom and bust of the 1920s, the growth of the middle sectors in the decades of the Keynesian period, and the return to rapidly rising inequality by 1987. It was in that immediate post-war period extending into the late 1960s and early 1970s that the incorporation of workers into formal labour market relations reached its highest level in the most advanced economies. In the United States, it helped bring down the share of total job earnings going to the top 10 per cent from 47 per cent at its height in the 1920s and early 1930s to 33 per cent from 1942 until 1987. The formalization of the employment relation in this period helped implement a set of regulations that, overall, protected workers and secured the gains made by often violent labour struggles. Not that all was well, of course. This formalization also entailed the exclusion of distinct segments of the workforce, such

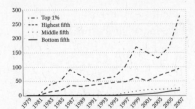

Fig. 5: Percentage change from 1979 levels in after-tax income in the United States, 1979–2007. *Data source: Sherman and Stone, 2010.*[19]

COUNTRY	DEBT PAYMENT (% government revenue)
Belize	28.1
Philippines	27.1
Bhutan	26.6
El Salvador	25.8
Sri Lanka	24.1
St Vincent	18.6
St Lucia	18.1
Angola	17.1
Maldives	14.4
Gambia	13.9
Paraguay	13.3
Guatamala	12.7
Indonesia	11.9
Laos	11.5
Pakistan	10.5

Table 2: Low- and lower-middle income governments with the highest foreign debt payments, 2012. *Data source: Jubilee Debt Campaign, 2012.*

as women and minorities, particularly in some heavily unionized industries. Whatever its virtues and defects, this golden period for organized labour came to an end in the 1980s. By 1987, inequality was on its way up again, and sharply. Figure 5 shows that the top 1 per cent of earners had a 280 per cent rise in their household income between 1979 and 2007, a trend that was confirmed in the 2010 census and continues today.

The Global South has had its own version of shrinkage, a subject I develop at greater length in Chapter 2 in *Expulsions*.[20] Very briefly, after 20 or more years of IMF and World Bank restructuring programmes, many of these countries now carry a far larger burden of debt to diverse private lenders represented by the IMF than they did before international financial intervention. Their governments now pay more to their lenders than they invest in basic components of development such as health and education. Table 2 presents data for some of the governments that owe the most.

These are some of the key destructive trends that began in the 1980s, took off globally in the 1990s, and reached some of their highest levels in the 2000s. Although many of them began before the 2008 crisis, they were not quite visible.

What was visible was the redevelopment and gentrification of vast urban areas, which produced an *impression* of overall prosperity, from Paris to Buenos Aires, from Hong Kong to Dublin. Now these formerly invisible trends have been exacerbated and have become visible. In their extreme forms they can function as windows into a more complex and elusive reality of impoverishment in the making, one partly engendered by what was mostly visible as explosive growth in wealth and profits, a 20-year process I have examined in great detail elsewhere.[21]

At the Systemic Edge

The point of inquiry in this chapter is the systemic edge. The key dynamic at this edge is expulsion from the diverse systems in play — economic, social, biospheric. This edge is foundationally different from the geographic border in the interstate system. The focus on the edge comes from the core hypothesis that the move from Keynesianism to the global era of privatizations, deregulation, and open borders for some, entailed a switch from dynamics that brought people in to dynamics that push people out. Such a switch from incorporation to expulsion might also be emerging in China and India; China, especially, has seen a massive incorporation of people into monetized economies, but now is also experiencing sharpening inequality, new forms of economic concentration at the top, and corporate bullying.

Each major domain has its own distinctive systemic edge — this edge is constituted differently for the economy than it is for the biosphere and the social. One of the organizing assumptions in this chapter is that the systemic edge is the site where general conditions take extreme forms precisely because it is the site for expulsion or incorporation. Further, the extreme character of conditions at the edge makes visible larger trends that are less extreme and hence more difficult to capture. I conceive of these larger trends as conceptually subterranean because we cannot easily make them visible through our current categories of meaning. Thus the importance of positioning my inquiry at the systemic edge.

I want to conclude with a question: what are the spaces of the expelled? These are invisible to the standard measures of our modern states and economies. But they should be made conceptually visible. When dynamics of expulsion proliferate, whether in the shape of the shrunken economy of Greece, the predatory elites of Angola, or the growth of the long-term unemployed or the incarcerated in for-profit prisons in the United States, the space of the expelled expands and becomes increasingly differentiated. It is not simply a dark hole. It is present. Also the spaces of the expelled need to be conceptualized. In *Expulsions*, I make a similar argument about the proliferation of stretches of dead land and dead water due to our toxic modes of development. These are also present. Thus, in a conceptual move aimed at making dead land present, I argue it should be conceived of as an informal jurisdiction. More generally, the spaces of the expelled cry out for conceptual recognition. They are many, they are growing, and they are diversifying. They are conceptually subterranean conditions that need to be brought above ground. They are, potentially, the new spaces for making — making local economies, new histories, and new modes of membership.

1   This essay is an excerpt from my book *Expulsions: Brutality and Complexity in the Global Economy* (Cambridge, MA: Harvard University Press, 2014), reprinted with kind permission of Harvard University Press.

2   Saskia Sassen, "A Bad Idea: Using a Financial Solution to the Financial Crisis," *Huffington Post*, 20 November 2008; idem, "Mortgage Capital and Its Particularities: A New Frontier for Global Finance," *Journal of International Affairs* 62, no.1 (2008): 187–212; idem, *Territory, Authority, Rights: From Medieval to Global Assemblages*, 2nd ed. (Princeton, NJ: Princeton University Press. 2008), chapters 4 and 7; and idem, "Global Finance and Its Institutional Spaces," in *The Oxford Handbook of the Sociology of Finance*, ed. Karin Knorr Cetina and Alex Preda (Oxford: Oxford University Press, 2013).

3   Oxfam, "Our Land, Our Lives: Time Out on the Global Land Rush," Oxfam Briefing Note (October 2012), 1–2; see also Anthony B. Atkinson, Thomas Piketty and Emmanuel Saez, "Top Incomes in the Long Run of History," *Journal of Economic Literature* 49, no.1 (March 2011): 3–71.

4   Sassen, *Territory, Authority, Rights*, chapter 5.

5   Saskia Sassen, *The Global City: New York, London, Tokyo*, revised 2nd ed. (Princeton, NJ: Princeton University Press, 2001), chapter 8; idem, *Cities in a World Economy*, revised 4th ed. (Thousand Oaks, CA: Sage/Pine Forge, 2011).

6   Saskia Sassen, *The Mobility of Labor and Capital: A Study in International Investment and Labor Flow* (Cambridge: Cambridge University Press, 1988).

7   David Cay Johnston, *Perfectly Legal: The Covert Campaign to Rig Our Tax System to Benefit the Super Rich — and Cheat Everybody Else* (New York: Penguin, 2005); idem, "Corporate Tax Rates Plummet as Profits Soar," *The National Memo*, 16 July 2013; GAO, "Corporate Income Tax: Effective Rates Can Differ Significantly from Statutory Rate" (Report to Congressional Requesters, Washington, DC, 2013); and CNNMoney Staff, "S&P 500 Above

1,800. Dow Hits Record Again," *CNNMoney*, 22 November 2013, http://money.cnn.com/2013/11/22/investing/stocks-markets/.

8   Johnston 2013 writes that a 1 July 2013 report to Congress suggests the rate on large profitable firms may be even lower than what is shown in publicly available IRS data. The 2010 net tax rate was really just 12.6 per cent, according to the Government Accountability Office — the investigative arm of Congress — which had access to secret documents.

9   Large corporate firms do extensive lobbying for laws and regulatory rules that get little or no attention in the mainstream news. GE spent US$39.3 million just on Washington lobbying in 2010, more than US$73,000 per senator and representative. ExxonMobil has spent on average almost US$23 million annually lobbying Washington between 2008 and 2010. Walmart has spent between US$6.2 million and US$7.8 million lobbying Washington each year since 2008. See also Lawrence Mishel, "Economy Built for Profits Not Prosperity" (Economic Policy Institute, Washington, DC, 28 March 2013).

10 Tax Justice Network, "The Cost of Tax Abuse" (November 2011).

11 For a short description of the report, see David Cay Johnston, "Where's the Fraud, Mr. President?" *Reuters*, 13 December 2011; Chris Isidore, "Corporate Profits Hit Record as Wages Get Squeezed," CNNMoney, 4 December 2012, http://money.cnn.com/2012/12/03/news/economy/record-corporate-profits/.

12 Sassen, *Territory, Authority, Rights*, chapter 5.

13 Ida Kubiszewski et al. "Beyond GDP: Measuring and Achieving Global Genuine Progress," *Ecological Economics* 93 (2013): 57–68.

14 Isabel Ortiz and Matthew Cummins, *The Age of Austerity: A Review of Public Expenditures and Adjustment Measures in 181 Countries* (New York: Initiative for Policy Dialogue & Geneva: The South Centre, 2013); see also Samir Amin, "Exiting the Crisis of Capitalism or Capitalism in Crisis?" *Globalizations* 7, no.1 (27 April 2010): 261–273; and Alejandro Portes, *Economic Sociology: A Systematic Inquiry* (Princeton, NJ: Princeton University Press, 2010).

15   This is a whole subject in itself, with a rapidly growing research literature; for one of the most comprehensive treatments, see John R Bryson and Peter W. Daniels, eds., *The Handbook of Service Industries* (Cheltenham: Edward Elgar Publishing, 2007). It is impossible to develop the subject here beyond a few summary statements (for a detailed discussion and extensive list of sources see Sassen, *The Global City*, chapters 5 and 6, and idem, "Global Finance and Its Institutional Spaces;" see also idem, "Interactions of the Technical and the Social: Digital Formations of the Powerful and the Powerless," *Information, Communication & Society* 15 (2012) on digital technology). In my reading, the growth in the demand for service inputs, and especially bought service inputs, in all industries is perhaps the most fundamental condition making for change in advanced economies. One measure can be found in the value of bought service inputs in all industries. For this purpose I analyzed the national accounts data over different periods — beginning with 1960 — for several industries in manufacturing and services. For instance, the results showed clearly that this value increased markedly over time. It has had pronounced impacts on the earnings distribution, on industrial organization, and on the patterns along which economic growth has spatialized. It has contributed to a massive growth in the demand for services by firms in all industries, from mining and manufacturing to finance and consumer services, and by households, both rich and poor.

16   For instance, data analyzed by Smeeding for 25 developed and developing countries showed that since 1973 the incomes of those in the top 5 per cent have risen by nearly 50 per cent, while incomes of those in the bottom 5 per cent have declined by approximately 4 per cent — see Timothy M. Smeeding, "Globalization, Inequality, and the Rich Countries of the G-20: Evidence from the Luxembourg Income Study (LIS)" (SPRC discussion paper no. 122, Sydney, University of New South Wales, 2002). According to the U.S. Bureau of the Census, from 1970 to 2003 the aggregate national income share of the top 5 per cent in the United States went from 16 to 21 per cent, and for the top 20 per cent from 41 per cent to 48 per cent. All these figures will tend to underestimate inequality insofar as the top earners also have non-salary-based gains in wealth, and the bottom of the scale tends to exclude many of the poor who lack any source of income and are dependent on friends and family, or become homeless and dependent on charities.

17   Lawrence Mishel, "Who's Grabbing All the New Pie? Economic Snapshots" (Economic Policy Institute, Washington, DC, 1 August 2007); Joseph E. Stiglitz, *The Price of Inequality* (New York: W. W. Norton & Company, 2012); and Max Fisher, "Map: U.S. Ranks Near Bottom on Income Inequality," *The Atlantic*, 19 September 2011.

18   Lawrence Mishel, Jared Bernstein and Sylvia Alegretto, *The State of Working America, 2004/2005* (Ithaca, NY: Cornell University Press, 2004), table 1.

19   Arloc Sherman and Chad Stone, "Income Gaps Between Very Rich and Everyone Else More than Tripled in Last Three Decades, New Data Show" (Center on Budget and Policy Priorities, Washington, DC, 25 June 2010).

20   Sassen, *Expulsions*.

21   Sassen, *The Global City*; and idem, *Cities in a World Economy*.

BOTTOM BILLION CAPITALISM: HOW INFORMALITY BECAME A GLOBAL MARKET

Ananya Roy

Ethicalizing the Market

It was the end of a long day at work. I had just finished shopping for groceries at Whole Foods Market in Berkeley, my cart piled high with striped heirloom tomatoes, lush eggplants and round Asian pears. Then I saw Felicita. She was smiling, a broad grin that was confident, and she bore in her hands a garment with vibrant embroidery. Felicita was the "micro-entrepreneur" featured that month at Whole Foods Market, her smiling face beaming at us from donation flyers. As I paid for my groceries, I had the option of adding $1 or $5 to my bill for use by the Whole Planet Foundation to "empower the poor through microcredit". But the flyer also told a story: of how Felicita, who lives in Guatemala, "runs an embroidery business and sells her products in the local marketplace". Curious to learn more I came home and browsed the "photo-story" of Felicita on the Whole Planet Foundation website: "Before receiving a microloan, she lacked the capital to buy enough raw materials to make more than a few blouses a week. Now, she has doubled her monthly production, enabling her to buy school supplies for her children."[1]

FELICITA

That was 2008. Felicita's photo-story is no longer featured on the Whole Planet Foundation website but there are numerous other such stories of entrepreneurial poor women displayed there. Each is photographed with her new enterprise launched through a microloan. Each is beaming a smile.

My encounter with Felicita was the opening move of my book, *Poverty Capital.*[2]

ETHICAL CONSUMERISM

I interpreted that encounter as symbolizing three broad processes. First, Felicita was one of millions of women worldwide who are today recipients of microfinance loans given out by a proliferation of organizations. Microfinance, the provision of financial services to the poor, has become a poverty panacea. Billed as the democratization of capital, microfinance seeks to remedy exclusionary systems of finance by extending credit to the poor. In this sense, microfinance is the iconic example of "bottom of the pyramid" markets. The idea of such markets comes from the seminal work of business school guru, C.K. Prahalad, who argues that it is possible to eradicate "poverty through profits".[3] In his early work, Prahalad envisioned the world's poor as vast and new markets, a source of renewed profits for corporations. Most significant, Prahalad argued that such an approach would break with paternalistic forms of aid to the poor. Covers of his book bore the phrase, "enabling dignity and choice through markets". But as noted by Elyachar, in his later work, Prahalad was to more ambitiously argue that the bottom of the pyramid was a "giant laboratory" where the "next practices" of business models and strategies could be found.[4] In short, multinational corporations could discover "new sources of value from the social practices of the poorest of the poor".[5] I term such efforts "bottom billion capitalism", a transformation of capitalism to integrate the poor not through well-worn formats of exploitation and dispossession but instead through new formats of inclusion and integration. Central to bottom billion capitalism is faith in the inherent entrepreneurialism of the poor, specifically in an entrepreneurialism that can convert informal economies of survival and subsistence into productive enterprises through the magic of financialization, in this case microfinance loans.

Second, Felicita is the microfinance client of Banrural Grameen Guatemala, a Whole Planet Foundation partner. In 2007, the Whole Planet Foundation, Banrural, and the Grameen Trust entered into an agreement to establish a microfinance organization in Guatemala. Headquartered in Austin, Texas, Whole Planet Foundation is a private, non-profit organization established by Whole Foods Market to address issues of world hunger and poverty. Banrural is Guatemala's largest bank. The Grameen Trust is a special arm of the Grameen Bank of Bangladesh, charged with the mission of replicating the Grameen microfinance model around the world. The Grameen Bank of Bangladesh is of course one of the pioneering organizations of modern microfinance. Implemented widely in Bangladesh, the Grameen Bank model is today a global phenomenon, bearing the powerful promise of alleviating poverty and empowering women. In recognition of such efforts, Muhammad Yunus and the Grameen Bank were awarded the 2006 Nobel Peace Prize. The prize committee credited them with the creation of "economic and social development from below". "Lasting peace," the committee noted, "cannot be achieved unless

CONSCIOUS CAPITALISM

large population groups find ways in which to break out of poverty. Micro-credit is one such means."[6]

Felicita thus belongs to a distinctive assemblage, one that articulates profit-making corporations with non-profit humanitarian organizations with financial institutions. This assemblage departs from previous formats of development in significant ways. On the one hand, it seeks to revolutionize philanthropy through the logic, discipline and metrics of capital investment, what Bishop and Green have celebrated as "philanthrocapitalism".[7] On the other hand, it seeks to ethicalize capitalism itself. Thus, co-founder and CEO of Whole Foods Market, John Mackey has called for a "conscious capitalism", a commitment to achieving social impact alongside reaping profits.[8] The idea bears striking resemblance to Bill Gates's vision of "creative capitalism", a transformation of capitalism to include and assist the billions it has left out.[9] But it is worth noting that key to philanthrocapitalism or conscious capitalism or creative capitalism is the "heroic spirit" — Mackey and Sisodia's phrase — of markets.

Third, Felicita is an example of the visible global poor, her photo-story enmeshed with the mundane and intimate routines of our lives. Her visibility is a crucial aspect of how spaces of consumerism, such as Whole Foods Market, are being transformed into ethicalized markets, portals of intimate transactions of conscious capitalism. But the production of her visibility — the seemingly ethnographic narrative accompanying her smiling images — indicates yet another set of transactions, those of global volunteers seeking to do good by helping the poor. In a strange irony, Felicita's photo-story was constructed by a young man called Alex Crane who spent a summer volunteering for Grameen Guatemala. As it turns out, Alex was also a student in my Global Poverty class at the University of California, Berkeley. Alex is part of a generation of "millennials" — college students and young professionals in both the global North and global South who are defining a global sense of self through the portals of volunteerism and humanitarianism. In these encounters with what Elwood and Lawson have described as "poor others", they make and unmake their own class ontologies.[10] Such encounters are replete with "affective surplus", a phrase I borrow from Adams who studies how the recognition of poverty and need generates an emotional urgency whose circulation becomes an "ethical inducement to action".[11] From the volunteerism of millennials such as Alex to the micro-donations added on to the payment for groceries, the affect economy is a key part of the ethicalization of the market and the renewal of capitalism's creativity. Technologies of visibility and portals of intimacy are in turn central to the affect economy.

But there is more to Felicita's story. Recently, I partnered with an artist, Abby Van Muijen, to create a series of short-length video animations, each taking up an issue related to global poverty. Combining critical social theory, improvised art, and graphic illustration, the #GlobalPov project stages an intervention in the age of Youtube.[12] Our second video, produced in 2013, is titled "Can We Shop to End Poverty?" Meant to examine the hegemonic formation that is bottom billion capitalism, the video explores popular strategies of ethical consumerism. Our storyboard for the video started with Felicita's story. Since Whole Planet Foundation had granted permission for her photograph to be reprinted in *Poverty Capital,* I assumed that similar permission would be forthcoming for the video. But I was mistaken. The Development and Outreach Director for the foundation insisted not only on reviewing the script but also on the power to veto segments of it. In particular, she objected to three aspects of our analysis: that we critiqued how the global poor were made visible as smiling women entrepreneurs; that we noted that Whole Foods consumers would never get to meet or know women like Felicita who they were asked to support through micro-donations; and that the script did not acknowledge the social impacts of Whole Foods Market's business model. Self-described as "inspired" by the "transformative power of microcredit" and eager to "create prosperity", this foundation director argued that women like Felicita smile in their photographs because they are proud of their micro-enterprises. The smile, she emphasized, is a statement of human dignity. Felicita, she also noted, need not be a stranger to me or other Whole Foods consumers. After all, Whole Planet Foundation had just launched "consumer volunteer" trips such that "conscious capitalists" could travel to the exotic sites of such microloans to witness firsthand the impacts of their donations. Finally, she asserted that Whole Foods Market, inspired by the philosophy of conscious capitalism, had pioneered a stakeholder business model, one committed to producing social benefit to the communities from which they sourced their products.

It was an intriguing set of arguments, providing rare insight into the workings of bottom billion capitalism. Was it so important to present the global poor as smiling Third World women? Why did it matter to stage numerous types of encounters with poverty? And what was at stake in the stakeholder business model? What, for example, was the main form of the social benefit created in stakeholder communities? Microcredit and its transformative power, of course. Financed how? Through the donations solicited by Whole Foods Market from its shoppers as they buy (expensive) groceries. In addition, its own store workers make millions of dollars in donations, often through a regular pay deduction. These are the funds utilized by Whole Planet Foundation to make microfinance loans in stakeholder communities. Needless to

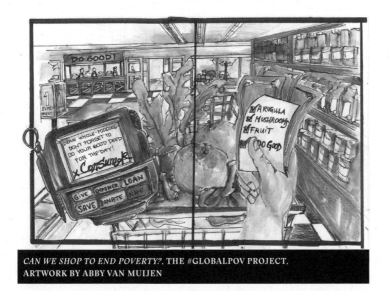

CAN WE SHOP TO END POVERTY?, THE #GLOBALPOV PROJECT.
ARTWORK BY ABBY VAN MUIJEN

say, this version of stakeholder capitalism cannot envision a stake for Felicita in the massive profits generated by this mammoth retail chain.

Here then is an excerpt from our revised script, sans Whole Planet Foundation permission and approval, sans Felicita:

Here then is my first provocation: that in a global world, we do not see invisible workers. Instead we see visible poverty.

A child living in poverty flashes a brilliant smile. Sponsor a child today.

Do the poor really smile this much? Bullshit.

Here is my second provocation: that what we see in the poverty spectacle is not the effects of our consumption but instead the poor whose lives can be saved by us.

Who is the us? Those with the resources and power to sponsor a child, make a Kiva loan, donate a heifer, buy a pair of shoes so that a second pair can be given to those who are barefoot.

This too is consumption. And this consumption is a relationship — at once intimate and distant — between benevolence and need, between donor and recipient.

Where does this relationship take place? Increasingly, in our everyday acts of shopping.

And thus my question to you: can we shop to end poverty?

Each week I shop for groceries at a fancy store in Berkeley. You know the type: fair trade goodies, organic produce, sky-high prices.

Each week I fill my grocery cart with organic, peppery arugula, delicate mushrooms, and luscious fruit. Yes, I am a foodie.

And each week the act of grocery shopping becomes the opportunity to do good. I can add $5 to my grocery bill to empower poor women a continent away; I can donate to end world hunger; I can make poverty history — quickly, conveniently, as I shop.

I am no longer just a consumer; I am now a micro-philanthropist.

Let me share a confession with you: I like this feeling. I like to make micro-donations. I like to feel that these donations have an impact on poverty and that these impacts can be measured and tallied and printed on the side of recyclable grocery bags. I like the feeling.

Poverty and Millennial Modernity

In 1989, at the height of free market ideology and practice, Francis Fukuyama published an essay titled *The End of History and the Last Man*. In it, he argued that "what we may be witnessing is not just the end of the Cold War... but the end of history as such: that is, the end point of mankind's ideological evolution and the universalization of Western liberal democracy as the final form of human government".[13] Fukuyama also went on to argue that "liberal principles in economics — the 'free market' — have spread", producing "unprecedented levels of material prosperity" around the world.[14] Although Fukuyama himself was to later cast doubt on the "end of history" thesis, at the time the paradigm signified the audacious utopia of free-market, global capitalism.

Yet, by the start of the new millennium, this seemingly unshakeable utopianism had given way to a grave and widespread awareness of global suffering. Writing against Fukuyama, Jacques Derrida in *Specters of Marx* drew attention to worldwide poverty, the "obvious macroscopic fact", that "never before, in absolute figures, have so many men, women and children been subjugated, starved or exterminated on the earth".[15] If the free market can be understood as a "stark utopia" — Karl Polanyi's term[16] — then now it was haunted by the spectre of poverty.

But this millennial concern with poverty is also utopian in its audacity and euphoria. If Fukuyama had proclaimed the end of history, interlocutors of millennial development now proclaim the end of poverty.[17] In my previous work, I have charted the remarkable emergence of this collective will to end poverty.[18] An unprecedented mobilization of global conscience, this millennial utopia has been fuelled by the global social movements of the 1990s — in the villages of Chiapas, on the streets of Seattle, at the barricades of Cancun, at the World Social Forum of Porto Alegre. It has involved a remaking of the global institutions of development, from the launch of the Millennium Development Goals of the United Nations to the incorporation of poverty alleviation as a key part of the mission of the World Bank. Organized against the stark utopia of the free market, this millennial utopia envisions a world where poverty will exist only in museums — a phrase often used by Muhammad Yunus, the 2006 recipient of the Nobel Peace Prize and founder of the Grameen Bank.

If millennialism rejects the free market as an organizing paradigm — indeed, the language of market failure dominates millennial development — then what animates this historical moment? The answer to this question, I argue, lies in the new visibilities of poverty. Of course, the concern for poverty is not new. At various historical moments, poverty has emerged as a public issue. At each of these moments, a distinctive visibility has attended the public character of poverty debates. For example, in the late nineteenth century, amidst the flurry of urban modernization, poverty became suddenly visible. From Baudelaire's prose poetry to the photographs of Jacob Riis, fin-de-siècle culture was necessarily constituted through the "eyes of the poor", through that encounter with "how the other half lives". The visibility of poverty was enabled by new social technologies, including the survey. Maps of poverty, for example those produced by social reformer Charles Booth in London, were at once a statistical order and a moral order, cataloguing the "deserving" and "undeserving" poor. Osborne and Rose rightly note that Booth's surveys of poverty should be seen as one of the great inventions of the social sciences, its role akin

AFRICA WORKS, UNITED COLORS OF BENETTON, 2009

to that of the telescope in the natural sciences.[19] In the new millennium, poverty is once again visible, and new social technologies, from internet portals to celebrity campaigns to an industry of volunteerism, mediate the visibility of poverty. Particularly significant is that poverty has become visible as a global issue, as an urgent problem that transcends national borders and economies, and that can be taken up by global citizens acting upon a newly constituted social category, the global poor. This is the story of Felicita that I sought to tell in the opening section of this essay.

But what is distinctive about the present historical conjuncture is yet another relationship between modernity and poverty: a conversion of the shadow economies of the poor into new frontiers of capital accumulation. Such an imagination is not limited to microfinance and its microloans but in fact is writ large. Indeed, it is an imagination about the world itself.

Fukuyama's stark utopia of the end of history required a geographical imagination of a flat world. The latter, a phrase coined by Thomas Friedman,[20] suggests a "level playing-field" of economic competition where old geographical separations and historical divisions are irrelevant, one where Bangalore, India, can compete neck to neck with Silicon Valley, California. This world, as imagined by Friedman, is one of mobile entrepreneurs, the instantaneous flows of capital and innovations, and an unprecedented time-space compression enabled by new technologies of information and transportation. But millennial modernity is concerned with market failure and poverty traps. It cannot imagine a flat world. Instead it imagines a world full of spaces of underdevelopment and backwardness, and yet one in which such primitivism can be transformed into productivity. Take the case of Africa. Once understood only in the language of crisis, as the heart of darkness, it is now what James Ferguson has called a place-in-the-world.[21] Take for example a Benetton "global communication campaign". Featuring Senegalese singer Youssou N'Dour, the campaign highlights a microcredit programme in Senegal supported by Benetton. N'Dour proudly states that "Africa doesn't want charity" but rather wants microfinance.[22] His declaration echoes a new set of "African" voices that seek to set Africa "free" — free from Western aid and state bureaucracies. This is the theme of Ayittey's treatise, "Africa unchained": Africa is poor because it is not free.[23] It is also the central idea in the influential work of Dambisa Moyo who claims that aid has encumbered economic development and entrepreneurialism in Africa.[24] The Benetton campaign's striking images promise freedom — economic freedom — transforming figures of African poverty into micro-entrepreneurs. They are the new "united colors of Benetton", a reconfigured global chic. But they are also, in the words of Alessandro Benetton the "new face of Africa".[25] They embody the truth that is the Benetton campaign slogan: that "Africa Works".

In his important intervention *On the Postcolony*, Achille Mbembe notes that "Africa still constitutes one of the metaphors through which the West represents the origin of its own norms, develops a self-image"; Africa is that which is defined as "radically *other*, as all that the West is not".[26] But what is at stake in millennial modernity is how ontologies of difference — notably poverty as the primitive other — comes to be absorbed and assimilated into a master narrative of development. In the Benetton advertisement, symbols of Africa's informal economy become symbols of global entrepreneurialism. The global poor symbolize difference and yet are now a part of the modern economy, indeed an integral part of the modern self itself. Nowhere is this more evident than in the popular sentiment that underpins many of the global poverty campaigns: that we are all Africans. For example, the July 2007 issue of *Vanity Fair*, was dedicated to Africa and guest edited by Bono. In it, we are introduced to Africa not so much via Africans as through American celebrities who care about Africa: Oprah, George Clooney, Madonna, Bill Gates, each photographed in stunning fashion by Annie Leibovitz. Particularly striking is a theme that runs through the entire issue: that we are all Africans. This theme echoes an earlier media campaign of the U.S.-based charity, Keep a Child Alive: *I am African*,[27] with celebrities such as Gwyneth Paltrow and Richard Gere, meant to draw attention to the ravages of HIV/AIDS on the continent. In the *Vanity Fair* issue, DNA samples taken from the editors and celebrities chart "individual ancestral paths from their starting point in East Africa". Editor Graydon Carter writes: "It is quite moving to see that every person on the planet is linked to this African tribe, and that, as the saying goes, we are all African."[28]

If we understand "bottom billion capitalism" as a set of dispersed but coherent efforts to construct a global economy where the world's bottom billion are integrated into circuits of capital accumulation, then the conversion of poverty from primitive alterity to the "next practices" of productivity is of vital significance. This is, as the title of this edited collection suggests, the making of informal market worlds. Microfinance is an especially interesting case because it is a peculiar type of bottom billion capitalism. The commodity that is being produced, traded, and valued is debt. The practices of calculation at work in microfinance are less a valuation of the labour of the poor or of the assets of the poor and more an assessment of the capacity to enact repayment. Not surprisingly, the microfinance mantra is that "the poor always pay back".[29] This is the speculative arbitrage that underlies microfinance: a calculation about the social habits of the poor and how they can be capitalized through the practices of financial discipline imposed by microfinance institutions. At a World Bank sponsored microfinance training workshop that I attended, one economist thus described microfinance as "the mystical and transcendental practice of monetizing the promise of a poor woman who has never before touched money". In another account, a microfinance consultant noted that microfinance can function "in places where Americans are scared to drink the water". Comaroff and Comaroff have appropriately argued that millennial capitalism is "magical" because it seems to have the capacity to yield wealth "purely through exchange [...] as if entirely independent of human manufacture".[30] Key to such exchange is how debt is made productive, and how in the generation of such productivity, the informal worlds of the bottom of the pyramid are monetized and financialized.

If we understand microfinance as an experiment in what Janet Roitman has called the "productivity of debt",[31] then it becomes apparent that microfinance, and other such forms of bottom billion capitalism are not the abandoned past of global finance capital but rather its future. Finance capital itself needs the tricks and techniques of microfinance — the "mystical and transcendental practice of monetizing the promise of a poor woman who has never before touched money", "in places where Americans are scared to drink the water". It is in this sense that microfinance has been branded as a cure for the crisis of capital. The cure that it represents is at once the ethicalization of the market and the "next practices" of making debt productive. As I have argued in previous work, such formations rely on the (re)articulation of territories and subjects of risk.[32] It is thus that Africa is being transformed from dark continent into primal human history. It is thus that the redlined informal economies of the poor are being transformed from the primitive other of global finance capital into its future. Put another way, subjects and territories once designated as high-risk are now being valorized and monetized as frontiers economies. Needless to say, not all forms of risk are thus valorized. In a recent essay, Rankin thus notes that while microfinance, anchored by the operative subjectivity of rational economic woman, is celebrated as a cure for the crisis of capital, massive defaults in U.S. subprime mortgages are narrated "in terms of the dangers of lending to 'publicly designated bad subjects'".[33] What are the epistemologies of poverty that make possible such constructions of risk and thereby of new market worlds? In the concluding section of the essay, I argue that central to these epistemologies of poverty is a specific understanding of informality. Once the realm of deproletarianized survival, informality is now the new economy of entrepreneurship, poised to be monetized and capitalized. Indeed, informality seems to hold the key to the fortune at the bottom of the pyramid.

The Creativity of Capitalism

The modern economy is a construction. From Polanyi to Foucault, social theorists have charted the emergence of this sphere. In an important analysis, Mitchell foregrounds the making of the modern economy, as "self-contained, internally dynamic, and statistically measurable sphere of social action, scientific analysis, and political regulation".[34] The birth of the economy, he argues, made possible "new forms of value, new kinds of equivalence, new practices of calculation, new relations between human agency and the nonhuman, and new distinctions between what was real and the forms of its representation". Such an analysis is particularly useful for an understanding of bottom billion capitalism as a distinctive format of the modern economy, one in which a new type of relationship is established between capitalism and poverty.

In an essay on the "global poor", Nancy Fraser argues that the term casts the poor as "passive victims instead of agents and potential political actors" and abstracts "from the social relations and processes that have generated their poverty".[35] She prefers the term, "transnational precariat", both to indicate exploitation, precarity, and vulnerability, and to mark multiple intersecting scales of justice. But Fraser's conceptualization exists in sharp contrast to the epistemologies of poverty that animate bottom billion capitalism. In this final section, I turn to the example of a new national policy unfolding in India, Slum-Free Cities, to provide an example of such epistemologies of poverty.

In India, two decades of slum demolitions and squatter evictions have given way to what at first glance seems to be a radical paradigm shift: a recognition of the slum as a vital part of Indian cities. A component of India's ambitious national urban renewal mission, Rajiv Awas Yojana, or Slum-Free Cities replaces regimes of urban dispossession with a new mode of governing: inclusive growth. Inclusive growth, as articulated in various discourses and agendas in India, is a vision of market-oriented inclusion, very much in keeping with the premises and arguments of bottom billion capitalism.

Like microfinance, Slum-Free Cities is simultaneously an ethicalization of the market and a new frontier of capital accumulation. On the one hand, Slum-free Cities signals what one of its main authors has titled a "new deal for India's urban poor", or safety nets for the urban poor.[36] On the other hand, the policy seeks to transform slum land into urban assets, in other words, to initiate slum redevelopment. At the core of these slum redevelopment plans is a radical idea: the assignment of legal title to slum-dwellers. Such a declaration of security of tenure for the urban poor is crucial, especially in India where slum evictions and demolitions have been commonplace. But the challenge with Slum-Free Cities is that these property titles for slum-dwellers are meant to enact social inclusion as well as create new markets. Inspired by policy guru, Hernando de Soto, India's then Minister of Housing and Urban Poverty Alleviation, in a talk titled "Inclusive Paradigms for Inclusive Growth" announced Slum-Free Cities by posing the following question: "How do we create a process by which the poor can convert capital from the extra-legal to the legal sphere and in so doing, contribute to the GDP at the bottom of the pyramid?"[37] It is thus that India's first urban social protection policy is also an endeavour to title and revalue property. It is thus that security of tenure in newly visible slum lands becomes the basis of slum redevelopment.

Hernando de Soto's understandings of poverty and informality are an important ingredient of the hegemonic formation I am calling bottom billion capitalism. Against apocalyptic renderings of a "planet of slums"[38] where a "surplus humanity" is warehoused in spaces of despair, de Soto presents the Third World slum as the place of "heroic entrepreneurs".[39] He writes: "Marx would probably be shocked to find how in developing countries much of the teeming mass does not consist of oppressed legal proletarians but of oppressed extra-legal small entrepreneurs with a sizeable amount of assets." What is important about de Soto's ideas is that he is not just providing a new global imaginary about poverty but also that this imaginary makes possible the conversion of economies of poverty into frontiers of capital accumulation. De Soto argues such economies are rich in assets, albeit in the defective form of dead capital. The "mystery of capital" is how such dormant and defective assets can be transformed into liquid capital. Of course, de Soto's authoritative narrative rests on a particular understanding of capital, one that conceptualizes capital not as the social relations of production but instead as a "representational process". For him the poor are not workers but rather latent entrepreneurs who own assets, albeit those rendered impotent by faulty representation.

In the West [...] every parcel of land, every building, every piece of equipment, or store of inventories is represented in a property document that is the visible sign of a vast hidden process that connects all these assets to the rest of the economy. [...] [Assets] can be used as collateral for credit. [...] Third World and former communist nations do not have this representational process. As a result, most of them are undercapitalized [...]. The enterprises of the poor are very much like corporations that cannot issue shares or bonds to obtain new investment and finance. Without representations, their assets are dead capital. The poor inhabitants of these nations — five-sixths of humanity — do have things, but they lack the process to represent their property and create capital. [...] This is the mystery of capital.[40]

Not surprisingly, India's Slum-Free Cities policy, and more broadly the inclusive growth approach, pivots on new visibilities of poverty. Indeed, central to market-oriented inclusive growth is the state's project of unique identification, *Aadhar*, spearheaded by Nandan Nilekani, a mogul of India's software industry. "Inclusive growth is giving identity," Nilekani has argued, "about giving every Indian an acknowledged existence and then letting them participate in the fruits of development".[41] For Nilekani, the *Aadhar* project marks a departure from previous state interventions in poverty:

> If 30 years back, we talked about *roti, kapda, aur makaan* (food, clothing and shelter) and in the last 10 years we have talked about *bijli, sadak, paani*, which is infrastructure (power, roads and water), then in the next 10 years, it is going to be about bank accounts, mobile numbers and *Aadhaar*.[42]

Nilekani's conceptualization of the "power of identity" bears striking resemblance to de Soto's arguments about granting legal identity to slums. Above all, these are a set of calculative practices meant to make poverty visible, and to thereby establish the foundations not only of social inclusion but also of a bottom billion capitalism able to capitalize the shadow economies of the poor.

But Slum-Free Cities is not just about new visibilities of poverty; it is also about a new epistemology of poverty, that of the poor as heroic entrepreneur, one able to convert slum lands into assets of global value. In sharp contrast to conceptualizations of poverty concerned with exploitation, dispossession, and spatial inequality, this epistemology of poverty is a vision of what a recent architectural exhibition described as "jugaad urbanism", a celebration of the brilliant bricolage of the urban poor, a display of the "inspired, duct-taped ingenuity" of slums.[43] From tin-can canopies to frugal latrines, the exhibition argued that the poor "make-do" and that such forms of making-do are a new idiom of urban ingenuity and entrepreneurialism.

In my previous work, I have argued that such valorizations of economies of poverty are now commonplace.[44] Take for example global architect, Rem Koolhaas who interprets the urbanism of Lagos as a "culture of make-do".[45] In his encounter with Lagos, part of Harvard's Project on the City, Koolhaas is taken with the inventiveness of its residents as they survive the travails of the megacity. He sees such experimental responses as generating "ingenious, critical alternative systems", a type of "self-organization" creating "intense emancipatory zones".[46] As Gandy has noted, such imaginations turn on the premise of "ontological difference", the African megacity situated outside the currents of world history.[47] Key to this understanding of difference — assimilable difference — is a conceptualization of poverty as ingenuity. And such "inspired, duct-taped ingenuity", I am suggesting, is a key idea in the making of bottom billion capitalism and its informal market worlds.

But bottom billion capitalism is fragile. In the case of Slum-Free Cities, it requires the difficult work of converting complex and informal systems of land ownership into cadastral property and ultimately into assets with globally legible value. Amidst slums replete with multiple regimes of tenancy and occupation, such a task is near impossible. Indeed, I interpret Indian cities as a generalized system of informality such that social differentiation must be located not in the distinction between formal and informal habitation but rather *within* informal habitation in the distinction between elite informality and subaltern informality. Elite informality, from farmhouses to commercial developments, is no more legal than the shantytowns of the poor. But as the encroachments of the rich, they are expressions of class power and can thus command infrastructure, services, and legitimacy in a way that marks them as substantially different from the landscape of slums. The Indian state has for decades, if not centuries, criminalized subaltern informality while legalizing elite informality. As an expression of bottom billion capitalism, Slum-Free Cities misses the urgent question at hand: Who is authorized to (mis)use the law in order to declare property a law and capitalize its exchange as a commodity?

To repoliticize informality, to challenge the aestheticization of poverty, it is necessary to return to such fundamental questions, specifically those of elite encroachments and the (mis)use of the law by the powerful. These are the shadow economies of unregulated wealth, too often rendered invisible by the affects of millennial modernity.

1 http://www.wholeplanetfoundation.org/partners/microen-trepreneurs

2 Ananya Roy, *Poverty Capital: Microfinance and the Making of Development* (New York: Routledge, 2010).

3 Coimbatore Krishnarao Prahalad, *The Fortune at the Bottom of the Pyramid: Eradicating Poverty through Profits* (Cambridge, MA: Wharton School Publishing, 2004).

4 Julia Elyachar, "Next Practices: Knowledge, Infrastructure, and Public Goods at the Bottom of the Pyramid," *Public Culture* 24, no. 1 (2012): 109–129.

5 Ibid., 110.

6 Ole Danbolt Mjøs, "Presentation speech: Nobel Peace Prize award ceremony," 2006, accessed 7 January 2007, http://nobelprize.org/nobel_prizes/peace/laureates/2006/presentation-speech.html.

7 Matthew Bishop and Michael Green, *Philanthrocapitalism: How the Rich Can Save the World* (New York: Bloomsbury Press, 2008).

8 John Mackey and Raj Sisodia, *Conscious Capitalism: Liberating the Heroic Spirit of Business* (Boston, MA: Harvard Business Review, 2013).

9 Bill Gates, "How to fix capitalism," *Time,* 31 July 2008, 23–29.

10 Sarah Elwood and Victoria Lawson, "Encountering Poverty: Space, Class and Poverty Politics," *Antipode,* published online (2013): 1–20.

11 Vincanne Adams, *Markets of Sorrow, Labors of Faith: New Orleans in the Wake of Katrina* (Durham, NC: Duke University Press, 2013), 1.

12 http://blumcenter.berkeley.edu/globalpov/

13 Francis Fukuyama, "The End of History?" *The National Interest* 16 (1989): 4.

14 Francis Fukuyama, *The End of History and the Last Man* (New York: Avon Book, 1992), xiii.

15 Jacques Derrida, *Specters of Marx: The State of the Debt, the Work of Mourning, and the New International* (New York: Routledge, 1994), 106.

16 Karl Polanyi, *The Great Transformation: The Political and Economic Origins of Our Time* (Boston, MA: Beacon Press, [1944] 2001), 3.

17 Jeffrey Sachs, *The End of Poverty: Economic Possibilities for Our Time* (New York: Penguin Press, 2005).

18 Roy, *Poverty Capital.*

19 Thomas Osborne and Nikolas Rose, "Spatial Phenomenotechnics: Making Space with Charles Booth and Patrick Geddes," *Environment and Planning D* 22, no. 2 (2004): 209–228.

20 Thomas Friedman, *The World is Flat: A Brief History of the Twenty-first Century* (New York: Farrar, Straus and Giroux, 2005).

21 James Ferguson, *Global Shadows: Africa in the Neoliberal World Order* (Durham, NC: Duke University Press, 2006), 6.

22 Benetton, "MFI Started by Youssou N'Dour Featured in Benetton's Latest Global Communication Campaign," 13 February 2008, http://www.benetton.com/africaworks-press/en/press_information/1_1.html.

23 George Ayittey, *Africa Unchained: The Blueprint for Africa's Future* (New York: Palgrave Macmillan, 2004).

24 Dambisa Moyo, *Dead Aid: Why Aid is Not Working and How There is a Better Way for Africa* (New York: Farrar, Straus and Giroux, 2009).

25 Benetton, "MFI Started by Youssou N'Dour Featured in Benetton's Latest Global Communication Campaign."

26 Achille Mbembe, *On the Postcolony* (Berkeley, CA: University of California Press, 2001), 2.

27 http://www.keepachildalive.org/i_am_african/i_am_african.html

28 Graydon Carter, "Editor's Letter: Annie Get Your Passport," *Vanity Fair* (July 2007): 28. http://www.vanityfair.com/magazine/2007/07/graydon200707.

29 Asif Dowla and Dipal Barua, *The Poor Always Pay Back: The Grameen II Story* (Bloomfield, CT: Kumarian Press, 2006).

30 Jean Comaroff and John Comaroff, "Millennial Capitalism: First Thoughts on A Second Coming," *Public Culture* 12, no. 2 (2000): 291–343.

31 Janet Roitman, "Unsanctioned Wealth; or, The Productivity of Debt in Northern Cameroon," *Public Culture* 15 (2003): 211–237.

32 Ananya Roy, "Subjects of Risk: Technologies of Gender in the Making of Millennial Modernity," *Public Culture* 24, no. 1 (2012): 131–155.

33 Katharine Rankin, "A Critical Geography of Poverty Finance," *Third World Quarterly* 34, no. 4 (2013): 547–568.

34 Timothy Mitchell, *Rule of Experts: Egypt, Techno-Politics, Modernity* (Berkeley, CA: University of California Press, 2002), 4–5.

35 Nancy Fraser, "Injustice at Intersecting Scales: On 'Social Exclusion' and the 'Global Poor'," *European Journal of Social Theory* 13 (2010): 369.

36 Om Prakash Mathur, *A New Deal for the Urban Poor: Slum-Free Cities* (Delhi: NIPFP, 2009).

37 Kumari Selja, "Inclusive Paradigms for Inclusive Growth," public address, 2010, http://www.ficci.com/events/20323/ISP/kumari_Selja.pdf.

38 Mike Davis, "Planet of Slums: Urban Involution and the Informal Proletariat," *New Left Review* 26 (2004): 5–34.

39 Hernando de Soto, *The Mystery of Capital: Why Capitalim Triumphs in the West and Fails Everywhere else* (New York: Basic Books, 2000), 216.

40 Ibid., 6–7.

41 Shaili Chopra, "Inclusive Growth is Giving Identity: Nandan Nilekani," *Economic Times,* 2 November 2010, http://articles.economictimes.indiatimes.com/2010-11-02/news/27602165_1_nandan-nilekani-inclusive-growth-flat-world.

42 Nandan Nilekani, "The Power of Identity," Skoch Group, n.d., http://www.inclusion.in/index.php?option=com_content&view=article&id=537&Itemid=77.

43 Kanu Agrawal, "Jugaad Urbanism: Resourceful Strategies for Indian Cities," 2011, http://cfa.aiany.org/index.php?section=upcoming&expid=136.

44 Ananya Roy, "Slumdog Cities: Rethinking Subaltern Urbanism," *International Journal of Urban and Regional Research* 35, no. 2 (2011): 223–238.

45 Okwui Enwezor, "Terminal modernity: Rem Koolhaas' discourse on entropy," in *What is OMA: Considering Rem Koolhaas and the Office for Metropolitan Architecture*, ed. Véronique Patteeuw (Rotterdam: NAi Publishers, 2004), 116.

46 Joseph Godlewski, "Alien and Distant: Rem Koolhaas on Film in Lagos, Nigeria," *Traditional Dwellings and Settlements Review* XXI, no. II (2010): 7–20.

47 Matthew Gandy, "Planning, Anti-planning and the Infrastructure Crisis Facing Metropolitan Lagos," *Urban Studies* 43, no. 2 (2006): 371–396.

ECODOMICS:
LIFE BEYOND THE NEOLIBERAL APOCALYPSE[1]

Ignacio Valero

— Nature Loves to Hide. *(Heraclitus)*

— It is easier to imagine the end of the world than it is to imagine the end of capitalism. *(Fredric Jameson)*

— TINA: There is no alternative. — There is no such thing as society. *(Margaret Thatcher)*

— "Then let me ask you this," he said. "Would a person on Earth be worse off if they weren't part of a society?" "Oh, for sure," I said "you don't have to explain that." *(Dante,* Paradiso, *Canto VIII)*

— Emancipatory politics must always destroy the appearance of 'natural order'. *(Mark Fisher paraphrasing Brecht, Foucault, Badiou)*

— To the declaration of war on nature and humanity by neoliberal globalization, there can only be a declaration of peace ... a planetary sense of ethics and spirituality ... the deepest meaning of the ecology of difference that aims toward worlds and knowledges otherwise. *(Arturo Escobar)*

— When I give food to the poor, they call me a saint. When I ask why are they poor, they call me a communist. *(Archbishop Dom Hélder Câmara)*

— Economics ... must become a *biopolitical science*. Economic engineering, as Amartya Sen, says, must turn to ethics. *(Antonio Negri)*

— Women do two-thirds of the world's work, receive 5 percent of world income, and own less than 1 percent of the world's assets. ... How can this sordid reality be changed? *(Marcus Rediker quoting Selma James)*

— Just 85 people now own as much wealth as the bottom half of the world's population. *(Oxfam.org.uk)*

This essay is a preliminary attempt to historicize anew[2] what today has become a default, naturalized system: neoliberal free-market capitalism. A rigorous search for alternative political economies cannot be made in a context-free vacuum that protects a frozen ideological status quo, even as it paradoxically engages in a 24/7 orgy of "innovation" and "creative destruction."

The 1980s phrase of British PM Margaret Thatcher: "There is no alternative", known by its acronym, TINA, still is operative today,[3] along with her "there is no such thing as society".[4] These lead to the question: *Why has it become "easier to imagine the end of the world than it is to imagine the end of capitalism"?* Though this end-of-times quote is a satirical statement, it is a profound reflection on the callous absurdity of our contemporary condition, which invites the obvious question: *Can we even imagine, or discover in plain sight, "ways-other" and "worlds-other"?*[5]

To answer this question, we need a corresponding level of genealogical inquiry that can unpack the naturalizing concept of "capitalist realism", and its implied idea that "there is no alternative". A genealogical exercise might help us break away from the ontological and ideological stranglehold of a naturalized capitalist worldview, and, potentially, from other default management and environmental history concepts like *natural capitalism, natural capital, nature's economy* and, surely, the *market economy* with its *free markets*, that seem to add to the confusion. The word "market" brings to mind the old "village market", with nostalgic echoes of innocent commerce and exchange. Locke and Adam Smith naturalize this nostalgia and, then, a veritable roster of economists, all the way to the apologists for the gigantic financial markets of today, giving the insidious impression that all "markets" are basically the same, only bigger and faster.[6] The market, tout court, is also given human agency, as in "the market likes this or dislikes that," isomorphic to corporations being defined as people with free speech. But, the question becomes even more intricate when we open up the Pandora's Box of "informal markets", which run the gamut from bona fide alternative post-capitalist markets,[7] to those that are mere pawns in the larger game of transnational capital and labour. Thus, a historical genealogy could bring us to ideas and practices better suited to transition from our contemporary crisis and its ideological substratum — thankfully, the goal of the present book.

The brief exploration I shall make inevitably has a history-of-"Western"-thought[8] accent, not because it is the universal, normative container that must encompass all other thought and practice in the world, but because "Western" became hegemonic in the last 500 years, largely through the long, techno-economic, colonial, patriarchal, and imperialist project. It is true that its tight Eurocentric and Euro-American grip on our imaginations and practices has lost much of its former power, both from (1) the massive amplification, diversification, and connectivity of the new information, communication, and transportation technologies; the processes of decolonization; the politics of ethnic, gender, and sexual acknowledgement; and the emergence of major new players on the world stage; and (2) the 2008 global crisis of capitalist accumulation and neoliberal globalization that brought back to the table the question of the legitimacy of the system, as we saw financial corruption and vast wealth concentration and class differentials, resulting in massive poverty and inequality.[9]

In a short period of 50 years, we went from a myriad of still relatively isolated societies, nations, and communities to a new global plurality of voices, powers and interests. Nevertheless, it would be naïve to think that this expanding global polity and diversity is not still greatly influenced by the recent colonial past, the neo-colonial free market ideology, or even by events and processes that took place long ago in the Mediterranean and Middle Eastern regions of the planet. It is imperative to understand this context precisely to demonstrate that the present outcomes are fully embedded in history and geography, *and are not set in stone*.

We can only hope that the growing assertiveness of a global *ecumene* capable of welcoming a plurality of voices — always already there, yet hidden by the neoliberal discourse — is shredding this occultation through a rising tide of global awareness and resistance.

Thus, to approach the twin questions of neoliberal naturalization and ways-other to capitalism, I suggest the following intertwined levels of analysis:

(1) The Neoliberal Naturalization of Capitalism; (2) The Nature/Culture dichotomy, or the ambiguous relation between "nature" (*physis*) and "culture" (*nomos*), originally problematized by the ancient Greeks; (3) Archaic Modernity: "Divine *Oikonomia*" and Apocalypse, or the question of the sacred and the profane; and (4) The sphere of *EcoDomics*[10], post-capitalist politics, democracy, *vis-à-vis* global neoliberal capitalism; that is, the contested contemporary realm of *nomos* (culture, law, custom, ethics, aesthetics, commons) and *physis* (the environment).

In sum, borrowing from Heraclitus' observation that "*Nature loves to hide*" I suggest that *Culture loves to hide,* too — an archaic ambiguity that allows one to hide behind the other, so that every time one of them gains ascendancy and becomes ideologically hegemonic, the other still leaves its ghostly shadow.[11]

1 - The Neoliberal Naturalization of Capitalism

— Capitalist Realism: the widespread sense that not only is capitalism the only viable political and economic system, but also that it is now impossible even to *imagine* a coherent alternative to it. *(Mark Fisher)*
— The belief that modern capitalist societies have natural reproductive cycles has been central to the development of economics and sociology. *(George Caffentzis)*
— Oh, boohoo. You can't afford water. Guess what? It falls from the sky all the time, and you can purify it with uv radiation from sunlight.
— This video is bullshit. Water is not disappearing, water can't leave the earth unless we send it into space. Just because poor people can't buy water doesn't mean that we should make it free! Water pumps and purification plants cost money! If you live in a place that doesn't have natural freshwater, that sucks for them! C'est la vie, whatever. Quit whining. *(YouTube comments on the 2006 uk documentary* A World Without Water*)*
— The current dominance of capitalist economic theory and practice is socially and ecologically destructive. New ways of theorizing and organizing economic systems are necessary if sustainable and equitable human societies are to be achieved. *(Frances Hutchinson, Mary Mellor and Wendy Olsen)*

The suggestion that there was "no other way" exploded with a particular vengeance after the collapse of the Soviet Union and the end of the Cold War in the late 1980s and early 1990s. It coincided with a major accumulation crisis of global capitalism that began in the 1970s, and is crucially illustrative of what lies behind Jameson's and Žižek's statements on apocalypse versus capitalism.

The "end of history" had arrived,[12] and the "elevation and *reification* of 'the economy' as a distinct and dominant social domain"[13] was now "complete".

Conservative Prime Minister Thatcher, influenced greatly by the thought of Austrian economist Friedrich Hayek, often used the slogan, "There is no alternative", (tina), namely: there is no alternative to neoliberal global capitalism, with its dogmas of free markets, free trade and ruthless competition; massive financialization and privatization; minimum taxation and a minimal social safety net; an ever expanding impoverishment and precariousness of the middle class and misery for the poor;

toxic environmental impacts, massive biodiversity loss, and climate change. These, together, resulted in a new and widespread round of enclosures of commons and primitive capital accumulation.

Closely related to TINA was another of PM Thatcher's (in)famous statements, which eventually led to the dismantling of the labour-capital compact that had been in effect since the Great Depression and World War II:[14]

> I think we have gone through a period when *too many* children and people have been given to understand "I have a problem, it is the Government's job to cope with it!" or "I have a problem, I will go and get a grant to cope with it!" "I am homeless, the Government must house me!" and so they are casting their problems on society and *who is society?* There is no such thing! There are individual men and women and there are families and *no government can do anything* except through people and *people look to themselves first* [...] *There is no such thing as society*. There is living tapestry of men and women and people and the beauty of that tapestry and the quality of our lives will depend upon how much each of us is prepared to take responsibility for ourselves and each of us is prepared to turn round and help by *our own efforts* those who are *unfortunate*.

The hyper-individualism of "people look to themselves first", together with private charity in lieu of social justice and true democracy, form a natural ontology. Rather than asking why there are "too many children and people" saying that they "have a problem", "I am homeless", how is it that Thatcher simply can say, tout court, that "people are casting their problems on society"? As if there were no connections whatsoever between a population and its social context, as if "problems" or misfortune were simply isolated data, floating single elements, without a historical grounding.

In PM Thatcher's world, the "homeless" and the "unfortunate" appear as a fact of life, a datum of nature, an ontological condition that is axiomatic, as do the fragmented individual and the inexistent society.

It is incongruous to hear PM Thatcher utter those statements, for we should do well to remember that the "unfortunate" do not pop out of the ether like pre-Pasteurian microbes. Marxist feminist Silvia Federici's well-documented studies on primitive accumulation through the enclosures of the commons, demonstrate how the immense contribution of women's reproductive labour has been a centuries-old massive subsidy in the accumulation of capital and a powerful instance of a patriarchal forcing of "culture", (women's material and social conditions) behind an essentialized feminine "nature". The fundamental role of women's silent nurturance in the household is debased and systematically ignored and naturalized, as well as their contributions outside the domestic sphere like their ability to foster community and care. The silk singer's song still rings true throughout many parts of the world: "Always spinning sheets of silk / We shall never be better dressed / But always naked and poor / And always suffering hunger and thirst."[15] But Federici also shows how women were a key support in the medieval movements for social justice and spiritual renewal, which though it took them to the stake and misery by the thousands, accelerated the demise of feudalism.

This is not to forget of course the misery, and naturalization, sustained by male peasants and workers throughout, but to emphasize the particular blind spot that critiques across the political spectrum have had about women's roles in the world. Both genders, though, are still fully subjugated to the pretences of capitalist "realism".

Alenka Zupančič, via Mark Fisher, from the perspective of Freudian/Lacanian psychoanalytic theorizations on the *reality principle*, "invites us to be suspicious of any reality that presents itself as natural:"[16]

> The reality principle is not simply some kind of natural way associated with how things are [...] The reality principle itself is ideologically mediated; one could even claim that it constitutes the highest form of ideology, the ideology that presents itself as empirical fact or (biological, economic ...) necessity (and that we tend to perceive as non-ideological). It is precisely here that we should be most alert to the functioning of ideology.

Melinda Cooper criticizes naturalism from the perspective of *biocapital*:[17]

> But perhaps it is not so much the implicit anti-environmentalism of these theorists that is remarkable in itself (it is after all of a piece with the ubiquitous free-market critique of state regulation) as the fact that it stems from a position that can only be described as vitalist. It is because life is neguentropic, it seems, that economic growth is without end. And it is because life is self-organizing that we should reject all state regulation of markets. This is a vitalism that comes dangerously close to *equating* the evolution of *life* with that of *capital*.

There is (1) a tendency to naturalize and universalize a global, capitalist status quo: namely, the ontological search for the stable "system", while, at the same time, there exists (2) a perennial investment in rapid "growth", billed as "innovation", a kind of hyped-up Schumpeterian fetish of "creative destruction", that looks suspiciously like the "planned obsolescence" of old, but neo-Darwinian, IT ornamentations. This developmental road from infancy to maturity is, paradoxically, leery of chance, emergence, and the unexpected. While this road acts on change, continuously exalting risk and speculation, it still wants a bailout in the end.[18] The critique of Friedrich von Hayek and others challenge the neoclassical equilibrium models from within the neoliberal paradigm, but it is, ultimately, intensely invested in the (brutal) linear passage from a pre-capitalist to a capitalist economy, from a *developing* to a *developed* condition — *progress* and never-ending growth.[19]

Again, this internal critique leads to a double bind, wanting to inhabit both a stationary flat-earth *and* a moving spherical-earth; to see capitalism as both the centre of an imagined Ptolemaic geometry *and* a Copernican Astronomy; to be strictly Newtonian but also Quantum Probabilistic.

But why is this unproblematic acceptance of such conditions taken at face value: the so-called "takers" robbing the hard-earned dollars of the "job creator" billionaires? The reality of capitalism as uncontested empirical fact, a "business ontology" equating life with capital — unravelling aspects of this seemingly-natural condition prompts me to turn to epistemology and some history of thought and political economy, for in this Western genealogical context there might be an additional interpretation of the enduring mind-set that helps reinforce the status quo of this toxic "realism".

2 – On the Nature and Culture Dichotomy

— All things are full of gods. (*Thales*)
— From earth water comes-to-be, and from water, soul. (*Heraclitus*)
— You would not find out the boundaries of soul, even by travelling along every path: so deep a measure does it have. (*Heraclitus*)
— *Physis Kryptesthai Philei*/Nature Loves to Hide (*Heraclitus*)
— Man *lives* from nature, i.e. nature is his body, and he must maintain a continuous dialogue with it if he is not to die. To say that man's physical and mental life is linked to nature simply means that nature is linked to itself, for man is a part of nature. (*Karl Marx*)
— Naturalist reductionism and semiological idealism are still alive and kicking, and they continue to form the pole of an epistemological continuum ... some will affirm that culture is a product of nature ... others will forcibly claim that, if left to itself, nature is always mute. (*Philippe Descola*)
— DNA is not the be all and end all of heredity. Information is transferred from one generation to the next by many interesting inheritance systems. Moreover, contrary to current dogma the variation on which natural selection acts is not always random in origin or blind in function: new heritable variation can arise in response to the conditions of life. (*Eva Jablonka, Marion J. Lamb & Anna Zeligowski*)
— Epigenetic regulation is an increasingly well-understood concept that explains much of the contribution of an organism's environment and experience to its biology. However, discussion persists as to which mechanisms can be classified as epigenetic. (*Veronica J. Peschansky & Claes Wahlestedt*)
— The myth of one humanity, based on universal values, an essential human 'nature' and human exceptionalism with regard to nonhuman others, has always worked to exclude *some* humans that didn't correspond to the ideal which tacitly underlies the apparent universalism: there have always been fine gradations within the category of the human, according to gender, race, class, culture, nation, etc. (*Stefan Herbrechter*)

This tendency to a reified naturalism is congruent with the way ancient Greek and Judeo-Christian thought approached the stasis-versus-change relations of world and humanity: the *nature/culture* or *nature/nurture* dichotomy. Whereas the Greek version struggled between the cyclical and teleological, the ancient Judeo-Christian went towards apocalypse and eschatology.[20] The European Enlightenment and Western modernity, direct heirs to the classical Greco-Roman and Abrahamic intellectual and political traditions, have continued to parcel out in this dualistic way what came to be designated as *reality*. Major debates continue on the related issue of *the One and the many*, or monism and pluralism, and the mind-body problem. These new iterations of universal grand narratives versus post-dialectical and post-structuralist skepticisms are reflected in current discussions of philosophy, neuroscience, anthropology, ecology, economics, feminism, and quantum physics.[21]

While Whitehead says that all of Western philosophy since Plato can be considered a series of footnotes to his thought, I see his work as more of a hinge between his ancestors and descendants. It mirrors the canonical inquiry on the nature of "reality" and "truth" initiated by the Greeks before him. Hellenic thought was a bifurcated discourse about: (1) the elemental composition (the "stuff") of the world, with which the pre-Socratic *physicoi* and *physiologoi* engaged, what Plato called later the *peri physeōs* (about nature) type of writing, and (2) the Socratic "Who are we?" with its attendant "care of the self" and "know thyself", directed by intentionality, *nomos* (tradition, custom, law) and *technē* (art and craft).[22]

Imagine fish without water, critters without air, or trees without soil: for them to have or to lack these essentials is to confront the very possibility of survival or annihilation. In the view of some, this is simply how natural things are, and our task is merely to discover them and study their precepts. The challenge of course is to find out whether something in particular is so, and if so how is it so: whether it is merely an empirical matter, a discursive one, or both and more; and/or how it may be related to a purported *reality*.

Gerard Naddaf, in his introduction to *The Greek Concept of Nature,* has described succinctly the origin of the debate:[23]

> The Greek notion of *phusis* (or *physis*), usually translated as nature (from the Latin *natura*), has been decisive for the early history of philosophy and for its subsequent development. In fact, it is often said that the Greeks discovered nature. But what did the earliest philosophers have in mind when they spoke of *phusis*? There is a formidable amount of controversy on the subject [...] [In Book 10 of Plato's *Laws* he] criticizes those who wrote works in prose or in verse of the *peri phuseōs* type. Plato's primary reproach is that the authors of these works never admitted the notion of intention (implied by *technē*) as the explanatory principle behind the order that governs the universe. This refusal, in Plato's eyes, is at the basis of the "atheism" of his time [...].

When one closely examines the contents of these works entitled *Peri phuseōs,* it is clear their primary aim is to explain how the *present* order of things was established. This, in fact, clearly follows from Plato's own analysis in *Laws* 10. These works propose a theory to explain the origin (and development) of the world, humanity, and the city/society. The structure of these works (even before undertaking a linguistic analysis of the word *phusis*) leads one to conclude that for the first philosophers, or pre-Socratics as we conventionally call them, the word *phusis* in this context means the origin and growth of the universe as a totality. And since humanity and the society in which they reside are also part of this totality, explanations of the origin and development of humanity and society must necessarily follow an explanation of the world ...

In sum, pre-Socratics were interested in a history of the universe: in an explanation of its origin (*phusis* as absolute *arche*), of the stages of its evolution (*phusis* as process of growth), and finally of its result, the *kosmos* as we know it (*phusis* as the result).

In this more encompassing reading of the pre-Socratics that includes the *physis* and *nomos* of the *peri physeos* type, the other element, *peri*, is also contributing to invisible overlaps and ambiguity.

Specifically, it is important to note that Anaximander of Miletus (ca. 610–546 BCE), the Ionian *physicoi*, probably the first to combine these two words, *peri physeos*, is the same person who theorized the concept of *apeiron* (the boundless) — connected

Pre-Socratic intersection of nature
& culture

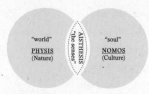

The platonic break
Nature and culture do not intersect

to the etymologically complex word *peirar* and *peirata* (plural), known to us through early Greek poetry, and variously meaning geographical "boundaries", Odysseus' "struggles", technical "skill", the determinants of victory, the "bonds" that tied Odysseus to the mast, "the boundary line of misery", direct quotations or "winged words", etc.[24] In Anaximander, *apeiron* becomes a philosophical term meaning the "unbounded", the "infinite origin" or beginning. Our modern *perimeter* is a semantic survivor of this old human struggle between the boundless and the limited, freedom and necessity. We can see why the thinkers engaged in this type of cosmic inquiry would include the entire realm of being and becoming, in their own thresholds, open and closed at the same time. As Heidegger points out, the one extant fragment "speaks of manifold being in totality. But not only things belong among beings. In the fullest sense, *'things' are not only things of nature.* Man, things produced by man, and the situation or environment effected and realized by the deeds and omissions of men, also belong among beings, and so do daimonic and divine things."[25]

Naddaf sees a tendency for cosmogony to absorb anthropogony and politogony into one single origin and whole. This absorption is Janus-faced: "culture loves to hide" is the obverse of "nature loves to hide", for we are still beholden to Plato's particular way of attempting to solve this situation. The pre-Socratic search for the primordial *elements* that make up the "stuff" of the world was still infused by the theogonies of the shamanic and epic and lyric traditions, where gods are derived from primordial entities (Chaos, Gaia, Eros, Tartaros, etc.). That is, divinities come into being *after* the existence of the world.

But Plato postulates that, unless "a divinity [is] present from the *beginning* and *independent of* the material on which it works, it is impossible to attribute the order that governs the universe to an intelligence."[26]

This Platonic break establishes an ontological and epistemological separation from within the world. It fractures the earth's immanent condition for a total transcendent *other*, and has meant ever since a recurrent pendular movement between these two poles, particularly after the convergence of the Hellenistic intellectual tradition with the transcendental Judeo-Christian monotheistic theological traditions during the late Roman Empire and the Middle Ages that accomplished a sort of aesthetic[27] alienation from world and self. It became further accentuated with the Cartesian *res extensa* and *res cogitans* split; the Protestant Reformation with its individualistic emphasis; the scientific revolution with its initial mechanistic and naturalistic taxonomies; the colonial and patriarchal Eurocentrism; the deisms, idealisms, and materialisms of the Enlightenment and modernity; and certainly with the development of capitalism.

And, like a dividing cell, a certain genealogy unfolds where Nature and Culture is now "mediated" by aesthetics, originally, the senses *(aisthesis)*. This somehow starts a fateful[28] oscillation between the "physical" world and the "soul" world of *Nomos* and *Psyche*. They are classificatory attempts squeezing the "territory" inside the "map", but roughly corresponding to what we today call the somatic, neuro-affective, emotional, environmental, and socio-cultural realms — after Aristotle's canonical categorizations, there ensues a long philosophical, theological and political history attached to these meanings, and the graphs "Genealogies" and "Aristotle: An Interpretation" on this page are only two of several possible semiotic genealogies. The Platonic break is further reflected today in the mind/matter split of modernity that has become, once more, pressing, with the 0/1 virtual binary logic of digital culture. Later in the essay it will become more clear the extent to which my loosely triadic interpretation of Aristotle influenced my initial *EcoDomics* proposal — not a mere antiquarian musing, but rather the new potential meanings this classification suggests.

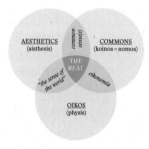

Genealogies

Aristotle: an interpretation

But living in both Plato and Aristotle is, of course, the legacy of the pre-Socratics, where Aristotle, the biologist and physician, though still anchored in metaphysics, tries to solve the dualistic philosophical idealism of his teacher, with his accent on the "real" and material. I would suggest that the atomistic-materialistic tradition,[29] attempting to bridge the divide between Parmenides' full and eternal Being and Heraclitus' Becoming — *panta rei*, "everything flows", and his maxim, *physis kryptesthai philei*, "Nature loves to hide"[30] is clearly in Aristotle's mind — but, this lasting inquiry has left us with a myriad analytical and practical possibilities and contradictions. One is the atomic "swerve" (*clinamen*) of Epicurus, a sort of nuanced, non-linear declension of the atom that gives rise to and keeps the world going.

Yet, this "hiding" begat, too, a reductionist and hierarchical tendency to find the ultimate, elemental building blocks of reality, the surface and the core: from the Parmenidean/Platonic ideas of "truth" and "appearance", to the unchanging "great chain of being" or nature's scale (*scala naturae*).[31] As heirs to this tradition, we tend to look for the "natural" workings of atomized "things", extricate what they hide, and follow their laws — analogous to how capitalist ideology "hides" its culturally constructed history behind an unquestioned atomized veneer of "naturalism". All we need to do is to "lift the veil"[32] that impedes the realization of an "always-there" capitalist form, and let it bloom.

Once more, Fredric Jameson's epigraph refers precisely to this way of viewing things: There is no beginning nor an end to capitalism, nor is a class struggle recognized trying to prevent "the establishment of the preconditions of capitalism" or "to transcend those preconditions once they are established". As George Caffentzis[33] argues:

Self-conscious capitalist ideologists, of course, do not recognize this structure and the struggles it intimates, since they are continuously engaged in an effort to posit only capitalism itself in the continuous past (as always already) and as the continuous future (always will be) [...]. It is a process of "externalization" characteristic of any idea that has been transformed in the course of historical struggles into a totality.

A classic example of this process is Adam Smith's identification of the beginnings of capitalism with the "very slow and gradual" workings of an "original principle of human nature": "the propensity to truck, barter, and exchange one thing for another".[34] This propensity is according to him, "common to all men" and is "the necessary consequence of the faculties of reason and speech". In other words, if one finds a being without these propensities, he/she/it is not likely to be human.

So the conditions of capitalism seem to merge with the conditions of human existence and the lineaments of human history, "shrouding it in myth or presenting it from the standpoint of the nursery tale as the one thing fit for all age-groups and all stages of development.[35]

> But capitalism has a beginning ... in fact [...] many beginnings. In the Marxist analysis, it is posed as the "secret of primitive (or original) accumulation". *Primitive accumulation's dirty little "secret", however, is that the preconditions for capitalism's existence were not, are not, and will not be eternally present.* The logical key to primitive accumulation is depriving people of non-capitalist access to the means of subsistence (metonymically described as the "enclosure of the commons") whenever and wherever this access arises.[36]

So, just as other historically organized social systems have been superseded in the past, there is no reason to assume that the same will not happen to capitalism or, for that matter, to any other systems that may follow it. We are past the triumphalism of the post-Cold War "end of history" avatars[37] regarding — in a sort of paradoxical Hegelian teleology — a liberal democracy and market capitalism, as the natural end point of human evolution, that at the same time expects to maintain endless growth.

3 – Archaic Modernity: Divine *Oikonomia* and the Apocalyptic Tradition[38]

— But if and when the entire planet Earth ceases to exist, all records of its existence will also cease to exist, and nothing (except for some bit of space junk, and perhaps a plaque on the moon with Richard Nixon's name on it) will remain for any future civilization to contemplate. *(Wheeler Winston Dixon, 2003)*

— The Apocalypse is no accident. Whenever the ongoing model of exploitation becomes untenable, capital has intimations of mortality *qua* the world's end. Every period of capitalist development has had its apocalypses. *(George Caffentzis, 2013)*

— The Increase of our Foreign Trade ... whence has arisen all those Animal Spirits, those Springs of Riches, which has enabled us to spend so many millions for the preservation of our Liberties. *(William Wood, 1719)*

— "Animal Spirits" denoted an adolescent attitude to authority that resulted in energetically and deliberately acting ... to the point of stretching the letter of any regulations involved to the limit ... to maximise short-term disruption. *(P.G. Wodehouse, 1909)*

— Animal Spirits — a spontaneous urge to action rather than inaction, and not as the outcome of a weighted average of quantitative benefits multiplied by quantitative probabilities. *(John M. Keynes, 1936)*

— Now that markets have regained their composure, it is time to be bolder. *("The $9 Trillion Sale: Governments should launch a new wave of privatisations, this time centered on property," The Economist, 2014)*

NATURALIZED
CAPITALISM
(physis)

"There is no alternative."
(to capitalism: TINA)

ALIENATED
CAPITALISM
(a-nomos)

"There is no such
thing as society."

APOCALYPTIC
CAPITALISM
(psyche)

"The End of the World
is more likely than the
end of Capitalism."

Neoliberal capitalism

— Economic Science Is Not a Science ... economists are not wise people. They should not even be considered scientists. They are much more similar to priests, denouncing society's bad behaviors, asking you to repent for your debts, threatening inflation and misery for your sins, and worshiping the dogmas of growth and competition. *(Franco "Bifo" Berardi, 2012)*

— In this context, some people continue to defend trickle-down theories, which assume that economic growth, encouraged by a free market, will inevitably succeed in bringing about greater justice and inclusiveness in the world. This opinion, which has never been confirmed by the facts, expresses a crude and naïve trust in the goodness of those wielding economic power and in the sacralized workings of the prevailing economic system. Meanwhile, the excluded are still waiting. *(Pope Francis, 2013)*

It is now necessary to briefly explore how the Judaic and Christian millenarian apocalyptic traditions themselves contributed to this hiding. It is also relevant to further understanding the chaotic "self-destruct" automaticity of contemporary neo-Schumpeterian neoliberalism, hiding material production and environmental destruction behind a "virtual" world wherein the so-called knowledge economy serves as a veil for the continued exploitation of workers both in the former colonized countries and in the old colonial countries, now in the clutches of post-Fordist precarity.

So, as the Greco-Roman collapses, it is superseded by a new syncretism that becomes one crucial bridge in this apocalyptic naturalization process: the transition from a religious-based worldview to a modern secular one, which — via the Patristic and Medieval adaptation of the classical concepts and practices of *politeia* and *oikonomia*, the Hellenistic *oikoumene* and the Roman *imperium* — led to a hermeneutic and institutional integration of a "divine economy" with an "ecclesiastical economy."

It becomes a grand unified theological and political canon and practice of government: the Divine *Logos*, the Son, incarnated in the world as the earthly Divine minister of the Father charged with implementing the Redemption. But it came with a heavy foundational load: since the ancient Greeks, it has conflated and confused the question of the state, the *hoi polloi*, and sovereignty, *with* the ministering of government, *and*, with the existence of a divinely created Cosmos administered by an angelical bureaucracy — through the Platonic split where "the notion of intention (implied by *technē*) becomes the explanatory principle behind the order that governs the universe".[39] It is the ontological and emotional estrangement from the world, setting up the conditions for an alienated, instrumental managerial rationality that eventually "hides" the cultural (theological and political), as well as the physical (the environmental), and it is primarily concerned with control and efficiency rather than active democracy.

Agamben reminds us how:

> The term democracy sounds a false note wherever it crops up in debate these days because of a preliminary ambiguity that condemns anyone who uses it to miscommunication. [...] it might mean one of two different things: a way of constituting the *body politic* ([...] public law) or a *technique of governing* ([...] administrative practice) [...] the form through which power is *legitimated* and the manner in which it is *exercised*. Since it is perfectly plain to everyone that the latter meaning prevails in contemporary political discourse, that the word *democracy* is used in most cases to refer to a technique of governing (something not, in itself, particularly reassuring) [...]. These two areas of conceptuality (the *juridico-political* and the *economic-managerial*) have overlapped with one another since the birth of politics, political thought, and democracy in the Greek polis or city-state, which makes it hard to tease them apart.[40]

In a revealing appendix on Adam Smith's "invisible hand", Agamben citing Linneaus, the famous naturalist, states that "given the strategic function that the syntagma 'economy of nature' will perform in the birth of modern economics", it is important to look at Linneaus' 1749 definition:[41]

> By "economy of nature" we mean the wise disposition *(dispositio)* of natural beings, established by the sovereign Creator, according to which they tend to common ends and execute reciprocal actions [...] Everything that falls within our senses, everything that is presented to our mind and deserves observations combines, through its disposition, to manifest the glory of God; that is, to produce ends that God wanted as the purpose of all his works.

Agamben, then, observes: "[The] derivation of the syntagma from the economic-providential tradition is here obvious and beyond doubt. *Oeconomia naturae* simply means — in perfect accordance with the theological paradigm that is familiar to us — the wise and providential *dispositio* that the creator has impressed upon his creation and through which he governs it and leads it to its ends". The nature/culture issue maintains that original visibility and invisibility, but now influenced by some views from Stoic thought:

"Christian Marouby has demonstrated the importance of the 'economy of nature' in Adam Smith. When it appears for the first time in the *Theory of Moral Sentiments* (1759), its links with the providential paradigm are entirely explicit." Agamben, further drives the point quoting Smith speaking about the ancient Stoics: "[...] the world was ruled by the all-ruling providence of a wise, powerful, and good God, every single event ought to be regarded as making a necessary part of the plan of the universe". The continued line to Patristics and to Smith's "invisible hand" is crystal clear in the voice of St. Augustine: "God *governs* and *administers* the world, from the great to the small things, with an occult hand sign ('omnia, maxima et minima, *occulto* nutu *administranti*')."[42] The "hidden wink" of God still reigns supreme in the glorious hall of money and power.

But between Augustine and Smith lies a roster of ideas, and historical developments, slowly transforming a postlapsarian redemptive "Divine *Oikonomia*" to an earthly Ecclesiastical *Oikonomia* to eventually the secular economics we have come to know. Through a figure closer to his era, Smith gets another strand of Stoicism via Hugo Grotius, the Renaissance Dutch jurist, much influenced by the Roman Stoics, particularly Cicero's school, notorious for its justification of *Imperium*, "just war" and Barbarian conquest. Grotius, a staunch defender of Dutch imperialism, develops important theologico-political arguments to defend his country's rights. His justification for free trade is basically the same one we have today. In a contest of wills and wits with the Spanish empire he develops a theory of providential *jus sanctissimum* or "sacrosanct law of free trade", that is seen as natural law and truly meta-political. "This choice of words and the structural conception of the Freedom of the Seas as a supreme principle clearly points to an analogue between Grotius' concept of international law and the Iberian medieval one against which he argues."[43] In the end it was a private fight between European colonial empires helping themselves to the rest of the world, bringing "natural law", God and the Greeks and the Romans, to justify their ruthless appropriations: "On the occasion of the donation of the Canary Islands, Pope Clement VI wrote: [...] By reason of their infidelity non-Christians lose their right to *dominium* [...] because of their lack of faith and morals [...] they are unfit to be rightful owners."[44] Here is the hand of Francisco de Vitoria's Salamanca school also arguing about "just war" and international relations.

In another mixture of sacred and profane, at the start of the fifth chapter of his *Second Treatise of Government*, John Locke, direct heir to Grotius — protégée of the First Earl of Shaftesbury, one of the seven Lord Proprietors of Carolina and President of the Council on Trade and Foreign Plantations — argues for the appropriation of indigenous lands because they were idle, and needed to be "improved" according to God's will at the start of the Creation, which eventually became his famous: *Thus in the beginning all the world was America.*

> It is very clear, that God, as King David says, Psal. Cvx. 16, "has given the earth to the children of men," given it to mankind in common. But, this being supposed, it seems to some a very great difficulty how any one should ever come to have a property in anything [...]. I shall endeavour to show how men might come to have a property in several parts of that which God gave to mankind in common, and that without any express compact of all the commoners.[45]

Now, there comes the question of how the religious apocalyptic eventually fuses with the secular apocalyptic, with the capitalist apocalyptic. Here the work of David Noble seems to connect well with Agamben's, for I believe the overt emphasis on administration, instrumentality, and (divine) outcomes, greatly facilitates converting the Christian Redemption into the salvific "useful arts" that will deliver us from the postlapsarian Fall — needless to say that this type of utilitarian view is ever more entrenched in our frantic, outcomes-oriented present.

A complex process emerged about a thousand years ago, when the theology of the Christian salvation and the Redemption became entangled with millenarian apocalyptic movements (heirs to the earlier Judaic apocalypses) and technology, what David Noble has so aptly called *The Religion of Technology*. Such dynamic is still at work today, for it strongly combines with the deliverance aims of capitalism itself, or better yet, it is really the other side of the same spiritual-material, mind-matter, coin, as we will reflect below. It is worth quoting him at length, as it highlights key elements of my overall argument:

> We in the West confront the close of the second Christian millennium much as we began it, in devout anticipation of doom and deliverance, only now our medieval expectations assume a more modern, *technological expression*. It is the aim of this book to demonstrate that the present enchantment with things technological — the very measure of modern enlightenment — is rooted in *religious myths* and *ancient imaginings*. Although today's technologies, in their sober pursuit of utility, power, and profit, seem to set society's standard for rationality, they are driven also by distant dreams, *spiritual yearnings for supernatural redemption*. [...] Perhaps nowhere is the intimate connection between religion and technology more manifest than in the United States, where an unrivalled popular enchantment with technological advance is matched by an equally earnest popular expectation of Jesus Christ's return. What has typically been ignored [...] is that the two obsessions are often held by the same people, many of them being technologists themselves. [...] Artificial Intelligence advocates wax eloquent about the possibilities of machine-based immortality and resurrection, and their disciples, the architects of virtual reality and cyberspace, exult in their expectation of *God-like omnipresence* and *disembodied perfection*. [...] All of these technological pioneers harbor deep-seated beliefs which are variations upon familiar religious themes. Beyond [...] are countless others for whom the religious compulsion is largely unconscious, *obscured* by a secularized vocabulary but operative nevertheless.[46]

Noble goes on to argue how this process started to unfold when the "useful arts became implicated in the Christian project of redemption". To be saved and return to the noble prelapasarian state, one had but to fervently use the tools at one's disposal or develop new ones, ultimately making technology a full-blown religious undertaking that would lead, it was expected, to the "recovery of mankind's lost divinity". And, so today, fateful heirs that we are, we are not just content with having our gadgets fulfil their functional use: "We demand deliverance." A deliverance that takes the form of the so-called "High-Tech", without usually giving much thought what and who is really sustaining that interminable treadmill — say, the geopolitics and hidden trails of a mobile smart-phone: wolframite, cassiterite, gold, *col*umbite-*tan*talite's bloody provenance, labour conditions, server farms' energy consumption and cooling, e-waste dumped on low-income countries, etc.[47] Informal markets and shadow economies handle most of this obscure and highly toxic trade.[48]

> For Marx, the capitalist factory system is a regime of avid vampirism whose victims are transformed into undead extensions of its own vast, insensate, endlessly feeding body. "*The automaton itself is the subject,* and the workers are merely conscious organs, coordinated with the unconscious organs of the automaton, and together with the latter subordinated to the central moving force" of capitalist production. The *worker* essentially becomes a cybernetic organism — *a cyborg* — prosthetically linked to a despotic, ravening apparatus.[49]

With *24/7: Late Capitalism and the Ends of Sleep,* Jonathan Crary adds a creepy corollary to this subjection, writing about the latest research trying to appropriate the world of sleep and dream for the capital (and military) *automaton.* Building on the migratory sleep habits of the tiny White-crowned sparrows, which gives them an ability to stay awake for more than 21 hours per day over the 4,000 kilometres trek from Alaska to Southern California: "Over the past five years the U.S. Defense Department has spent large amounts of money to study these creatures."[50] Crary reports that there are "massive ongoing efforts by the scientific-military complex to develop forms of '*augmented cognition*' that will enhance many kinds of human-machine interaction [...] including the development of an anti-fear drug". This could potentially create "death squads of sleep-resistant, fear-proofed commandos [...] needed for missions of indefinite duration". He ominously concludes: "As history has shown, war-related innovations are inevitably assimilated into a broader social sphere, and the *sleepless soldier* would be the forerunner of the *sleepless worker* or *consumer*." Research that otherwise may be helpful to alleviate mood disorders and other human suffering is outsourced to some form of sci-fi *terminators.* The brutal connection between a panoptical power and a chaotically programmed capitalism proceeds at apocalyptic speed.

With Cooper's *Life as Surplus*, Latham's cyborg youth, and Crary's *24/7*, we have come full circle where the natural and the virtual intertwine with the instrumental and chrematistic, the spectacular and the vampiric, the godly and the ungodly, the apocalyptic and the make-believe creative aesthetic and materiality of innovation and technology. It is an increasingly automatic machine whose anaesthetic semiotics is relentlessly trying to colonize and naturalize the planet and its peoples into a dystopian *Society of Control*.[51]

4 – *EcoDomics*: An Art of Making and Living (in) Common(s)

— Dans son ouvrage *De abstinentia* (ii, 32), Porphyre, en citant Théophraste, parle de la 'terre' (Ge), qualifiée de 'notre nourrice et mère' (os trophoi kai metros emon). La terre, dit le texte, est 'le foyer commun des dieux et des hommes' (theon kai anthropon estia), et il faut que tous ... nous lui chantions des hymnes et la chérissions comme celle qui nous a enfantés (os tekoysan). (*Stella Georgoudi*)

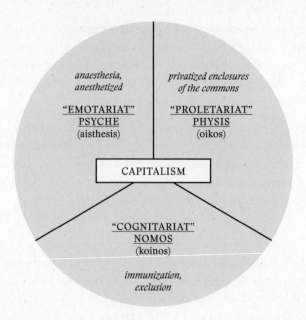

anaesthesia,   *privatized enclosures*
anesthetized   *of the commons*

"EMOTARIAT"   "PROLETARIAT"
PSYCHE   PHYSIS
(aisthesis)   (oikos)

CAPITALISM

"COGNITARIAT"
NOMOS
(koinos)

immunization,
exclusion

Conditions of alienation, exploitation, and debt

— "Becoming-Earth": The creation of sustainable alternatives geared to the construction of social horizons of hope, while at the same time doing critical theory, which implies resistance to the present. *(Rosi Braidotti)*

— New ethical and political challenges and the extension of the demand for social justice to include all humans and non-humans call for new 'ecologies' of how these increasingly complex environments may be shared 'sustainably' in the face of ... a globalized capitalist system that seems to be destined to pursue its path of destruction until everything is consumed. *(Stefan Herbrechter on Rosi Braidotti)*

— In many ways, while capitalism was selling us the hope of personal success, we bought into a sense of profound separation masked as individual importance. Just as any recognition of animation was extracted from the Earth, just as humanity was extracted from the worker, so was the individual extracted from the community. *(Amaryllis Moleski)*

— Capital has managed to overcome the dualism of body and soul by establishing a workforce in which everything we mean by the Soul — language, creativity, affects — is mobilized for its own benefit. Industrial production put to work bodies, muscles, and arms. Now in the sphere of digital technology and cyberculture, exploitation involves the mind, language and emotions in order to generate value — while our bodies disappear in front of our computer screens. *(Franco 'Bifo' Berardi)*

I have suggested, thus far, that historically in the "West", ancient Greek thought about nature and culture — combined with the early Judeo-Christian tradition of "divine *oikonomia*", and its apocalyptic millenarian views on science and technology as salvation — has contributed to the naturalization of capitalism.

The efforts of artists, thinkers, activists, and social movements concerned with issues of post-coloniality, subaltern studies, coloniality, decoloniality, and *buen vivir*, as well as the widening experiences and conceptualizations of the global, North-American and Latin American environmental justice movement, comprise another, equally important body of reflection and practice that make the hidden visible and influence my work.[52]

Unfolding from the above context, and from my environmental policy and academic experience, I have embarked on a long-term study that I call *EcoDomics*, *(oikodomia)* imagined as an (already-existing) "art of making and living (in) common(s)", a ways-other contribution to resist neoliberal capitalism. In the concluding part of this chapter, I will outline some of its main elements and principles.

But before doing so, it is important to remember in a very succinct manner, the issue of the *precariat* or precariousness of labour under neoliberal capitalism, that combines secular and more recent forms of alienation and exploitation. Roughly corresponding to the nomenclature *Physis-Nomos-Psyche* I have been utilizing thus far, I combine them with two neoliberal moments: (1) alienation: the privatized physical and cultural enclosures of the common(s), the immunitary exclusion from the *Nomos*/common(s), and the anaesthetic estrangement from the *psyche*/soul; (2) exploitation: *Proletariat, Cognitariat,* and *Emotariat.* These latter terms borrow from the old Roman-Law concept of the *proletarius*, denoting the propertyless social class who only had their "offspring" *(proli)* to offer, and became the backbone of the Roman army in the latter part of the Republic and during the Empire. Marx, a serious student of the classics, coined the term *proletariat* to signify the propertyless, penniless person, who has only his physical body to offer, as labour power, in the production and capital accumulation process of industrial capitalism — *proletariat* that bears the traces of "Hegel's rabble", as Frank Ruda argues: "[T]he transition from Hegel to Marx is, I want to claim, the transition from the rabble to the proletariat."[53] Or as, Žižek prefaces, "because there is too much excessive wealth — the more society is wealthy the more poverty it produces ... gradually dissolving [the legal frame of equality] with the rise of the new forms of social and political exclusion: illegal immigrants, slum-dwellers, refugees, etc. It is as if, in parallel to the regression from profit to rent, in order to continue to function, the existing system has to resuscitate premodern forms of direct exclusion."[54]

More recently Italian and French theorists in particular, have used *cognitariat* to denote the 24/7 exploitation of knowledge and creative workers under "cognitive capitalism" or "semiocapitalism".[55] In turn, I am coining the term *emotariat*, to denote the deep anguish that has always haunted the precariousness of those who have nothing but their bodies, minds, and hearts to offer to the owners of the means of production, the top managerial class, and the financial rentiers. It is inscribed within the substantive literature on affect, emotion, desire, and want, and concurrent political economy. It would seem helpful to refer to the troubling increase of

Precariousness of labour under contemporary capitalism

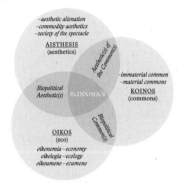

EcoDomics/Oikodomia

mental illness and addictions of all types, and the frenzied hyper-consumerism and hyper-indebtedness of the capitalist "society of the spectacle". Multiple *cognitariat* writings include the question of affect in their critiques, but I feel that it is important to give those questions an added emphasis, that might otherwise be lost in a more neuro-cognitive or semiotic approach[56] — moreover, I would argue that contemporary global capitalism can place most of us, recurrently, or occasionally, at once in these three moments of alienation and exploitation, or consistently, in at least two of them.

I suggest the above, because contemporary global capitalism appears in all manner of hybrid shades at once: (1) "industrial", emphasizing its material (*physis/oikos*) base and corresponding alienation, (2) equally for the "semiotic" and its *Nomos/Koinos* field, and (3) the "consumerist" with its emotional, affective, and aesthetic/sensuous alienation. This intrusive and flexible neo-Schumpeterian "creative" destruction, is supposed to magically even out in the end — except that it is the many that always pay the bill of the very few, this new 1%. The diagram on top of this page tries to synthesize some of these hybrid interactions.

Departing from the above considerations, I "update" the ancient *oikodomia* (building, constructing) to a proposed living synthesis, because I want to envision it as an embodied, practising/thinking art, and not just a technique — a living engagement inviting us to "come to our senses" in ever-expanding "communities of sense", out of the chaotic anaesthesia of neoliberal consumerism.

Succinctly, it encompasses three main areas of integrated activity and reflection: (1) *OIKOS* (house, household, hearth), comprising: (1.1) *oikonomia*, (political economy, ecological economics, feminist economics), (1.2) *oikoumene* (ecumene, ecumenical, earth democracy), (1.3) *oikologia* (ecology, political ecology, biopolitics); (2) *AISTHESIS*: Aesthetic(s), comprising: (2.1) Aesthetic Alienation, (2.2) Commodity Aesthetics, and (2.3) the Aesthetic(s) of the Common(s); and, (3) *KOINOS*: (3.1) the common, and (3.2) the commons. 2 and 3 combine to form: "aesthetic(s) of the common(s)". Aristotle's *Aisthesis Koine* (common senses, *sensus communis*) partly inspired this concept and my initial ecoDomic approach: In this iteration I have used the Greek (and Latin) words because they help reveal a genealogy of concepts and practices that are active in today's global political economy, but in no way exhaust other immensely rich indigenous traditions like *pachamama, popol, ch'ixi, suma qamaña, suma kawsay, ubuntu,* and others, that in fact are being integrated into the *EcoDomics* project.

Inspired by *oikodomia* and these alternative traditions, I thus see *EcoDomics* within an anthropology and genealogy of building/making/praxis, starting from our animal and plant ancestors to the myriad *Homo habilis* (handy man), *Homo ergaster* (working man), *Homo erectus* (upright man) and the like, which lead eventually to the *Homo sapiens* (knowing man) species, and finally to our own, the only extant modern human sub-species, *Homo sapiens sapiens*, some 200,000 years ago. Throughout that long early dawning of humanity we learned how to make tools and tame fire, live in social groups, thrive and survive, honour our ancestors, build shelters, scavenge and hunt and gather, and, key for accomplishing the above — develop the arts of languages and the languages of art. And, assuming the recent "tether hypothesis", it seems that these communal abilities were furthered not only by brain size, but also by complex multi-sensory neuronal connectivity:

In our smaller-brained ancestors, the researchers argue, neurons were tightly tethered in a relatively simple pattern of connections.

> When our ancestors' brains expanded, those tethers ripped apart, enabling our neurons to form new circuits. [...] As they got bigger, their sensory and motor cortices barely expanded. Instead, it was the regions in between, known as the *association cortices*, that bloomed. Our association cortices are crucial for the kinds of thought that we humans excel at. Among other tasks, association cortices are crucial for making decisions, retrieving memories and reflecting on ourselves.[57]

This associative hypothesis gives additional weight to what is discussed below: *transversality* (Guattari), *oikeiosis* (Stoic school) and *oikeiotes physique, Gaia/Ge* (Theophrastus, Braidotti) *oikeios topos* (Theophrastus, Moore), as well as Aristotle's *Aisthesis Koine* — his reflection on the greater perception our common senses develop when, within their perimeter (*peiras*), they act together.

To expand some of the proposed interactive levels of the *EcoDomics* triad:
I – *OIKOS* / *Oikeios Topos, Oikos Polis*: hearth, home, household, *pachamama*, is the general dimension of sustainable stewardship. It encompasses:

1.1 *Oikonomia,* understood as an economics that is not chrematistic; it stems from the key Aristotelian distinction in *De Republica* between *oikonomia* (provisioning of the home) and *chremata* (pecuniary or money-based accumulation, circulation, and interest), whose influence gave rise to the Christian prohibition of usury. Alberto Toscano[58] brings attention to a crucial reference in volume one of Marx's *Capital*:

> Aristotle opposes Economic to Chrematistic. He starts from the former. So far as it is the art of gaining a livelihood, it is limited to procuring those articles that are necessary to existence, and useful either to a household or the state. [...] There is, however, a second mode of acquiring things [...] Chrematistic, and in this case there appear to be no limits to riches and possessions. [...] there are no bounds to its aims [...]. Economic not Chrematistic has a limit [...] the object of the former is something different from money, of the latter the augmentation of money [...]. By confounding these two forms, which overlap each other, some people have been led to look upon the preservation and increase of money ad infinitum as the end and aim of Economic.

This relentless "production of money" (*poietike chrematon*) Aristotle denounces as a veritable "diabolical" undertaking (*dia chrematon diaboles*). Relentless production that is even more relevant today, being at the base of financial capitalism. Ecological economist Herman Daly and theologian John B. Cobb, Jr, capture the tenor of the *oikonomia* I have in mind, which, intended or not, has a clear Marxian-Aristotelian ring:

> [Chrematistics] can be defined as the branch of political economy relating to the manipulation of property and wealth so as to maximize short-term monetary exchange value to the owner. Oikonomia, by contrast, is the management of the household so as to increase its use value to all members of the household over the long run. If we expand the scope of household to include the larger community of

PROBLEM	SOLUTION	DESIRED OUTCOME
AISTHESIS (aesthetics) *alienation, spectacle, anesthesia, debt*	coming to our senses	
KOINOS (commons) *immunitas, exclusion, debt*	communitas, "communites of sense" aesthetic(s) of the common(s)	EcoDomics An art of living and making (in) common(s)
OIKOS (eco) *privatized enclosures of the common(s), debt*	protection and expansion of the common(s)	

EcoDomics as practice

the land, of shared values, resources, biomes, institutions, language, and history, then we have a good definition of "economics for community".[59]

1.2 *Oikoumene* (ecumene, ecumenical, earth democracy) defined the original Greek *perimeter* as "our world". When Classical and Hellenistic Greece expanded, they began to speak of "the known world", and eventually, "the world", by the time Romans took over. Ecumene, later taken up by the Church and political philosophy, has survived as a mixture of cosmopolitanism and ecumenical tolerance, and I see it as a counter to an impersonal and instrumental *globalization*. It could be grounded on a new *Gaia/Gê/oikeios topos*, what Vandana Shiva regards as "earth democracy", and Rosi Braidotti calls "Becoming-Earth".[60]

1.3 *Oikologia* (ecology, political ecology, biopolitics), or a practice of ecology that would go beyond a mere technocratic management and pollution abatement, and other forms of massive geo-engineering and green washing that leave in place the circuits of appropriation and accumulation, to embrace an empathic political ecology, ecological feminism, and environmental justice, in the manner of Guattari, Escobar, Agrawal, Moore, and others, as well as indigenous ecological and cultural conceptions like *ch'ixi* and *pachamama*. It is the power *of* life superseding the power *over* life.

2 – *AISTHESIS / Aesthesia, Aesthetica*: sensuousness, aesthetic(s), matter, senses, sensitivity, sensual, sensibility, taste and subjectivity. It contains three levels: (2.1) *Aesthetic Alienation*, a type of "anaesthesia" that estranges from the world, from each other, and from self, deeply impacting our affect and sensibility but also our survival and sense of commons, what J.M. Bernstein views, too, as the "art and truth" split; (2.2) *Commodity Aesthetics*, or the society of the spectacle, desire, affect, emotion, and hyper-consumerism that, expanding on Marx's discussion of "commodity fetishism", is theorized by Wolfgang Fritz Haug, and, (2.3) as a response to the above two that continuously help enact the enclosures of the commons of neoliberal privatization, through a consumerist, anaesthetized, and mechanistic subjectivity — the support and expansion of those counter-hegemonic practices

of resistance, common sense, and critical awareness rising up throughout the world, expressing revitalized base communities of sense, a new *Aisthesis Koine*, or *aesthetic(s) of the common(s)*.[61]

3 – κοινος / *Koinos Bios, Koinos Topos, Koinos Logos, Koinonia, Pachakuti*, or sociality, living in community, cenoby, sharing, society and its political economy, science and technology, culture and the common(s).[62] In this context, the engaged plurality of different aesthetics, cultural common, and material commons would join in the *aesthetic(s) of the common(s)*. They would challenge alienation and anaesthetic torpor, nurturing community, social activism and social movements, and a liberatory cultural production. To recall how *immunitas*, immunization, separation, distance, exoticism, stand in contrast to *communitas*, empathy, connection, conviviality, and sharing, as human constants and physical and cultural dynamics and tensions.[63] Alienation from the sensible segregates us at the great price of social cruelty and injustice, personal indifference and environmental degradation.[64] This estrangement, as argued, was already at work in patriarchal proto-modernities and still is present in capitalist modernity.

The graph above depicts in schematic fashion some of the main interconnected processes involved in tackling the set of problems encountered at each of the main three fields studied, concluding on a hoped for dynamic and transversal synthesis: *EcoDomics*:

Later in my research I was pleased to find Félix Guattari's *Three Ecologies*, whose proposed *ecosophy*[65] reads similar in substantive points to my tripartite *EcoDomics*, and I am now incorporating many of these ideas:

The earth is undergoing a period of intense techno-scientific transformations. If no remedy is found, the ecological disequilibrium this has generated will ultimately threaten the continuation of life on the planet's surface. Alongside these upheavals, human modes of life, both individual and collective, are progressively deteriorating. [...] It is the relation between subjectivity and its exteriority — be it social, animal, vegetable or Cosmic — that is compromised in this way, in a sort of general movement of implosion and regressive infantilization. Otherness [*l'altérité*] tends to lose all its asperity. [...] Political groupings and executive authorities appear to be totally incapable of understanding the full implications of these issues. [...] [T]hey are generally content to simply tackle industrial pollution and then from a purely technocratic perspective, whereas only an ethico-political articulation which — I call *ecosophy* — between the three ecological registers (the environment, social relations and human subjectivity) would be likely to clarify these questions.[66]

EcoDomics, in its ethico-political-aesthetic-cultural-ecological articulation, can potentially live in Guattari's "*ecosophy*", just as *ecos, common(s)*, and *aesthetic(s)* can abide in "the environment", "social relations", and "human subjectivity".

The base triad of *EcoDomics* aims to address the fragmentation, which constantly impacts true democracy and everyday social practices, and to contribute to the body of work that resists this alienation — with an approach close to what Guattari calls *transversality*. "As Deleuze explains, one of [his] most significant contributions is the political idea of '(non-hierarchical) transversal relationships'."[67] "Transversality is a dimension that strives to overcome two impasses: that of pure verticality, and a simple horizontality. Transversality tends to be realized when maximum communication is brought about between different levels and above all in terms of different directions."[68] Hence, transversality serves to undo power's long-time strategy to divide and conquer (*Divide et Impera*), with which it maintains a stranglehold on conquered peoples and territories. The task, then, is to make visible the diversity of natures and cultures, as conceptual and practical projects of resistance.

By way of closing, I want to refer to two theorizations, one ancient and one contemporary. Based on derivations from *oikos* (hearth) and *gaia/ge* (earth, mother and nurturer), they connect with a sense of belonging, intimacy, and familiarity extended to all — what could be regarded as a concentric local to cosmopolitan common: the stoic concept of *oikeiosis* (affinity, endearment), Theophrastus' *oikeiotes physike* (natural fellowship extended to non-humans) and *gaia/ge*, or "Becoming-Earth," via feminist political philosopher Rosi Braidotti and, again, Theophrastus' *oikeios topos* (intimate, familiar place), via Jason W. Moore.

It is "life in accordance with nature that was the sole object of *oikeiosis* in Stoic ethics [...]. Nature causes human beings to feel they are part of fellow humankind through the power of their rational faculties, and this makes *honestum* and virtuous conduct appear natural. In the same way virtue is shown to correspond to Stoic requirements with respect to *summum bonum*."[69] The "supreme good" fostered by *oikeiosis* is the "beginning of justice" and guides us through the collapse of the walls that separate us from each other, as we understand ourselves, and the world, better.

Oikeiosis is:

(S)omething like an act (sometimes preconscious) by which a being identifies itself with an object, either its own body or beings beyond its own body. The first form of oikeiosis is the animal's orientation to its own self-preservation. (Stoics did recognize oikeiosis at this level as common to humans and nonhuman animals.) But for humans oikeiosis can extend outward to other humans, even to concern for the whole human species.[70]

Oikeiosis thus exemplifies the expanding circle of affinity and affiliation that develops during the life of a person as s/he matures virtuously according to the laws of nature. It becomes one of the bases for achieving a wider *ecumene* or cosmopolitanism, a form of global justice and endearment.[71]

Jason W. Moore, particularly his *Oikeios* conceptualization of "environment-making" and "capitalist world-ecology", opens up "a perspective that joins the accumulation of capital and the production of nature in dialectical unity. This perspective begins from the premise that capitalism does not act upon nature so much as develop through nature-society relations. *Capitalism* does not have an ecological regime; it *is an ecological regime.*"[72]

Moore's *Oikeios* draws its inspiration from *oikeios topos*, a concept developed by Aristotle's heir, philosopher-botanist Theophrastus, denoting a "favourable place" for a plant species and its environment to relate, akin to today's idea of ecological niche. It is semantically related to *Oikos*, and in its making/creative emphasis is close to my own *EcoDomics* as well. Moore conceptualizes *Oikeios* as:[73]

a way of naming the creative, historical, and dialectical relation between, and also always within, human and extra-human natures. [...] We can, through the *oikeios*,

implicate the widest range of meta-processes in the modern world as socio-ecological, from family formation to racial orders to industrialization, imperialism, and proletarianization. [...] As such, environment-making is the decisive concept. Nature can neither be saved nor destroyed; it can only be transformed. In this way, the *oikeios* represents a radical elaboration of the dialectical logic immanent in Marx's concept of metabolism (*Stoffwechsel*). *Stoffwechsel* signifies "a metabolism of nature ... in which neither society nor nature can be stabilized with the fixity implied by their ideological separation". [...] All life makes environments. All environments make life. [...] We are looking at the *relations* that guide environment-making, and also the processes that compel new rules of environment-making, as in the long transition from feudalism to capitalism. [...] To say that capitalism is constituted through the production of nature, the pursuit of power, and the accumulation of capital is not to identify three independent blocks of relations that may then be interconnected through feedback links. Rather, these three moments interpenetrate each other in the making of historical capitalism — and in its unraveling today.

Finally, from Latin America, breaking down the vicious circle of naturalization, the rising alternative voices of "living in plenitude" or *buen vivir*, from the Aymara *suma qamaña* or the Quechua *suma kawsay*, resonate through Rolando Vázquez's own listening:[74]

In our mind the recognition, the avowal of those who have been denied existence in the present, leads to an understanding of the past as a force of liberation. The decolonial critique of time seeks to liberate the past from the hegemonic representation of history. The discourse of history, in its affirmation of modernity, the negation of its exteriority and the disavowal of the "other", has been a key mechanism of the modern/colonial control over representation. History as the monumentalization and in-scription of the past in textuality, produces a narrative of the past that functions as a teleology of the modern hegemony of the present. Through it modernity makes possible the representation and the naturalization of the present as the whole of the real. This very same mechanism allows a form of temporal discrimination in which the "other" is relegated as either being in the past (as barbarian, underdeveloped ...) or simply negated as outside of history.

And, eloquently, the words of a young Brazilian writer, Juliana Barreto, sum up in a poetic and hopeful way the search so many of us are making for worlds-other.[75] Her intuitive flash gives us a path.

ECODOMIA*

Nossa geração é a primeira a ter de engendrar, não sem alegria e sem dor uma ecodomia* familiar, regional, e planetária; ao mesmo tempo econômica, ecológica e ecumênica.

Despertar, resistência e responsibilidade serão as palavras mestras desta nova ecodomia. Seja bem-vindo!"—* Do grego "construção".

1   I would like to acknowledge the gracious editorial support I received in the early draft from writer Lenore Norrgard, and to thank artist and designer Daniel Lorenze for helping me transform my multiple original sketches into fewer, more pleasant, and clear diagrams. In a felicitous link I also acknowledge anthropologist, artist, and border theorist Fiamma di Montezemolo, anthropologist and cultural theorist Tarek Elhaik, social architect Teddy Cruz, and professors Peter Mörtenböck and Helge Mooshammer, supporters of my work all along. And, mom, I put much heart and hard work, as you reminded me to do always, on that final conversation we had six Novembers ago.

2   This historicizing vs. naturalizing is akin to Jacques Rancière's argument that he has "always fought against the idea of *historical necessity*. [...] What I mean is, history isn't some entity that acts or speaks; what we call history is what is woven by people as they construct a situation in time out of their own lives and experiences." Quoted from "Democracies Against Democracy," in *Democracy In What State?* Giorgio Agamben et al. (New York: Columbia University Press, 2001), 80, emphasis added. When a specific power/class formation becomes invisible by reason of an imposed ideology, we are in the presence of a naturalized or "historical necessity", that must be shed the light on.

3   On a major policy speech of PM David Cameron, "Economy: There is no Alternative (TINA) is back," 7 March 2013, http://www.bbc.co.uk/news/uk-politics-21703018.

4   This much-debated quote extracted from her speech to the 1982 Conservative Party Conference, alone, and when read in the context of the full paragraph, exemplifies the political and economic reductionism of neoliberal capitalism.

5   Cf., inter alia, Arturo Escobar, "Other Worlds are (Already) Possible: Self-Organisation, Complexity, and Post-Capitalist Cultures," in *World Social Forum: Challenging Empires*, ed. Jain Sen, Anita Anand, Arturo Escobar, and Peter Waterman (New Delhi: Viveka Foundation, 2004); see also J.K. Gibson Graham, *The End of Capitalism (As We Knew It): A Feminist Critique of Political Economy* (Minneapolis, MN: University of Minnesota Press, 2006 [1996]), and *A Postcapitalist Politics* (Minneapolis, MN: University of Minnesota Press, 2006); Judith Blau and Marina Karides, eds., *The World and U.S. Social Forums: A Better World is Possible and Necessary* (Leiden and Boston, MA: Brill Academic Publishers, 2008); David McNally, *Another World is Possible: Globalization and Anti-Capitalism* (Winnipeg: Arbeiter Ring Publishing, 2007 [2005]) and *Global Slump: The Economics and Politics of Crisis and Resistance* (Oakland, CA: PM Press, 2011). See also Agamben et al., *Democracy In What State?*; Peter Sloterdijk, *In the World Interior of Capital: For A Philosophical Theory of Globalization* (Cambridge: Polity Press, 2013); and, Philippe Descola, *Beyond Nature and Culture* (Chicago, IL: University of Chicago Press, 2013 [2005]), and *The Ecology of Others* (Chicago, IL: Prickly Paradigm Press, 2013).

6   A classic treatment of this question is Karl Polanyi's *The Great Transformation: The Political and Economic Origins of Our Time* (Boston, MA: Beacon Press, 1957 [1944]). A Vienna-born economic historian and public intellectual, Polanyi had to flee the fascist onslaught. He became an Oxford University professor. For a naturalized reading of market lore, see Stanford's John McMillan's *Reinventing the Bazaar: A Natural History of Markets* (New York and London: w.w. Norton & Company, 2003).

7   See note 4 above, and also, William I. Robinson, *Latin America and Global Capitalism: A Critical Globalization Perspective* (Baltimore, MD: The Johns Hopkins University, 2008), and Sandro Mezzadra and Brett Neilson, *Border as Method, or, the Multiplication of Labor* (London and Durham, NC: Duke University Press, 2013)

8   Western is in quotes to denote that it is a term burdened by a definite historical and geographic, colonial, political, and ideological context.

9   Friedrich Hegel, in his *Philosophy of Right* already spoke of *grosser Reichtum* (massive wealth) and *grosse Armuth* (massive poverty). And that was not of course the first instance of someone speaking against massive poverty and inequality. One has just to read some history to realize that, but this new "Gilded Age" has an entirely new planetary dimension.

10 *EcoDomics* from *oikodomia* (building, making): "an art and practice of living (and) making (in) common(s)", is a concept that I have been developing in the recent past years, which combines a transversal relation between *oikologia* (ecology and biopower), *oikonomia* (ecological economics), and *aisthesis koine* or aesthetic(s) of the common(s). More below.

11 This "hiding" reflection commences with the early presocratic investigations "On Nature" or *peri physeos*.

12 The canonic argument of this current is, of course, Francis Fukuyama's *The End of History and the Last Man* (New York: Simon & Schuster/The Free Press/Avon Books, 2006 [1992]). To be sure, Fukuyama tried to balance his neoconservative stance with some Nietzschean angst, reviewing his more radical triumphalism after the Iraq debacle. See also José Gabriel Palma, "The Revenge of the Market on the Rentiers: Why neo-liberal reports of the end of history turned out to be premature," Faculty of Economics, University of Cambridge, https://www.repository.cam.ac.uk/bitstream/handle/1810/229494/0927.pdf?sequence=2, shorter version in *Cambridge Journal of Economics* 33, no. 4 (July 2009).

13 Frances Hutchinson, Mary Mellor and Wendy Olsen, *The Politics of Money: Towards Sustainability and Economic Democracy* (London: Pluto Press, 2002), 2, emphasis added.

14 http://blogs.spectator.co.uk/coffeehouse/2013/04/margaret-thatcher-in-quotes/, emphasis added.

15 In Silvia Federici, *Caliban and the Witch: Women, the Body, and Primitive Accumulation* (New York: Autonomedia, 2004), 52.

16 Mark Fisher, *Capitalist Realism: Is There No Alternative?* (Winchester and Washington, DC: Zero Books, 2009), 17–18.

17 Melinda Cooper, *Life as Surplus: Biotechnology and Capitalism in the Neoliberal Era* (London and Seattle, WA: University of Washington Press, 2008), 42, emphasis added.

18 Palma, "The Revenge of the Market on the Rentiers."

19 There is ample literature addressing this contradiction including the now classical analysis of Arturo Escobar, *Encountering Development: The Making and Unmaking of the Third World* (Princeton, NJ: Princeton University Press, 2011 [1995]), the work of Naomi Klein, *The Shock Doctrine: The Rise of Disaster Capitalism* (New York: Picador, 2008); David Harvey, *The Enigma of Capital and the Crisis of Capitalism* (Oxford: Oxford University Press, 2011), Melinda Cooper's challenge to a brand of non-linear economics in *Life as Surplus: Biotechnology and Capitalism in the Neoliberal Era* (Seattle, WA: University of Washington Press, 2007), George Caffentzis, *In Letters of Blood and Fire: Work, Machines, and the Crisis of Capitalism* (Oakland, CA: PM Press, 2013). Even *The New York Times* talks now of "The End of the 'Developing World'. [...] 'Lean' Societies approach consumption with scarcity in mind. [...] Nothing can be taken for granted or wasted. But resource constraints have provoked an astonishing bounty of homegrown solutions. [...] If necessity is the mother of invention, lean economies have a distinct advantage." Dayo Olopade, http://www.nytimes.com/2014/03/01/opinion/sunday/forget-developing-fat-nations-must-go-lean.html.

20 http://en.wikipedia.org/wiki/Geocentric_model

21 Cf. Sloterdijk, *In the World Interior of Capital*, 4, and his monumental *Sphären* project; see also Evan Thompson, *Mind in Life: Biology, Phenomenology, and the Sciences of Mind* (London and Cambridge, MA: Harvard University Press, 2007); Descola, *The Ecology of Others* and *Beyond Nature and Culture*; Karen Barad, *Meeting the Universe Halfway: Quantum Physics and the Entanglement of Matter and Meaning* (London and Durham, NC: Duke University Press,

2007); Timothy Morton, *Ecology without Nature* (Cambridge, MA: Harvard University Press, 2009); Kenneth Worthy, *Invisible Nature: Healing the Destructive Divide Between People and the Environment* (Amherst, NY: Prometheus Books, 2013); Nikolas Rose and JM Abi-Rached, *Neuro: The New Brain Sciences and the Management of the Mind* (Princeton, NJ: Princeton University Press, 2013).

22 Cf. Michel Foucault, *The Hermeneutics of the Subject — Lectures at the Collège de France 1981-1982* (New York: Picador, 2005).

23 Gerard Naddaf, *The Greek Concept of Nature* (Albany, NY: SUNY Press, 2005), I, II, 64.

24 Ann L.T. Bergren, *The Etymology and Usage of Peirar in Early Greek Poetry*, American Classical Studies Number 2, The American Philological Association (New York: Oxford University Press, 1975), 21ff., 115ff.

25 Martin Heidegger, "The Anaximander Fragment," in *Early Greek Thinking: The Dawn of Western Philosophy* (San Francisco, CA: HarperSanFrancisco, 1984 [1975]), 21, emphasis added.

26 Naddaf, *The Greek Concept of Nature*, 2, emphasis added.

27 *Aisthesis, Aesthetica*: senses, sensuous, sensate, of the senses.

28 Cf. J.M. Bernstein, *The Fate of Art: Aesthetic Alienation from Kant to Derrida and Adorno* (University Park, PA: Penn State University Press, 1992). The diagrams below capture suggested paths, but there is no room in these pages to get into more refined arguments.

29 This is a point that interests Marx very early, as his erudite doctoral dissertation demonstrates: "Difference between the Democritean and Epicurean Philosophy of Nature," in *Collected Works*, Vol. I (Marx: 1835-1843), Karl Marx and Frederick Engels (New York: International Publishers, 1975), 25-107, 403-509; see also Lucretius *De Rerum Natura*, "On the Nature of Things," a Roman *peri physeos* that saved for posterity Epicurean atomism; Stephen Greenblatt, *The Swerve: How the World Became Modern* (New York: Norton, 2011); Paul M. Schafer, ed., *The First Writings of Karl Marx* (Brooklyn, NY: Ig Publishing, 2006), and Dane R. Gordon and David B. Suits, eds., *Epicurus: His Continuing Influence and Contemporary Relevance* (Rochester, NY: RIT Cary Graphics Arts Press, 2003).

30 Cf. Pierre Hadot, *The Veil of Isis: An Essay on the History of the Idea of Nature* (Cambridge, MA: Harvard University Press, 2008). See also Parmenides *Peri Physeos* Poem, http://philoctetes.free.fr/parmenidesunicode.htm; http://plato.stanford.edu/entries/parmenides/; Robert Collingwood, *The Idea of Nature* (Oxford: Clarendon Press, 1945); Naddaf, *The Greek Concept of Nature*; Clarence J. Glacken, *Traces on the Rhodian Shore: Nature and Culture in Western Thought from Ancient Times to the End of the Eighteenth Century* (Berkeley, CA: University of California Press, 1976).

31 Arthur L. Lovejoy, *The Great Chain of Being: A Study of the History of an Idea* (Cambridge, MA: Harvard University Press, 1936); see also Amy Franceschini and Michael Swaine, *A Variation on Powers of Ten* (Berlin: Sternberg Press, 2012).

32 "The lifting of the veil" or "revelation" are the original meanings of *apocalypse*.

33 George Caffentzis, *In Letters of Blood and Fire: Work, Machines, and the Crisis of Capitalism* (Oakland, CA and Brooklyn, NY: PM Press/Common Notions/Autonomedia, 2013), 88.

34 Adam Smith. *Wealth of Nations* (Amherst, NY: Prometheus Books, 1991 [1776]), 19, quoted in Caffentzis, *In Letters of Blood and Fire*, 88.

35 Karl Marx, *Capital: Volume I*, 874, quoted in Caffentzis, *In Letters of Blood and Fire*, 88.

36 Ibid., emphasis in Caffentzis.

37 See note 12 above.

38 This section is part of an ongoing investigation and pedagogy on what I call "archaic modernity", the continued co-existence of archaic and modern I have alluded to already.

39 See Naddaf, *The Greek Concept of Nature*, italics in original.

40 Giorgio Agamben, "Introductory note to the Concept of the Democracy," in Agamben et al., *Democracy in What State?* 1-2, emphasis added, except in: "the word *democracy* is used [...]"

41 Linneaus, *Specimen academicum de oeconomia naturae* (Uppsala: 1749), quoted in *The Kingdom and the Glory: For a Theological Genealogy of Economy and Government*, Giorgio Agamben (Stanford, CA: Stanford University Press, 2011), 278-279, italics in original.

42 Ibid., 283-284, emphasis added.

43 Johannes Thumfart, "On Grotius *Mare Liberum* and Vittoria's *De India*, Following Agamben and Schmitt," *Grotiana* 30, no.1 (2009): 77.

44 Ibid., 73.

45 Roland Boer, "John Locke, the Fall, and the Origin Myth of Capitalism," http://www.politicaltheology.com/blog/john-locke-the-fall-and-the-origin-myth-of-capitalism/; see also Ignacio Valero, "How Free is 'Free'? Property, Markets, and the Aesthetic(s) of the Common(s)," in *What We Want is Free: Critical Exchange in Recent Art*, ed. Ted Purves et al. (Albany, NY: SUNY Press, 2014).

46 David Noble, *The Religion of Technology: The Divinity of Man and the Spirit of Invention* (Harmondsworth: Penguin Books, 1999), 1-6, emphases added.

47 "Blood Coltan," http://topdocumentaryfilms.com/blood-coltan/; "High Tech Misery in China — National Labor Committee," http://www.globallabourrights.org/reports?id=0006; "Worker's Rights Protection in Mexico's Silicon Valley," http://dspace.mit.edu/handle/1721.1/69456; *SMART 2020: Enabling the Low Carbon Economy on the Information Age*, http://www.smart2020.org/publications/; "How E-Waste is Becoming a Big, Global Problem," http://www.npr.org/2013/01/11/169144849/how-e-waste-is-becoming-a-big-global-problem; "E-Waste: A Global Issue with Local Solutions," 31 October 2013, http://www.kiosk.tm/thinking/e-waste-a-global-issue-with-local-solutions/; while "high-tech" registers 2.43 billion Google results, "salvation" clocks a subdued 24.8 million, and "blood Coltan" a mere 93,200.

48 Cf. http://www.transwaste.eu/file/001274.pdf; http://www.marcobulgarelli.com/galleries/e-waste-bangalore#myGallery1-picture(2); Mike Ives: "For decades, hazardous electronic waste from around the world has been processed in unsafe backyard recycling operations in Asia and Africa. Now, a small but growing movement is seeking to provide these informal collectors with incentives to sell e-waste to advanced recycling facilities," http://e360.yale.edu/feature/in_developing_world_a_push_to_bring_e-waste_out_of_shadows/2736/.

49 Rob Latham, *Consuming Youth: Vampires, Cyborgs & the Culture of Consumption* (Chicago, IL: University of Chicago Press, 2002), 3, emphasis added.

50 Jonathan Crary, *24/7: Late Capitalism and the Ends of Sleep* (London: Verso, 2013), 1 ff., emphasis added; see also http://www.nature.com/news/2004/040712/full/news040712-5.html; http://www.plosbiology.org/article/info%3Adoi%2F10.1371%2Fjournal.pbio.0020212

51 Cf. Gilles Deleuze, "Postscript on the Societies of Control," *October* 59 (1993): 5; see also Michael Hardt, "The Withering of Civil Society," in *Deleuze and Guattari: New Mappings in Politics, Philosophy, and Culture*, ed. Eleanor Kaufman and Kevin Jon Heller (Minneapolis, MN: University of Minnesota Press, 1998), 23-39.

52 See note 4, but also: Rolando Vázquez, "Towards a Decolonial Critique of Modernity: *Buen Vivir*, Relationality and the Task of Listening," in *Denktraditionem im Dialog*, Vol. 33, ed. Raul Fornet-Betancourt (Aachen: Wissenschaftsverlag Mainz, 2012); Walter Mignolo and Arturo Escobar, "On Decoloniality," Center for Global Studies and the Humanities, Duke University (2007), https://globalstudies.trinity.duke.edu/wko-v2dr; Pheng Chea, "The Limits of Thinking in Decolonial Strategies," The Doreen

B. Townsend Center for the Humanities, UC Berkeley, http://townsendcenter.berkeley.edu/publications/limits-thinking-decolonial-strategies; Escobar, *Encountering Development*; Immanuel Wallerstein, *The Modern World-System IV: Centrist Liberalism Triumphant, 1789–1914* (Berkeley, CA: University of California Press, 2011), *World Systems Analysis: An Introduction* (Durham, NC: Duke University Press, 2004); Vine Deloria, *The Metaphysics of Modern Existence* (New York: Harper & Row, 1979); Abhijit Banerjee and Esther Duflo, *Poor Economics: A Radical Rethinking of the Way to Fight Poverty* (New York: Public Affairs/Perseus Books Group, 2011); Amartya Sen, *Development as Freedom* (New York: Alfred A. Knopf, 2001); Raul Zibechi et al., *Territories in Resistance: A Cartography of Latin American Social Movements* (Oakland, CA: AK Press, 2012); Alvaro Reyes (Special Issue Editor), "Autonomy and Emancipation in Latin America," *South Atlantic Quarterly* 111, no.1 (Winter 2012); Gayatri Chakravorty Spivak, "Can the Subaltern Speak?" in *Marxism and the Interpretation of Culture*, ed. Cary Nelson and Lawrence Grossberg (Chicago, IL: University of Illinois Press, 1988), 271–313.

53   Frank Ruda, *Hegel's Rabble: An Investigation into Hegel's Philosphy of Right* (London: Bloomsbury, 2011), 5.

54   Ibid., XV, XVII.

55   To be sure, *cognitariat* is a controversial term among some respected scholars like George Caffentzis, but there is no room here to get into the rich arguments that he offers. But I modestly prefer to maintain a certain difference between the two connotations, particularly since I seem to be coining the term *emotariat*. *Emotarian* has been used since late 2013 in certain political, musical, and lifestyle discussions and performances that have nothing to do with the issue at hand.

56   In this regard, Franco "Bifo" Berardi's *The Soul at Work: From Alienation to Autonomy* (Los Angeles, CA: Semiotext(e), 2009), is a piece that insightfully brings back the "archaic" soul into new currency that certain strands of behavioural, evolutionary, and cognitive psychology and neuroscience don't even begin to tackle. It has been a special source of inspiration for my *emotariat* coinage.

57   Carl Zimmer, "In the Human Brain, Size isn't Really Everything," *The New York Times*, 26 December 2013, http://www.nytimes.com/2013/12/26/science/in-the-human-brain-size-really-isnt-everything.html?ref=science, emphasis added.

58   Karl Marx, *Capital, Volume One, A Critique of Political Economy* (Mineola, NY: Dover Publications, 2011), Part II, Ch. 4, 170; Alberto Toscano, "Divine Management: Economy and Secularization in Agamben's *The Kingdom and the Glory*," *Angelaki* (Journal of the Theoretical Humanities) 16, no. 3 (September 2011): 131, emphasis original; see also, Agamben Symposium, http://agambensymbosium.blogspot.com/2012/07/agamben-symposiumadam-kotsko.html; José Manuel Naredo, *La Economía en Evolución: Historia y perspectivas de las categorías fundamentals de las ciencias económicas* (Madrid: Siglo XXI, 1987); Hutchinson et al., *The Politics of Money*.

59   Herman E. Daly and John B. Cobb, Jr., *For the Common Good: Redirecting the Economy Toward Community, the Environment, and a Sustainable Future* (Boston, MA: Beacon Press, 1994 [1989]), 138ff.

60   Cf. Vandana Shiva, *Earth Democracy: Justice, Sustainability and Peace* (Cambridge, MA: South End Press, 2005); Robinson, *Latin America and Global Capitalism*; Peter Sloterdijk's *Sphären* project, op. cit.; J. Timmons Roberts and Nikki Demetria Thanos, *Trouble in Paradise: Globalization and Environmental Crisis in Latin America* (London and New York: Routledge, 2003); Eric Voegelin, *Order and History, Vol. IV: The Ecumenic Age* (London and Baton Rouge, LA: Louisiana University Press, 1974); and Stella Georgoudi, *Gaia/Gê. Entre mythe, culte et idéologie*, https://digitalt.uib.no/bitstream/handle/1956.2/2952/Gaia%2

Ge_Georgoudi.pdf?sequence=1; Rosi Braidotti, "The Ethics of Becoming Imperceptible," http://deleuze.tausendplateaus.de/wp-content/uploads/2008/01/trent-final.pdf, and *The Posthuman* (Cambridge: Polity Press, 2013).

61   On this very topic, I recently wrote: "How 'Free' is Free? Property, Markets, and the Aesthetic(s) of the Common(s)."

62   In this topic, besides the experiences of the Latin American groups, theorists, and social movements, I am influenced by Jacques Rancière on the "politics of aesthetics" and the "sharing of the sensible", Baruch Spinoza's ethical and political ideas on the "multitude", and the practice and theories on the common of post-Autonomist theorists and activists like Antonio Negri, Paolo Virno, Franco "Bifo" Berardi, and Roberto Esposito. *Midnight Notes Collective*'s ideas from George Caffentzis ("commonization"), Silvia Federici ("reproducing commons"), and Peter Linebaugh's "communing" are also influential.

63   Cf. Roberto Esposito, *Communitas: The Origin and Destiny of Community* (Stanford, CA: Stanford University Press, 2010), see also his *Immunitas: The Protection and Negation of Life* (Cambridge: Polity Press, 2011).

64   The level of carbon dioxide has surpassed 400 parts per million, "passing a long-feared milestone...reaching a concentration not seen on the earth for millions of years", Justin Gillis, "Heat-Trapping Gas Passes Milestone, Raising Fears," http://www.nytimes.com/2013/05/11/science/earth/carbon-dioxide-level-passes-long-feared-milestone.html?hp&_r=0.

65   *Ecosophy* is a word used both by Guattari and Norwegian philosopher Arne Naess, who coined it, but each gives it a different meaning. In Naess *ecosophy* and *deep ecology* are a largely synonymous environmental discourse, expanding identity into the non-human world in order to create a self-identified empathy for nature. Guattari's works by dissolution, "becoming other," Naess' by "self-realization." Moreover, Guattari's *ecosophy*, is a political ecology that strongly criticizes global neoliberalism, what he calls IWC, Integrated World Capitalism.

66   Félix Guattari, *The Three Ecologies* (London and New York: Continuum, 2008 [1989]), 19–20, emphasis in original; see also Félix Guattari, *Chaosmosis: An Ethico-Aesthetic Paradigm* (Bloomington, IN: Indiana University Press, 1995 [1992]), particularly "The Ecosophic Object," 119–135.

67   Gilles Deleuze, "For Félix," in *Two Regimes of Madness* (New York: Semiotext(e), 2006), 382, quoted in Gary Genosko, "Transversality and Politics," in *Félix Guattari: A Critical Introduction*, Gary Genosko (New York: Pluto Press, 2009), 51; see also Janell Watson, *Guattari's Diagrammatic Thought: Writing between Lacan and Deleuze* (New York: Continuum, 2009), 22–31.

68   Ibid.; see also Félix Guattari, *Chaosmosis*, and *Schizoanalytic Cartographies* (London: Bloomsbury Academic, 2013 [1989]); *Félix Guattari in the Age of Semiocapitalism, Deleuze Studies* 6, no. 2, ed. Gary Genosko (2012); John Tinnell, "*Transversalising the Ecological Turn: Four Components of Félix Guattari's Ecosophical Perspective*," http://eighteen.fibreculturejournal.org/2011/10/09/fcj-121-transversalising-the-ecological-turn-four-components-of-felix-guattari's-ecosophical-perspective/.

69   Benjamin Straumann, "Oikeoisis and appetitus societatis: Hugo Grotius' Ciceronian Argument for Natural Law and Just War," *Grotiana* (New Series) 24/25 (2003/2004): 48, 52–53.

70   http://people.wku.edu/jan.garrett/stoa/stoinuts.htm

71   Cf. Sloterdijk, *In the World Interior of Capital*, 143ff.; see also Voegelin, *Order and History, Vol. IV: The Ecumenic Age*, 114ff., 272ff.

72   Jason W. Moore, "Transcending the Metabolic Rift: A Theory of Crisis in the Capitalist-World Ecology," *The Journal of Peasant Studies* 38, no. 1 (January 2011): 1.

73   Jason W. Moore, "From Object to *Oikeios*: Environment-Making in the Capitalist World-Ecology," http://www.jasonwmoore.com/uploads/Moore__From_Object_to_Oikeios__for_website__May_2013.pdf, 2, 6–7.

74 Vázquez, "Towards a Decolonial Critique of Modernity," 7.

75 "Our generation is the first called to give birth, not without joy nor pain, to an *ecodomia** of the family, the region, and the planet, at the same time economic, ecological and ecumenical. Awakening, resistance, and responsibility will be the very words of this new *ecodomia*. May you be welcome! * (Greek: construction)" Juliana Barreto, http://jubarreto.wordpress.com/sobre/. I came across these inspiring verses after I had enunciated my first thoughts on *ecoDomics* at a conference, "Rising Tide: The Arts and Ecological Ethics," http://risingtideconference.org, a poignant synchronicity!

INFORMAL MARKETS

Gayatri Chakravorty Spivak

I wrote the embedded text in response to a request from the Occupiers of Wall Street in their initial phase. The editors of this collection allowed me to include this piece because, in their words, it "interrogate[d] the broader political situation in which informal markets are embedded". My words to them had been that, "although I enthusiastically supported informal markets, I did not think they were a major force in transforming global relations". I want to write a few opening words to bring these two statements together.

If the international civil society is taken for granted, informal markets do indeed change global relations in so far as the global North thinks that the global South should be only the recipient of top-down philanthropy for their needs, and/or military intervention for "peace-keeping", and/or sanctions for containment. One of the best examples of the informal market in this sense is the M-Pesa, discussed vigorously in Dayo Olopade's The Bright Continent: Breaking Rules and Making Change in Modern Africa.[1]

If, on the other hand, one looked behind the international civil society into the decimation of the modern state and its transformation into management of capitalist globalization, with the sanction of the North-in-the-South, informal markets would remain competitive within the ruling view of the world that can no longer think democracy. It makes its place within the contemporary disappearance of the democratic. My own work has therefore been to produce the intuitions of democracy, above and below, rather than work in the acceptance of a world without it. For lack of time, and not only for lack of time, I do not want to elaborate these matters here.

I must however say that the Occupiers, with their question about the connections between Wall Street and Washington, required a robust long-term systemic answer for the possibility of good global governance, not an acknowledgement of superb reactive solutions.

Keep this in mind as you read what follows. The "you" is the Occupiers, the readers of this collection are overhearing:

What is to be Done?

You have asked me this hard question. You have also asked how Washington and Wall Street — politics and economics: political economy — are connected. That connection is through the international banking system, anchored by central banks of various nation-states, secretly protected by entities such as the Bank for International Settlements, the International Organization of Securities Commissions and the World Economic Forum, and supported by non-banking financial institutions. This network controls Washington.

Interest in the international capital network began in the middle of the nineteenth century. But for our purposes, we can begin after World War II, when organizations facilitating the internationalizing of political economy were established: the International Monetary Fund (IMF), the International Bank for Rural Development or the World Bank and, through the operation of the General Agreement on Tariffs and Trade, the World Trade Organization (WTO) in 1995, 50 years down the line.

Most of these organizations secure the connection between the nation-states of the world and the international banking system. The WTO regulates trade. Its goal is not people but business: to help producers of goods and services, exporters, and importers conduct their business. The United Nations, with its militarized Security Council, provides the ideological justifications for nation-state agreement and conflict within this international network.[2]

Rather than the end of imperialism (*post*colonial digital multitudes or social networks), globalization is a new stage of imperialism. When we celebrate social networking, we must not forget that the telecommunication companies — China Mobile, Deutsche Telekom — were the first ones to break state control and privatize, cross borders to encourage investment in foreign currencies not necessarily located in their country of origin, thus changing the nature of the connection between the state and global capital, making the state serve capital rather than people located within its boundaries. Globalization, information-intensive and working at high electronic speed, has improved, not only the seeming political possibilities of social networking, but also the possibility of trade in foreign exchange — the differences among hard currencies and between hard and soft currencies — the currencies of the global North and the global South — minute, incessant (24/7 because of the world's time-zones), hard to track electronic manoeuvres. This "finance capitalism", has a much higher daily turnover or circulation, which makes capital grow exponentially over against world trade. World trade itself has been "financialized" through futures trading and derivatives. Already ten years ago, U.S. Gross Domestic Product was less than 2 per cent of the finance capital transaction volume. In addition to this, the so-called service industries have grown in volume over manufacturing as well. Electronic capitalism has also managed to "pulverize the factory floor," and made it impossible for Labour-based general strikes to achieve more than limited and topical results. This is one of the reasons why the citizen-based (rather than labour-based) general strike (we will not move until our demands are met) that is the Occupy Wall Street movement fits the times.

Lenin's "What is to be Done?" recommends vanguardism in the face of consolidated opposition from world imperialism. Even without the depredations of Stalinism, vanguardism could not lay the basis of a just society. At best, it built up a counter-imperialism (neither more nor less "evil" than any other) supported by state capitalism and a "nationalist" education. Although Lenin spoke of bringing the masses to full class consciousness, there was no time for this, and certainly, the building up of a will to social justice generation after generation within the speed required by the ceaseless strategizing demanded in turn by the incessant workings of the vanguardist control of political economy was not on the agenda. The emphasis was on explaining political information, not on an attempt to change habits of mind.

Without the general nurturing of the will to justice among the people, no just society can survive. The Occupy Wall Street movement must attend to education — primary through post-tertiary — at the same time as it attempts to the uncoupling of the connection between specifically capitalist globalization and the nation-state. This is an almost impossible task to remember, especially when there are such complex and urgent immediate tasks lined up! But it must be repeated:

without this attention, there is no chance of survival — as we have seen in the case of the Soviet Union, China, and other post-revolutionary societies.

Indeed, Mao Zedong tried to solve this problem by the once-and-for-all solution of the Cultural Revolution, whereby he simply reversed the hierarchy that inhabited Chinese society — only to prove that without the patient and continuous system of education, the mind of a people cannot be nourished, and without robust mental resources, we are at the mercy of brainwashing.

The dismantling of the connection between the citizen and the state that we are now witnessing in the U.S. context is basically a dismantling of the New Deal established by Franklin Roosevelt between the two world wars, during the Great Depression brought about by a crisis of over-production. Roosevelt's Labor Secretary, Frances Perkins, ran the committee that was responsible for planning the New Deal in its detail. It was my great good fortune to live across the hallway from her as a graduate student at Cornell University in the sixties, in the honour society called Telluride House, where I was the first woman student to be given a lodging scholarship. Madame Perkins was the permanent faculty resident. We were the two women living in the house with 32 male undergraduates and three male graduate students (among them Paul Wolfowitz). I believe I can say that the idea of devising a welfare state in the United States was so capably protected because it was in the hands of a supremely intelligent and feminist *woman*. I am not someone who believes that women as an essence possess some direct gift of nurture. But it is true that one of the unintended consequences of keeping women separate from gainful employment, keeping them forcibly responsible toward other human beings all their lives, and idealizing them in polite society, historically produced in superbly educated brilliant women a propensity towards other-directed behaviour much more readily than in men of comparable class-production, whose ambition could take a self-directed path to success. (Post-feminism is quickly taking care of this, of course.)

It is certainly true that the working class enabled by the New Deal went to fight in World War II, which was inevitably an imperialist war. To write off the welfare state as a result of this is like writing off Socialism because the German Social Democrats, at the time the most powerful socialist party in Europe, voted in war credits in 1914.

The Reagan-Bush era in the United States, together with Thatcher's regime in the United Kingdom saw the beginnings of the dismantling of the welfare state that we are witnessing today.

In globalization, the sovereignty of the state is compromised as a result of the removal of barriers between national and international capitals, leading to a restructuring of governance commonly called economic restructuring or "neo-liberalism". In the best concept of the democratic nation-state, the state's chief function is the redistribution of revenue for social welfare according to the constitution. After restructuring, the state's role becomes managerial of capitalist globalization. Thus the state becomes accountable to business rather than to people, the predicament of the 99% versus the 1%. It goes without saying that this cannot be redressed simply from within the democratic electoral mechanism of a state. The law can forever be changed in favour of business rather than people, if the entire polity is not educated to desire justice for all. The randomness of informal markets has no connection with this.

To repeat, then: the largest sector of global capital is finance capital. Finance capital is basically trade in foreign exchanges. The more often (finance) capital turns over or circulates, the more its volume increases. For financial globalization to work, the world must remain unevenly divided between the global South and the global North, so that there can be constantly fluctuating differences in the value of hard currency and soft currency, so that financialization can operate. The banks in all nation-states are clued into this game and so must turn over money as often as possible — borrowing and lending fast and playing one sort of investment over against another. World trade turns over less often because it is connected to material goods and services. But world trade also has a very large "futures" trading sector that plays into finance capital. Since the Reagan-Bush era the barriers between national capital — in our case federal regulations — and this play of global capital have been slowly relaxed, until the collapsing of investment banks and commercial banks in 1999 effectively removed conflict of interest prohibitions between investment bankers serving as officers of commercial banks took control away from government controlled enterprise, and gave it over to global capital flows. It is because of the demand that capital flows in and out as fast as possible that, even when human beings were suffering and being beaten down into the 99%, as a result of the housing crisis, banks had to be "bailed out" so that they had enough funds to continue in the inflow and outflow of capital that makes finance capital turn over. (The IMF regularly bailed out banks when nation-states were in debt-crises.) This is an insane, inhuman and seductive game, which needs to be controlled so that it can be medicine — in the interest of social productivity — rather than poison. As the U.S. General Accounting Office said in its generally ignored 2004 report on "predatory lending": "The Secondary Market [where previously issued financial instruments such as stocks, bonds, financial futures, and loans are bought and sold] May Play a Role in Both Facilitating and Combating Predatory Lending." The connection with Washington comes clear if we look at the past few years when states fought bitterly to have some kind of regulation and the federal government fought back strongly to squelch these efforts. We must also take into account the so-called non-banking financial institutions — *insurance firms*, *pawn shops*, *cashier's check* issuers, *check cashing* locations, *currency exchanges*, *microloan organizations* and the like —, which are free of any national and international regulatory efforts. In order to correct political economy, we cannot rely on politics alone.

It so happens that traditionally (Northern) Democrats are more into regulation and Republicans less — but it is not really a question of party politics. It is much rather a question of an educated electorate that understands what it is that is involved in the undoing of a bad connection between Washington and Wall Street and is not simply focused on self-interest. There is no guarantee of this in the organization of informal markets, however they might undermine the authority of the ruling class.

What we must also understand is that real estate came to be the field in which this kind of insane global flow of capital would be encouraged because it happened to be the field which was the least protected, in the powerful and gendered ideology of a "home". In other words, the abstract areas which capital inhabits are not necessarily controlled by human decisions to do specific kinds of harm. In such a situation, unless the polity is educated to want social justice, it can be taken in by many different kinds of slogans. It is not a question of subject matter alone, nor of gathering information. It is a question of making minds that will read the information right. It is a question of educating in such a way that the intuitions of democracy and justice for everyone, rather than just self-interest, become habitual: working for standards not necessarily motored by competition; not being reward-ed for leadership; not encouraging role models; one could go on. The pursuit of happiness must be somewhat curbed in in the interest of justice for all. And liberty must not be confused with capital flow for a financialization that need create jobs only so people will borrow. Mitt Romney accused Obama of "putting free enterprise on trial". When the state is subservient to global capital, flowing in and flowing out at the highest possible rate, private enterprise is not "free". An ill-educated society can be persuaded with the obvious lies of trickle-down economic advantage in jobs created by capitalists rather than if the state has a robust structure of redistribution. Small business is no longer an unquestioned good, when venture capital regularly promises global connections as quickly and as broadly as possible. Metaphors can then be negotiated as literal truth. Any attempt of the state to serve the citizen can be misrepresented as a design on the part of the state to control. Every attempt to save the nation-state economy so that there can be socially just redistribution can be described as state-control of private lives. All efforts by the state to serve business and not people, giving everything over to make capital flow in the interest of the financialization of the globe, can be called "free" enterprise. Therefore, in addition to the legal involvement on the national and international levels, we must continue to emphasize the need persistently to construct a mindset to desire justice for all, from the primary to the post-tertiary level, if a just society is to prevail. This is not an impractical or "individualistic" lesson. The electorate must learn to read well enough, generation by generation, so the play of metaphors is seen clearly. Social networking is useful only with a mindset willing social justice.

This is not a situation of either state control or small is beautiful. What we have to learn to do is demand and protect such laws as will see to it that the federal gov-ernment will not work only in the interests of the play of finance capital, but also in the interest of good lives for the welfare of human beings.

Another slogan to watch out for is "giving back". As the volume of turnover decreases, so called diasporic investment across borders, especially in the country of origin, can raise the amount greatly. This activity can take the form of foreign direct investment being ideologically justified through culturalism and heritagism. In the name of globalizing education, there is now also a trend toward foreign direct investment in for-profit education that can be justified by these unexamined slogans.

If one wants to bring about equal justice within the nation-state alone, through electoral politics alone — although this is extremely important —, one ignores the fact that the banking system, with its global connections, now has far superior powers than a democratically structured state that must turn over its executive leadership at regular intervals. The jurisdiction of the Supreme Court in general is more tied to the Constitution, which belongs to another era — today's global politics being to a surprising extent released from constitutional obligations. It is very important to remember that Washington lobby politics is well organized by and for the apologists for seeking globalization as the only goal. To engage with them is not only a question of winning through verbal violence and managing votes. However idealistic it might seem, it is also and perhaps only winnable through a sustained argument advanced by people trained into an intelligent analysis of what political/economic moves are good for the general public. Lenin's "What is to be Done" concentrated on the party. Our "What is to be Done" must concentrate on the mindset of the electorate. For times have changed. The citizen cannot afford to be taken in by the old slogans: job creation, small is beautiful, freedom from state control, economic growth, heritage. The vanguard has sold out to unregulated capital in- and out-flow; putting all kinds of debts together and selling them at high risk. Student loans, like women's microcredit, are features of this. When we think about education we must therefore keep in mind that if business administration is given into the hands of people who are untrained in the necessity for social justice, it cannot lead to the world for which we are striking. Most business ethics courses teach the maximum of business sustained by the minimum of ethics. If material gains within political economy are not supplemented by an other-directed and just culture that protects the fragility of the public use of reason, there is no hope for the future. We must ensure that the public sector become accountable for social welfare. The only way to ensure this is through bringing back regulatory laws. The trend now is to praise individual benevolence. Good rich people helping out the poor. The will to social justice, sustained by education, engaged in electoral activism, using regulated capital for social productivity and individual fulfilment, is not to be equated with this; *and the ebullience of the energy of informal markets can at best be integrated within this hegemony, with class, race, and gender relations altered rather than seriously transformed.*

1   Dayo Olopade, *The Bright Continent: Breaking Rules and Making Change in Modern Africa* (Boston, MA: Houghton Mifflin Harcourt, 2014).

2   Today, the countermove by BRICS (Brazil-Russia-India-China-South Africa) should be considered, in broad strokes, as a way to compete in this control.

PART II   GLOBAL INFORMALITY

GLOBAL INFORMALITY: BOTTOM-UP TRADE AND TRANSNATIONAL REALIGNMENTS

Peter Mörtenböck

The recent period of accelerated globalization and liberalization has seen new forms of informal economic activity that have shifted informality much "closer" to centres of power.[1] This shift involves a two-way dynamics: on the one hand, global flight and migration are being met with urban segregation in Western cities while, on the other, global corporations are persistently extending their market interests into "developing" countries. In different parts of the world informality has become viral and is tied to political agendas in ways that seem to elude the explanatory frameworks offered by prevalent structuralist and legalist approaches. This expanding grey zone of informal economic activities in which an ever increasing number of regions, groups of people and areas of life are becoming involved cannot be explained solely by structural un-employment and income inequality — as the International Labour Organization (ILO) tends to argue — or by the legal barriers that advocates of micro-entrepreneurship argue are necessitating an immersion in informality. From the new ethos of exper-imental, self-generated enterprise in the Western world to flexible approaches to land-use rights and nation-state affiliation, from financing platforms based on social media to mobile-phone-based microtrade between Asia, Africa and Latin America, we are seeing a spread of technologies that are creating new relationships between spaces, people and cultures. As a result, informal systems have attained a dimension that spans the world, one that encompasses the structuring of social relationships, the configuration of living environments and participation in political and social processes, as well as the generation of individual incomes and cultural production.

Such bottom-up strategies, which emerge wherever the forces of the institution-alized economy are unable to operate directly, indicate not only changes in scale but also changes affecting critical conceptual, institutional and operational levels of what we commonly understand as "economic transactions". The symptoms of this shift include new citizenship arrangements and the production of a diverse spectrum of migrant subjects as well as the "worlding" practices of neoliberal urbanism, the consequence of which is an accelerated circulation of models, protocols and prac-tices of city-making.[2] With this expandable repertoire, the metropolis is replacing the factory as the primary spatial reference for a globalized production of goods, ideas and values.[3] In this context, urban growth and informal patterns of trade are mutually reinforcing one another. Influential actors in this world-spanning space of informality include new financial institutions in developing economies established to provide financing for infrastructural development that is not tied to loans from the world's leading economic powers. An example found at the highest level is the New Development Bank set up by the BRICS countries as an alternative to the IMF and the World Bank, which serves an economic area containing almost half of the world's population.

Such applications of informality as a grey area, reserve capacity and infrastructural frontier circulate across different domains and pervade social life with imperatives of informal production such that everything, including the independent-minded realm of the arts, becomes infested with a new kind of "economic thinking" distilled in innumerable "laboratories" that engage an ever-willing audience in their operations. The allurement of informal lifestyles binds existing desire smoothly and inconspicuously to the promise of economic returns. This process is increasingly being steered by remote control rather than direct action: whether in the form of remote diagnoses of violations of commercial agreements, which are used by governments to apply political pressure, state surveillance of immigration areas and border regions using remotely controlled drones, or the current planning rhetoric of urban "acupuncture" in informally settled urban areas. In the context of the neoliberal politics of globalization, the art of controlling informality, as discussed below, consists in maintaining a distance from its "natural" development while selectively siphoning off the returns it can bring.

In an interview with architects Urban-Think Tank (U-TT) a couple of months before they were awarded the prestigious Golden Lion at the Venice Architecture Biennale 2012 for their project *Torre David/Gran Horizonte* about the — now evicted — community that squatted Venezuela's third-tallest but only half-built skyscraper in downtown Caracas,[4] I asked them how they felt about the fact that in recent years a specialized repertoire of spatial practices seemed to have developed that was able to link very different experiential worlds with one another — local populations with urban expertise, the "one-to-one laboratory" of the Global South with the academic sphere. They replied that their own experience had shown them how little will there was for genuine cooperation and that they therefore had no illusions that the relationship between the Global North and South would fundamentally change except as a result of the economic shifts that are now directing our attention to cities like Caracas, São Paulo and Mumbai, in which U-TT and other like-minded actors are aiming to realize the urban experimental field of the twenty-first century.[5] Whether or not we will see some changes in the global world order as a result of economic shifts, it seems to be the very act of spatializing informality as a globally distributed patchwork of unfettered urban frontiers that is driving the spread of contemporary myths of informal entrepreneurship, self-financing and self-employment. Responding to the expansionary practices of capitalist market relations, this spatialization entails systematic and well-placed operations, techniques of interruption and evasion, accumulated protocols and rituals, radical gestures and expressions, coded values and aesthetics. Any attempt to trace the current frontiers of global informality will therefore need to take into account the role in transnational realignments being played by experimentation with entrepreneurial schemes, aesthetic trends, organizational techniques and civic enterprises.

In light of these territorial and conceptual mobilizations, my intention in this essay is threefold: first, to situate urban informality at the intersection of economic, political and cultural vectors that reference a global struggle over the constitution of subjects as citizens; second, to locate informal markets within the manifold ways in which space is produced in relation to new arrangements between state and non-state technologies; and, third, to focus on some of the transnational practices mobilized by different actors to intervene in this fabric. An important reference point in this context is the postcolonial world order and the production of transnational spaces associated with it, spaces characterized by a precisely calculated but apparently boundless mobility of labour power, worldwide data traffic, the uninhibited flow of capital and the proliferation of hybrid lifestyles. These cross-border flows are steered by the economic calculation of "location intelligence", outsourcing and geomarketing, supported by economic and trade agreements, and brought about by labour migration, the flight of business and politically-motivated expulsion. New worlds emerge wherever these flows are bundled — at the numerous nodes of advanced capitalism, where human capacities are combined with physical and intellectual capacities to form hybrid resource agglomeration and massive infrastructural concentrations that facilitate the worldwide dissemination of goods. An important role in the rhythms of these circulations is played by high-growth metropolitan regions, whether classic global cities orientated to the virtual management of financial capital or super-sized urban agglomerations in emerging world regions. These entities all constitute chess pieces in the contest for the best location, newly formatted territories whose particular and capricious logics endeavour to bring state and private stakeholders under control in order to achieve success in the global competition between "city-worlds."

Citizenship Arrangements: From Territorialized Rights to Exchange Values
In recent years, these dynamics have brought to the fore a new kind of urban system that has arisen from the multi-directional movements of transnational urban deregulations and realignments: the "extended city" as a cluster of networked sites produced by technology, laws, political pressures, migratory movements, disciplinary measures, and other translocal forces that are acted out locally. These landscapes of "lateralized market power" are not purely an effect of accelerated globalization but a set of situated cultural practices and interactions between particular emergent assemblages.[6] They have become manifest as a range of trans-territorial spatial articulations that fuse multiple politico-economic interests with processes of subject formation. Sites as diverse as special economic zones, informal border markets, squatted building complexes, refugee centres and migrant workers' camps have begun to populate both physical and mental landscapes on a global scale. On a conceptual level, this has highlighted a critical shift in our understanding of notions of mobility, citizenship and land use, which are now seen as interrelated, flexible and contingent practices rather than as defined by administrative or regulatory means. It also demonstrates how new modes of citizenship are being produced at the intersections of international corporate interests, the differentiated exercise of state power and the contingent struggle of citizens themselves, and thereby extending the concept of citizenship beyond the idea of the enjoyment of territorialized rights.

"Before the law all citizens were equal, but not everyone, of course, was a citizen."[7] — Robert Musil's concept of the citizen is only applicable in modified form to the strangely unresolved hybridities confronting us today: the "man without qualities" of the twenty-first century is characterized by the question not of whether someone counts as a citizen but of *which components* of citizenship are part of an individually claimable package. The life without qualities can no longer hope for stability especially given the permanent erosion of the prospect of overcoming crisis situations by means of a decisive event. Mobility has become a fundamental constant of globalization and with it the compulsion to be constantly cognizant of the accumulation of strategic values that make one a worthy citizen. A discourse of citizenship has thus taken shape that is almost exclusively orientated to the ability of citizens to contribute to economic growth. Central to this transformation is the destabilization of previously exclusive links between nation-state territories and citizenries in favour of a "contractualization" of citizenship aligned to the quid pro quo principles of market relations[8] — economic viability, efficiency requirements, competitive pressures and terms of trade. In the context of the ongoing economic crisis, the way in which labour forces are absorbed into economically successful regions is increasingly orientated to the profit that can be generated with them. The creation of zones governed by various forms of sovereignty, the flexible bestowal of graduated legal titles and the specification of immigrant contingents based on professional qualifications are some of the consequences of this development.[9] A new variant is represented by the immigrant investor programmes (IIPs) being offered by an increasing number of states, which promise wealthy immigrants the accelerated granting of comprehensive citizenship if they are prepared to invest in the national economy.

While this denationalization of citizenship[10] has pushed the spatial parameters of the relationship between nations and citizens formerly clearly marked by respective state borders into the background, the growing symbolic and political significance of entrepreneurial citizens is spatializing new power relations and exchange relationships. In this transformation of economic contexts, space as such has certainly not become dissociated from the construct of citizenship; however, it is generated anew out of this association as a means of flexibly steering populations. In this process, as Saskia Sassen has argued, the tightly packaged and naturalized multi-component "bundle" of citizenship rights is contested, unbundled and "sold off" in a variety of new configurations as appropriate counterparts to different levels of economic status. *One* space of immigration thereby becomes *many* spaces of immigration, meticulously crafted along specific market demands — spaces of low-wage workers, IMF citizens, IIP citizens, Sans Papiers and "paper citizens"[11]. As a consequence, while firms and concerns are accruing ever more citizenship rights, individuals are increasingly being deprived of them.[12]

In light of this development, migrant subjects now exist in a state of multiply graduated legal situations shaped by the character of informal spaces whose elasticity inspires a sense of the possibility of alternative identity projects and forms of social integration beyond the reach of state control, even though the chances of realizing such alternatives are relatively modest. Such "grey spaces", as Oren Yiftachel calls interim spaces that are maintained as informal on an ongoing basis, in which the boundaries of acceptance and rejection are deliberately kept blurred, are forming a new political geography in which urban colonial relationships are recoded.[13] Grey spacing, the associated process of producing new social relationships, which involve not only weak and marginalized communities but also powerful state and private actors, creates locally focussed zones of exception characterized by ongoing conflicts over which relationships are desirable, tolerated or criminalized — conflict spaces whose geographical isolation obscures the fact that they are significant indicators of structural relationships unfolding throughout the world.

The postcolonial theorist Achille Mbembe regards one consequence of these dynamics to be an increasing particularization of the conflicts besetting our epoch. The extension of the informalization of the economic sphere across the entire spectrum of our social and cultural realm of imagination, he argues, has led to durable political processes being replaced by a mosaic of individual struggles.[14] The entwinement of the political concerns embodied by trade union federations, associations and other traditional institutions is disappearing, and questions of spontaneous alliance formation and the improvised coordination of interests are taking centre stage. Informal organization in the form of short-lived, direct and unstable agreements is thus coming to constitute a dominant way of life in which work, culture, education and the social are beginning to orientate themselves to global economic interests and their mechanisms to such a degree that the market orientation of social relations Karl Polanyi saw as a corollary of the industrial and bourgeois political revolution[15] becomes an all-encompassing idea.

Government Power and the Economy

The ongoing "growth" of the world (population, urbanization, resource use, etc.) has made space one of the most important subjects of the practices of economic instrumentalization. Issues of land use are at the heart of contestations over the informalization of cities. Informal markets, in particular, play a pioneering role in the appropriation of intermediate times and spaces. Of late, enormous influence over informal urbanism has been exercised by means of banking, financialization and fiscalization. Finance economies have become a powerful motor not only of urbanization in gentrified or segregated areas of major cities, but, more generally, of patterns of growth in the metropolitan fabric. In parallel with this development, the institutions of the global financial markets are propagating a planning policy the purported aim of which is to integrate people from the informal sector into formal environments. In this context, informal urbanity is seen as a challenge for the modern city as such. Corresponding policies operate on the basis of the assumption that informality is to be understood as exclusively temporary, as an auxiliary mechanism whose creativity can be drawn on in order to achieve an improved situation. From this perspective, informality represents a space of exception, one that can only be confronted with the aim of introducing a system-compatible transformation that retrospectively legitimizes existing norms and regulations.

An important influence on this interplay of state, population and market is exerted by the connection between government power and the economy that has been established in the course of the development of Western modernity, a link elucidated in detail by Giorgio Agamben in his book *The Kingdom and the Glory*.[16] Agamben sees this connection as originally deriving from theology, more precisely from the doctrine of the Trinity. While the concept of governmentality developed by Foucault, whose work Agamben partly builds on, focuses above all on fathoming characteristic rationalities of control,[17] Agamben's frame of reference — government and the Christian doctrine of the Trinity — aims to show how the economic orientation of the Christian Trinity served as a laboratory for the formation of the modern Western machinery of government. According to Agamben, the concept of economy denotes a progressive extension of the (divine) sphere of power's application beyond power's own limits — a force that governs and administers from within. In this sense economy is a praxis that applies outside the realm of politics, a praxis that arranges, divides, represents and implements, and with these processes simultaneously establishes the dominant power.

In the context of the flexible positioning of informal markets, Agamben's argument is above all interesting in the sense that the process of secularization he speaks of is not to be understood in a Weberian sense as denoting the increasing demystification and de-theologization of the modern world but rather — as in the case of Foucault — as a signature that moves signs and concepts from one field to another.[18] This mechanism helps us to understand how easy it is to transplant forms of power between differently classified economic arrangements (formal/informal, permitted/unpermitted, etc.) without abrogating the existing pattern of meaning. In this way, economy has become the figure that defines the general principle on which all aspects of our public existence are based. Under its influence, the exercise of power rests on a form of substitution that produces not only a separation between being and praxis, within which many forms of urban informality are generated, but also a displacement of classical ontology (i.e. an original, substantive core of power) by an *economic* paradigm in which nothing is original apart from the relationship between power and government. As a consequence there is, as Agamben writes, "no substance of power, but only an 'economy,' only a 'government.'"[19]

Just as government invokes the power for which it deputizes, this power draws its validity from the execution of a substitutive praxis. Making this possible requires a complex coherence between the coordination and simultaneous fracture of being and acting[20] in which praxis in a certain sense becomes liberated and anarchic because it does not operate *according to instructions* but merely *within the framework* of the economy. Free action in the sense of self-determined praxis and free trade in the sense of the unrestricted movement of goods are in this sense not substantively but nevertheless economically controlled. An important role in this control is played by the political space of the border and its confrontation with the economically orientated regulation of transnational space.[21] Many informal markets forge cross-border economies that form crucial corridors for transnational undertakings, made up of the activities, people and goods that circulate within them while also functioning as a means of exerting influence on impenetrable territories. These illicit economies accommodate a multi-level network of "operators", "intermediaries" and "marketeers" who provide the spatial and political context for access to and control of hitherto untapped markets.

A particularly instructive example of this phenomenon is presented by informal markets in North Korea. Since the beginning of the present century, black markets have been emerging there, especially in Pyongyang and in the northern provinces close to China, where goods are smuggled over the border. In their reports, a range of Western think-tanks, including the Peterson Institute for International Economics in Washington, celebrate groups of people conducting illegal informal street trade in North Korea as "little revolutionaries", although similar activities in countries such as Paraguay, Mexico and China are condemned as "criminal". These different assessments of informal marketplaces have less to do with the number or gravity of legal violations than with the strategic-political and economic interests in a particular region. In the case of North Korea, as the Peterson Institute for International Economics writes, there is an interest in transforming the political-economic system of North Korea through the influence of external actors, and, in the longer term, in possibilities for the development of external economic relations with the USA.[22] The hopes being placed in such a development therefore require locally acting "grass-roots capitalists" who are prepared to take risks and who, as the driving force of this burgeoning "second economy", are prepared to embrace ongoing political changes and manage this developing market informally (or, put another way, "anarchically").

When in November 2009 the North Korean government radically devalued the official state currency in order to undermine informal markets and the infrastructure associated with them (private snack food stands, taverns, sewing rooms, financial services, etc.), the result was in fact an acceleration of informal economic development. Despite the government's intense efforts, these markets proved resistant to monetary intervention, above all because many people had already begun trading using foreign currencies instead of pricing their goods and services in the national currency. Ironically, it were actually the internationally well-networked traders who profited most from this government campaign, while law-abiding citizens, who had no access to large sums of foreign currency, bore the real burden of these measures. According to constantly updated U.S. military reports, informal markets in North Korea have in the meantime developed into an extremely sophisticated and complex network. This underground structure plays such an important role in the everyday lives of people in North Korea that it has become a source of important information about the changing political situation in the country.[23] Access to this dense web of political and socioeconomic relationships is therefore seen by decision-makers in the USA as a central mechanism of endeavours to gain political and economic influence.

This example illustrates the complex enmeshment of informal marketplaces with the lives of millions of people. One element of this complexity is the development of a specific type of knowledge as the result of engagement in informal trade. The appropriation of this knowledge is in turn part of a political mechanism that probes informal marketplaces in order to identify possibilities for the reconfiguration of global relationships. In the case of North Korea, different processes are contributing to this enterprise. These include direct investigations commissioned by governments, analyses of reports by defectors, think-tank operations as well as scholarly conferences such as the one held in 2011 by the American Institute of Peace in Washington, which was devoted to the question of how informal markets in North Korea could expand and what role new technologies, particularly mobile telephony, could play in extending the scope of activities of informal markets in North Korea in terms of both type and scale.[24]

All these enterprises point to the fact that this perspective on informal markets is not concerned with legality or illegality per se. It is also not motivated by the goal of improving a certain type of economic praxis or eliminating injustice. And it is certainly not concerned with recognizing the economic efforts made by the local population in a disadvantaged region in order to ensure their survival. Strategic efforts to gain access to informal markets from outside are tied to the exercise of power in the form of an economy. This kind of access entails what Agamben calls the division between a "general" and a "particular" economy, the split between intellectual knowledge and praxis, eternity and temporality, remote authority and governmental action.[25] Put another way, state interventions in informal markets are orientated to a dual form of economy: on the one hand, to a "general" economy from the perspective of which trade operating outside conventions is regarded as a breach of law, and, on the other, to a "particular" economy for which the extraneous represents a space of expansion that can be annexed by substitutive forces. This distinction forms the basis on which power is unfolded and exercised from a distance. Commenting on the apparent contradictoriness of the hegemonic logic of the Western world that rests on this distinction, Agamben writes:

> Independently of whether what is at stake is the breakup of pre-existing constitutional forms or the imposition, through military occupation, of so-called democratic constitutional models upon peoples for whom these models turn out to be unworkable, the basic point is that a country — and even the entire world — is being governed by remaining completely extraneous to it.[26]

The introduction of this dual economy into political praxis and the "collateral effects" produced by the economic paradigm are well illustrated in the case of North Korea's "second economy" by a YouTube clip posted in 2011. The video features a pizza restaurant in Pyongyang serving cans of Coca Cola to a group of international guests. This pictorial "evidence" of a Western presence in North Korea appeared to confirm rumours that the soft-drink concern was already doing business with the communist country. However, because such a step would contravene current U.S. laws and economic regulations, Coca Cola had to deny the rumours reported by many media outlets. On the other hand, in order to avoid completely denying the existence of a potential market for soft drinks in North Korea, local black marketers were deemed responsible for illegally bringing the product into the country.

When it comes to steering public attention towards the incidence of economic "violations", North Korea is certainly not an isolated case. Providing an overview of such infringements is the aim of the so-called "Special 301 Reports" prepared annually by the Office of the United States Trade Representative under Section 301 of the U.S. Trade Act of 1974. These annual reports contain meticulous descriptions of physical marketplaces referred to as "notorious" because they reputedly violate the intellectual property rights of US companies or citizens. This annually performed assessment of selected informal marketplaces as "notorious markets" follows a predictable pattern, which centres on corporate interests and is driven by a combined effort of industry sponsored research and state institutions. While informal markets in growth regions such as the tri-border area linking Paraguay, Argentina and Bolivia, and Bangkok's "red zones" regularly appear on the list of "notorious markets",[27] no attention is paid to the equally notorious underground markets in Cuba and North Korea.

This praxis involving political instruments such as the Special 301 Report clearly illustrates the construction of informal markets as a territory under observation, the assessment of which takes place remotely and in more controllable spaces such as the offices of the United States Trade Representative in Washington, where each year a public session draws on evidence that has been collected and comprehensive witness interviews to determine which countries should be listed as offenders. Such accessing of informal markets in legal-political terms is opening up a transnational arena for activities by means of which informal business can be seamlessly linked to political speculation and strategies. In this way, the policies of the world's leading power are able to exert a direct influence on the structure of the many local publics connected with informal market trading. Every incident noted in the country descriptions contained in the Special 301 Report becomes an individual conflict with the ever vigilant "world authority". As a result, a report that officially has only a recommendatory status has become one of the politically most influential instruments used to steer hundreds of nodal points of informal trade and to model the dependence of many thousands of people whose existences are inseparably bound up with these markets.

Worlding Practices: The Counterpublics of Informal Markets

A decisive requirement for the informal economic instrumentalization of global relationships is the availability of spontaneously structurable and easily accessible spaces in which material and social capital is exchanged and a transfer of values can take place. Neither integrated nor eliminated, these spaces represent not merely defenceless peripheries but also sites at which new mobilizations and innovative tactics of resistance emerge to combat contempt, expulsion and the withdrawal of citizenship rights. In these zones of intersection between globally effective (de) regulations and locally emerging bottom-up processes, informal markets assume a special place. They are at once delinquent space, application zone and production facility. The way informal markets "become world" is orientated not to a universally applicable doctrine of world-making — to global branding, product placement, marketing and endorsement — but to the reciprocal influence of different forces that rub against one another and generate new and various forms of change when they come into contact. As AbdouMaliq Simone writes, these erratic movements constitute a way of urbanizing relationships by foregrounding "the dynamic that is created when different histories and logics of urban operation are allowed to work. This bouncing off things is movement, and it is a rough-and-tumble game, and not the smooth fantasies of easy circulation where everything blends and moves on."[28]

The informal market lives from a plurality of possibilities, which different actors can access to different degrees. It relies not on uniform expectations, logics and mechanisms but rather on situational needs, initiatives and opportunities. In this way, informal markets illustrate how little a single concept can determine the make-up of urban worlds, irrespective of how seductive the promises inherent in commercial images of modern urban lifestyles are. The capacity of informality to embrace a multiplicity of structural connectivities and the reciprocity of possibilities of exerting influence anchored in real-life conditions opens up an ethical perspective on global interaction that Rosi Braidotti has termed "becoming-world"[29] — a renunciation of moral and cognitive universalisms in the conception of world in favour of a process-orientated perspective in which the multiple relationships and uniqueness of every subject is seen as a building block of complex world structures. These transactions, which are sustained by an urge for change, and the geographies traced by them are, as Aihwa Ong has argued, "experiments with the future" situated in everyday life, spatializing and signifying gestures that create alternative "worlds" — different forms of being global.[30] The ambition of "worlding" practices orientated to alternative configurations renders informal marketplaces and the agglomerations emerging around an important arena for insights into global transformations but also a setting and target of different "worlding" projects.

While this raises the prospect of inscribing anew and transforming prevailing power relations, it has to be remembered that prevailing power and representational interests are also always involved in every new inscription. The idea that informal trade takes place on "empty ground" is at best a naïve one but also one that is often instrumentally deployed as a means of "worlding" that, as Gayatri Chakravorty Spivak has argued, masks the privileging of First-World perspectives that inscribing oneself on a supposedly uninscribed territory entails. "Worlding" in this sense denotes the way in which colonized space is brought into the world in the form of narratives, policies and representations, "the reinscription of a cartography that must (re)present itself as impeccable." [31] It follows that precisely those regions in whose economic dependence the influence of the colonial past is deeply inscribed repeatedly stand out as arenas of a frontier mentality that regards informal markets as an "undiscovered" space in need of more precise knowledge and description because it is ultimately of interest as an emerging market. Informal market worlds are in this sense the locus and expression of a struggle between one's own and other interests, historical and contemporary influences, and globally and locally determined forms of exchange.

In the face of this type of "economic instrumentalization" of informal markets, what possibilities are available for the creation and cultivation of self-determined transnational spaces? Decisive for these sites of congregation is the supra-individual character of the efforts made to shape market environments in which trustworthiness, security and solidarity are paramount principles. This development is often founded on a close interweaving of economic and social interests. Based on a common struggle to survive and a shared historical experience, numerous informal markets are so tied to the existing social fabric of the areas in which they operate that their trading activities cannot be separated from other aspects of daily life. One example of this phenomenon is Tepito in Mexico City, a centrally located neighbourhood that emerged from structures of self-organized trade at the beginning of the twentieth century in the wake of the Mexican Revolution. Informal production, trade and retail continue to constitute an important aspect of community life and class consciousness within this quarter, although or precisely because the traded goods are often counterfeit articles, pirate copies and recycled products. In the U.S. Trade Representative's "out-of-cycle review of notorious markets" Tepito is consequently classed as a central storage and distribution node for illegal products destined for numerous other markets throughout Mexico.[32]

However, it is precisely this collectively practised way of dealing with *originals* — the appropriation of forms of cultural capital such as music CDs and feature-film DVDs — that constitutes a source of pride for the residents and traders of Tepito. They are part of a dense social fabric that has developed here around work and culture that locals have collectively taken into their own hands, both in spite of and because of the hostility they experience from the system of norms and values imposed by the global economy. This makes Tepito more than just a marketplace whose informality is an expression of collective self-determination and political resistance. It is also a place where all this is structured into its public facilities, institutions, rituals, forms of behaviour and relational patterns — resulting in what can be described as a counterpublic.[33] Sites such as the local Centre for Tepito Studies play an important role in shaping this counterpublic by offering institutional support, helping to explain political and economic contexts and thereby ensuring orientation within the fleeting world of informal trade over the longer term. In a similar way, art and literature contribute to the cultivation of an expanded perspective on local informality, for Tepito is also known for its many self-initiated literature circles, newspapers and galleries that engage creatively with the everyday culture of the neighbourhood and have in the process developed their own forms of artistic expression. This public-orientated and at the same time extra-economic engagement not only forms a focus within the emergence of the complexly structured reality regime of informal markets but also creates a level of negotiation that can be utilized in cases of conflict between traders and government authorities.

Such extra-economic processes also play a role in the generation of a level of communication between market traders. Radio stations are often found at informal markets with interactive programming that provides news about what is happening in the market as well as a mouthpiece for people involved in the market's operation. By such means, alliances can be built and the different interests involved in the market can find a public form of expression without triggering an escalation of latent conflicts. Along with the organization of such public services, the competence of collective self-organization on informal markets is also expressed in enterprises that include the establishment of communally used infrastructure such as sanitary facilities, water supply, electricity connections and street lighting. Not all markets are equally well equipped in this respect, but community facilities in which information is exchanged, techniques are learned and advice is acquired are found at many markets that have existed over a longer time. Trade union premises and improvised venues for religious assemblies are just as often part of this repertoire in larger market areas as are special spaces for gatherings of women, young people and other groups.

The constant threat to informal markets from business associations, local authorities, private investors and the real-estate industry is consequently also experienced as a threat to self-created niches in which autonomous communities are able to form.

In order to guard against these dangers, numerous local organizations have been established that lobby for the continued existence, protection and infrastructural improvement of informal markets. At the national level there are also organizations in many countries that not only regulate disputes between individual market actors and lobby for the social recognition of informal markets but also present concrete proposals to governments on how informal street trade can be better integrated into the use of public space. Associations such as the Kenya National Alliance of Street Vendors and Informal Traders (KENASVIT), the National Alliance of Street Vendors of India (NASVI) and the National Federation of Korean Street Vendors (NFKSV) work together with authorities and government representatives to formulate, among other things, guidelines for cultivating a better dialogue between informal markets, street traders and other urban actors. A genuinely transnational level of action has only emerged very recently with the founding of international organizations that, as umbrella associations, are able to influence other bodies such as the ILO and international trade unions. For instance, the StreetNet International alliance, which was founded in South Africa in 2002, comprises dozens of member organizations, most of which are based in African, Asian and Latin American countries.[34]

One of the central concerns of StreetNet International is the implementation of the *Bellagio International Declaration of Street Vendors*, which was drawn up in Italy in 1995 at a meeting of street vendor organizations, activists, lawyers and researchers from 11 countries. A key focus of the declaration is the development of national strategies to protect and strengthen the rights of street traders. These strategies should improve the legal status of vendors, ensure their access to urban space, increase the level of consideration given to informal trade in urban development planning and, not least, develop adequate mechanisms for ensuring that street vendors are included as equal partners in discussions about claims to the use of public space with other public agents (governments, administrative authorities, NGOs, police, etc.). In terms of its tone and content, the street vendors' declaration formulated in Bellagio is aimed at state and city government forces. However, it also seeks to contribute to the generation of a public in order to expose deficits of prevailing policies pertaining to legality and to lend weight to the concerns of street vendors. Thus, while the direct addressees of the declaration are state actors and the international policies connected to them, the statements contained therein are also addressed to social actors whose attitudes, relationships and actions have decisive implications for the genesis of transnational publics: social networks and movements, NGOs and similar associations as well as numerous other platforms of engagement by civil society that are increasingly structuring the transnational space. A declaration of this type is thus both an appeal directed at political decision-makers (i.e. elected representatives of the public) and a constitution of publicness wrought by the declaration itself. As such, the *Bellagio International Declaration of Street Vendors* sets its sights not only on the articulation of political demands but also on the formation of a public sphere in which these demands are supported and implemented. Aspects raised for discussion in this process include relationship structures, spatial configurations and transnational trajectories of different kinds of informal trade as well as their relationship to other economic models, whether these be solidarity economies, gift economies, resource-based economies or economic experiments in the context of artistic and cultural production.

All these facets of the struggle around spaces for political action make it clear that the development of alternative economic alliances in the shadow of the global economy is not a uniform movement but a process that is being driven forward by many actors, both hegemonic and non-hegemonic. Insofar as the interplay between economic interest groups and local informants, governmental forces, juridical authorities and media reports exerts an influence on our concepts of socially useful production, legitimate goods traffic and honest commercial behaviour, dissident ideational worlds and alternative political spaces can also develop in the transnational collaboration of street vendors with trade unions, activists, researchers and many other groups that are part of a global pursuit of social and economic justice. International conferences, education circles, demonstrations, cultural and artistic production[35] number among the many ways in which these intertwinements are currently taking form.

This dynamic is being accompanied by decisive changes in the paradigms, reach and conditions of economic power. One of the most important experiences engendered in this context is that of the increasing economic instrumentalization and unassailable negotiability of relationships on every level. In this particular economy, everything is put into circulation: people, policies, principles. The quest for economic power furthers a kind of informal politics in which all market constituents are subjected to situation-based modification: from market-driven political discourse to the flexibilization of citizenship as a means of managing the mobility of people to the fragmentation and commodification of life itself. A skilful handling of indeterminacy becomes key to success in these regimes of infinitely adaptable interests. The seizure of opportunities momentarily up for grabs forms an endlessly malleable fabric in the fashioning of transient arrangements that influence the form, diffusion and distribution of social interaction. Informal markets are a ubiquitous expression of these dynamics. Their everyday realities yield a plethora of creative ways of making use of whatever resource they can get hold of that is potentially tradable. Yet, despite, or because of, their embracing of a market mentality, informal markets are drawn into fierce struggles around their raison d'être. From local issues to international diplomacy, a broad range of fronts link up to oppose and dissolve attempts to establish such bottom-up economic relationships. Informal markets may not produce an alternative political economy all by themselves, but it is precisely through their contested existence that they point to the necessity of such a political economy.

1   For a detailed description of this development in the context of Latin American, Southeast Asian and Middle Eastern countries see, for example, Nezar AlSayyad, "Urban Informality as a 'New' Way of Life," *Urban Informality*, ed. Ananya Roy and Nezar AlSayyad (Lanham, MD: Lexington, 2004), 7–30.

2   Ananya Roy, "Urbanisms, Worlding Practices and the Theory of Planning," *Planning Theory* 10, no. 1 (2011): 6–15.

3   Michael Hardt and Antonio Negri, *Commonwealth* (Cambridge, MA: Harvard University Press, 2009), 244–260.

4   According to the Biennale press release, "the jury praised the architects for recognizing the power of this transformational project. An informal community created a new home and a new identity by occupying Torre David and did so with flair and conviction. This initiative can be seen as an inspirational model acknowledging the strength of informal societies."

5   Interview by the author with Urban-Think Tank, published in *konstruktiv* 284 (December 2011): 20–26.

6   Aihwa Ong, *Neoliberalism as Exception: Mutations in Citizenship and Sovereignty* (London and Durham, NC: Duke University Press, 2006).

7   Robert Musil, *The Man Without Qualities*, vol. I (London: Secker & Warburg, 1953).

8 Margaret R. Somers, *Genealogies of Citizenship: Markets, State-lessness, and the Right to Have Rights* (Cambridge: Cambridge University Press, 2008).

9 Aihwa Ong, *Flexible Citizenship: The Cultural Logics of Transnationality* (Durham, NC: Duke University Press, 1999).

10 Saskia Sassen, "Towards Post-National and Denationalized Citizenship," in *Handbook of Citizenship Studies*, ed. Engin F. Isin and Bryan S. Turner (London: Sage, 2002), 277–291.

11 Kamal Sadiq, *Paper Citizens: How Illegal Immigrants Acquire Citizenship in Developing Countries* (Oxford: Oxford University Press, 2009).

12 Saskia Sassen, *Brutality and Complexity in the Global Economy* (Cambridge, MA: Harvard University Press, 2014).

13 Oren Yiftachel, "Critical Theory and 'Gray Space': Mobilization of the Colonized," *City* 13, no. 2–3 (2009): 241–256.

14 Achille Mbembe, "Sovereignty as a Form of Expenditure," in *Sovereign Bodies: Citizens, Migrants, and States in a Postcolonial World*, ed. Thomas Blom Hansen and Finn Stepputat (Princeton, NJ: Princeton University Press, 2005), 153–154.

15 Karl Polanyi, "Our Obsolete Market Mentality: Civilization must find a New Thought Pattern," *Commentary* 3 (February 1947), 109–117 [reprinted in *Primitive, Archaic and Modern Economies: Essays of Karl Polanyi*, ed. George Dalton (Garden City, NY: Doubleday Anchor, 1968)].

16 Giorgio Agamben, *The Kingdom and the Glory: For a Theological Genealogy of Economy and Government — Homo Sacer II.2* (Stanford, CA: Stanford University Press, 2011).

17 Michel Foucault, *Security, Territory, Population: Lectures at the Collège de France, 1977–1978* (Houndmills, Basingstoke: Palgrave Macmillan, 2009) and *The Birth of Biopolitics: Lectures at the Collège de France, 1978–1979* (Houndmills, Basingstoke: Palgrave Macmillan, 2010).

18 Michel Foucault, *The Order of Things: An Archaeology of the Human Sciences* (New York: Pantheon, 1970), 24–29.

19 Agamben, *The Kingdom and the Glory*, 139.

20 Ibid., 66.

21 For a more extensive analysis of informal cross-border economies, see also the introductory text to the section 'Border Markets' in the sister volume of this publication, the *Informal Market Worlds Atlas*, 132–135.

22 Stephan Haggard and Marcus Noland, *Witness to Transformation: Refugee Insights into North Korea* (Washington, DC: Peterson Institute for International Economics, 2011), 125.

23 Andrew Chack, John V. Farr and James H. Schreiner, "A Systems Perspective of Foreign Intervention with Regards to the Democratic People's Republic of Korea," White Paper 2012-1 (West Point, NY: Center for Nation Reconstruction and Capacity Development, United States Military Academy, June 2012) 14.

24 Informal Markets and Peacebuilding in North Korea, international conference organized by the Institute of Peace, Washington, 19 July 2011.

25 Agamben, *The Kingdom and the Glory*, 141.

26 Ibid., 140.

27 See the section '"Notorious" Markets' in the sister volume of this publication, the *Informal Market Worlds Atlas*, 24–91.

28 AbdouMaliq Simone, *City Life from Jakarta to Dakar: Movements at the Crossroads* (London and New York: Routledge, 2010), 189.

29 Rosi Braidotti, "Becoming-world," in *After Cosmopolitanism*, ed. Rosi Braidotti, Patrick Hanafin and Bolette B. Blaagaard (London and New York: Routledge, 2013), 8–27.

30 Aihwa Ong, "Worlding Cities, or the Art of Being Global," in *Worlding Cities. Asian Experiments and the Art of Being Global*, ed. Ananya Roy and Aihwa Ong (Malden, MA: Wiley-Blackwell, 2011), 12.

31 Gayatri Chakravorty Spivak, *A Critique of Postcolonial Reason. Towards a History of the Vanishing Present* (Cambridge, MA: Harvard University Press, 1999), 228.

32 United States Trade Representative, 2013 Out-of-Cycle Review of Notorious Markets (12 February 2014), 17.

33 Alfonso Hernández, "El mercado de Tepito," *Informal Market Worlds Atlas. The Architecture of Economic Pressure*, ed. Peter Mörtenböck and Helge Mooshammer (Rotterdam: nai010 Publishers, 2015).

34 http://www.streetnet.org.za. See also Caroline Skinner, "Street Trading Trends in Africa: A Critical Review," in *Street Vendors in the Global Urban Economy*, ed. Sharit Bhowmik (New Delhi: Routledge, 2010), 201.

35 Apart from international conference events such as the conference *Contesting the Streets: Street Vending, Open-Air Markets, and Public Space*, which was held in Los Angeles in May 2010, and the symposium *Markets: From the Bazaar to eBay*, which took place at the University of Toronto in March 2008, recent years have seen numerous artistic projects that have lent visibility to the function of informal markets as spaces of encounter between different social interests, including Joanna Warsza's extensive works on *Jarmark Europa in Warsaw* (2006–2009), Tadej Pogačar's *Street Economy Archive* (2001–2007), Oliver Ressler's documentary video work *Alternative Economics — Alternative Societies* (2003–2008), Jesús Palomino's installation of an informal market in Panama City (2003) and Kate Rich's artistic intervention in food cycles through direct trade in food products via social networks (*Feral Trade*, since 2003).

FIELDS OF INCLUSION: NOTES ON TRADITIONAL MARKETS IN JAKARTA

AbdouMaliq Simone
Rika Febriyani

Selling and Buying in the Interstices of the City

The night street produce and meat market at Kebayoran Lama in Jakarta is one of the world's largest, with over 1,000 stalls scattered across the streets and lanes that radiate from the "official" market. This site, perhaps more than any other, embodies the capacity of the poor, the working class, and the "barely" middle class — still the majority of the 14 million people who live in Jakarta and its immediate suburbs — to viably reside there. This is a city that exists on small margins and incremental accumulations, always with the exigency to keep costs down. This is a city where hundreds of thousands of residents exist selling and preparing food.

As such Kebayoran Lama is a site of various temporalities. Premium produce is circulated in just-in-time circuits of delivery to local markets, as various gradations of freshness and quality assume different positions downstream. Thousands of truckers, porters, cleaners, sellers, and brokers have long rehearsed the intricate choreographies and financial transactions necessary to convert this four-square-kilometre area into a vast nocturnal trading floor, with its array of locational advantages, costs, spatial arrangements, words of mouth consumption, and networks of supply and distribution. There can be few mistakes and contestations, few grand manoeuvres for competitive advantage, as a vast number of livelihoods rely upon the market's seemingly seamless performances.

At six in the morning, there are very few traces that this trading floor ever existed. As such, it is one of the few major operations that works in a city that otherwise appears enmeshed in congestion, confounding rules and regulations, and widening class segregation. It is a city desperately in need of efficiencies, planning, and rational land disposition, but also where the confusions and the mess become important guarantees of the city's plurality.

The diversity of markets in Jakarta thus reflects various forms of social heterogeneity — its fault lines, segregations, mixtures, and spatial realignments. Processes of making, selling, discarding, servicing and dissimulating all intersect in various proportions according to a wide range of official and unofficial regulatory mechanisms, spatial and social complexions, and varied sense of economic efficacy. This discussion will look primarily at the operations of two markets, Pasar Tambora and Pasar Jatinegara. It does so in order to highlight their capacities to generate particular singularities and relational fields, which in turn serve as important mechanisms for intensifying an experience of *cityness* in trajectories of urbanization that would seem to make "the city" increasingly irrelevant. The chapter attempts to amplify the notion of markets as devices that not only elaborate transactions that maintain livelihoods but ensure the life of the city as *just the city* — something that always slips away from the grasp of its human inhabitants, and of which we can never be certain of exactly what will show up or in what form, or what will forever disappear.

Pasar Tambora, is one of Jakarta's most dynamic produce markets. Like many markets in Jakarta it straddles a both intensely marked and ambiguous frontier as to whose ambit the market really belongs. Does it fall within the jurisdiction of legally constituted market authorities as specified by the municipality, is it an "informal" operation, or an intersection of varying logics, each pushing and pulling at the other in a constant process of mutual accommodation? Or it is simply a kind of "parallel play", where different operators converge in the same space, but essentially leave each other alone to pursue their own way of doing things?

Parcels and Layers of Time: Operations in Pasar Tambora

Tambora is particularly complicated in that it refers to several different markets simultaneously, which operate at different times of day, and which spread out across four distinct *kelurahan* — local government districts. As each district is also constituted by a score of subdistricts, *rukun warga*, there are also at least eight distinct sub-districts that also have something to do with Tambora's realities. The market is thus folded into a profusion of various local authorities and their distinct styles of administration, but more importantly, these authorities are folded into the market, where the market absorbs many different ways of doing politics, as well as networked relationships to the larger city.

Tambora is not an easy place in which to come up with some kind of overarching view or sense. Conversations with a trader, a local government leader, *preman* (unofficial enforcer), transporter, trucker, municipal official, vendor, or long-established authority figures that have no official function amass layers of opacity. Street sellers who seemingly violate official regulations by selling in street areas will always point out that sub-district authorities facilitate their business. They also point out that these same authorities will offer sellers located in the official market facilities places on the street so that they can expand their businesses. Sub-district officials deny any such involvement even as they do the daily rounds to collect "fees" from the sellers.

Each participant will emphasize that they either have no real idea about what is going on or simply a partial view, and usually conversations end with a referral to speak to someone else who will more often than not pass you along in such a way that you end up with the first person you spoke to in the beginning. Part of the haze can also be attributed to the visibility of Tambora. It is a well-known place situated in a district long renowned for its floating residential population, its toughness, and dangerous densities — e.g., it is an area plagued by repeated fires.

The character of the operations is not easy in itself. The real action occurs primarily on the weekends and then deep into the night. In order to attract a high volume of customers, it also has to include a high volume of vendors, themselves connected to brokers who have cultivated a network of suppliers from farms at the periphery of the urban region. Abi, for example, is a vegetable seller who lives in

OFFICIAL MARKET AREA IN TAMBORA (2 P.M.–2 A.M.)

Puncak-Bogor at the periphery of Jakarta. He has opened a retail stall for himself but also supplies stock for several other sellers. He owns a small farm in Puncak, but also brings produce from neighbouring farms to sell directly or distribute to other sellers. The freshness of produce and price affordability have to operate in tandem, in a mixture of just-in-time delivery, facilitated by avoiding peak truck traffic times in Greater Jakarta, and retailing that circumvents the higher costs of being placed completely within a formal market structure.

Additionally, the retailing itself is less geared to individual consumers, but rather restaurants of various sizes, from simple eating-places to some of the city's most prominent hotel kitchens. Abi depends upon sales to a franchise restaurant, which has been his client for the past five years. 70 per cent of the markets turnover is generated by these relationships with restaurants, while the rest comes from individual customers and small food stalls. He spends the bulk of his time then delivering produce to the restaurant's main reception centre and has hired workers to staff his stall in the market for sales to individual customers.

There are thus various scales of pick-ups and deliveries, all of which have to get in and out fairly quickly along arteries that have been increasingly encroached upon by spin-offs from the produce trade to include clothing, cell phone, and toy stalls, to cite a few. Most vegetable deliveries are made around 2 p.m., just prior to the time that sellers push their carts to their designated spots in the market's parking area. Street sellers dealing mostly in non-produce items must wait until the stores close at 5 p.m. This means that the brokerage of traffic circulation constitutes a major power in the market, a source of rent-seeking, and a task largely captured by *preman* who work for various groupings arranged in various alliances with local authorities, the police, the military, and ethnic associations.

The market spans across the main artery of Jalan Kh. Moch Mansyur and down intersecting small lanes. There is a premium on space. While it is possible for a commercial operator to aggrandize discrete "plots", pay to eliminate competition, or organize some kind of overarching syndicate, that the market abuts not only different local government jurisdictions, but districts of distinctive histories and "real" governmental practices requires a certain inclusivity of different players. But this is not an inclusivity of clearly delineated representations, not a count of clearly defined interest groups, sectors and occupations. Inclusivity entails a capacity to provide opportunities for the interests and aspirations of particular sub-territories of the market, specific players, and trades to outweigh those of others at particular times and for reasons that will not always be clear or apparent. These trade-offs and oscillating interests do not of course sit easily with each other and generate different effects that cannot be anticipated or even assessed. Part of effective modulation requires not only that these interests have an opportunity to be expressed but that the resolution of tensions and conflicts is not perceived as emanating from any specific authority all of the time.

Like any big market in Jakarta, Tambora consists of at least three distinct operations. First, there is the commercial activity that takes place within the official market building. This operation and the facility are managed by a company established by Jakarta's government, Pasar Jaya, and commence early in the morning. But the real activity does not begin until after 2 p.m. and takes place outside the market facility and lasts until the early hours of the morning. Second, these official market facilities are usually situated in a larger commercial district. In Tambora, these stores specialize in plastic housewares and kitchen equipment. They open at 10 a.m. and close at 5 p.m. When the stores close, street sellers will trade in front, usually until 10 p.m. Third, there is a produce market geared toward local household consumption that runs from 4 a.m. to 9 a.m., just after the more wholesale oriented market has closed in the area surrounding the market building and before the stores open at 10 a.m. Many different local authorities, including local government officials, manage all the activities taking place outside the market building. Municipal by-laws stipulate that all marketing activities should be subsumed under the *Pasar Jaya*, but clearly this is not the case.

The work force that cuts and chops and cleans vegetables in the basement of the market's formal structure, the vendors who crowd the parking lot in front which becomes the main trading space, the scores of men who load and unload the produce from trucks, the stalls that sell tea and cakes and prepared food, the stalls selling various clothes and other goods, the unofficial brokers who navigate traffic, the cleaners who collect and store refuse, the committee that runs the mosque on the roof of the market, the various "security forces" paid and reporting to different sub-district offices, the unofficial council of elders (long term residents) who infuse the memory of decades of transactions into current operations — all must be accorded operational space where they feel they can sustain, recalibrate or transform the way they do things. This is not a matter of concurrence but alternating cycles.

One of the reasons why "unofficial brokers" play such a big role in the market is because they can act as if they have no vested interests, they have the manoeuvrability to listen to the stories that different kinds of participants tell them, they actively cultivate a willingness to have stories told, and then intersect these stories with narrative lines that they deem useful and effective, either a particular time of day, month or so forth.

On the other hand, this sense of making room for different kinds of interest to operate is why participants are reluctant to provide definitive representations of the market, or to claim that they know what is taking place in its entirety.

The operations of the market appear to be stabilized by agreements forged among many different parties. But they are also replete with unpredictable changes. Constant adjustments are required in order to balance out the prerogatives of long-time sellers with the need to introduce new opportunities for other players. Uwi, a "local security officer", with no official position in such agreements nevertheless brokers these adjustments, which sometimes include payments by some sellers to lessen the competition by getting rid of other sellers. But for the most part these practices of brokerage are aimed at providing opportunities for as many sellers as possible.

In part, this flexible production corresponds to the larger area in which the market is situated. It is an area with many migrant labourers inserted into residential and entrepreneurial networks with deep histories of collaboration and suspicion. The districts in the area — Tambora, Jembatan Lima, Krendang Utara, and Tanah Sereal — embody the convergence of a long-term creolization of ethnic influences and trading networks with an intensely urbanized sensibility that tries to ward off strict territorial categorizations by class, ethnic and religious affiliation in often highly peculiar ways. In one sense, these districts are massive "factory floors" cut up into hundreds of distinct operations. They are part of the game of low-end textile production that nevertheless provides a significant proportion of domestic consumption, and which is managed by big Indo-Chinese networks with hegemonic access to imports, machinery, political influence, and supply chains. Most of the fabrication that takes place is based on shifting subcontract relationships, with small firms seemingly locked into highly disadvantageous terms of trade.

But the mixtures of small operations, some highly transparent, open to the street, and others hidden behind the screens of household gates and nebulous looking structures attempt to balance out the need for residents and workers in these districts to garner and circulate knowledge, at the same time as to "muddy the waters" as means to create spaces of manoeuvre and adjustment. Much of the opacity is used to cover up the fact that fabrication is taking place in structures not officially sanctioned for this work, that workers are being paid exploitative wages, and being housed in overcrowded conditions. Some of it is to hide the fact of production from more powerful networks that would view this as undercutting their control. Still, some of it is a kind of safety valve, i.e. contexts where large orders are shared or passed on without leaving tracks.

While the production game is usually skewed in the interest of those with investment capital and influence, parallel opportunities do exist which instil both dynamism and tension into the process. These opportunities depend on the practices of workers themselves to spread work around through sharing orders, splitting shift work, or organizing themselves into competitively viable production units. They also can entail productive contestations among local political authorities and entrepreneurial groupings that redistribute opportunities and assets. There are times when certain synergies are attained in various interactions of sub-contracting, finishing, piecework, and marketing that allows the scores of small outfits involved to forge insertions

STREET HAWKERS IN TAMBORA (4 A.M.–9 A.M.)

into new markets collectively, acting with some autonomy from the patronage and corporate structures to which they otherwise "belong". In other words, each unit at times, given the circuits of information exchange, informal sharing of workers and work, can exist in "separate worlds", i.e. working for particular paymasters and brokers as well as working for "themselves" on the side. While the Tambora market is a different operation, it too, must exhibit some of the atmosphere of inclusivity that operates in tandem with the hard-fought struggles to control that are a feature of these districts.

On the other hand, this sense of inclusivity does not obviate the need for certain codes and procedures. Vendors are required to pay specific fees in order to gain the right to sell, and then a series of fees for sanitation and "operations", which are essentially pay-offs to local officials, police and military. These are collected, assembled and distributed at various scales and with the responsibility of different brokers — some to collect, some to aggregate, some to distribute to the relevant recipients.

The Public Secret of Markets

The official Pasar Tambora building that would conventionally be assumed to anchor the market was built 50 years ago. Since 1980, not much takes place within it, at least in terms of the usual marketing activities. Usually, when a formal market structure no longer seems to have much of any function, the premises are torn down and their staff is redeployed. Except the floor of the vegetables section, some 80 per cent of the market interior has been vacated. For example, Kasih Ibu is a store that sells baby equipment. It is being rented for a price that includes free access to all of the goods within the store since the past tenants simply abandoned it because of limited sales. Other tenants may leave because they simply cannot afford the rent.

There is a great deal of speculation involved in the disposition of commercial space within the official market facility. Some entrepreneurs are offered extremely low rents for inopportune locations within the facility, which they use primarily to

OLD STALLS IN JATINEGARA

store goods. The managers, however, use the fact that even these spaces are rented as a way of trying to entice retailers to rent out more prime locations for larger amounts of money. Managers have been known to borrow goods to stock in unrented spaces in order to create the appearance of a thriving atmosphere. For example, a single woman unlocks the doors of the four abandoned stores and drags out racks of clothing, arranging them across the public access ways, every single morning. The entirety of the collection could fit into a single store, yet the meagre volume is distributed across the facility. The clothes do not and will not sell; they have probably been in storage for many years. But these tricks seldom work for long, and so very little revenue is generated from within the walls of the market itself. But the structure remains, as do its staff.

During the morning and early afternoon hours, the main trading floor — the "parking lot" of the market building — is full of sleeping bodies, and the parking lots in front of the building are used for their designated purpose, at least from 6 a.m. to 2 p.m. By mid-afternoon, those in the parking lot will have received the shipments of fresh vegetables and fruits, as the lot is organized into 104 selling units, which will work through the night, into the early hours of morning, generating enough visibility and perhaps income to keep the game of the market going.

Meanwhile, in the morning around the corner on the side streets, another market geared toward local consumptions is in full swing, usually between the hours of 4 a.m. to 9 a.m. Hardian, one of the sellers, explains that this market is not under the official market authority. Rather, the local district officials either allocate space or reauthorize space that sellers, such as Hardian, have "inherited" from their families who were conducting some kind of trade for long periods of time.

The official regulations stipulate that the trade on the outside, in the parking lot, should be taking place inside — in facilities whose official price exceeds what any trader could afford, particularly as indicated previously, rents are coupled to a host of other "fees" and extractions. While the traders on the outside are exempt from prohibitive costs, they also operate outside most any official regulative structure that might apply. The weak attempts at dissimulation — to make it seem that the interior of the market remains capable of generating income for the municipality — simply signal the operation of another game.

The deals with big hotels and restaurants are in part brokered by the market staff of the Jakarta metro. For example, Warno, an employee of Pasar Jaya, indicates that Hotel Mulia, a five-star Jakarta hotel, is one of the largest consumers of the Tambora produce market. He claims to manage this relationship, although it has little to do with his official position in the market, and rather stemmed from the fact that he had nothing really to do with the operations that take place in the parking lot after 2 p.m. but had to be at his post anyway, so tried to figure a way to be a player in the game. Even the official cleaning staff never want to talk about their jobs and instead constantly offer to broker produce deliveries for you. This is something that their official job description would not allow them to do.

But since the deals come together outside the official trading area, in a parking lot where things are not supposed to be sold, they can legitimately claim that they are not in violation of the rules. This is despite the fact that only this violation enables them to generate sufficient income for the municipality in order to keep the market open. Again, the deception hides nothing. Like most public secrets, it is simply a necessary gesture that enables the formal market to operate as a phantom, where it can, as phantom, do much of whatever it wants to do.

Usually a key facility, business, or attraction anchors the dispersal of activity all around, such as a famous building or monument, or even a market. The trading area surrounding this market continues to expand and become more central as a critical source of supply for a wide range of goods and services. But the central building at the origin of the market itself does not appear to have any kind of density capable of exerting gravitational force. Squatters fill the upper storeys and the basement which, when it is not flooded, is used to peel and shuck making the produce presentable. Everyone knows that the official market is "dead"; that the real action is elsewhere, and for the traders surrounding it, they know it is in their hands.

Again, in conversations with traders, truckers, customers, security guards, cleaners, brokers, local authorities and those that keep the traffic flowing, there is widespread denial that they have much influence in determining what goes on. In part, this uncertainty is a creation of their very own ingenuousness, which contributes to the uncertainty by installing a feigned lack of confidence as a key operating procedure. Part of what keeps this game going is the practice of making continued reference to the "market" as if it is a coherent entity embodied by the formal market building, which no longer operates as a real market from the outside, but is very much a real market because of these different actors are what makes it happen.

During times of confusion on the street or incipient conflict, people wonder what "the market might think", as if it still was some kind of command structure. Even as power and efficacy have been distributed across a complicated network of authorities, unofficial regulators, and brokers, reference is made to the sentiments and inclinations of something that has been thoroughly hollowed out. Rather than influence exerted as a function of an ability to define and impose, whatever is left of the official market registers its power in the way it induces speculation, i.e. the ways in which traders, customers and neighbourhood residents alike wonder what happened to the market and what it is "up to" now, even when the games it may be playing appear to be well known. But no matter how much knowledge may be in circulation, the hollowing out of the market in face of apparent thriving everywhere around it makes participants feel uneasy. Even as the arrangements of power and money throughout the surrounding street may be crystal clear, there remains a sense amongst all involved that things are not completely settled.

In a situation where the "central market" seems to continue an ability to control without possessing any of the conventional pre-requite components to control, thus instilling a pervasive unease in otherwise tightly defined market activities, the exigency is for individuals to assume no one particular role, but to act in an interval among them.[1] At the same time, roles make an individual visible, they put them on the map; they enable them to come to the stage in a particular way. As such, individuals could not seemingly be long-terms residents and strangers, sellers and buyers, mediators and the mediated all at the same time in any instrumental fashion.

For such occupations would be incommensurable, as distinct roles are defined in contrast to each other or follow and evolve from each other in a linear narrative sequence. But by trying to insert themselves in-between clear roles while maintaining the distinction between them, such incommensurability provides cover for jumps in "scale", in how far specific actors might reach across the landscape of power-laden transactions. Sastra, who owns one of the vegetable stalls in the official market and also places his stock out on the street, believes that many of the customers initially come for the plastic furniture, hardware, and kitchen appliances from the stores next to the market. His own business is mostly supported by one restaurant that found Sastra after having bought some restaurant equipment down the block. So many of the sellers with these kind of restaurant deals will encourage them to spread the word about the good quality, not of the vegetables, but of the restaurant equipment. These leaps may come off simply as a means to maximize opportunity at any expense. But, they also put together a sense of collective modulation, of give and take, of an ability for the overall arrangement of trading spaces to "breathe", to incorporate new information and practices and, as such, ward off atrophy and sedentary repetitions.

In Tambora, each participant has a job to do. They try not to step on anyone's toes while doing it, even if in the hustle and bustle, and the need to pursue agendas that do not always fit easily together, many toes will inevitably be stepped on. This largely concerns the ethnic territorialization of trades. Most storeowners that sell plastic furniture and household appliances are Indo-Chinese, while vegetable sellers mostly come from Banten in Java. Sastra, who came to Tambora 20 years ago from Banten, reiterates the common assumption that the Indo-Chinese and the Banten have a highly antagonistic relationship. There is little social engagement, yet Sastra claims that he appreciates that the Indo-Chinese are present. Because they tend to earn more than most Indonesians, yet are also demonized for this capacity, Sastra claims that there are many opportunities for the Banten to politically open up space for the Indo-Chinese, not only by helping to protect their stores, but also in running interference for their efforts to expand their local economic power. The Indo-Chinese in turn help to capitalize the night markets through the backdoor since having a twenty-four trading floor makes the Indo-Chinese feel more secure as both residents and entrepreneurs in the area.

The density of street markets is something familiar; it is a redundant celebration of chaos in circumscribed quarters; we know it will only go so far. Small entrepreneurs set up shop, they have their products and customers, their graduated fees and rents, and for the most part, little expands or contracts. Trying to figure out the different relations at work always incites mapping both on paper and in people's heads. The forward and backward linkages, the locational advantages, the platforms for reciprocal witnessing, and the proliferation of quiet calibration of entrepreneurial performance are well known features of such markets.

These occasions for gathering up of things and bodies, for the thickening of externalities to accompany prices kept just lower than anywhere else act as "sensation" machines. They are devices for stimulating purchases of goods and generating hundreds of silent promises of future accumulation. This is the infrastructure which sellers consider important. Tambora is a complete mess in many ways. The drainage is bad, and during the rainy seasons the market is often flooded. But most sellers do not consider the need for these kind of infrastructural repairs. Sastra states that such repairs would only increase the rents and fees, and thus the price of the products. He also does not trust those with the capacity to improve infrastructure to appreciate the feeling of the market and the way that the ability of the market to operate across frequent adversity strengthens the confidence of sellers.

Moreover, these more sensate infrastructures are ways of coaxing something else besides buying and selling. But they are also the methodical, often mundane, instruments that aim for long-term stories, for an endurance capable of absorbing the pressures and pulls, the incessant anxieties about having enough, of having to implicitly share the burdens and benefits of doing the same old thing in intense proximity with others. Whatever form the street market generates must be grasped over the long haul, in its ability to fold in and ward off, its seeming tolerance for accommodations of all kinds, but its equally stringent intolerance of things getting out of hand.

The prevalent idea about markets is that they aim for some kind of equilibrium. Such equilibrium could be that between supply and demand deploying the device of price; it could be equilibrium of sectors, supply chains, or identities. Additionally, equilibrium could refer to temporalities of exchange, to forestall manipulated shortages of goods, excessive dumping of low quality products, or to smooth out accelerating or lagging discrepancies in income. Whatever its object or aspiration, the practice of markets gears itself toward a continuous articulation of the volatile and the stable.

While all markets may pass through or even perpetually dwell in such a phase state, there are some that seem to head for an inevitable wearing away of their capacities. Here the accumulating intensities of different actors, materials, spaces, forces, and scenarios impacting on each other posit the immanence of decimation. This endgame may occur slowly over prolonged periods of time and without discernible tipping points, just as the redundancies of daily transactions may at some juncture seem to speed the destructive impetus along. There is no telling, although precipitous declines — in profit margins, efficiencies, customer bases, and entrepreneurial will — may generate prolific stories about possible causes and effects, or about the exigencies of compensation and of needing to make alternative plans.

Market Specters: The Long Road to Nowhere for Pasar Jatinegara

Pasar Jatinegara seems to be literally sinking in the weight of its overcrowded conditions, deteriorating infrastructure, escalating tensions, and loss of comparative advantages. Located at the confluence of key routes that link East Jakarta to the city centre and to one of the main north-south corridors, the market is part of an area with a long history of retail dynamism. This was anchored by Jatinegara's pre-colonial status as a platform for battles against the Dutch waged by Banten aristocracies, and then during the colonial periods as a critical space of expansion from the "incivilities" of the old core. This was a place where the Dutch and a nascent working and middle class could be sufficiently proximate and removed from the wheeling and dealing of Jakarta's version of the *cité*, to which is was, nevertheless, directly connected by an important train line. The built environment within and around the market still reflects the colonial heritage as well as the stamp of Chinese commercial arrangements, as it was the Chinese who configured the important linkages between wholesale and retail.

The market is enabled by the now classic spatial syntax that emphasizes both an intensive localization formed at the interior of multiple intersecting transportation routes and modalities and the opening out onto a prolific series of entrances and exits. Thus, the market takes advantage of the morphological possibilities of spatial concentrations capable of adding density to transactions, keeping them with multiple vantage points, overlaying them with a plurality of reciprocities, responsibilities and history. It also takes advantage of carrying these densities outwards into new spheres of influence, as well as diffusing and disentangling them across a wide landscape of potential use.

As is the usual story when such physical density is combined with the uncertain trajectories of effects, the market has experienced several debilitating fires that have required substantial reinvestment but also the concomitant loss of interest. As Jakarta has grown in ways that have outpaced the availability of public transportation, the market is particularly affected and bogged down by the city's near-gridlock. As with most of Jakarta's markets, the management of Jatinegara is subcontracted to a semi-private company, where the municipality is a secondary shareholder to that of major property developers. While the official market structure remains crammed with clothes and household items of all kinds, unlike many other official structures that are near empty, this state of being crammed becomes the predominant feature for customers who hurriedly may have to acquire a diverse series of items at one go. Otherwise, specific targeted acquisitions such as electronics, household appliances, clothing, hardware or various accessories are shopped for elsewhere at centres with specific specializations. The "go-slow" of internal circulation has been worsened when the managing agency, Pasar Jaya, erected a six-storey parking facility in the centre of the market.

While a section of the market provides for food produce, with a range of special foodstuffs, the site is not convenient for daily shopping, and the majority of the entire market's customers are those who usually buy in bulk or make needed acquisitions at the end of the month when they are paid. Large sections of the market are barely-hanging-on residuals of former flourishing trades. For example, there is a large section that specializes in agricultural implements, tools and machinery, which persists in face of the extensive corporatization of agriculture, through the needs of a new generation of niche farmers at the periphery of the urban region. These are the farmers that supply Tambora. From here, one enters into a dark maze of narrow corridors filled with thousands of used pulleys, cartwheels, nails and screws, hinges, used typewriters, and batteries — all of which border more on refuse than viable second-hand goods. Again, this sector holds on through the large numbers of the poor and near-poor who depend on repair and improvisation. This sector is also a screen for deals of other kinds, where the materials are just an excuse to trade in anything illicit, but without great commitment or specialization. If there were 20 stalls specializing in nearly everything metal to be discarded, it would be easy to conclude some kind of viability, but when the stalls number close to 100, with many being "owned" by a single pair of hands, multiplicity takes on a strange opacity.

For both sellers and customers it is a game of small margins and awkward synergies. Along the eastern entrance of the market are a series of important bookstores specializing in religious texts and paraphernalia, and their presence ensures a steady stream of customers coming from many different parts of Jakarta, who could also without much additional effort be drawn into paying attention to a wide range of other goods of uncertain origins, quality, and even use. Some established retailers broker arrangements with hawkers to use the pavement frontage to sell sundries, apparel accessories and cooked food, while other hawkers simply usurp "available" space. Many sellers seemingly working for themselves work for commission and which guarantees some limited protection from shakedowns or even competition, while some sellers are expressly left on their own by some implicit "corporate agreement" that does not want to tie up all operations into discernible alliances and patronage systems. Some operators must be accorded the space to work out singular practices within a fabric of transactions already overburdened with excessive scrutiny and obligations.

As mentioned in our discussion of Pasar Tambora, the actual running and decision-making takes place largely through a process of usurpation rather than delegation. There are the formal designations and structures of accountability. But as these usually only extend to the frontiers of official facilities, it does not fold in the surrounding areas to which the market has been extended and where the bulk of daily trading takes place. Commercial agents may have many operations and stalls within and outside the formal structures, and may act as if there exists a seamless interweaving amongst them. But, the movement between inside and outside still must pass its way through swarms of cars, small trucks, motorbikes, foot transporters, and pedestrian traffic circulating inside the market area, the constant movement of boxes and goods, and all of the near collisions of things coming in and those going out, relationships between inside and outside require constant mediation. Since different mediators and tasks affect this, there are meta-mediations that must take place without seeming to prioritize particular trades, functions, traffic, and activities over another.

All of this wear and tear on the fabric, psyche, and economy of the market creates the sense of some kind of downward spiral. There are of course significant hints that collapse may not come anytime soon even as the bulk of the infrastructure progressively advances in its dilapidation. Seemingly simple, even gestural repairs or sprucing up are not made, which under certain conditions such as frequent rainfall, makes simple transactions and navigation even more difficult. But then in the midst of decay, someone will build a new edifice, or a new bank branch may open. Of course for the most part, letting things wear away reflects a conclusion about just how long commerce may viably last or that the profit margins are so slim that it just is not worth the refurbishing. While commerce can spill over in all kinds of directions from a central node, creating vague interstitial spaces, when the official authorities wish to do so they can still apply a prohibitive gaze and accompanying sanctions on those enterprises perceived as being too confident in their capacity to flaunt specific regulations and institutions. Even when such enforcement is basically empty, and dependent upon variegated shadows in order to persist, public secrets themselves remain important modalities of jurisdiction. Authorities do not authorize anything but are still absolutely required as authorities, and so forth.

As a processing of wearing down becomes more visible, actors must be seen as exerting both a willingness and capacity to at least compensate. The tricky part for an outside observer is always trying to at least vaguely discern the extent to which compensations are "real" or part of the spectacle. Attempts to share markets and orders, to share networks of customers according to specific consumer needs and locations, deferred payments and unofficial credit, extending favours and cultivating any kind of small indebtedness, joining religious and political organizations, importing low-cost labour from rural areas, lowering wage bills through an array of in-kind affordances — all are various ways of compensating for apparent market decline. But the extent to which these are activated, sustained over any significant time period is often unclear, and may simply be a "show" of determination where there is actually little.

But such a show may be an integral aspect of an overall market performance where the increased uncertainties as to the future of this form of commercial activity increase — given the expansion of mega-retail outlets, escalating land-values, the imposition of new regulatory systems, and the declining aspirations of youth to pursue this kind of commerce. These uncertainties also diminish the kinds of social anchorage, largely forged through implicit interweaving of social and commercial relations and the correspondence of family network to commercial activity, which enabled participants to garner an overall view that helped them sustain confidence in what they were doing. As neoliberal regimens have accentuated the importance of individual efficacy and disentangled social relationship as a medium through which aspirations were enacted, it has become more difficult for urban residents in any occupation to orient themselves within a larger picture.

The wear and tear of the market, the way in which almost all of its discrete spaces and operations seem to bear the traces of the density of more laborious efforts all around them, could also be an important signalling of the fact that the market still "remains together." Perhaps for the most part, the status of commerce is now that of "remains", i.e. of leftovers, of capturing customers' leftover from all of the other

STREET HAWKERS IN JATINEGARA

big retailers either because of cultural tradition, affordability, or the intentional targeting of the near-poor. On the other hand, the market remains together because the impact that its actors and activities have on each other, directly and indirectly is registered in the visual landscape itself, the surface of its wearing down. Here, commerce is not only tied together through the burdens of sharing a decrepit physical plant, the informal mechanism of actual "rule", the intensive physical proximity of everything, or the specific acts of collaboration and trade-offs, but also by the ability of any participant to view the exertion of impact itself. This active viewing then, regardless of the particular vantage points, affects, and ideas that accompany it, becomes a kind of collective compass where participants eke out some kind of workable certainty for what they are doing, crammed as they are into the extremely labour-intensive game of trying to make trade.

There are also possibilities that not only do the compensations attempt to head off the inevitable decline, pluralize the ways in which the market could implode, but that there are no compensations at all. It may be that a tipping point is reached where suppliers, sellers and their actions act on each other in such a way that the effects not only exceed compensation but reflect an implicit recognition that the players no longer believe they have any livelihood or specific interest to sustain. Even when some players indicate that it is still possible to eke out a living, others concede, even joyfully, that they are simply "getting rid of everything to which they were once committed". They seem too anxious to "shed their skin" in some expectation that in this wear and tear something will emerge that will take them and others "away from this place and themselves". It is an attitude not dissimilar to how Benjamin Bratton writes about the presence of the post-Anthropocene as a parasitical design within the present,[2] not as a running things into the ground in a rapid return to an inorganic phase state, but rather as an indeterminable sequencing of realignments among material, body, atmosphere, and chemistry that will not produce anything that can be named or recognized in the present.

SECOND-HAND MARKET JEMBATAN ITEM, JATINEGARA

This sense of what remains together in the midst of apparent demise is also complimented by a kind of heterotopic remainder in this market. One day, it was raining hard, and we took temporary refuge underneath the over-roofing of a small *toko* (store). The front of the building had seemingly not been altered in a century. Looking through the barred window, there was a small foyer in front with a Chinese altar of fine wood. But looking down the interceding passage was an elderly man with his back turned toward us sitting in a chair engaged in some activity impossible to discern. In front of him was an enormous space with no other objects, just a wide interior expanse that seemed to reach across the length of the market, as we could not make out the existence of an anterior wall.

It would be expected in an old former Chinatown to note the remnants of no longer occupied workshops or trading halls, but it was nevertheless striking that this emptiness seemed to now be at the heart of the market. Only 15 minutes later, deep into the interior of the market itself, we were struck by the refreshing vitality of an all-purpose goods store, well stocked with many customers. We noticed however, that the space extended beyond a partial back-wall, and we angled ourselves to try to glimpse a view of what was behind. There was another large space, completely empty with the exception of four octogenarian looking women sitting far apart from each other hunkered over four small tables applying ink on parchment, as if the official record keepers of the spectral events, also at the heart of this market's life.

Concluding Note

Tambora and Jatinegara, in their own ways, try to affect a politics of inclusion. This is not just by finding ways to eke out work from spare space, from interwoven relationships outside formal institutional domains, or from the exigencies of managing the intricacies of these relationships. This is not just in providing affordable goods for large numbers of residents operating on small incomes. Inclusion is also the elaboration of a field of visibility, of interweaving discordant elements that make clear-cut delineations of roles, functions, and events ambiguous, sometimes opaque.

These ambiguities and opacities are not simply manoeuvres to operate under the radar of official scrutiny or to cover up illicit activities or trade secrets. They are also the by-product of an atmosphere charged with contradictions that circle around each other, that put off easy resolution, that intermesh efficacy and failure, growth and decay. It is an atmosphere that provides participants a platform on which to earn a modest and steady income but also a vantage point from which to continuously have the possibility of rearranging their activities in terms of those surrounding them. Inclusion then is inclusion of the discordant and unsettling, of the possibility of extended reach across different actors and networks from the negotiations entailed in knowing one's place, of having a place to operate. In the midst of often highly circumscribed routines, many different times are at work — things are falling apart, being renewed, often without clear trajectories. Orientation is less following the right way of doing things, of kicking money up through the right channels, or of knowing what your designated spot allows you to do. Rather, it is constantly learning how to inhabit a world where price is an opening salvo into uncharted waters, where selling is a way of operating between the lines, and where everything is yet to be worked out.

1   Morten Nielsen, "Temporal Aesthetics: On Deleuzian Montage in Anthropology," in *Transcultural Montage*, ed. Rane Willerslev and Christian Suhr (Oxford and New York: Berghahn, 2013).
2   Benjamin Bratton, "Some Trace Effects of the Post-Anthropocene: On Accelerationist Geopolitical Aesthetics," *e-flux journal* 46 (2013).

NATIONAL MARKET, BANGALORE

Lawrence Liang

As with any map that gives you a bird's eye view of a space, the view that one gets of the National Market in Gandhinagar, Bangalore on Google Maps is a deceptively flat one — for one thing, it locates the National Market in space and not in time — so we should perhaps begin by stepping inside the National Market and taking a walk around to see what's on offer. While the space is still pretty lively, it does not seem to have the same buzz that it did a few years ago when it was the prime market for pirated DVDs in the city. Any visitor to the market five years ago would testify to a palpable buzz and excitement of a kind that can only be generated by a hint of illegality. The few hundred shops making up the market are of a more or less similar size — rectangular stores measuring three feet by five feet. Given the small size of the shops, the question of what you stock becomes an important strategic decision based on balancing the size of your investment against the potential returns. In the 1980s, for instance, it was lucrative to stock foreign video cassette players and tapes despite the fact that they took up a fair amount of space because these were not otherwise available. Similarly, when VCD and DVD players were initially introduced, shopkeepers stocked them, but as their price dropped National Market traders found them unprofitable. By the early 2000s the entire market had shifted to stocking pirated DVDs. These were easy to obtain, easy to stock, there was a very high demand for them, and in the event that they were confiscated during a raid, the loss was not terribly significant.

As long as the internet was slow in India, markets like the National Market were the primary source of illicit films, but with most people now preferring to download films in the comfort of their own homes the market has had to diversify and traders have shifted to phones, tablet computers and other products, although a few continue to sell DVDs and Blu-ray discs.

The reason that the National Market remains interesting for us is that it is in many ways representative of many such markets that exist in cities across India, including the Palika Bazaar in Delhi and the Burma Bazaar in Chennai. Moreover, along with the markets themselves, the spaces around them also tell an interesting story, since, like the goods they sell, these markets exhibit a viral quality, with one market breeding another.

As you step out of the National Market in Bangalore, you are faced with a cartographic puzzle. Diagonally opposite is the Bangkok Plaza; a few metres away, there is the Burma Bazaar and, across from it, the New Hong Kong Bazaar, announced on a not-so-new signboard whose "Kong" is a matter of educated guess. While globalization is supposed to have redrawn boundaries, you still are not quite prepared for this distorted sense of Asia, as you leave "National" to encounter "Bangkok", "Burma" and "Hong Kong", all specialist outlets for non-legal media commodities — phones, DVDs and software. The bane of global policing institutions such as the World Trade

AUTHOR BROWSING FILMS IN THE NATIONAL MARKET

Organisation and the World Intellectual Property Organisation, these grey-market bazaars are also appropriate metaphors of the contemporary, where rules of property collide with unofficial cultural flows.

There are various versions of such unofficial Asian maps, and in fact the International Intellectual Property Alliance has also moved into the business of cartography, as evidenced by its annual "Special 301 Reports", which reveal a consistent interest in Asia.

In globalization's early days, travel writer Pico Iyer set out to track what he despairingly called the Ramboization and Coca-Colonization of Asia, joining the numbers arguing against the hegemonic spread of American business and culture across the globe. And yet, in bootleg DVD shops across the country, you find not just your standard Hollywood and Bollywood fare, but also a range of films from countries whose cinema has no circulation in India. These include cult classics like the Korean film *Oldboy* (directed by Chan-wook Park, 2003), which was remade in India as the non-incestuous *Zinda* (directed by Sanjay Gupta, 2006), as well as lesser-known films from other parts of the world.

Chua Beng Huat, arguing for the importance of conceptualizing an East Asian popular culture, says:

> In contrast to the very uneven and abstract presence of Confucianism, since the 1980s popular cultural products have criss-crossed the national borders of the East Asian countries and constituted part of the culture of consumption that defines a very large part of everyday life of the population throughout the region. This empirically highly visible cultural traffic allows for the discursive construction of an "East Asian Popular Culture" as an object of analysis. [...] [The] dense traffic of popular culture products across the national/cultural boundaries in East Asia has far exceeded the analytical boundaries that are determined by any focus on a specific location.

There are a number of exciting possibilities being opened out by this new cinephilia,[2] which is seeing the rapid development of a far greater interest in Asian films than in Hollywood or even European art-house movies. While the immense popularity of filmmakers such as Wong Kar-wai, Tsai Ming-liang and Hou Hsiao-hsien stems from their visibility on the film festival circuit, there is also demand for a range of films from Korea, Thailand, Japan and even Cambodia, which have found their way onto the pirate markets. Unlike national cinema categories, illicit media always spills over national boundaries and has always had a transnational feel to it (whether in the form of the ubiquitous foreign blue movie or the circulation of a wide range of art-house and commercial films on video and DVD). In Jianjun He's low budget film *Pirated Copy* (2004) about the circulation of pirated films in Beijing, a pirate DVD seller tries to interest a customer in Bergman, Tarkovsky and Fellini.

MARVELS OF THE BAZAAR

The customer says he has never heard of them and enquires whether Tarkovsky is a Russian composer. He then asks for the Korean film *My Sassy Girl*.

Cinema Paradiso at the National Market: Prashant's Story

Prashant was one of my regular suppliers of DVDs at the National Market. His shop was constantly packed with cinephiles and was considered Bangalore's mecca of world cinema. Even for filmmakers, artists and cinephiles visiting India from abroad, his store was one of the city's must-go-to places. So how did an average pirated DVD store become a cinema paradise?

This is Prashant's story (transcribed interview):

I began working at the National Market in the late 1990s when a cousin got me over from Kerala to Bangalore. This was a time when the new technology of VCDs had just been introduced. There was a great demand for VCDs and business was flourishing at the National Market. My cousin felt he needed a helping hand to look after the store when he was away sourcing films. The business at this time was already getting intense but there was still enough demand to ensure that everyone had a chance to make some money. Timing was key to our work. If you managed to get a copy of a film which no one else had, it gave you an advantage of a few days before the same film would be found with everyone else in the market. Sometimes we would also help other sellers whom we were close to, and who were not doing as well, by passing them a few "exclusive" VCDs that we had got in. But the real action started with the introduction of DVDs. Initially, when DVDs were introduced into the market, it was only the very affluent clients who asked for them, since they were being sold at a pretty high price. We could charge anywhere between 300 and 500 rupees per DVD,

Because of this market, there are now many markets like this in Bangalore.

THE VIRAL MARKET, STILL FROM *COPYRIGHT THIS*, SANJAY BHANGAR AND
SRAVANTHI K, 2005

but when the price of players started dropping, we also had to start lowering the cost of our DVDs. We generally sourced our films from people in Chennai, who in turn got them either from Malaysia or Singapore. As you can imagine, there was a lot of demand for pornographic films, which we used to keep under the counter and would only show to customers who we knew to be trustworthy.

I had a number of filmmakers who used to come to my shop since it was conveniently located right at the entrance of the National Market. I started noticing that some of my regular customers, who were very knowledgeable about cinema generally, got very excited when they came across some films that I had assumed to be regular porn films. Later, as my own knowledge of world cinema increased, I realized that these were films like Bertolucci's Last Tango in Paris *and Nagasi Oshima's* In the Realm of the Senses. *I started categorizing these films in my mind as "story porn" since when I saw them I realized that they were not just about sex but generally had complicated storylines. This is how my knowledge of world cinema started. Every time someone came and seemed to want some slightly offbeat films, I would show them this collection and they would get very excited and start asking me if I either had other films by the same director or had films whose names I didn't know. But I started making notes of some of the titles and filmmakers that they asked for.*

One day, a very famous Kannada film director, who has won national awards, came to my store and gave me a list. He asked me which of the films in the list I had. I was happy that I had at least a few of the films that he wanted. He left the list with me and asked me to try and locate as many of the films on the list as I could. This list was the Sight and Sound top 100 films. When I managed to find other films on the list, he also gave me other similar lists and that is how I started building my own collection of world cinema. Names like Godard, Truffaut and Bergman but also more contemporary names like Wong Kar-wai and Takeshi Kitano became more familiar to me. I even tried watching some of these films to educate myself, but I have to say that I did not enjoy many of the filmmakers that people seemed to love. My personal favourite is Kitano and I also particularly enjoy Zaitochi. Knowing at least a little bit about the films that you are selling is crucial in our business since

NEW HONG KONG BAZAAR

everyone has more or less the same set of films, and if you can demonstrate that you know something about cinema or that you are able to fulfil requests, then your reputation spreads through word of mouth and you are no longer shop no. 23 or 47 but instead known by name. I am proud to say that many people come to the National Market and ask for Prashant's shop. Over a period of time, after I got to know some of my customers better, I would even ask them if they had DVDs which I did not have or ask them to tell me the names of more obscure films and directors, since by that time others in the shop had also got a little more familiar with people like Bergman and Godard. Some of these customers started lending me copies of films from their personal collection and a few even gave me hard discs to copy films from. One customer gave me a hard disc which some friends of his from Berlin had given him, and he asked me to make copies of films by a director called Harun Farocki, which, I think, was the first time that anyone in Bangalore had copies of Farocki. A few years later, when Harun Farocki came to Bangalore, an artist and filmmaker brought him to my store and introduced him to me. I showed him DVD copies of his films and he even bought a few copies of his own films from me.

When I realized that there were people coming to my shop from places like Bombay and Delhi, I decided to expand my business and got another cousin to help me set it up. Since I did not have enough contacts in other cities to be able to get a place like the one in Bangalore, I decided that we would do direct supplies instead. Through my initial contacts, I got the numbers of many ad filmmakers and feature filmmakers in Bombay and my cousin would go with an entire suitcase of DVDs to Bombay. He would then make a selection of films and carry them in a bag to the customers' house after we had called them and fixed a time to meet at their homes or office. I even went to Calcutta once and supplied films to a well-known film studies department in the city.

What I enjoyed most about specializing in world cinema was the respect that it brought me. While earlier I was considered as just another film pirate, I was now being treated with respect by so many creative people, many of whom I was on a first name basis with and some of whom would even call me before coming to the store to check if I was there. When the raids in the National Market started increasing and there was almost one raid a week, our business was being affected. The bribe that we had to pay had also increased. I decided that it would be a good idea to figure out an alternative arrangement, and what I did was to arrange for a long car to be parked near the National Market in which I stored my entire stock of films. Whenever a client came on a day when there was a raid or when we feared

SAME BUT DIFFERENT

a raid, I would get one of my boys to take them to the car where they could sit comfortably and did not have to worry about the police turning up. They would choose their films in the comfort of the air-conditioned car and we would conduct our transaction without them having to even come to the shop. The other thing that I started doing was to order films from Amazon.com. Some of my clients in the advertising industry had started asking me for collections of short films or DVDs which were about the best ads in the world and these were not easy to source, but once I started ordering them from Amazon it became easier. While they were expensive to buy, I would rip them, make multiple copies, and very easily recover my investment.

Nowadays, the market is not the same as before. People prefer to download films and we rarely have people who come in to buy DVDs like they used to. We still manage to get by, selling Blu-rays, but that has not caught on in the same way in Bangalore as DVDs did and I have lost most of my old clients. So apart from the money, what I miss is talking and interacting with different film lovers.

The advent of VCDs and DVDs represents one of the key developments in the rise of these "Asian" electronics markets. Sony and Philips jointly introduced VCD technology in 1993 to record video on compact discs. It was cheap, digital and convenient, and it seemed to be setting the standard. At the same time, however, the development of the technologically far superior Digital Videodisc (DVD) was already underway. From the outset, Philips was well aware of the pending arrival of the high-density DVD and the threat it would bring to the VCD, and as a result the firm decided to stop working on improving VCD technology. Together with Sony, Philips decided to launch VCD in China, since it was "a technology that was fit for a poor cousin in laggard developing countries instead of cutting edge economies".[3] The introduction of VCDs into China created the biggest boom to date in the field of cheap reproduction technologies, although, ironically, the industry believed that CDs would prove an effective tool in the fight against video piracy.[4]

While there has been a great deal of hype around the idea of transnational cultural flows, it is unclear what the nature and impacts of these flows have been, and, more specifically, what sites are providing the context for them. How should we conceptualize these unofficial flows? One interesting aspect is the rapid expansion of such flows beyond East Asia. Indeed, the East Asian presence in Indian media markets is adding a whole new facet to the idea of a transnational cinema.

A large number of Asian markets adopted it enthusiastically, bypassing global distribution networks in order to "steal" enjoyment. Darrell Davis calls VCD a form of cockroach capitalism because of its proliferation. Within a short period of time, VCD became the major movie carrier in many developing countries. In 1998, there were 16 VCD players per hundred Chinese households; by 2000, there were 36.4 VCD players per hundred households. In 2000, 14.5 million units were manufactured, but by 2001, this number had fallen to 1.2 million units as manufacturing moved into DVDs.

VCD technology spread rapidly from East Asia to other parts of Asia, and within a few years of their introduction, VCD replaced VHS as the standard format in most Asian countries. In India, for instance, while the price of the VCR never fell below 10,000 rupees, a VCD player could be purchased for as little as a 1,000 rupees. VCD culture also spread from Asia into other parts of the world very rapidly. In Nigeria, which incidentally has the largest film industry in the world (producing more than 1,200 films a year), most films are only available on VCD and DVD. However, given its complete absence in the Western market, there seems to be something distinctly "Asian" about VCD technology.[5]

However, this technological emulation of East Asia by other parts of Asia in the case of the VCD has a deeper history, and it is perhaps here that we can start considering the question of Asia in relation to piracy, technology and cultural flows. Since the East Asian miracle and electronics boom, many countries in the region have become the symbol of a type of electronics modernity that other countries seek to emulate. But this is also a very distinct modernity, one that does not necessarily take the West as its point of reference. Indeed, it could be argued that the Western model can be leapfrogged in favour of a distinctly Asian model of technological development.

As is well known, the technological miracle was also strongly fuelled by Cold War interests and technology transfers. However, these were transfers that moved far beyond the official routes conceived for them. The technological history of East Asia during the 1980s is also one of a "copy culture" that saw the emergence of very strong manufacturing capabilities, which borrowed and adapted Western technology for the Asian region.[6]

Interestingly, the media landscape of many South Asian countries is a landscape chiselled out of another Asia of the mind. This is an imagining of the modern for which the point of reference is not the European Enlightenment or industrial revolution but the almost magical transformation of Southeast Asia. This is an Asian modernity in which the copying countries of Southeast Asia serve as the original role models for countries in the rest of the region. Tracing these trajectories creates a map of transgressions, one that does not use the idea of a map in the "disenchanted" sense of seeing national territory within a "techno-rational" grid. Our map belongs to the genre of enchanted maps, in which the imaginary overwhelms the real and opens out fantastical possibilities of seeing. This is our map of an Asian commons of copy culture.

But if we were to try to trace this story over a longer arc and go back to the question of why it is that country names such as Singapore, Burma and Dubai came to signify another kind of electronics revolution, we would have to address a much longer history of the informal trade routes and kinship networks that have forged this heterotopic space.

Take, for instance, the Tamu Bazaar — a border bazaar that lies between Burma and Manipur in India: It is a border bazaar that served as a space for people trading between Burma and India long before national boundaries were settled and in which people continue to trade today. In a similar way, due to the large Tamil diaspora in Southeast Asian countries and the Malayali working class diaspora in the Middle

East, these networks became a source of cheap electronic goods at a time when many foreign goods were either unavailable in India or were only available at a very high cost after the imposition of customs duties. The two-in-one player popularized by Sony (followed by its introduction of the Walkman), bottles of Tang orange powder and Charlie perfumes were all highly sought-after commodities which were only available in these illicit markets.

These markets were the non-spaces that provided relief from the frugal modernity enforced by the post-colonial state, which disavowed consumption since it led to a waste of precious natural resources. If the modernist mission of the postcolonial state sought to filter the sensual experience of citizens, then in contrast to the idea of utopia these were heterotopic spaces — a term with its origins in medicine (referring to an organ of the body that had been dislodged from its usual space) and popularized by Michel Foucault both in terms of language as well as a spatial metaphor.[7] If utopia exists as a nowhere or imaginary space with no connection to any existing social spaces, then heterotopias in contrast are realities that exist and are even foundational, but in which all other spaces are potentially inverted and contested.

Foucault later developed a greater spatial understanding of heterotopias in which he uses specific examples such as the cemetery (at once the space of the familiar, since everyone has someone in the cemetery, and at the heart of the city but also, over a period of time, the other city, where each family possesses its dark resting place). Indeed, the paradox of heterotopias is that they are both separate from yet connected to all other spaces. This connectedness is precisely what builds contestation into heterotopias. Imaginary spaces such as utopias exist completely outside of order. Heterotopias by virtue of their connectedness become sites in which epistemes collide and overlap. They bring together heterogeneous collections of unusual things without allowing them a unity or order established through resemblance. Instead, their ordering is derived from a process of similitude that produces, in an almost magical, uncertain space, monstrous combinations that unsettle the flow of discourse.

And while at the moment people are lamenting the fact that spaces such as the National Market are going to decline, it is too early to think of them as ruins. In fact, the fortunes of the National Market are currently being revived as people turn to informal intermediaries again in the face of official efforts to impose an excessive legality on the Internet and bring it, as it were, out of the shadows.

Appendix

In this appendix, I take four texts that to my mind approximate to four different kinds of map and allow us different entry points into the world of informal markets. The first two extracts are from the PPHP (Publics & Practices in the History of the Present) project that was run by Sarai at the Centre for the Study of Developing Societies (CSDS). It was an ethnographic research project that attempted to map out urban transformation in Delhi by closely studying its various media markets. Rakesh's texts give us a sense of the Palika Bazaar, one of Delhi's largest illicit media markets, which is located in the heart of the city. The second of these texts provides an account of a typical raid on Palika. The subsequent two extracts are

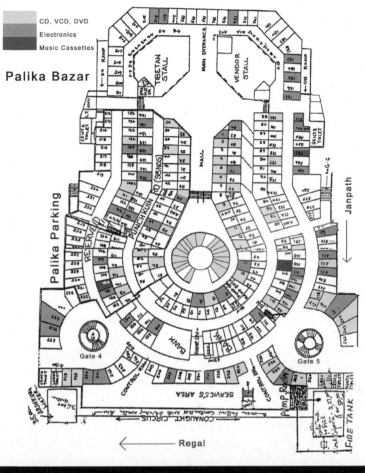

Palika Bazar

CD, VCD, DVD
Electronics
Music Cassettes

"PALIKA BAZAAR LOOKS TIRED AT THE AGE OF TWENTY-THREE"

about borders in South Asia: the first one is an extract from an account by Kanak Mani Dixit, which describes the realities of how borders work over long periods of time, while the second is an extract from Amitav Ghosh's novel *Shadowlines* and describes the epiphanic encounter that the young protagonist has with the reality and fiction of borders. My reason for choosing these texts is that they serve as useful landmarks in our navigation of the informal markets of our own times: if borders are fictions policed by barbed wire and armies, then surely intellectual property is a fiction guarded by armed police. Just as merely crossing over a line in the first instance renders the border superfluous, copying a media product renders irrelevant the lines drawn between the licit and the illicit.

Palika Looks Tired at the Age of Twenty-three [8]
Rakesh Kumar Singh

Palika Bazaar people tell you that Sanjay Gandhi had this dream of transforming Delhi into Hong Kong. An underground market which is fully air-conditioned. So, New Delhi Municipal Corporation (NDMC) made a plan during the Emergency. The plan was to shift the shops from Panchkuiyan Road to Palika. People were told the city would look beautiful. Tourism would get a boost. The area between Janpath and Central Circle connected to Regal was selected for the market which came up in 1978 when the Janata Government was in power. Spread over 123,000 square feet, the area occupied by the shopping complex came to be 64,000 square feet. The rest of the area was converted into parking. The total number of shops was 314, out of which 28 had water connection and 61 had a loft. There were 31 show windows, too. Allotment started towards the end of 1978 in which Panchkuiyan men were given priority. But only 79 shopkeepers agreed to move. Tenders were invited for the rest. By the year 1979, the market got operational although it is yet to be formally inaugurated.

Dealing in altogether 45 goods and services, the market was divided into five zones. The Central Hall, the Mall, the Mezzanine Floor, Inner and Outer Circle and the Mini Market near gate no. 4 and gate no. 5. The Mall was a major centre for handicrafts and jewellery. On the Mezzanine floor, there were shops selling toys, gift items, cameras, handicrafts and audio/videos. In the Central Hall, shops sold furniture and household goods. Readymade garments, leather goods, tailors and drapers, and other household items were on the Inner and Outer Circle.

Hairdressers, health and cosmetics, and travel agencies were placed adjacent to gate no. 4, while gate no. 5 came to be known for national and intercontinental food. The area occupied by vendors and Tibetan stalls (fully reserved for Tibetan refugees) was named Mini Market. Mehra Saheb says, "The Mini Market was a free zone, there was freedom to trade anything here. Even today. This is why here you have tea/coffee, paan shops, cheap clothes and eating joints apart from repair shops."

Palika vindicated its planners. Tourists started pouring in. Whosoever came to Delhi made it a point to visit Palika along with historical monuments. It was the same with foreign tourists, who took a liking to cotton, woollen and leather garments. Sales increased and the market bore a busy look. Traders say that Russians came especially for woollen clothes. The shopkeepers and salesmen acquired working fluency in many foreign languages like Russian, French, German, etc. Palika also provided a cool haven from the heat of the Delhi summer.

Times change. In a span of four to five years, the cracks emerged in the system. NDMC did a shoddy job in maintaining cleanliness and air-conditioning. The rentals shot up five times from the original official values. The shops were being rented out with increased frequency rendering the zoning system futile. Responding to trade pressures, occupations changed. There was a proliferation of audio/video shops. Show windows became sale counters. Shopkeepers improvised and created two to three counters within a single shop. And each counter became a fresh source of enhanced rent.

Very soon, encroachments became a pattern. What began as demonstrations in front of stalls quickly became mobile shops in common areas selling socks, purses, readymade garments, belts and electronic items. Free for all bargaining became a culture. Sensing unfair bargaining and foul play customers became insecure.

All the same, Palika participated in and benefited from the ongoing revolution in media technologies. When digital technology replaced the analogue, the market soon switched over to selling CDs, DVDs and MP3s. Right from fresh Friday releases to hottest pornos, everything is easily available. A salesman claimed, "anything that comes to any market in India or abroad today will be available in Palika the next day." With the big companies tightening the noose around informal trade practices, Palika came to figure prominently on the crime map of the Delhi Police. Raids became a frequent phenomenon.

The last decade was full of ups and downs for Palika. Domestic tourists kept coming but the number of foreign tourists declined. The business witnessed a slowdown. The shops verged on surrender. Now, Metro rail is about to reach gate no. 1. The air is rife with speculation ranging from "it may turn out to be a good omen" to "it will destroy the market." Old shop-keepers admit, "excess rise in rentals and wrong methods of shopkeeping are responsible for the tired image of Palika in its young age of twenty-three ..."

Palika Raid Report, 19 October 2002[9]
Rakesh Kumar Singh

Around 11.20 a.m., suddenly there was hue and cry all around the mezzanine floor. A lot of shops were pulling down their shutters. Plainclothes personnel from the Crime Branch, wielding dandas *(sticks), had already seized some shops. Some were chasing the shopkeepers and sales boys who were trying to run away. Meanwhile, a boy jumped down from the upper floor. Many of the shopkeepers and sales boys managed to escape the clutches of* dandadharis *(stick-wielders) and gathered in the central hall. Now it completely became the affair of shops no.* M-9, M-12, M-13 *and the raiding party. Within few minutes, it was completely 'house full' in the central hall. Barring a few outsiders like me, the rest of the audience consisted of shopkeepers and their respective staff. Suddenly, someone from the hall whistled, which was followed by voices hurling profanities such as "Maro saale ko, iski bahan****... (Hit the bastard, sister-f****...)". And with this, people started moving towards the stairs, which had been taken over by the* dandadharis. *The crowd started pushing the police, which resulted in a minor* lathi *charge. Since the police had already blocked off both exits, it was difficult for the crowd to disperse.*

Now it was time for the raiding party to leave the Bazaar with the seized materials (pirated/pornographic CDS). Here again the crowd, about 300 people, started shouting against the raiding party. It became difficult for them to push through. Finally, they got out their revolvers. The crowd scattered, but within a few seconds it started abusing the raiding party and pelting them with glasses and bottles. However, they managed to move out of the Bazaar with four or five big jute bags of seized materials. And, of course, they took two or three guys away with them.

12 p.m., central hall
I returned to the central hall after watching the entire episode, and looked around for someone with whom I could discuss it. Suddenly, I noticed Mahesh (name changed), who sold cheap men's wear in shop no. 45. I asked him about the incident. He said, "Brother, you have seen how raids are carried out here. Today the police escaped, but usually whoever is trying to raid this place gets beaten up. Last time three policemen were injured and the market people left another one half-dead. This raid must have had some big planning, otherwise we get to know in advance that a raid is about to happen. Do you know that from shop no. M-9 the cop on the local beat gets 2 rupees lakhs? ... yet the sisterfucker betrayed us."

After listening to Mahesh, I went towards a small group of youths. Sanjay (the owner of shop no. M-1) was giving his sales boys tips in Punjabi about how to close shop during raids. "First of all we should try to push the goods-counter inside and then think of pulling down the shutter. Now I will bring a long stick to push the counter inside ..."

I went again to the central hall and observed the surroundings. The mezzanine floor had a completely deserted look. Sales boys were sitting in small groups. The goods-counters are the prevailing sales structures in the Palika Bazaar today. Almost every shop has three or four counters. *Generally, counter attendants, vendors and salesmen are worst affected by such raids. True to form, today's raid was yet another nightmare for these people.*

I toured the whole of Palika and, with the exception of the Eagle and T-Series shops, found that most of some 100 CD and VCD outlets were closed. Moreover, they seemed to have been closed for several weeks.

12.30 p.m., Palika parking in front of gate no.1
A group of more than 50 people stood on the road discussing the matter. Apart from sharing a preference for hurling abuse at the raiding party, they all had different opinions about the day's raid. Some of them thought that this was a result of internal politics while others saw the hand of some Mini Market wallah behind the raid. However, all of them were looking for a way to restore normality following this traumatic event. One person suggested that they should lodge a complaint of dacoity (banditry), and, in order to support their case, one boy from each shop should tear his cloths and slash his body. Others suggested that they should block the road around Connaught Place to force the police to release their arrested relatives. Unable to reach a consensus, some members of the crowd then moved off towards the Delhi Police Crime Branch Headquarters located in the R. K. Puram complex. I realized later that they were the ones whose shops had been raided and whose relatives had been taken away.

Porous Societies, Sealed Frontiers: What Would Lalon Fakir Have Said?[10]
Kanak Mani Dixit
Several seemingly contradictory forces have transformed the demographic makeup here: open migration, forced migration and prevented migration due to the closure of frontiers.

In southeast Nepal, the roadside cemeteries are primarily of the Tibeto-Burman Kirant hill migrants, with many of the graves ornately designed replicas of mountain dwellings. More than 120,000 Nepali-speaking Lhotshampa refugees are huddled here in refugee camps. It has been 12 years since they were ousted from their native Bhutan, and regional geopolitics blocks their return.

The syncretistic mix of cultures in Nepal's Jhapa is nowhere in evidence 40 kilometres away as the crow flies in Bangladesh. The cemeteries here are all Muslim: many of the Hindus have left since Partition and creeping Islamization makes them more vulnerable. Only the place names remind of the once-upon-a-time demography: Rangpur, a dynamic marketplace before the borders were drawn in 1947 is now a backwater.

[...]

The Nepal–India border is open, a kind of frontier that does most justice to the shared history of all South Asia. The Bangladesh–India frontier has been closed since the rise of East Pakistan but remained porous for decades. Today, it is in the process of being sealed. India's fence-building frenzy to keep out Bangladeshi migrants has reached Changrabanda. To the south stretches an impregnable line of barbed wire, steel pillars, concrete and a service road. Some contractors have made good profit.

This is one alternative for a South Asian future, where weak governments dependent on vote bank politics will take the course of least resistance. But building a fence will only make societies more rigid in their own identities and certitudes. One wonders whether sharply defined frontiers will ever work in South Asia. Instead, is there a lesson to be taken from the open Nepal–India frontier just a few miles away?

Shadow Lines[11]

Amitav Ghosh

A few months after I had made my discovery in the Teen Murti Library, I found, at the bottom of my bookshelf, the tattered old Bartholomew's Atlas in which Tridib used to point out places to me when he told me stories in his room. Mayadebi had given it to me many years before.

One day, when it was lying open on my desk in my hostel room, quite by chance I happened to find a rusty old compass at the back of my drawer. It had probably been forgotten there by the person who had lived in the room before me.

I picked it up and, toying with it, I placed its point on Khulna and the tip of the pencil on Srinagar.

Khulna is not quite 100 miles from Calcutta as the crow flies: the two cities face each other at a watchful equidistance across the border. The distance between Khulna and Srinagar, or so I discovered when I measured the space between the points of my compass, was 1,200 miles, nearly 2,000 kilometres. It didn't seem like much. But when I took my compass through the pages of that atlas, on which I could still see the smudges left by Tridib's fingers, I discovered that Khulna is about as far from Srinagar as Tokyo is from Beijing, or Moscow from Venice, or Washington from Havana, or Cairo from Naples.

Then I tried to draw a circle with Khulna at the centre and Srinagar on the circumference. I discovered immediately that the map of South Asia would not be big enough. I had to turn back to a map of Asia before I found one large enough for my circle.

It was an amazing circle.

Beginning in Srinagar and travelling anti-clockwise, it cut through the Pakistani half of Punjab, through the tip of Rajasthan and the edge of Sind, through the Rann of Kutch, and across the Arabian Sea, through the southernmost toe of the Indian Peninsula, through Kandy, in Sri Lanka, and out into the Indian Ocean until it emerged to touch upon the northernmost finger of Sumatra, then straight through the tail of Thailand into the Gulf, to come out again in Thailand, running a little north of Phnom Penh, into the hills of Laos, past Hue in Vietnam, dipping into the Gulf of Tonking, then swinging up again through the Chinese province of Yunnan, past Chungking, across the Yangtze Kiang, passing within sight of the Great Wall of China, through Inner Mongolia and Sinkiang, until with a final leap over the Karakoram Mountains it dropped again into the valley of Kashmir.

It was a remarkable circle: more than half of mankind must have fallen within it.

1   Chua Beng Huat, "Conceptualizing an East Asian Popular Culture," in *Inter-Asia Cultural Studies Reader*, ed. Kuan-Hsing Chen and Chua Beng Huat (New York: Routledge, 2007), 117–119.

2   Moinak Biswas, "Film Studies, Film Practice and Asian Cinema: Points in Re-Connection," (paper prepared for the Asian Cinema Conference, cscs, Bangalore, February 2007), http://mail.sarai.net/pipermail/reader-list/2007-April/009144.html.

3   Shujen Wang, *Framing Piracy: Globalization and Film Distribution in Greater China* (Lanham, MD: Rowman & Littlefield, 2003).

4   Shujen Wang and Jonathan Zhu, "Mapping Film Piracy in China," *Theory, Culture, and Society* 20, no. 4 (2003): 97–125; Laikwan Pang, *Cultural Control and Globalization in Asia: Copyright, Piracy, and Cinema* (London: Routledge, 2006).

5   Kelly Hu, "Made in China: The Cultural Logic of OEMS and the Manufacture of Low-Cost Technology," *Inter-Asia Cultural Studies* 9, no. 1 (March 2008).

6   Ibid.

7   Michel Foucault, "Different Spaces," in *Aesthetics, Method, Epistemology*, ed. James D. Faubion (New York: The New Press,

1998), 179; For Foucault on language and heterotopias see *The Order of Things: An Archaeology of the Human Sciences* (New York: Pantheon, 1970).

8   *Rakesh Kumar Singh*, "Palika Looks Tired at 23," PPHP (*Publics & Practices in the History of the Present) Broadsheet* 2 (The Media Fabric of the Contemporary City), Delhi (2003): 5; Sarai archive, http://archive.sarai.net/files/original/007d5f2ffb817aa797e49ef-cd813f5e0.pdf.

9   Rakesh Kumar Singh, "Palika raid report, 19/10/02," in *Sarai Reader 05: Bare Acts*, ed. Monica Narula et al. (Delhi: Centre for the Study of Developing Societies, 2005), 281–282; Sarai archive, http://preview.sarai.net/journal/05_pdf/05/03_pphp.pdf

10 Kanak Mani Dixit, "Porous Societies, Sealed Frontiers: What Would Lalon Fakir Have Said?," South Asia Beat, *Nepali Times* 230, 14–20 January 2005, http://nepalitimes.com/~nepalitimes/news.php?id=1339#.VGVFoE1yatU.

11 Amitav Gosh, *The Shadow Lines: A Novel* (New York: Mariner Books, 2005 [1988]), 226–227.

INFORMAL CHINA:
A HISTORY OF CONTROL
& OUT-OF-CONTROL

Jiang Jun

To research China, we must look at its means of control. It is very difficult to find another civilization in history like China's, which has been extremely meticulous about control for thousands of years. This control is not only on political and ideological levels, but is also present in material and spatial realms: from macro-scale urban planning, meso-scale traditional construction rules, to countless micro-scale details of daily life. In an integrated archetype of traditional Chinese society, control is almost omnipresent. In this context, a discussion on "informal China" cannot be limited only to the "informal" aspect, but should look at the dialectical interaction between "control" and "out-of-control": if we regard one force as the counterforce of the other, then countless scattered, trivial counter-forces can make up the mirror image of the force. Through this verification that approaches the centre from the margins, what we see is not only the mechanism of the emergence of informal forces, but more importantly, in which manner and in what context of control this mechanism operates. If control constitutes one aspect of China, how do "informal forces" constitute the other aspect of it?

770 B.C.E.–206 B.C.E. [Qin vs. Qi]

Centralization and Capitalism in ancient times

Chinese civilization was precocious: it developed a whole macroscopic and complete theory on system and its change rather early, and built its primary civilization during the Warring States Period (475–221 B.C.E.) before it accomplished unification for the first time. Its macro-vision gave expression to the idea that "everything has the same origin" in philosophy, and "centralization" in politics. This primary civilization gradually crystallized through free expression and exchange of thoughts, as well as cruel wars and annexations among the feudal states, and became the prevailing ruling system. Ever since, China has not been able to break away from this framework.

In this war, the state of Qi, located in the eastern part of the central plains of China (in today's Shandong Peninsula), offered an alternative model that was different to "the legal system" or "the ritual system" of the period of unification after it. With its geographical proximity to the ocean, Qi not only built a vast and high-level cross-regional commercial network and market economy by taking advantage of its resources in fish and salt, but also witnessed the emergence of ancient China's most influential merchants and capitalists. This system was totally different from that of other feudal states in the same period, in particular Qin that pursued power politics, oppressive ruling and militarism, and later completed the unification of China.

Qi attached little importance to the *Rites of the Zhou* (a classic compiled during the third century B.C.E., describing the ritual procedures carried out during the Zhou Dynasty), encouraged the liberation of thought and feelings, and took part in actively creating a market. While other states were still engaged in fierce wars in order to annex more territories, Qi was waging an economic war; the big capitalists on the top of the pyramid structure monopolized the whole market through linking up with political power. Although the market was still under the guidance of the Qi government, the relatively large economic freedom allowed its cities to develop a more informal and outward character in comparison with other feudal states that "valued agriculture and restrained trade". Moreover, the cities of Qi also showed a better adaptation to the fluctuations of the market, population and the scale of the city.

Thanks to its strategy that resembled state capitalism, Qi for a time became the leading power among the states of the Spring and Autumn Period (770–476 B.C.E.). The competition between Qi and Qin was essentially between gold/finance-based capitalism and land-based feudalism. Moreover, it was also a competition between two ruling procedures, that is to say, between appropriate decentralization and high centralization. However, following the unification of China, this alternative model was dismissed overnight. The fact that the model of Qi did not develop in the prevailing civilization makes many historians who like to make hypotheses feel regret. However, to some extent, it was perhaps predestined that the model of Qi could never become the prevailing system in Chinese history: with its intrinsically informal character, i.e., economic laissez-faire and freedom, land and social wealth were automatically concentrated in the hands of a small group of people, resulting in the polarization of society. This was always a danger for a big country in ancient times, when there was no constraint by international contracts. On the other hand, the vitality and creativity brought by market economy to society was also what the rulers needed. As a result, Chinese history shows a subtle and interesting cycle regarding its attitude toward a free market: laissez-faire / restraint / laissez-faire again / restraint again, but with the condition that it must be in the context of a unified country. This reflects fundamental thinking in ancient Chinese philosophy, i.e., "seeking common ground, while allowing for minor differences". "Informal China" exists precisely in the "minor differences" in the context of "seeking common ground".

618 C.E.– 1279 C.E. [Chang'an (Xi'an) vs. Bianjing (Kaifeng) / Lin'an (Hangzhou)]
Curfew and the Lift of Curfew

If we consider Qi and Qin as the extremes of "laissez-faire" and of "restraint" respectively, the city form in different periods of China following them vacillated between these two extremes. Different measures of control over "minor differences" would result in different city forms. As the principal public space, the street is host to all of the informal variables—it is a hotbed of free market forces, but is also fraught with hidden dangers, such as mob riots. The form of this space can reflect the strategy and the force the government uses to control the city.

During the Tang and the Song Dynasties, between the eighth and the thirteenth centuries, China built international metropolises with a population of more than one million people, the biggest in the world at that time: from Chang'an in the Tang

Dynasty to Bianjing (today's Kaifeng) in Northern Song Dynasty and Lin'an (today's Hangzhou) in the Southern Song Dynasty. However, their measures of control were totally different, resulting in different city forms. Their differences were especially crystallized in the public space. The rulers of the Tang Dynasty implemented the strict "*Lifang* (Alley and Lane) street unit system" in their capital. Although Chang'an was the starting point of the "Silk Road", the world's largest and longest-lasting international trade route at that time, and enjoyed an extremely flourishing city life, the informal contents including the market and the "red light district" were all divided into groups and then assigned into specific checkerboard-like spaces. Moreover, through the enforcement of curfew at night, the time for these activities to take place was also fixed in a strict manner. It was forbidden to open windows on the façade facing the street; the streets were only used for traffic during the daytime; at nightfall, when the curfew was called, even walking in the streets would be punished. The Song Dynasty lifted restrictions on these informal activities in terms of time and place. The lifting of curfew in the streets and the disintegration of the *Lifang* system enabled the Song Dynasty's capital to develop thriving and prosperous scenes rapidly, as described in the *Qingming Shanghetu* (the "Upper River during Qingming Festival" scroll painting): the market went from the "alley" to the "street"; its working hours were extended from the "daytime" to the "evening"; the facades on the street side were turned into attractive and showy commercial interfaces; residential and commercial districts blended into each other; the principal function of the city was also transformed from being an administrative centre in the Tang Dynasty to being an industrial and commercial centre in the Song Dynasty. This was in sharp contrast to the introverted and confined streets in the Tang Dynasty. On the other hand, this contrast was precisely the contrast between the city forms in Qi and Qin.

In the same way, the "governance by means of doing almost nothing" of the Song government and the strong control of the Tang government were also reflected in their management of street space. The vast administrative organization of the Tang government had infiltrated every corner of every street, whereas the relatively weak management of the street by the Song government mainly relied on basic-level neighbourhood organizations and the "*Baojia* system" (a system organized on the basis of households and used for guaranteeing local security), by maintaining order in the street through substantial decentralization and neighbourhood self-government. This self-government provided the basis for the peaceful mixing and coexistence of different social classes in the public space of the street; it also helped develop lively street life and street culture. The Song Dynasty offered a model of loose control: even though power was still concentrated in the central government as in a pyramid structure, the looseness of its basic-level organizations created gaps for its large and diverse population to initiate informal activities by themselves. The social vitality thus resulted from this contributed to create the "unprecedented" city that so impressed Marco Polo in the early Yuan Dynasty.

1271 C.E. – 1368 C.E. [Dadu of Yuan (Beijing)]

Nomadic Pastoralism and Farming

The entire history of ancient China was fraught with wars with the surrounding nomadic peoples for territory. It was paralleled to the macro-history of the struggle between civilization and barbarism on a global scale, and developed following the rise and fall of one or the other. The so-called barbarians were mostly nomadic peoples, and the differences between them and farming peoples lied in a fact: the land for the former was grassland, whereas for the latter was farmland; the development of the former depended on obtaining the right of seasonal mobility between different lands, whereas the latter needed the right to permanent settlement on the same land. These two totally different land use mechanisms developed totally different types of city, state and society: the former almost never had, and never wanted to have, boundaries; their social organizations were limited to mobile, scattered tribal units. Because they never settled in one place, wealth was unable to be accumulated in form of a large-scale city; consequently, it was impossible to develop a vast and complex state machine with a closely interrelated distribution of interests. On the other hand, farming peoples constantly set up boundaries through constructing walls, and accumulated wealth from agriculture, commerce and handcraft industries within the state, cities and families which were separated from each other by walls (the Great Wall, city walls and moats, and courtyard dwellings). In order to manage this wealth, a strict and tight bureaucratic system and a rigid culture of officialdom were created. Moreover, their ways of fighting wars were also totally different: the former preferred to launch attacks, while the latter attached more importance to defence. The great difference between their wealth made the nomadic peoples, who were comparatively poor, concentrate even more on improving the military machine, and attacking and occupying more territories.

In the thirteenth century, as an informal force fighting against central China's formal, orthodox order, the Mongols in the north gained victory in the long-lasting military struggle between nomadic peoples, frontier countries and farming peoples, and became the first regime in Chinese history to be ruled by a different ethnic group other than the Han. From what was originally a simple idea, Genghis Khan from the steppes applied his worldview throughout Eurasia, included the territory within the Great Wall, and tried to turn Eurasia into his own vast pastureland by eradicating all farming civilizations; he even came up with a genocide project to exterminate the Han people. In the end, this project was not carried out completely; however, it revealed the incompatibility between nomadic and farming civilizations. The regime that evolved from pastoral tribes and was based on a system of military slavery was intrinsically incompatible with farming societies: previously, its distribution of interests derived mainly from the principle of booty distribution, and the equal status among nomadic warriors resulted in the absence of social stratification and polarization. However, as soon as some of them were appointed to rule a mixed country where nomadic pastoralism and agriculture coexisted, the warriors who constantly moved about in search of pasture in grasslands and the warriors who settled in their fiefs started to separate from each other little by little because of unequal payoffs between them. After becoming familiar with the rationality of the farming system and enjoying its advantages, the lifestyle of the latter gradually became "un-nomadized" and "Han-nized" (integrated into the Han culture). China as a country did experience a regime change, however, its means of control continued to exist by being attached to the agriculture-based mode of production. It clearly shows that Chinese civilization that knows the essence of the maxim: "willows are weak yet they bind other wood" has had an invisible enlightening and civilizing effect on barbaric forces from outside.

"Dadu of Yuan" was built where Beijing is today. It was not only the centre of the Yuan Dynasty, but also the heart of the Mongol Empire's worldwide territories. The rulers of the Mongol Yuan Dynasty consciously chose the *Rites of the Zhou* as the guide to carry out an integral plan of the capital city—The fact that this capital city that maintained the purest ritual lineage in Chinese history was built by a foreign ethnic group that was once belligerent and committed countless killings is undoubtedly irrefutable evidence of this in-depth enlightening and civilizing influence. On the other hand, the mobility of nomadic tribes also injected fresh vitality into Chinese society—like most cross-regional wars, at the same time as the Mongol Empire easily conquered all of Eurasia with its brave horsemen, it also created free-flowing, unimpeded free trade routes between the East and the West in the gap left by the great purge. This enabled the Yuan Dynasty to carry out an all-round opening toward the outer world on the commercial base established by the Song Dynasty. From an inland city in the Far East, Dadu of Yuan suddenly became the centre of international trade across the Eurasia Steppes, and was transformed artificially into a "port city" through its connection to the sea by canals, and became the terminal of the "Silk Road on the Sea" along with a series of seaport cities on the south eastern coastline. Highly developed maritime trade and navigation technology offered China the possibility of becoming the leading power at sea in the following century.

1368 C.E.–1843 C.E. [Guangzhou]
The Ban on Maritime Trade and the "Special Zone"

When the trade routes across Eurasia were interrupted following the collapse of the Mongolian Empire, the inextinguishable globalization boom was continued by sea.

In the early fifteenth century, the first navigator recorded in history, Zheng He, a eunuch specially appointed by the Ming emperor, led the largest fleet of ships in the world at that time, sailed from China to the West, thus marking the beginning of the great navigation era. However, after entering the Ming Dynasty ruled by the Han, the maritime economy that had started to emerge in the State of Qin in the Spring and Autumn Period, had developed in the Song Dynasty, and had attained its climax in the Yuan Dynasty, was subsumed into the central government's tribute-paying system with the promulgation of the "ban on maritime trade". Even though China was far ahead of the West in terms of maritime supremacy, the ban on maritime trade destroyed the possibility of civil people developing trade by themselves. At the same time, the fact that maritime trade and the "tribute-paying system" were monopolized by the government not only seriously limited the flow maritime trade was supposed to have, but also greatly increased its cost. Although Zheng He's expedition to the Western oceans demonstrated the Chinese emperor's strength and tolerance by means of rituals and technology, its economic or military effects were nearly nil. As a result, when Zheng He died of an illness during his last voyage, the conservative Ming government put an end to the project on account of its high cost. Maritime activities that once allowed China to dominate the world were laid aside overnight; China entered an era of a strict ban on maritime trade.

At the same time as this closed-door policy, the Ming Dynasty started to cut back its navy forces; the navy that had gradually built up over the Song and Yuan periods started to decline generally. One century after Zheng He's expedition to the Western oceans, as Western navigators started to sail around the world, the Ming government started to destroy all its vessels, in order to prevent these state-of-the-art technologies from falling into the hands of laymen. Ironically, at the same time that this was taking place, overseas Chinese, composed of unscrupulous and brave people who fled abroad at the end of the Ming Dynasty started to come together informally to make up a force rivalling the Ming government in coastal waters. These people, who later became the pioneers of "Chinatown", joined forces with other ethnic groups and pirates from neighbouring countries, and became smugglers and pirates raging on the sea. They opposed the Ming government's strict ban on maritime trade by carrying out illegal trade and taking loot. Seen from the other side, their highly capable equipment and weapons reflected "Zheng He's legacy" that had failed to be handed down to the next generations in the Ming Dynasty.

This ban on maritime trade continued off and on until the Qing Dynasty. The threat of pirates was in contradiction with the need of maritime economy. The desire to reconcile this contradiction resulted in the creation of the "integrated customs clearance in one single port" system. After the mid-eighteenth century, Guangzhou became the only "special zone" to enjoy this preferential policy. In comparison with the special zones set up by Deng Xiaoping in later times, the Qing government created the "Guangzhou Special Zone" more or less out of passive acceptance, instead of Deng Xiaoping's active choice with experimental flair. From a perspective of world trade, "integrated customs clearance in one single port" was a constrained policy; however, it helped to build Guangzhou into a popular international city of trade, and to create a group of extremely wealthy feudal broker-merchants. These "official merchants", who held trading licenses issued by the government, traded with foreign merchants from all over the world in the "*Shisanhang* trading houses" in the western part of Guangzhou near the Pearl River. Their concentration in one area and the commercial network that developed in the wake of it triggered the unprecedented development of a guardian town: Xiguan (Western Gate). This city was created because of commerce, and quickly spread out from Guangzhou's Western Gate. Its organic and vital character was in sharp contrast to the classic and orderly town of Guangzhou located within the walls. Undoubtedly, this "free" trade was still under the central government's strict surveillance and control, but it enabled a city to emerge in an informal and spontaneous manner. Perhaps this was precisely what the Qing government worried about: Will the "minor differences" within the "common ground" develop into "big problems"?

1843 C.E. – 1949 C.E. [Shanghai]

Foreign Concessions and Gang Organizations

The Opium War changed the conservative character of China. Guangzhou's monopolist position was replaced by the port cities opened by a series of unequal treaties, and foreign concessions were gradually established within these cities. In the surroundings of every old feudal city, a new colonial town made up of several foreign concessions was created, turning it into a society with a half-feudal, half-colonial double character. Western architecture, which had been regarded simply as an exotic landscape and had been reserved for corners of imperial gardens to please the emperor, now became "islands" and "countries within a country".

Twice in the history of China, Shanghai has played the role of Guangzhou's successor and substitute. The first time was in the colonial period, after the Opium War in 1840, and the second time in the post-colonial period, after the development of Pudong in 1992. Whether looking at the colonial Shanghai in turbulent times or the Pudong Developmental Zone in flourishing age now, they are in no way an exact replica of Western order. Instead, they express a combination of Western order with local forces, in order to overcome its in-adaptation in this unfamiliar world, and to accomplish the translation of Western rules within a Chinese context.

For the foreign concessions in Shanghai, it was unlikely for this combination to be realized through official governmental channels, as was true for the Pudong Developmental Zone later. In the half-feudal, half-colonial era, the Chinese government and the foreign concessions held, by nature, irreconcilably opposed positions; therefore, the foreign concessions could only turn to local grassroots forces. As conflicts and wars started to spread throughout the world in the early twentieth century, the world outside the foreign concessions became increasingly chaotic and full of animosity; on the other hand, the relative stability in the foreign concessions turned them into refuges in turbulent times, oasis in a desert of anarchy. Through its intervening and mediating role among foreign cessions, the Chinese government, and the bottom of society, these grassroots forces, supported and indulged by foreign concessions, linked up to form a powerful and complex gang organization in an informal and spontaneous manner. With foreign concessions backing them, and money, sex and violence as their means, they controlled every brothel, every gambling house, every smoking house and every lane of the entire city through installing their informers and hired thugs in every corner. The government's laws were undermined by the underground power's hidden rules; its policy-making could be influenced by the will of gangs. By the 1920s and 1930s, this invisible power originating from the bottom of society had already successfully infiltrated the political, military and commercial circles at the top of society. It was precisely this unusual combination between informal forces and power that made this particular period become the golden era in the history of Shanghai, when Shanghai was a very prosperous, but also decaying city.

The diversity and the unstableness of Shanghai made it become the "paradise for adventurers". The club of adventurers made up of gold-diggers, missionaries, revolutionaries, etc., who spoke different languages and held different political views, represented in different organizational forms, such as corporations, associations or parties, came to join this both exciting and frightening paradise one after another, including the Chinese Communist Party that later successfully seized power, and became the largest party in the world.

1949 C.E.–1978 C.E. [China]
Planning and Informal Generation
Among Shanghai's adventurers, there was one radical revolutionary who later changed the world: Mao Zedong. He was the embodiment of the revolutionary spirit throughout

his whole life. He carried out political and military revolutions in the first part of his life, and economical and cultural revolutions in the second. The same strategy was applied in all these revolutions: to seize and use informal and spontaneous forces.

As early as in the 1930s, he used the maxim "a single spark can result in an inextinguishable fire" to explain how a self-generating spark can become a destructive power. It was a strategy inspired by the lever principle: to trigger an immense informal force through a smaller control force, so as to fight against another greater control force. He used this grassroots strategy to overthrow the old regime that was superior to him in terms of equipment, and built up a centralized communist country. After entering the period of peace, this "human wave" tactic that had mobilized informal forces during the war was turned into a series of "mass movements" to carry out his various grandiose and romantic experimental ideas in economics, politics and culture.

One of his ideas was inspired by the view he had from the gate tower in Tiananmen Square. At that time, he saw a ruined ancient city left by feudal dynasties, and a flat skyline melting into the distance. However, what he wanted to see were factories; he wanted to "see chimneys everywhere from the tower in Tiananmen". A few years later, he used a more informal way to implement this idea. He started China's industrial "Great Leap Forward" by urging the whole country to take part in steel production. In the end, chimneys did not stand in great numbers in front of Tiananmen Square; instead, backyard steel furnaces were set up in every corner of the country—concentration was replaced by dispersion, and machines by manpower. Ten years later, this strategy was once again employed in the "Cultural Revolution", to destroy the entire state machine systematically: this time, he not only mobilized people from the bottom of society, but also conferred real power on them, allowing them to turn the whole hierarchical system upside down with the slogan "Revolt is Justifiable", and to break down the power pyramid with "Bombarding the Headquarters". Undoubtedly, Mao was still the core of control, but he no longer needed the intermediary segments in the hierarchical system. Through powerful propaganda, now he passed instructions directly down to the bottom of society, and further destroyed the intermediary segments he no longer needed, using the bottom of society. People from the bottom of society experienced a short but delightful feeling of emancipation in this informal deconstruction of the state, history, culture and the old system of control.

Obviously, these highly ideologicalized mass movements were totally different from the highly planned mass movements prior to them. Previously, mass movements had been expressed in militarized and orderly collective actions; millions of people were systematically organized into groups, and were engaged cohesively in important tasks in the vast Chinese territory, such as "People's Communes", "the Great Leap Forward", "Up to the Mountains and Down to the Villages", "the Third Front Construction", etc., and anyone expressing a dissenting view would become the object of severe punishment in the name of class struggle. This mode of control that had originated in Russia relied mainly on an organizational network with a clearly demarcated hierarchy; the instructions from the top were passed down level by level via the Party and State apparatuses. However, in the "Cultural Revolution", the communication function of the Party and State apparatuses was replaced by propaganda media such as broadcasting, newspaper, printed tracts, badges, carved statues, etc. The *Selected Works of Mao Zedong* became the "Little Red Book", the Bible of Red China; its great success enabled Mao to earn thousands of millions of dollars. However, the "Little Red Book" did not offer a clear frame of reference about revolution; its unsystematic structure of quotations and its loose editing left room for different interpretations. There was a common scene in the Cultural Revolution: two sides engaged in the struggle lifting up the "Little Red Book" while each sticking to their own argument — the little red book was used as a weapon of discourse. However, this space within the discourse also became a space where insults, lies, rumours, and gossip raged, and made the "struggle by reasoning" that put the two parties in opposing positions turn into the "struggle by force" that ended with the two parties trying to kill each other. Previously, people's informal forces had been pulled together to resist foreign enemies; here, they were being used in continual infighting. Even Mao Zedong himself had not expected this level of out-of-control.

In his political fiction *Yellow Peril*, the scholar and writer Wang Lixiong describes an apocalyptic diaspora in China, a world disaster caused by the collapse of the country's superstructure. However, the chaos of the Cultural Revolution did not leave the country totally out of control, for the simple reason that the control force of the army had not been too shaken, despite the fact that Mao had tried to suppress the "hierarchical system" in the army. The centralized control of party, government and military power constituted the pillar that guaranteed that this vast country with a population of more than one billion would not go completely out of control; it was also the basic tenet that needed to "be adhered to, without changing for one hundred years".

1978 c.e. – 1997 c.e. [Shenzhen]
Armed Forces and Special Zones

Strict control or laissez-faire? Both Mao Zedong and his successor, Deng Xiaodong, experimented with this issue; however, the experimentation of the latter was more pragmatic.

If we compare the choices of Mao and Deng regarding the places to build a city, Mao nearly always chose relatively hidden hinterlands and mountainous areas, whereas Deng was inclined to choose outward-looking coastal areas; Mao's idea was always an action realized by the whole population in the entire territory of the country, whereas Deng was more cautious, and preferred to proceed step by step — he would first choose several places to test his idea, then judge the feasibility based on the result, and decide whether he could apply it to the whole country or not. Shenzhen was one of several test sites chosen by Deng Xiaodong. Its success made it become the most famous and the most exemplified Special Economic Zone (SEZ).

There was nothing accidental about Shenzhen's success; the geographical advantage it enjoyed by being located close to Hong Kong eclipsed other SEZs. However, it was also because of its proximity to the capitalist world that the Chinese Communist Party remained particularly vigilant with it. The strictly designed space of Shenzhen is the expression of the outcome of the combination of control and opening: it is a city located between two walls—"the first front" between the SEZ and Hong Kong and "the second front" between the SEZ and the interior; these two "fronts" were set up respectively by Mao Zedong in the 1950s and by Deng Xiaoping in the 1980s. In the early days, the first front was set up to ensure China's separation from the outer world; later, the second front was set up to allow for a relative opening of the first front to the outer world. Shenzhen became a transitional space. The huge economic gap between the interior and Hong Kong, as well as a preferential policy on custom duties that SEZs had, made Shenzhen spread into a long and narrow linear city extending along the border between Shenzhen and Hong Kong, looking towards Hong Kong, and resulted in prosperity between the first and the second fronts.

Shenzhen gradually developed from a small fishing village into China's largest and youngest immigrant city. Informal and spontaneous risk-taking was allowed here; it was regarded as part of the pioneer spirit of the SEZ, and was encouraged for this reason. However, the whole zone of Shenzhen was still under strict surveillance and control, in order to ensure that only "minor differences" existed within the "common ground". For two decades, in the 1980s and the 1990s, after the creation of the SEZ, people from the interior needed to hold a "border permit" to enter Shenzhen; they passed through the "second front" check-post guarded by the army and underwent border checks. Shenzhen became a "beleaguered city" of the new era, experiencing a free economy and the chaos that ensued between two well-guarded walls. Very quickly, the rapid emergence of this new town was accompanied by all sorts of decayed and corrupt capitalist byproducts: corrupt deals, smuggling and the sex industry. This original accumulative process that was "tainted with blood and dirty things" seriously shook the high-ranked Chinese government officials' faith in SEZs. In 1992, when the then-retired Deng Xiaoping paid an open inspection tour to southern China, he sent out a "do-not-throw-away-the-apple-because-of-the-core" message to the central policy-making body: "socialism or capitalism" is not the issue, "only development is the absolute principal"; the absolute control of military forces is the guarantee of the communist origin of SEZs. Consequently, the Shenzhen model was officially regarded as "Socialism with Chinese characteristics". In the same year, a large-scale portrait of Deng Xiaoping was set up in the most prominent place in the centre of Shenzhen. On the portrait, he was showing the Creator's love and looking at this city in the background that was entirely designed by his hand; above the city was written: "Adhere to the Party's basic line, and without changing for one hundred years".

The signals conveyed by Deng's investigation tour to southern China were soon taken up by the whole country, and one after another, almost every city started to build its own "small special zone": "developmental zones" supported by tax revenues. Ironically, in the same period, China's largest economic zone, Hainan, lost its strong position in an economic bubble created by the real estate market and became a failed experiment—a "rotten city" with thousands of square metres of unfinished building sites. However, the "Hainan Lesson" did not spread to the whole country like the "Shenzhen Experience" did. Obviously, when development zones were flourishing throughout the country, some cities became "little Shenzhens", while some others became "little Hainans". This showed the double-edged effect of an informal economy.

On 1 July 1997, the first garrison of the People's Liberation Army forces entered and stationed itself in Hong Kong. This colony previously governed by the British and Hong Kong government finally became a special administrative region under

China's policy of "one country, two systems", after one and a half centuries following the Opium War. Shenzhen-Hong Kong became a "twin city" made up of a Special Economic Zone (SEZ) and a Special Administrative Region (SAR). The change of sovereignty, as well as the reduction of the economic gap between Shenzhen and Hong Kong, the progressive spreading of "special zones / developmental zones" from the coast to the whole country, the emergence of the Pudong Developmental Zone, and China's deeper involvement in international affairs, were all factors in making Shenzhen enter a more open "post-SEZ" era. The simplification of the customs formalities between Hong Kong and Shenzhen, and between Shenzhen and the interior — the weakening of the "first front check-post" and "the second front check-post" shows that local experiments under severe surveillance and control are approaching their end. China, which is opening up in every direction, is now receiving and adopting a new means of control.

2001 C.E.-... [China]

Globalization and Communism

The value of Shenzhen's experiment does not lie in the creation of a new city, but in the invention of "Socialism with Chinese characteristics", which is the Communist model within a context of globalization. It is the product of Communist China facing the capitalist world: for Shenzhen, this context is mainly embodied in its geographical proximity to Hong Kong; whereas for China, it represents a world that is heading towards economic globalization. It is also the contemporary expression of "seeking common ground while allowing for minor differences": the variables that are likely to be brought by globalization can all be tackled as elements with "Chinese characteristics" and be taken into the constant of "socialism"; it combines firm domestic policies and flexible diplomacy, and enables China to take part in international affairs actively and in a more orderly and stable manner.

In September 2001, China concluded all bilateral negotiations with World Trade Organization (WTO) members, and officially put an end to its 15-year-long accession process that began in July 1986. This is the first time in history that the Chinese government had intervened in the world system with such an active and patient role. The final document on China's term of membership to the WTO is more than 800 pages long; the numerous elaborated treaties and commitments listed in this document represent the common consensus humanity has reached after experiencing various world wars in the last century: it is better to cooperate than compete, a win-win situation is better than killing each other, but with the condition that all parties must play by the rules of the game that they set up together. Now these rules have become the rules that Communist China voluntarily abides by. The centralized model of one-party rule is put into a diverse network of interests, where all parties are kept in check by each other; Communism is locked within the world economy. Communism uses the economic system's informal mechanism to constantly improve, to overcome its inherent inertia in the political system; it uses exterior forces to realize self-enforcement; and it uses economic revolution to realize political reform, while at the same time keeping the advantages of one-party rule regarding the avoidance of internal exhaustion and high governing performance.

The 65 years of communist China's history can be divided in two phases — the revolutionary phase and the reformist phase. In the former phase, all national resources were highly centralized, whereas in the latter phase they were redistributed throughout society. Every period of such redistribution — of land, housing, revenues and nationally owned resources — has proven to be a stimulus for reform in a serious historical crisis. The revolution that centralized power and turned private ownership into public ownership took place from above and very rapidly, whereas the reverse transformation that is turning public ownership into private is occurring only slowly. However, just as the former movement would not have found popular support without an authoritative revolutionary leader, the latter transformation could also collapse without strong reformers. The incremental progress of reform from Deng to Xi is both a democratic transition driven by strongmen and a complement to the strategy of fostering autonomous development.

15 years after joining the WTO, China is now close to qualifying for full market economy status. To achieve this end, China needs to complete its process of self-adjustment, which includes restructuring its economy and legal system. This process is being pushed by external forces, but it is also a result of improvements in the country's superstructure being driven by its rapidly developing economic base. In 2006, the government officially changed the term *Five Year Plan* to *Five Year Planning*. This one-word difference is indicative of the decision taken by the Chinese government to reposition itself within the market economy and to transform its quantitative control of the national market into a strategy of dynamic adjustment combining strategic deployment and macro-control as a means of adapting to a mutually inclusive global political and economic environment. At the same time, China's GDP has become the second-highest in the world, and the sense the country now has of its own strength is seeing the focus of government expanding beyond the national economy to include social, ecological and cultural issues. In the cases of ecology and social policy, a more active form of government is required, while the fields of the economy and culture would seem to require more passive government. How China manages to balance these seemingly contradictory demands will become evident over the coming decade.

FROM INFORMALITY
TO PARAMETRICISM AND
BACK AGAIN

Vyjayanthi Rao and Vineet Diwadkar [1]

Since being coined in the 1970s by anthropologist Keith Hart,[2] the concept of informality has referred to a diverse set of phenomena and practices operating at different scales. It has been used by scholars and institutions alike to characterize a range of heterogeneous practices. In fact, the distinction between "formal" and "informal" practices may be largely conceptual and impossible to identify empirically with any degree of precision. To invoke a metaphor from linguistic anthropology, the concept of informality is a shifter or a deictic category, highly mobile and applicable to a practice by means of locating it within a particular time-space configuration, simultaneously demarcating and locating the formal by contrast.

As a number of scholars have observed, so-called informal practices can be comprehensive, use institutions and rely upon non-state norms for regulation, implementation and valorization. This contradiction is specifically present in the idea of informal markets. Markets, by their very nature, presume the institutionalization of relations of trust required to complete market exchanges and transactions in the absence of contractual relations governed by judicial institutions. In the Indian context, the bazaar signifies such a pre-modern site of personalized exchange. A significant body of scholarly literature on the bazaar emphasizes kinship, caste, ethnic and religious community as dominant idioms of market organization. This historical and anthropological literature focuses on elaborating the textures of meanings that constitute market practices in order to discover organizational protocols rather than privileging the functional role of rational calculation by abstract, rights-bearing subjects engaging in exchange.[3]

Early use of the concept of informality such as in Hart's work on Ghana contrasts pre-colonial forms of organization and labour with emergent forms of governance in the post-colonial period of former colonial societies. In this context, informal activity exists in a continuum with post-colonial migrations of "traditional" populations into modernizing cities in Asia, Latin America and Africa. Informality thus also signifies pre-colonial cultural practices that continue to operate in modern urban centres. These cultural protocols and meanings are given form in spatial practices at odds with modern planning norms seeking to sanitize and cordon off space for specific uses. As a result, the proliferation of street vending and similar forms of occupation of public spaces, which are ubiquitous in most postcolonial cities, constitute concrete sites where "informal" practices become visible and targets for intervention by state authorities and other regulatory agents.

Work on markets as concrete sites and built environments has largely remained the domain of architects, for whom markets are directly connected to consumption

and the consummation of various forms of exchange and circulation, both material/
tangible and abstract/intangible.[4] Architectural writers provide the most powerful
and direct descriptions of what architecture does. As urban design and architectural
critic Michael Sorkin puts it, "All architecture distributes: mass, space, materials,
privilege, access, meaning, shelter, rights."[5] Thus, physical sites where markets are
performed are themselves forms of media, like money, through which exchange
is possible at least as a quasi-public act, with or without the sanction of the state.
Confronted with the abstraction of physical territory from analyses of government
and discipline and the emergence of abstractions like economy and society as an
object of governmentality, architectural discourses enter a contradictory terrain of
analysis when attempting to connect the physical to the political directly.

We suggest that the contemporary discourse on informality, as distinct from
earlier, postcolonial and culturally inflected understandings of informality, can
be located within this complex relation between the governance of populations
and that of territory. In addition, we suggest that the problem of locating informal
practices precisely is an artefact of dominant discourses of government and we ask
if an alternative, structural understanding of informality itself is possible. Here, we
are interested in moving beyond reifying informality as a "logic" that informs other
spheres such as practices of governing and planning. Instead, we are focusing on
the logic by which a set of practices is identified as informal and problematized. This
logic, we believe, is connected to the naturalization of the market as the dominant
mechanism for organizing governance and to the corresponding rise of uncertainty
as a problem for governance.

In her book on market expansion in Egypt, anthropologist Julia Elychar explains
how neoliberal governance offers micro-enterprise projects as solutions to intractable
problems of poverty as the state withdraws from welfare provision.[6] Under the tutelage
and advocacy of international organizations, micro-enterprises, deploying existing
networks amongst Egyptian craftsmen as "social capital", attempt to transform the
small-scale enterprises of traditional communities into new instruments of debt and
capital generation. The analysis of this type of "formalization" represents an important
step in the development of our understanding of how informality comes to be treated
as a "problem" for governance in the contemporary world. Following Elyachar, it
can be argued that such poverty-alleviation projects, which build on the social and
cultural networks of the poor, are one strategy for identifying and "formalizing"
networks otherwise outside the purview of the state in order to create and circulate
new forms of debt-based capital. Based on this example, we argue that informality
does not exist a priori as a logic to be discovered and codified by scholarship but
rather emerges as networks, structures and institutions whose relationship to the
state is an uncertain one — outside of existing laws of enterprise-formation, taxation
and spatial practice are "formalized" through a variety of interventions. In turn,
the logic of formalization, within which "informality" is identified and applied to a
variety of structures, spaces, networks and institutions, is intimately connected to
the rise of market paradigms and uncertainty in the practice of governance. Thus,
in contemporary discourse — in particular in relation to the question whether informality is treated as an instrument for the expansion of micro-enterprises and a

locus of debt formation or as an aesthetic problem — informal worlds are precisely those sites that demand intervention and ordering since they pose the threat of uncertainty to market-based governance. A key feature of such governance, in turn, is the existence of a knowable and governable "public" whose transactions can be measured and rewarded or punished as the case may be.[7]

The focus on informality, we argue, has shifted from identifying practices within a moral framework of modernization to identifying practices that threaten order and governability because they cannot be accurately measured and thus not valued according to standardized regimes of value associated with state-governed markets. Ambiguous notions of value in turn pose a threat to measured order and rules of valuation. In the physical space of informal markets dominated by consumers who are typically priced out of such state-governed and taxed markets, such practices range from the occupation of spaces reserved for other uses — such as pavements and bridges — to the sale of pirated or counterfeit goods and the proliferation of betting and gambling activities that often take place on the margins of these markets.

Sympathetic understandings of informal practices involving, for instance, land settlement, infrastructure provision, or the distribution of resources position these practices as filling gaps in availability by repurposing common resources, commandeering underutilized private resources or creating new methods of exchange.[8] Such practices then encounter regulatory and governmental interventions in a variety of ways.

In this essay, we focus on two major forms of intervention – representational interventions and regulatory interventions. Representational interventions are ones that posit these practices as disorderly, chaotic, anarchic, unruly and ungovernable. Corresponding to these representations are forms of governable subjectivity made possible by imagining society as a public collective of exchanging, contracting actors and a private sphere within which differences of belief and practice are contained. A second form of intervention involves bringing to bear new forms of regulation that price and fix the values of these practices within state-governed regimes of value and taxation. Both forms of intervention rely on aesthetic judgements about desirable order and desiring subjects. But the very need for such interventions on a global scale is itself tied to the emergence of the market as an abstract, ethico-political space and its ascendance as a natural mechanism for organizing governance in the post-World War II period.[9] In other words, regulatory interventions — whether spatio-legal regulation or regulations of abstract rights tied to the products of human labour — are themselves an artefact of the rise of the market as a mechanism for organizing governance.

In practical terms, some of the most visible interventions involve the production of desirable order and desirable forms of subjectivity through the design of space and commodities, largely based on the belief in the capacity of forms to determine systemic organization and behaviour.[10] Physical market sites — where the design of both commodities and space is highly visible and communicative — are therefore sites of intense contestation.

Crucially, formalizing processes that intervene in spaces and practices permissible within demarcated limits depend on the idea that informal practices are those that *cause* turbulence and volatility and introduce uncertainty within orderly spaces or

A LABOURER SORTS THROUGH WASTE IN THE DRAINED,
CONCRETE-WALLED 'RIVERBED' OF THE SABARMATI
RIVERFRONT DEVELOPMENT PROJECT, AHMEDABAD,
JANUARY 2014.

within systems of value-generation such as self-regulating markets driven by predictable processes of demand and supply. This representation of causality in turn has a genealogy related to the simultaneous emergence of the concepts of informality and the market as the natural site for organizing governance on a global scale. In his lectures at the College de France in the 1970s, Michel Foucault traces the rise of self-regulating markets as the natural site for organizing governance in his remarks on the Chicago School of Economics.[11] This form of governance in turn depended on gauging and valuing the uncertainty inherent in large, contract-based modern societies in terms of the rationality of the demands of heterogeneous populations with their own private beliefs and freedoms.

Thus, the rise of what we commonly understand as neoliberalism as a form of government has depended on constantly *regarding as suspicious* the practices of what Partha Chatterjee terms the "governed" and on the concurrent development of technologies for gauging different regimes of value and putting them in place through regulation and governance. Formal and informal then are the recto and verso of processes of governing value through a focus on eliminating uncertainty — the informal is not so much the *cause* of uncertainty in contemporary practices of democratic governance as a sign of anxiety about the unknown and the uncertain, about that which is absent, that which cannot be gauged, and a space for cultivating technologies for dealing with unknowability. Perhaps for this reason, informality is being applied to an ever-expanding and shifting universe of practices.

Our argument here is based on ethnographic research conducted in two cities in western India — Ahmedabad and Mumbai — where we have observed processes of urban spatial and social transformation over nearly a decade. While our research was focused broadly on the development, production and understandings of infrastructure, it included specific engagement with the development of trading infrastructure in cities marked by the violent and forced displacement of large numbers of vulnerable citizens and spatial redevelopment to accommodate real estate investment and new forms of urban organization. Our vantage point offers us a unique understanding of the ways in which processes are marked as "informal" and eliminated through displacement and enclosure into parametrically ordered spaces. New forms of enclosure and space-making are increasingly being guided by parametric logics and design practices the politics of which are complex and emergent.[12] Our use of "parametric" is specific, as is evident in our case studies. For us, parametric architecture refers to forms of architecture generated by algorithms and formulae that optimize the interaction between given and imposed parameters — such as the eviction and resettlement of residents from historically occupied settlements and the denomination of new forms of exchange value for land.

Ahmedabad

The Sabarmati riverbed has functioned as a civic and ecological *maidan*[13] commons throughout Ahmedabad's history, supporting the livelihoods of many launderers, cloth washers, dyers and printers, petty traders, carpenters and farmers.[14] Three generations ago, many poor families residing along the river grew melons and pumpkins there to sell in Ahmedabad's produce markets. However, by 2004, 18 highly polluting industries had made the river ecologically incapable of supporting crops.[15] Other labourers borrowed from low-interest banks to buy donkeys, seeking economic subsistence in the river's sand, which they would carry to nearby construction sites.[16] Access to this resource has since been cut off by the damming and flooding of the nine-kilometre stretch of the Sabarmati River that runs through Ahmedabad. Furthermore, the closing of the city's 64 textile mills resulted in lay-offs for the majority of Ahmedabad's workforce. It is estimated that 75–80 per cent of the city's working population, many of them women, depend on open markets and street vending as major sources of sustenance.[17] Many of Ahmedabad's poor have also settled along the river as a result of state-sponsored evictions and the subsequent denial of access to rehabilitation and relocation processes mandated by law.

The history of Ahmedabad's Gujari Bazaar includes many years of use of the riverbed as a commons, dispossession by the recent Sabarmati Riverfront Development Project (SRFDP) and the struggle of bazaar traders to participate in Ahmedabad's urban transformations. Founded by Ahmed Shah three years following the city's establishment in 1414 C.E., this lively market developed into a self-governed space for the weekly exchange of primary products among low-income residents in the region. Having first used the *maidan* in front of Bhadra Gate, the traders' association began leasing 2,600 square yards (2,170 square metres) of *maidan* on the Sabarmati River in 1954 for a mere 151 rupees per year.[18] The market was legendary for its capacity to furnish an entire lower-income family's home in just one visit. Up to 200,000 customers and 2,400 traders[19] met on any given Sunday, buying and selling, among other things, cooking utensils, clothes, furniture, books, hardware, electronics, antiques and handcarts. With women making up 40 per cent of traders, and another 40 per cent self-identifying as Dalit, the Gujari Bazaar has been representative of socially and economically progressive attitudes in Ahmedabad.[20]

Traders' co-dependence has provided stability throughout the city's history of communal riots. While Ahmed Shah originally organized the market to operate in accordance with the weekly call to prayer at the Jama Masjid, the traders' decision in 1944 to regulate themselves through the Ahmedabad Gujari Association prioritized economic over communal affiliation. The 600-year history of trader solidarity and cooperative dependence on customers and weekly access to the Sabarmati riverbed highlights the efficacy of this socio-spatial structure. With such relationships of material exchange, which were previously based in the city's commons, now being reconfigured as competitive binaries between communities — be they elite/poor, with/without land tenure, upper-caste/Dalit or Hindu/Muslim — the tipping points and consequences of social and economic exclusion are becoming increasingly violent.

A second strength of the Gujari Bazaar's socio-spatial structure was its openness: it could accommodate more than 1,000 ad-hoc traders each week, who set up in drier areas on wet days or sited themselves around other channels in the riverbed to provide seamless functionality within a monsoon-fed river landscape. By enclosing, policing and charging high rents for a section of the waterfront, the SRFDP abrogated the market's flexibility. The project's designers have expressed interest in replacing the self-organized petty trade of the Gujari Bazaar with a "world-class" conference

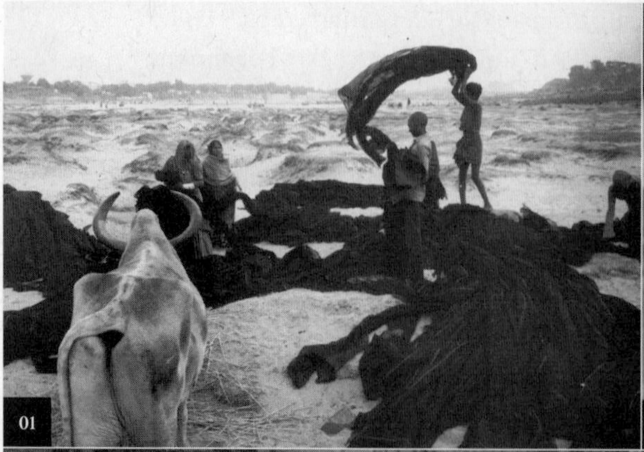

01

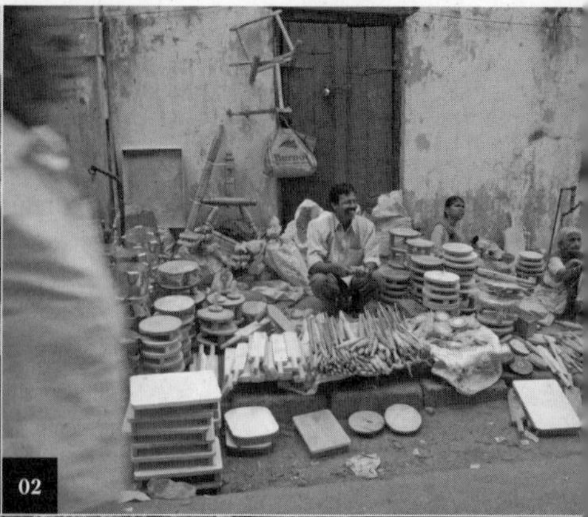

02

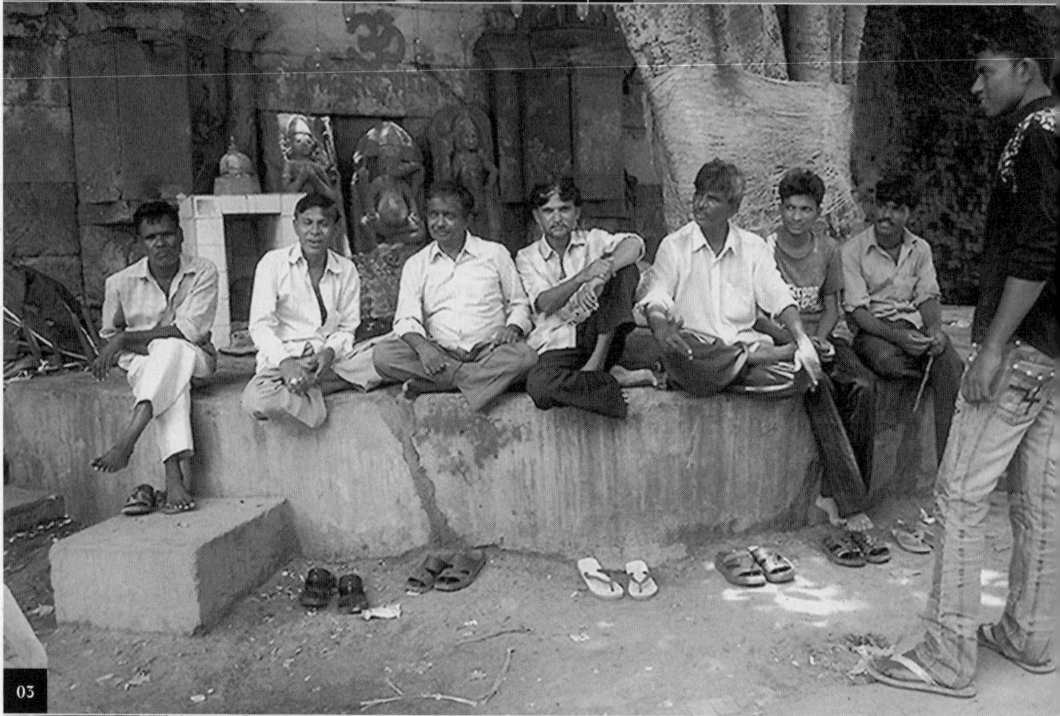

03

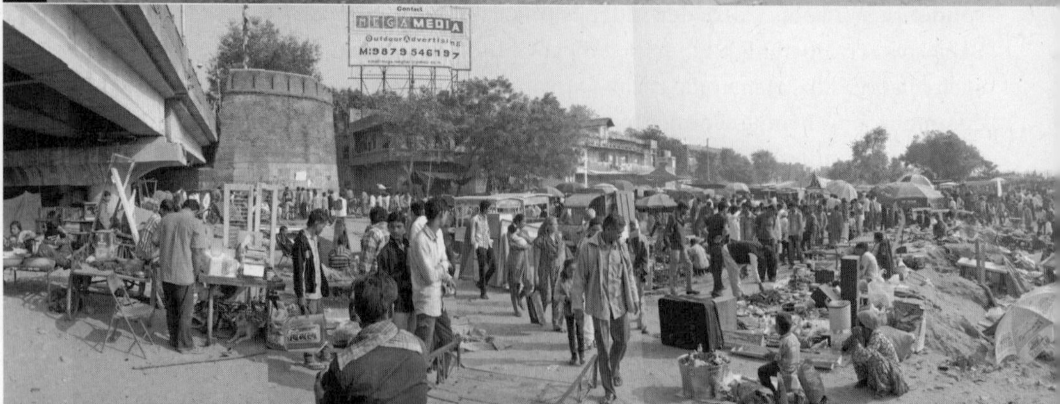

04

01 Henri Cartier-Bresson captured indigo dyers drying cotton in the Sabarmati riverbed in 1966.

02 A wooden utensils trader sets up between Ellis Bridge and Victoria Garden.

03 Men gather under the canopy of a sanctified tree, surrounded by idols and a plinth, below Ellis Bridge. The Gujari Bazaar extends, along the bridge's shade to the riverbed below.

04 Remains of the Gujari Bazaar in January 2014 following years of illegal demolitions by the Ahmedabad Corporation and the dumping of debris from the adjacent Sabarmati Riverfront Development Project. Trading continues despite dramatic topographical changes, a reduction by half in the occupiable area and the lack of a rehabilitation plan.

05–07 A boy sells roosters on the edge of the bazaar. Such illicit traders are not members of the traders' association and depend on access to the margins of exchange sites.

08 Families of hardware and knife traders have been associated with the Gujari Bazaar over multiple generations, living bearers of the city's 600-year-old cultural heritage.

FROM INFORMALITY TO PARAMETRICISM AND BACK AGAIN

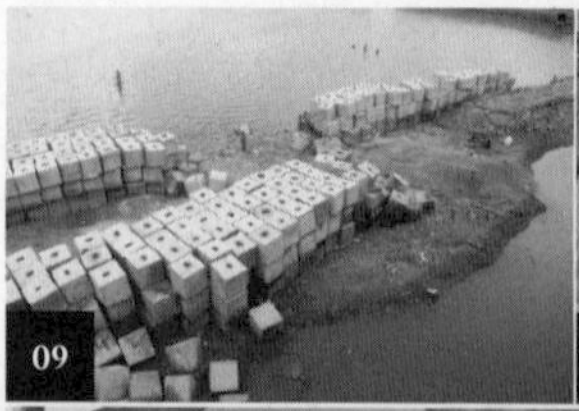

09

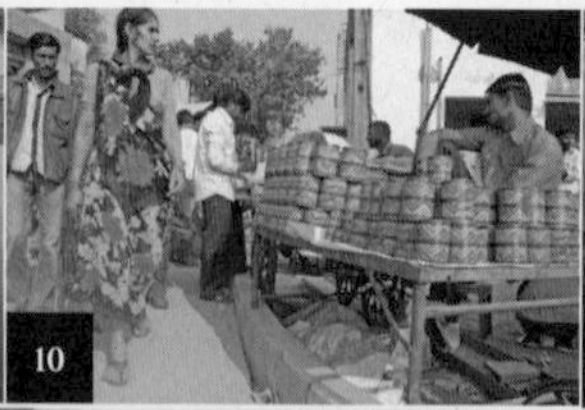

10

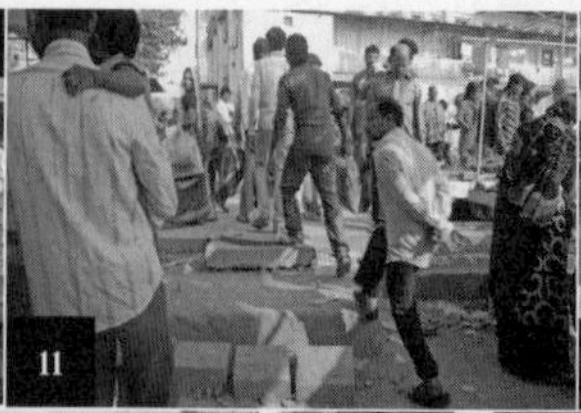

11

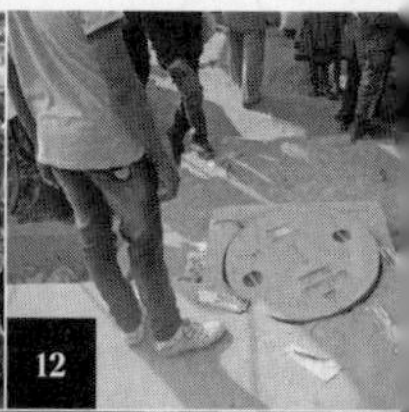

12

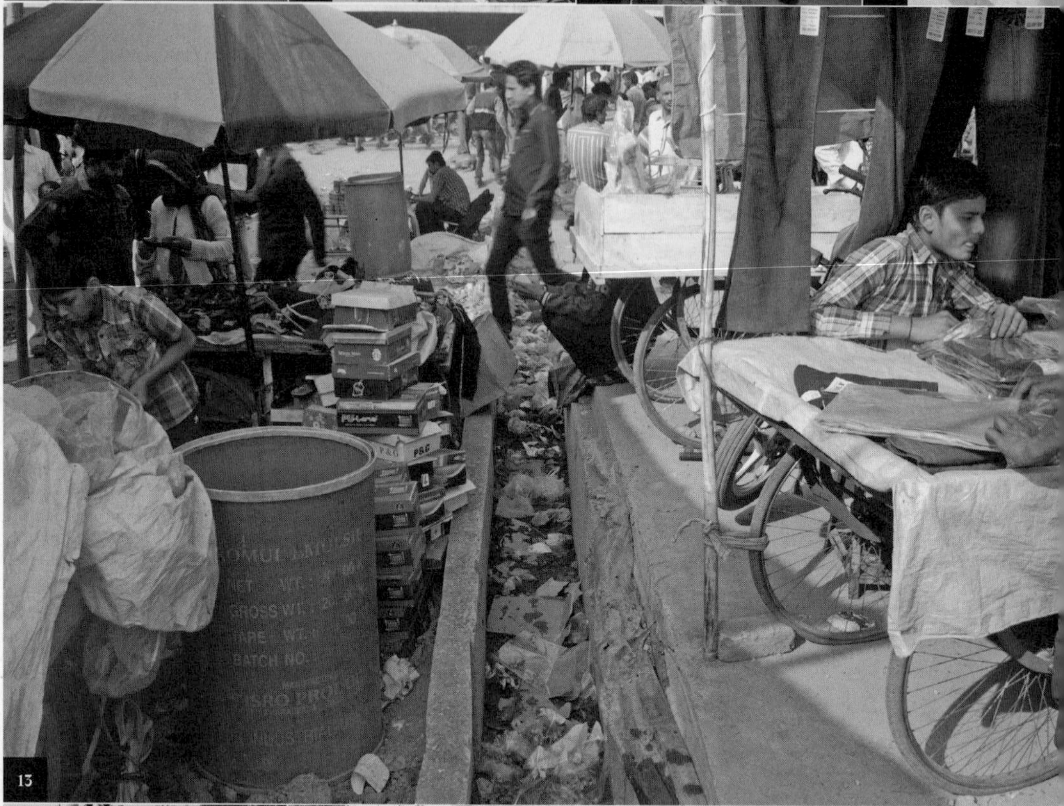

13

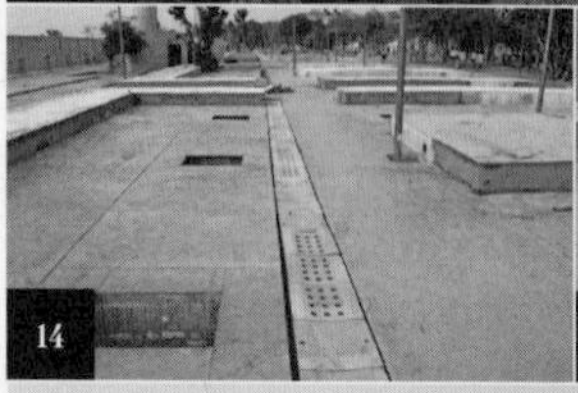

14

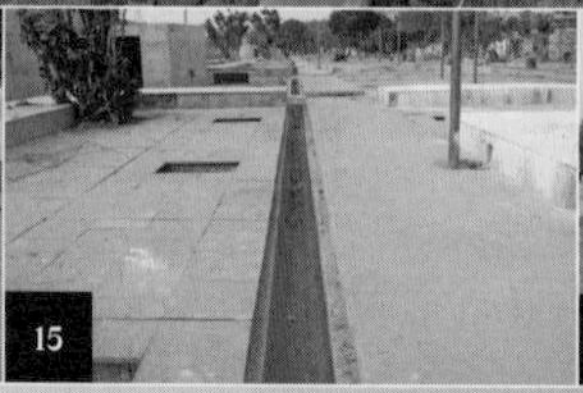

15

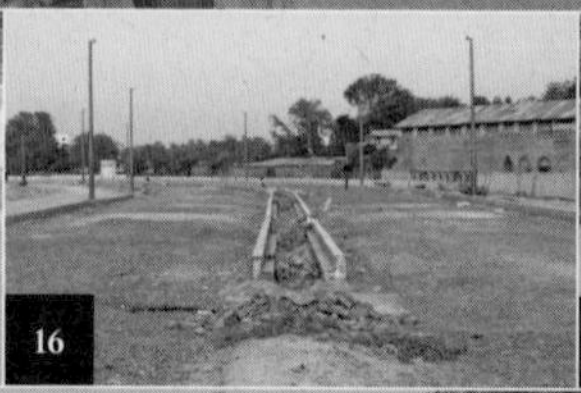

16

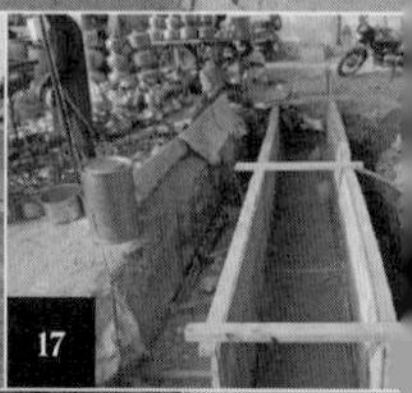

17

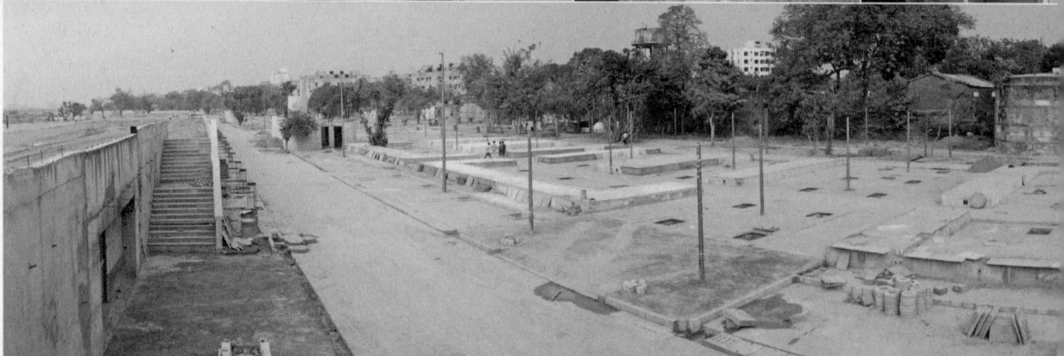

09-13 During construction activity connected with the Sabarmati Riverfront Development Project, materials were deliberately deposited and debris dumped on the site of the Gujari Bazaar to conform with an image that suggested the creation of a "world-class" urban environment. Prior to occupying the new market, which was only attained as a result of public interest litigation, traders continued to meet amidst ongoing construction activity.

14-17 High modernist design characterizes the construction of a convention centre and parking lots on the market site, rationalizing the riverbed and the governance of exchange activity occuring there.

18 The new site for the Gujari Bazaar during completion of construction in January 2013.

19-22 Traders organize on and around construction materials, selling durable and second-hand goods, books, clothing and tools to mostly working poor customers.

23, 24 Traders allot selling areas beneath Ellis Bridge during construction activity. Following completion of the Sabarmati Riverfront Development Project, they will not have access to the riverbed or its banks.

centre and antiques trade in a sanitized market in line with the self-image of those aspiring to be part of a world-class city.

Ahmedabad's administrators have interpreted informal uses of the commons as transgressive of their totalizing authority, confirming sociologist Amita Baviskar and geographer Vinay Gidwani's claim that the "destruction of common resources and the communities that depend on them is a long-standing outcome (some would argue prerequisite) of capitalist expansion" in India.[21] While this commodification of common resources is lauded as emancipatory for the imagined beneficiaries, this erasure of the commons devastates urban populations living with thin survival margins. The Sabarmati riverbed, along with Ahmedabad's streets, garbage dumps, open markets and other sites liminal to authority, has become an ecological and civic commons occupied by the working poor in resistance to their own dispossession.

The liberalization of India's economic policies that began in 1991 has seen Indian architects become central players in the homogenization of urban form as a means of projecting efficiency and competence in order to appeal to the investment of what architect Rahul Mehrotra describes as "impatient capital".[20] Economic liberalization has also catalyzed Ahmedabad's shift towards entrepreneurial urban governance,[23] giving rise to city imagineering practices including city branding, the staging of mega-events, and the construction of flagship urban projects to move discourse away from the blatant anti-Muslim rhetoric and violence of Hindutva politics and towards reassuring images of the state as generative of economic and developmental progress.[24] Implementation of these projects through the Jawaharlal Nehru National Urban Renewal Mission has encouraged Ahmedabad's administrators to evict slum dwellers in order to open up riverfront land to gentrification and associated speculation.[25] Through the seemingly irrefutable rhetoric of the sanitary, predictable and efficient modernization of Ahmedabad, a nexus of landowners, builders, designers and city administrators has profited tremendously while the non-compliant urban poor have been criminalized for pursuing survival practices in the face of state-imposed restrictions.[26] The spatial products of this gentrification mirror one another: on the one hand, they include infrastructure-intensive, gated enclaves with public spaces programmed for leisure and consumption and, on the other, peripheral relocation sites with minimal infrastructural services and lack of access to previous livelihood and community networks.[27] This trend toward entrepreneurial governance and its associated spatial products can be seen extending to other places in Gujarat as well as across metropolitan India.[28]

In 2010, the Ahmedabad Municipal Corporation began the illegal demolition of the Gujari Bazaar without providing notice or rehabilitation plans to the 1,400-strong traders' association, 1,000 ad-hoc traders, or the extended livelihood networks of craftsmen, daily-wage supply chain labourers and their collective family dependents. The traders' association responded by initiating the design of a rehabilitation plan for the market and drew on the support of faculty members, students and researchers from the Indian Institute of Management and National Institute of Design to present this community-based design process before the Gujarat High Court in order to demonstrate the feasibility of their inclusion in the design process and a technologically modernized form of trading activity. As a result, the association was able to halt demolition until the SRFDP design team could provide an in-situ rehabilitation plan. However, since the completion of construction and the recent occupancy of the modernized Gujari Bazaar in 2014, preliminary observations suggest that power within the traders association has been consolidated and that the organization of the market is also being shaped by the presence of several wholesale traders operating from the new market site. Those traders not absorbed by the new site and consolidated leadership still meet to sell their goods at the previous Ellis Bridge site, just north of the new parking lot planned for a new convention centre. For the traders at this ghost market, it is still an open question whether they will subject themselves to the terms of the shifts within the traders association, relocate elsewhere, or adopt other livelihoods altogether.

Mumbai

In sea-locked Mumbai, urban renewal policies[29] provide legal grounds for opening up land to different uses. In this process, it is people who form the currency of exchange as they are displaced from desired to less desired land, which results in a range of outcomes and experiences. A second form of exchange incentivizes actors with large amounts of capital at their disposal to take advantage of this transformation of land: the government-sanctioned transfer of development rights to profitable northern suburbs has generated a shadow economy around transfer certificates, in which powerbrokers such as politicians, real estate developers and criminals — who are often the same person — have the direct power of disposal over this transformative potential. In this pixelated economy of new buildings and internal spaces, the state and its big-capital beneficiaries utilize these land policies to employ spatial allotments as a means of dispossessing the poor of land, claiming it for other profit-seeking uses and forcing the poor into state-regulated "relocation and rehabilitation" housing.

Housing advocates lament the rationed and poor structural quality of such accommodation, which ranges from 225 to 270 square feet (21 to 25 square metres) in size. However substandard their previous living conditions were, people were able to incrementally extend their floor areas vertically to support livelihood and community-related activities and production. The administered parametricism of "rehabilitation" architecture dislocates people's autonomy with regard to their economies of space, replacing it with tenuous footholds in the city's administered classifications.

These spatial parametrics also scale upwards and outwards: from the 225-square-foot room into a double-loaded corridor with eleven units on each side, to a ground-plus-seven-storey building, to a parcel of land packed with buildings separated by 20-foot buffers. The provision of daylight, air circulation, and areas for play spaces, markets, and gatherings do not figure directly in policy algorithms. Residents now employ a different calculus, absorbing a range of activities into one 225-square-foot room, renting additional 225-square-foot rooms from others at market rates, re-appropriating ground plans in this new vertical geography, or seeking other means by which to fulfil their needs and desires. These emergent practices create infrastructures for living and market exchange in much the same way that such infrastructure is created in the slums of Mumbai. In our images, we document and explain some of these emergent practices that are attempting to subvert the totalitarian underpinnings

LALLUBHAI COMPOUND, MUMBAI, JULY 2013.

STRUCTURES & DRAINAGE
25 Residents in Lallubhai
Compound use concrete stepping
stones to bridge street-side water
pooling between dirt entry alleys
and higher elevation sections of
the asphalt street.

26 Residents in Panjrapole
Settlement use blue tarpaulin
as barriers to prevent water
from entering under doorways.

27 Residents relocated from
Panjrapole settlement to Lallubhai Compound modify their
225-square-foot allotments with
a marine plywood partition wall.

28, 30 Exterior curbs and raised
plinths divert monsoon rains
downslope to maintain dry
interior spaces.

29 Mobile petroleum-powered
water pumping units with hoses
drain water away from building
entryways in Lallubhai
Compound.

WATER SUPPLY
31, 33, 34 Residents of the Rafinagar
and Panjrapole settlements
gather water barrels for filling
during irregular visits by private
tankers. Tarpaulins hung from
roofs also harvest rainwater
during monsoon months.

32, 35 The ad-hoc above-ground
bundling of 50 mm water pipes acts
as a form of collective infrastructural planning. Traders and
pedestrians treat this surface
as part of a continuous terrain.

36, 37 Private water tankers fill
above-ground cisterns and collected
barrels. Residents use hoses and
jugs to distribute water through
the Rafinagar and Panjrapole
settlements.

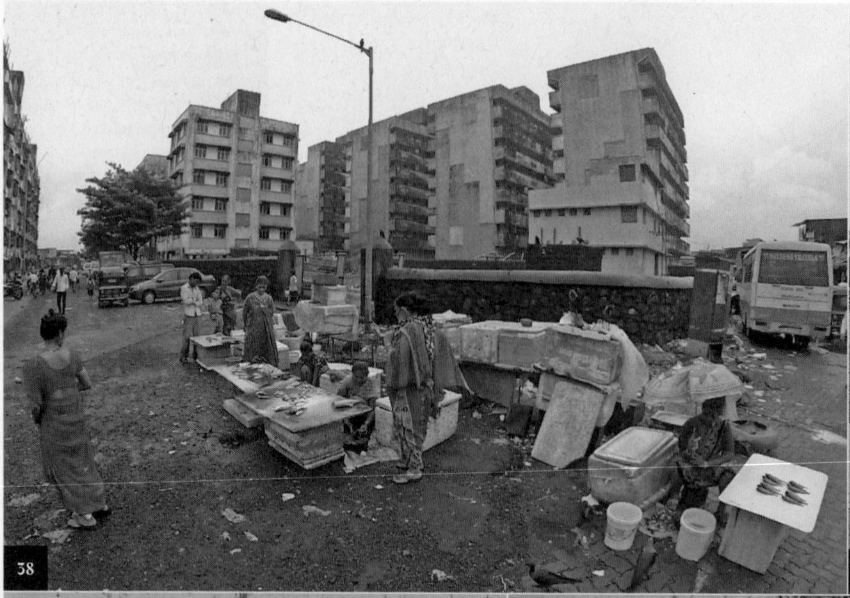

38

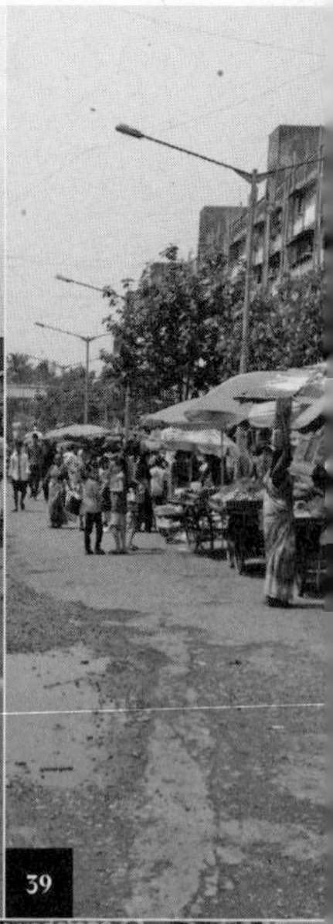

39

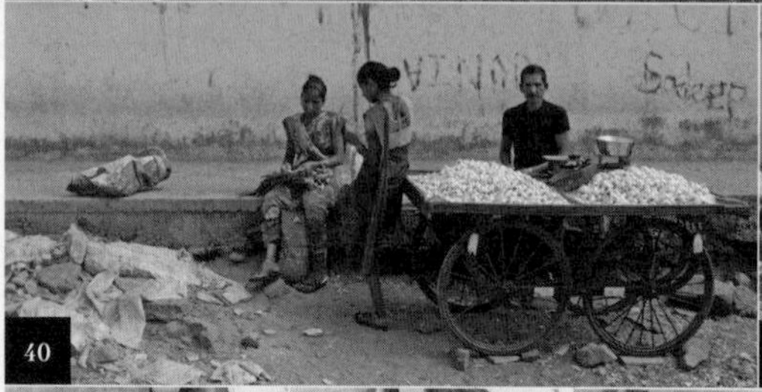

40

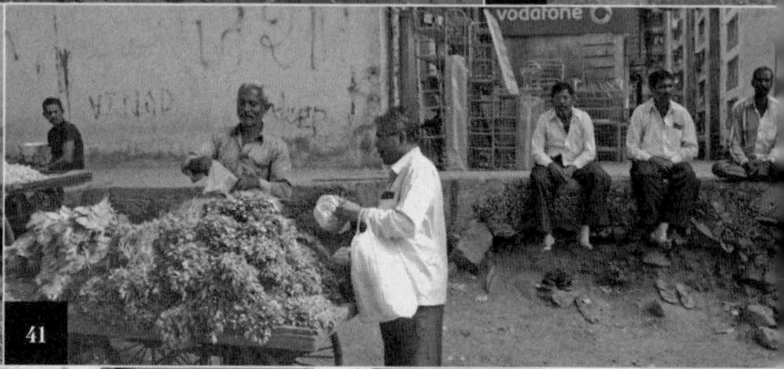

41

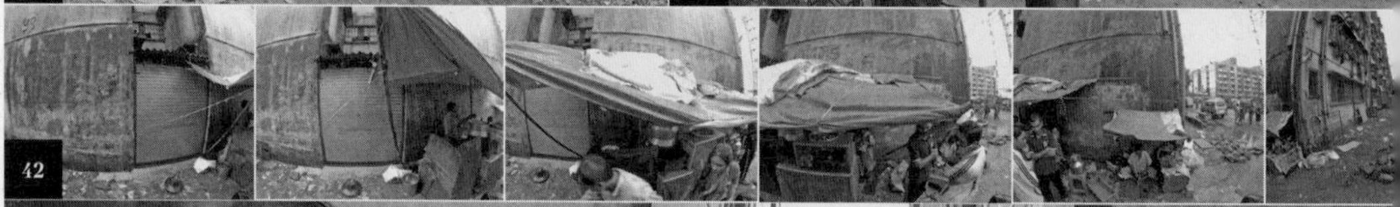

42

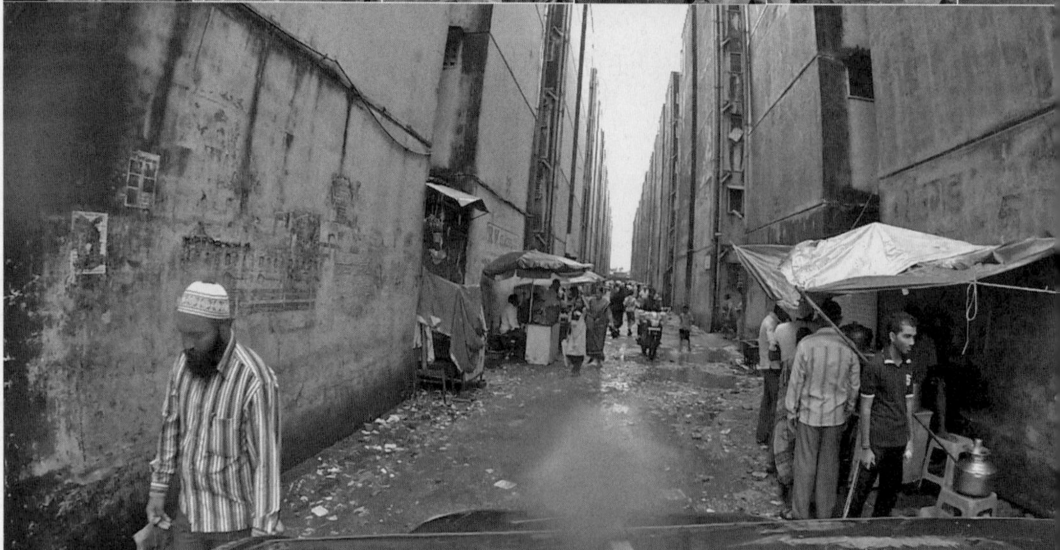

43

MARKET ACTIVITY

38 Without adequate space for trading activity, carts, coolers, crates and tarpaulin fill Lallubhai Compound's streets with produce, clothing and fish sellers.

39 Beach umbrellas both shade Sathenagar's vendors and advertise logos for real estate and cellular services.

40, 41 Traders in a Chandivali SRA project use building foundations as trading surfaces.

42, 43 Everyday markets for produce and tea stalls line Lallubhai Compound's 20-foot-wide access lanes.

MARKET ACTIVITY

44, 51, 52 Without adequate space for trading activity, carts, coolers, crates and tarpaulin fill Lallubhai Compound's streets for produce, clothing and fish sellers.

45 A small general supplies store and a flour mill are situated beneath the entry ramp to the elite residencies within the Imperial Towers, India's tallest residential buildings. The stores serve residents in the SRA component of the project who were relocated into adjacent 225-square-foot allotments.

46, 51 Some stalls and platforms are elevated above the level of monsoon flooding in the Lallubhai Compound.

47–50 Residents in a Chandivali SRA site construct stationary plywood and sheet metal trading stalls. These attach to existing buildings for storing and trading; others fit the depth of existing gutters and sidewalks. Some of these include real estate brokerages in addition to produce, clothing, hardware and stalls that provide a range of other services.

of these parametric architectures. New marketplaces occupy territories reserved for circulation and trade in everyday as well as "forbidden" goods — numerous real estate brokers' offices signify a vibrant marketplace for these "free" spatial allotments, which residents are legally prohibited from selling in the "free" market.

On a recent field trip, we interviewed traders occupying the main thoroughfare of the Lallubhai Compound in northeast Mumbai, where most of the images used in this essay were shot. Additional fieldwork was conducted in a settlement in northwest Mumbai. In our photo essay, we contrast conditions in the Lallubhai Resettlement Compound with those in Panjrapole, a typical "informal" settlement that was partially demolished to make way for the Eastern Freeway connecting northeast Mumbai with south Mumbai. Most residents from Panjrapole were moved to Lallubhai, which also houses many thousands of residents displaced from other parts of Mumbai after being evicted from sites taken over for transport projects by the Mumbai Metropolitan Region Development Authority (MMRDA). Lallubhai is one of several resettlement sites scattered across the city's northern suburbs and mainly constructed on the brownfield sites of former factory complexes such as the Lallubhai Aminchand industrial complex.

In Lallubhai, a daily vegetable and fish market is held on the edge of a street where it runs into a less developed tract that leads to a large slum settlement. On this edge, the liminal space where the road tapers off, vendors set up their stalls in the afternoons when parents typically go out to pick up their children from school. Many of the vendors come from outside the settlement and are prepared to move in and out as quickly as possible in order to give way to other uses of the space. Vendors pay off organizers who live in the settlement and the local police to maintain their spaces. Stalls are made of very light, generally plywood planks set up on plastic cans or four-wheeled hand carts, which allow for a hasty retreat from the street should the police show up. One visually striking element are the beach umbrellas used for shade from the unrelenting autumn sun. This already indicates a degree of confidence in the security of this spatial occupation, and the umbrellas feature logos of popular consumer brands and advertise services from real estate brokerage to mobile phone recharging.

Vendors' use of this street and some of the other wide-access streets within the Lallubhai Compound — streets that offer transport access and therefore attract a lot of foot traffic — has coded the space with a degree of predictability, since the markets are set up and dismantled in a fairly regular rhythm. More than a physical site, the market is a set of operations that captures potentials in space, not only for trade and commerce but also other activities. For example, one recent September afternoon, just before the state assembly elections, vendors packed up their stalls early to make way for a political rally. Moreover, a few days prior to this, the ad-hoc market site was doubling as a gathering place for public celebrations of major Hindu and Muslim religious festivals. However, interviews revealed the still ephemeral nature of relations between vendors, who are only tied together by their autonomous mobilization of contacts and networks from previous worlds. Unlike Gujari Bazaar, there is an impermanence to these non-contractual and ad-hoc market gatherings, where vendors may tacitly support each other against outside authority yet are not knitted together in the forms of association that one finds in large markets like

Gujari Bazaar, which cater to a large and heterogeneous group of consumers and where creating and maintaining the infrastructure for the market itself produces durable networks of solidarity.

Here, in the resettlement colonies, markets are fulfilling local needs while also functioning as points of convergence of the thin lines of attenuated networks that the displaced populations bring with them. Over time, as the density of adjacencies increases and changes, these tenuous markets may gain heft and become more permanently established. For now, their principal activity is to give form to exchanges that are not accounted for within the parameters of resettlement. For the residents who now find themselves on an urban periphery, cut off from transportation, the former lack of even basic market structures represented a significant deficit, one that completed their isolation.

Thus, in an ironic twist, spaces created to control informal development are proliferating market forms that trade on the uncertainties saturating these new forms — from uncertainties regarding the provision of goods not accounted for in planning to uncertainties about the fitness of residents to maintain and uphold these architectural forms.

Conclusion

Space and the forms used to shape it are inescapable — after all, the dimensions and desires of the body have a spatial character. "Informality" aspires to an infinitely flexible form that twins the affordances of the existing "ecology of the city"[30] with affordability in a highly unequal market economy. Such twinning has produced a stunning archive of forms, which are visible across the cities of India in which dispossessed communities have actualized occupation in places where there are explicit sanctions against human presence. Along the sides of major roadways, drainage canals, garbage dumps, dry riverbeds and hillsides new forms of occupation have proliferated throughout postcolonial India's urban history. With the emergence of market governance and the commodification of previously common resources for private use, a variety of strategies have emerged for dealing with this ecology of forms. We chose a comparative format, studying developments in two closely related cities specifically in order to highlight the diversity and historical specificity of "informal" situations and their transformations.

In a volume about informal markets, we chose to focus on how informality is brought into the world as a calculus for charting and dealing with uncertainty in the face of the rise of market governance. This calculus is formally played out at the many physical market sites explored in the *Informal Market Worlds* publications.[31] Numerous scholars are examining the emergence of new forms of selfhood developing at these sites where ambiguous legalities and hegemonic capital intersect and demand different kinds of performances from itinerant sellers and consumers.[32] If markets are fundamentally sites where economy and law intersect to iterate public and shared meanings, then we would suggest that they are also sites where the meaningful spatial practices and cultural performances of actors developed to establish concrete relationships to the abstractions of law and economy are *suspected* of exceeding and moving beyond these regulated iterations. In this dialectic of performance and suspicion, the logic of uncertainty that drives the market-based governance of publics as consumers becomes ever more acute.

Our essay focuses primarily on the parametrically embodied intentions of designers who have intervened in spaces deemed to be outcomes of informal and decentralized methods of infrastructure-making. These projects take highly diverse and contested "urban design ecologies"[33] as their ground zero and sanitize them through a seemingly irrefutable logic of necessity into a predictable set of forms that mirror similar attempts elsewhere. The geographies and ecologies that are being acted upon are themselves speculative ventures, combining elements with untapped potential to create unexpected connections with hegemonic forms of practice. They anticipate but also restlessly attempt to move beyond enumerated and monitored outcomes. In this type of speculative practice lies their potential threat to the purported hegemony of markets which rule and thrive by managing the potential uncertainty of practice. For progressive spatial practice, the "informal" is at best an impotent bridge from the primacy of material to that of exchange. What even progressive practice cannot capture is the ever-present generative potential of even pre-determined forms that arises fundamentally from exchange. Nowhere is this movement more sharply visible than in the formalizing markets of the post-colonial world.

1 This essay is based on collaborative visual and ethnographic investigations conducted by the two authors. Its theoretical framing draws on Vyjayanthi Rao's work on *The Speculative City*, a book manuscript that explores speculative spatial practices in the context of Mumbai's rapidly transforming and turbulent economic, policy and natural landscapes. The book frames speculation as a key analytic in understanding the ways in which people cultivate new forms of life, practice and selfhood to respond to the legal and economic regulations of late liberal market governance, which opens the space of the city to unpredictable and turbulent flows of investment, information and objects. Primary fieldwork in Mumbai was conducted by Rao between 2006 and 2012, and in 2013–14 visual research was conducted in collaboration with Vineet Diwadkar. Vineet Diwadkar's work as a designer and researcher in Ahmedabad forms the basis of our reading of the ways in which traders, city officials and technical design contractors participated in the eviction, contestation and eventual absorption of the Gujari Bazaar into the Sabarmati Riverfront Development Project. Primary fieldwork in Ahmedabad was conducted by Diwadkar between 2009 and 2014, during which time the city was dramatically transformed through large hydrological infrastructure and speculative real estate development projects.

2 Keith Hart, "Informal Income Opportunities and Urban Employment in Ghana," in *Third World Employment — Problems and Strategy: Selected Readings*, ed. Richard Jolly, Emanuel de Kadt, Hans Singer and Fiona Wilson (Harmondsworth: Penguin, 1973).

3 In her pioneering historical work on law, culture and market governance in colonial India, Ritu Birla summarizes this literature locating the bazaar within the formation of colonial knowledge about India. See Ritu Birla, *Stages of Capital: Law Culture and Market Governance in Late Colonial India* (Durham, NC and London: Duke University Press, 2009).

4 Despite the widely accepted "spatial turn" in the social sciences, the relationship between government and physical space specifically has a complex genealogy. For a detailed analysis of this genealogy, see Andrew Barry's essay "Lines of Communication

and Spaces of Rule." In it, he outlines Foucault's account of the emergence of forms of the modern State at the end of the eighteenth century. There was, according to Foucault, a break between a form of police state whose political rationality operated through architecture and new forms of political rationality whose concern was not territory but society. Barry writes: "At the centre of the concerns of the forms of political rationality that developed in the nineteenth century was not the city or the territory but *society*. The governmental State was no longer defined in relation to its physical territory, its surface area, but in relation to its social geography, its population and its economy." Andrew Barry, "Lines of Communication and Spaces of Rule," in *Foucault and Political Reason: Liberalism, neo-liberalism and rationalities of government*, ed. Andrew Barry, Thomas Osborne and Nikolas Rose (Chicago, IL: University of Chicago Press, 1996), 126.

5 Michael Sorkin, "Afterword: Architecture Without Capitalism," in *Architecture and Capitalism: 1845 to the Present*, ed. Peggy Deamer (New York: Routledge, 2014), 217.

6 Julia Elyachar, *Markets of Dispossession: NGOs, Economic Development, and the State in Cairo* (Durham, NC: Duke University Press, 2005).

7 Birla, *Stages of Capital.*

8 See Asef Bayat, *Life as Politics: How Ordinary People Change the Middle East* (Stanford, CA: Stanford University Press, 2010) and Ravi Sundaram, *Pirate Modernity: Delhi's Media Urbanism* (London and New York: Routledge, 2010).

9 See especially Timothy Mitchell's essay, "The Properties of Markets." Mitchell explores the boundary between formal and informal through an analysis of the boundary between activities that appear to exist outside the market. He writes: "The idea persists that capitalism has a boundary. There appears to be a limit, not just to particular markets but to the market in general. This limit is particularly significant in countries beyond the West, where large areas of material activity and resources seem to exist outside the formal boundaries of capitalism. The idea of a boundary between the capitalist and non-capitalist provides a common way not just to think about these kinds of countries but to diagnose their problems and design remedies." It is this

relationship between the formal and informal as separate but interactive spheres that informs the rationality of contemporary capitalism, as actors seek to both expand the sphere of the market while also maintaining a zone outside it as a potential lever for the reproduction of capital. Timothy Mitchell, "The Properties of Markets", in *Do Economists Maker Markets?: On the Performativity of Economics*, ed. Donald MacKenzie, Fabian Muniesa and Lucis Siu (Princeton, NJ: Princeton University Press, 2007), 244–275.

10 As an aside on the relation of form to process, we would point to an argument made by architectural critic Sanford Kwinter in an essay on architecture as a technique of formalization. Kwinter writes: "Our environment is being reworked in depth, no one denies this. Buildings, however, are not oases from history (unless explicitly and brutally organized to be so, and then at best only incompletely) but rather relays in a comprehensive cultural system of management, administration, and engineering of human affect and historical unfolding. Like the coils of an anaconda, loop after loop of the soft infrastructural mesh is drawn daily around us, not to crush, but merely to restrict expansion in unsanctioned directions, to guide movements subtly but uncompromisingly towards other ends." We bring this up here because our focus is on markets as built environments and thus on building as a technique of formalization.

11 Michel Foucault, *The Birth of Biopolitics: Lectures at the College de France 1978–1979* (New York: Picador, 2008) and *Security, Territory, Population: Lectures at the College de France 1977–1978* (New York: Picador, 2009).

12 See Keller Easterling, *Extrastatecraft: The Power of Infrastructure Space* (London and New York: Verso, 2014).

13 Landscape architect Anuradha Mathur characterizes the *maidan* as an accommodating grounds that is nomadic, collective and supporting of indeterminacy. See Anuradha Mathur, "Neither Wilderness nor Home: The Indian *Maidan*," in *Recovering Landscape: Essays in Contemporary Landscape Architecture*, ed. James Corner (New York: Princeton Architectural Press, 1999).

14 Achyut Yagnik and Suchitra Sheth, *Ahmedabad: From Royal City to Megacity* (New Delhi and New York: Penguin Books, 2011), 300.

15 United Nations Development Programme (UNDP), *Human Development Report 2004* (New York: UNDP, 2004).

16 Ela Ramesh Bhatt, *We Are Poor but So Many: The Story of Selfemployed Women in India* (Oxford and New York: Oxford University Press, 2006), 114.

17 Navdeep Mathur, "On the Sabarmati Riverfront: Urban Planning as Totalitarian Governance in Ahmedabad," *Economic & Political Weekly* 47, no.47–48 (2012): 65.

18 Shonali Vakil, *Gujari: A Concept of Contemporality* (thesis, Ahmedabad: National Institute of Design, 1995), 11.

19 The Ahmedabad Gujari Association has 1,400 member-traders, who were joined by between 1,000 and 1,200 ad-hoc traders each Sunday.

20 See Navdeep Mathur and Arpita Joshi, dir., *Global Sites, Local Lives* (film, Indian Institute of Management-Ahmedabad, 2009). Selling stainless steel cooking utensils and second-hand clothes, a number of women members of SEWA rely on the market as a vehicle of economic independence. See Vakil, *Gujari*.

21 Vinay Gidwani and Amita Baviskar, "Urban Commons," *Economic & Political Weekly* 46, no. 50 (2011): 43.

22 Rahul Mehrotra, *Architecture in India since 1990* (Mumbai: Pictor; Ostfildern: Hatje Cantz, 2011), 49.

23 Renu Desai, "Entrepreneurial Urbanism in the Time of Hindutva: City Imagineering, Place Marketing, and Citizenship in Ahmedabad," in *Urbanizing Citizenship: Contested Spaces in Indian Cities*, ed. Renu Desai and Romola Sanyal (Thousand Oaks, CA: Sage, 2012).

24 This strategy has continued in the wake of the 2002 riots, as indicated by Chief Minister Narendra Modi's statement on the *Vibrant Gujarat* website that the state is safe for investment and "with its all inclusive, sustainable and rapid growth, is emerging as a globally preferred place to live in and to do business." See Narendra Modi, *Vibrant Gujarat Summit 2013*, http://www.vibrantgujarat.com.

25 Renu Desai, "Governing the Urban Poor: Riverfront Development, Slum Resettlement and the Politics of Inclusion in Ahmedabad," *Economic & Political Weekly* 42, no. 2 (2012): 52.

26 Amita Baviskar, "What the Eye Does Not See: The Yamuna in the Imagination of Delhi," *Economic & Political Weekly* 46, no. 50 (2011): 53. Bimal Patel, director of the SRFDP, confirmed this nexus during a recorded public discussion, recognizing the design team's use of participatory rhetoric to obfuscate a refusal of actual participatory processes. See Bimal Patel, Navdeep Mathur and First Saturdays Meeting Group, "Dark Side of Planning: Riverfront Development of Ahmedabad," public discussion at First Saturday Meetings, St. Xavier's Social Service Society, Ahmedabad, India (January 2012) and Vineet Diwadkar, "Entrepreneurial Governance and the Ahmedabad Gujari Bazaar: Erasure of the Sabarmati River as Commons," *Revista Materia Arquitectura* 7 (2013): 69–79, 110–115.

27 Mathur, "On the Sabarmati Riverfront," 69.

28 See Charul Bharwada, and Vinay Mahajan, "Gujarat: Quiet Transfer of Commons," *Economic and Political Weekly* 41, no.4 (2006): 313. Gujarat's drive to modernize its wastelands has resulted in the transfer of wasteland commons — used for sustenance by the state's large nomadic population — to larger corporate enterprises, which will lease the land at prices beyond the nomads' reach.

29 Urban renewal policies include post–1991 Development Control Regulations, specifically DCR 33(7), DCR 33(9), DCR 33(10), DCR 33(11) and DCR 58.

30 Ecosystem scientist Stewart Pickett argues that designers need to understand the ecology *of* the city rather than ecology *in* the city as a basis for developing models and prototypes. He develops the idea from Aldo Rossi's call for a turn from investigating architecture *in* the city to investigating the architecture *of* the city. Stewart T. A. Pickett "Ecology of the City: A Perspective from Science," in *Urban Design Ecologies*, AD Reader, ed. Brian McGrath (Chichester: John Wiley & Sons, 2013).

31 See also the sister volume of this publication: Peter Mörtenböck and Helge Mooshammer, eds., *Informal Market Worlds Atlas* (Rotterdam: naio10 Publishers, 2015).

32 In an unpublished paper, sociologist Carlos Forment, writing about the Feria la Salada in Buenos Aires, remarks that participation in the market offered the residents of this impoverished neighbourhood the opportunity to cultivate the new forms of selfhood encouraged by neoliberal governmentality. He also remarks how, "in the course of negotiating with public officials, local residents gained for the first time in their lives a practical understanding of the way interpretive conflicts among groups in daily life, to borrow from Robert Cover, are constitutive of the 'Rule of Law." Carlos Forment, "Plebeian Neoliberalism and the Political Practices of the Ungoverned: Buenos Aires's La Salada and Emergent Forms of Subaltern Democratic Life," (paper presented at the Wenner-Gren Foundation for Anthropological Research Symposium 2013), 26. Similarly, Jordanna Matlon captures the emerging relationship between capital and masculinity in the practices of male street vendors in Abijan with the term "complicit masculinity", which entails specifically deploying practices of bypassing the state and its rule of law (see http://jordannamatlon.com/publications/ for her publications on the subject).

33 Brian McGrath, ed., *Urban Design Ecologies*, AD Reader (Chichester: John Wiley & Sons, 2013).

SPECULATIVE FUTURES: SOCIAL PRACTICE, COGNITIVE CAPITALISM AND/OR THE TRIUMPH OF CAPITAL

Matias Viegener

Artists have long been interested in the social and economic spheres, bringing their attention to focus on the everyday world, those ordinary things we need to survive, such as food, company, shelter and income.[1] Unlike them, art is not necessary though often much desired, thus creating a counterpoint to what we might call the ordinary. The questions of commodities and labour are often central here, both the labour to make and the labour required to buy the commodity, and then even the affective labour invested in the product, service, or indeed experience itself. This artwork is often overtly political, and even when it is not, it has a worldly "investment" that is at odds with a more aesthetic strain of art that reflects nothing other than its own formal qualities, a dialogue about materiality and aesthetics.

Much of this work today comes under the heading of social practice or sometimes participatory practice. It engages the audience in ways that undermine both the so-called autonomy of the art work and its basis as a commodity. Among the artists I will examine through this lens are Stephanie Syjuco,[2] the Institute for Figuring,[3] Martha Rosler,[4] and e-flux,[5] as well as a second grouping whose project involve the production of food, among them Fallen Fruit,[6] Oscar Murillo[7] and Superflex.[8] Each represents different forms of oppositional work that interrogates both the capitalist mode of production and inherited ideas of the art work. By deploying ordinary objects and alternative forms of exchange or gifting, their projects critique the basis of commodity capitalism and reflect upon the current circumstances of what might best be called cognitive capitalism.

The conjoined transformation of industrialization and photography in the nineteenth century initiated a crisis in art that impelled artists to make new claims about the work of art. Chief among them is the claim for autonomy, which originates in Kant's *Critique of Judgement* as the philosopher's argument for a form of art that serves no practical function, is devoid of purpose and thus free of instrumental value.[9] Taken up in the nineteenth century under the slogan of "art for art's sake", moving into Modernist formalism, it advocated the repression of referentiality and context beyond the context of art itself. It asks less what art is, as an object of value, than "what it *does*".[10] Art historians trace this lineage back to eighteenth century French salons and the onus placed on cultivating one's distinctive and autonomous taste, part of creating a bourgeois political subject. Later, there are Marxist and politically inflected concepts of autonomy that are instrumental to a degree, in that they designate

BROWN CHANEL, *THE COUNTERFEIT CROCHET PROJECT*,
STEPHANIE SYJUCO, 2006-ONGOING

art as a distinctive capacity, as a valuable practice that does something no other form (philosophy, religion, science, etc.) can do: help us understand the world — and perhaps begin to change it. Many of the artists I discuss here reject the former kind of autonomy in favour of the latter, creating work that makes interventions in a world moving into post-commodity capitalism.

Industrialization loosened the flow of commodities and was superseded in the twentieth century by Fordism, a term first coined by Antonio Gramsci in his *Prison Notebooks*. Henry Ford's strategy was to expand productivity by standardizing output, using conveyor-belt assembly lines, and breaking the work into smaller de-skilled tasks. With costs minimized and profits maximized, productivity and worker's salaries went up (in exchange, he says, for their putting up with the monotony and degradation of the work). Gramsci saw Fordism as a "rationalized" practice deriving "from an inherent necessity to achieve the organization of a planned economy [...] marking the passage from the old economic individualism to the planned economy".[11] He was the first to acknowledge the possibility that Fordism was a strategy that could also serve communism, seeing Fordism as the "ultimate stage" of the socialization of the forces of production.[12]

Elsewhere, Fordism is credited with creating the post-war boom in standards of living, economic equality and social justice, also called socialized or liberal capitalism. Much of the work I discuss here touches upon these questions in some form, as well as tracing the shift from a Fordist to a post-Fordist economy, with which each artist has a complex and nuanced relationship. Among their foci of the work are the shimmer of commodities and their afterlife, assembly lines, excess, trash, barter, gift economies, and especially intangible economies, which have to do with the growing immateriality of how we live, which brings with it a predominance of service labour, cognitive labour, and affective labour. This work asks how we get these desired (or unwanted) objects, where they go, what alternatives there might be, and what consequences both intangible and material arise from their passage.

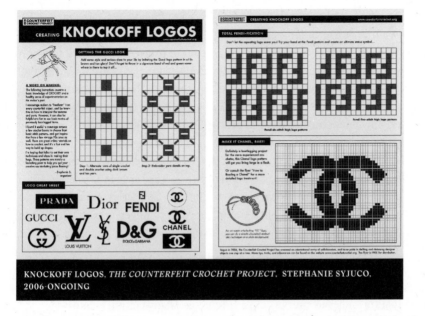

KNOCKOFF LOGOS, *THE COUNTERFEIT CROCHET PROJECT*, STEPHANIE SYJUCO, 2006-ONGOING

Much of it is tinged with a utopian impulse, the wish for new forms of art that make new forms of life possible.

***

Looking more like a store than a gallery, a brightly-lit window is filled with hand-made luxury handbags flashing cc's, f's and gg logos for brands such as Chanel, Fendi and Gucci. On closer sight, one sees they are all homemade, crocheted out of wool with meticulous but off-scale detailing. They are made through an ongoing participatory project by San Francisco-based artist Stephanie Syjuco in her *Counterfeit Crochet Project (Critique of a Political Economy)*, 2006–ongoing. When Syjuco launched a website to solicit participants to join her in hand-counterfeiting designer handbags in 2006, she attracted the attention of the craft community, in this case mostly women who crochet, which is considered the stepchild of the finer crafts of embroidery, needlepoint, and knitting. The handcrafted articles stage a collusion between high-end luxury items and humble domestic craftwork, and in their misfit quality, they radiate a strange kind of commodity fetishism behind which lurks a subtle perhaps anarchist critique. From afar they look quite conventional, especially when seen in a well-lit gallery window, but as one approaches them a certain cognitive dissonance arises. Presenting themselves as craft, they none-theless shimmer with consumer desire. Presented as luxury objects, they not only fall short of consumerist desire, but offer a subtle though sharp commentary of it.

The counterfeits play the line between naiveté and critique, never settling com-fortably at either. The care put into their creation echoes the kind of charismatic quality that luxuries exercise over consumers, but once their counterfeit nature becomes evident, the fetish is put into quotes, into a kind of suspension. Syjuco tips her hand with the project's parenthetical subtitle, *Critique of a Political Economy*, which is the subtitle of Marx's *Capital*. Presented in an art context, most often artist-run or alternative spaces, the work itself is not for sale; the pieces belong to the individual makers, who are free to enter into commerce with their works, presented of course as art or craft, not as brand-name originals. The critique may or may not be evident, based on the position of the viewer, but the act of provocation is hard to ignore.

The *Counterfeit Crochet Project* has been exhibited in the Philippines and Beijing, China, locations which add a particular resonance to the topic of both piracy and concepts of consumer luxury. The counterfeit is always a challenge to our material values: the appearance of things comes to supersede any concrete meaning, the ultimate manifestation of exchange over use value. It's not so much the appearance of luxury items as their signification of wealth and taste; the fetishism of the commodity is easy to read, but the operation of taste — a key term in aesthetics — is more complex. Syjuco situates this work through three axes, craft, commodity and art, and calls these articles (though I would also call them gestures or performances) counterfeits rather than piracy, referring to them as a kind of "jamming," a reference to culture jamming.

A tactic used by many anti-consumerist activists to disrupt advertising, consumerism and media culture, culture jamming is an attempt to expose systems of domination and even spur progressive change. Many culture jams are intended to provoke questionable political assumptions behind commercial culture, and its tactics include re-figuring logos, fashion statements, and product images as a means to challenge the idea of coolness in relation to assumptions about the actual "freedom" behind unfettered consumption. Culture jamming is a form of *subvertising*, related to the Situationist tactic of *détournement*. Naomi Klein speaks of the power behind branding to create the concept of lifestyle, rootless and consumerist in base; especially for young people caught in its embrace, it reflects not so much the absence of a literal space to occupy "so much as a deep craving for metaphorical space: release, escape, some kind of open-ended freedom".[13] This craving might be said to have found an outlet in the Occupy movement, which indeed was spurred by the Canadian activist group Adbusters, which describes itself as "a global network of artists, activists, writers, pranksters, students, educators and entrepreneurs who want to advance the new social activist movement of the information age".[14]

Art gallery itself is a site of strange commerce: Syjuco notes that one major component difference between the *Counterfeit Crochet Project* and an existing fashion structure is that there is no "store", since nothing — not even materials, instructions, patterns, nor finished products — is for sale. "This discrepancy is a purposeful and pivotal change in the structural model of production and consumption. The 'buyer' is essentially the crafter-producer, closing the loop on who has access to the means of production."[15] Syjuco also notes that the *Counterfeit Crochet Project* proposes a model of participation against that of temporary labour, of skill-sharing against management, and of cultural capital against wages.

Participatory crocheting also forms the basis for The Institute for Figuring's *Crochet Coral Reef*, (2005–ongoing) conceived of by Christine and Margaret Wertheim. This unique fusion of art, science, mathematics, handicraft and community practice may well be the largest community art project in the world. The vast majority of participants are women, recruited through the website and by word of mouth; most of them think of themselves as crafters more than artists, and even the Wertheims

TOXIC CORAL REEF (DETAIL). INSTITUTE FOR FIGURING. 2009

play with the designation by calling themselves an institute, an organizational body of research and study. The inspiration for making crochet reef forms began with the technique of "hyperbolic crochet" discovered in 1997 by Cornell University mathematician Dr. Daina Taimina. Initially experimenting with crochet as a way to express mathematical formulas of hyperbolic space, the Wertheim sisters adopted Taimina's techniques and elaborated upon them to develop a whole taxonomy of reef-life forms.

Loopy "kelps", fringed "anemones", crenelated "sea slugs", and curlicued "corals" have all been modelled with these methods. The basic process for making these forms is a simple pattern or algorithm, which on its own produces a mathematically pure shape, but by varying or mutating this algorithm, endless variations and permutations of shape and form can be produced. The crochet reef project became an on-going evolutionary experiment in which the worldwide community of Reefers brings into being an ever-evolving crochet "tree of life". As with Syjuco's counterfeit project, the participants own their work, except on the occasions that the IFF buys it; the work may enter the art market, or more likely become part of the non-profit Institute's archive. It is a distributed collaboration that forges a transnational consciousness of the power of whimsical representations to communicate the urgency of climate change.

The direct referent for the crochet reef is the endangered Great Barrier Reef, along the coast of Queensland, Australia, where the Wertheim sisters grew up. Originating in 2005, for the first four years of its life the reef took over their home, gradually expanding to become the dominant life-form in their house. At the same time the project began to expand into other cities and countries until it has become a worldwide movement that engages communities across the globe from Chicago, New York and London, to Melbourne, Dublin and Cape Town. As a totality, the *Crochet Coral Reef* has grown far beyond its original incarnation so that today it is made up

BLEACHED CORAL REEF, INSTITUTE FOR FIGURING, 2007

of many different "sub-reefs", each with its own colours and styling. Some of these are local, like the London reef, but others are thematic, including the Bleached Reef, the Beaded Reef, the Branched Anemone Garden, and the Kelp Garden. In addition to these delicate woollen reefs there's also a massive Toxic Reef crocheted from yarn and plastic trash — a part of the project that responds to the escalating problem of plastic trash that is inundating our oceans and choking marine life.

It is this last reef, made entirely of refuse and recycled plastics, that comments most on the global economy of waste as it feeds into climate crisis and environmental precarity. The Toxic Reef stages the relationship between coral reefs endangered by global warming and the Great Pacific Garbage Patch, a swirling gyre of mostly plastic garbage just north of the Hawaiian Archipelago. Estimates of its scale runs from the size of France to 20 times bigger, making it the largest repository of garbage in the world. Through craft, the Toxic Reef dramatizes the human role in global pollution as well as raising questions of value and global economy; if art fulfils the role of the sacred, trash represents the profane. "Detritus has ideological, social, political contexts and associations. Anyone forced to work with other people's garbage — from office cleaners to sewage workers — recognizes this."[16] Artists have been overtly combining the two since the 1950s, beginning with assemblage that re-uses found material that follows the model of artist as bricoleur, with a consciousness of how economies of wealth are always shadowed by excess, invisible labour, planned obsolescence, and waste — trash itself is an integral part of capitalist economies.

Mierle Laderman Ukeles, an early social practice artist who started working with New York City garbage men in the late 1970s, created installations and critical documentation of the role of trash and maintenance work which she calls "maintenance art". One can still draw a connection to Gramsci's optimism here, his certainty that the future lies with the "new man". The "humanity" and "spirituality" of artisan labour has been destroyed, but this is precisely the archaic "'humanism' that the new industrialism is fighting", so that the destruction of artisanal work and craft unionism is progressive. But the "deskilling" of labour does not turn the worker into Taylorism's notorious "trained gorilla". "Once the process of adaptation has been completed, what really happens is that the brain of the worker, far from being mummified, reaches a state of complete freedom."[17] Fordist forms of labour predominated through the 1970s, though they had begun its gradual eclipse, marked in the West by the triumph of Reaganism and Thatcherism.

***

For her first solo exhibition at The Museum of Modern Art in 2012, native New York artist Martha Rosler presented her *Meta-Monumental Garage Sale,* a large-scale version of the classic American garage sale, in which Museum visitors could browse and buy second-hand goods organized, displayed, and sold by Rosler herself, with dozens of assistants. The installation filled MOMA's Marron Atrium with unusual and everyday objects donated by the artist, the museum's staff, and the general public, creating a lively space for exchange between Rosler and her customers as they haggle over prices. The project also included a newspaper and an active website, and if customers agreed, they were photographed with their purchases. Pictures of them with their purchases were posted to the exhibition's photo stream on Flickr.

Unveiled in 2004, four years after the Tate Modern's Engine room, MOMA's atrium reflects museological trends toward outsize spectacles and entertainment park aesthetics. At four stories of precious space, the atrium has been criticized as both too corporate and too much like a shopping mall. Notoriously difficult to activate, Rosler filled the space with 14,000 pieces of well-organized junk. On the atrium's oversized walls was clothing of all types, from bras and panties arranged by colour, to T-shirts with feminist or anti-war slogans. If these held no appeal, there was Rosler's record collection, including such enduring favourites as Burl Ives's greatest hits and cast albums from the musicals *Kismet* and *Pajama Game.* There was a child-sized piano, a Macintosh Classic, stuffed animals, old pornography, and a yellowed, still-talking PeeWee Herman doll, watched over by an enormous U.S. flag suspended above, also for sale. You could take home a washing machine or a US$4,000 black Mercedes station wagon from the 1980s, with frayed upholstery and no engine because MOMA refused to have it on the floor; but delivery was offered neither through the artist nor the museum.

The *Meta-Monumental Garage Sale* at MOMA is a successor to a work originally held (as *Monumental Garage Sale*) in the art gallery of the University of California at San Diego in 1973. The work was advertised simultaneously as a garage sale in local newspapers and as an art event within the local art scene. A chalkboard on site bore the legend "Maybe the Garage Sale is a metaphor for the mind", and a slide show of a seemingly typical white family, bought at a local estate sale, played continuously while an audiotape loop offered a meditation on the role of commodities in suburban life. Held over eight times since then in museums in Vienna, Barcelona, Stockholm, London and elsewhere, the garage sale implicates visitors in face-to-face transactions within a secondary, informal cash economy — just like garage sales held far outside any art setting.

A sign at the entrance announced "everything clean, nothing guaranteed", and indeed MOMA required Rosler to fumigate the 14,000 items before the show, lest insects or fungi migrate upstairs into Picasso's "Demoiselles d'Avignon". In this flea

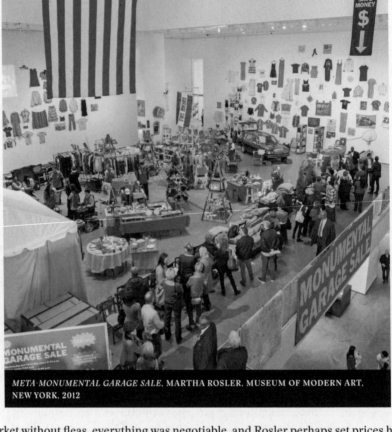

META-MONUMENTAL GARAGE SALE, MARTHA ROSLER, MUSEUM OF MODERN ART, NEW YORK, 2012

market without fleas, everything was negotiable, and Rosler perhaps set prices high to set the haggling process off with vigour. She was on site every day for two weeks, willing to let some things go at reasonably low prices, while fending off low bids for other, seemingly equivalent items. With money changing hands in plain sight, the art space becomes a transactional place, exposing not just consumerism but the re-valuation of formerly un-valued and unwanted things. "One of the main issues in an art gallery is value," said Rosler. "The price tags are not visible and yet you know they are there."[18] These two forms of value are juxtaposed, a dialogue between the sacred and the profane, highlighting a system that designates the same things as priceless art or junk. It is one legacy of Duchamp's readymade, but while his work is an argument around the autonomy of art, work such as Rosler's repositions ordinary objects in relation to the political economy of art and is lodged in a broad critique of social, cultural and economic values.

Before staging her first *Monumental Garage Sale* in 1973, Rosler "was struck by the strange nature" of local garage sales, "their informal economic status and self-centeredness, but also the way they implicated the community in the narrative of the residents' lives". Speaking to MOMA curator Sabine Breitwieser, Rosler states that her first sale was designed to create a space "where the question of worth and value, use and exchange, are both glaringly placed front and centre and completely represented and denied".[19] Rosler points out that the work originated during the oil shock of 1973, when gas rationing was imposed and the U.S. economy entered a recession and "stagflation" that led to the slow dismantling of the socialized liberal economy that had created the great prosperity of the post-war years. In 1973, alternative modes of economic exchange still held a degree of promise, but by 2012, they work in the shadow of a rampant neoliberal economy that has remade not only the forms of value, but those of labour.

While Rosler's garage sales echo older forms of mercantile exchange-based economies, a wave of time bank projects initiated by artists in the last decade investigate systems of exchange that do away with money entirely. My local *Time Bank*, the Echo Park branch, was founded in 2008, and it addresses both a real world and online community in which hours of service, help and expertise are exchanged on a purely equal basis. For example, I can trade an hour of revising your manuscript for an hour of John Doe's help in cleaning my garage. Time banking operates on principles of reciprocity, based on the proposition that everyone is an asset and deserves respect, that some work is beyond monetary price, and that social networks are necessary. It can be described as a form of social banking, and it is an exercise in radical equality: "Time Banking builds relationships by connecting untapped resources with unmet needs. Through reciprocity we celebrate that everyone has unique gifts to share."[20]

While time-based exchanges date back to the socialist movements of the early nineteenth century and were the subject of anarchist Peter Kropotkin's 1902 *Mutual Aid*, in the last decade they have permeated art world discourse. Julieta Aranda and Anton Vidokle of e-flux created their *Time/Bank* in 2010, though their website stresses that it was conceived of as much as two years earlier, betraying a bit of authorship anxiety attached to a rather anarchic project. Their "currency" is designed by no less than conceptual artist Lawrence Weiner, a kind of name "brand", and it can be exchanged for other currencies, biological time, ideas, services, and commodities.

Though originally conceived of as a social exchange of services, Aranda and Vidokle's provocation is to include the commodity of art in the purview of the time bank and to train their focus on the "creative class". *Time/Bank* was preceded by e-flux's 2008 *Pawnshop*, which placed over 60 artist's works in a pawnshop just as the financial crisis began. Artists in financial need were given cash in exchange for their work, which if not retrieved after 30 days was available for purchase. Two contradictory models of value collide, transforming a holding pen for pawned objects into a gallery space. "A pawnshop is a stage where merchandise and money dance in a choreography that could have them circle back and cancel each other out, but in fact rarely does. What better place to question how the value of the artwork and the worth of money might be set, and reset."[21]

Aranda and Vidokle insist that the basis of *Time/Bank* is not barter. Their hope was to create "an immaterial currency and a parallel microeconomy for the cultural community, one that is not geographically bound, and that will create a sense of worth for many of the exchanges that already take place within our field—particularly those that do not produce commodities and often escape the structures that validate only certain forms of exchange as significant or profitable".[22] They evoke a kind of distributive justice, a socially just allocation of goods in a society. Envisioning an alternative economy not bounded in space but still measured in time, their desire is both utopian and pragmatic, seeking to validate intellectual or art work that primarily produces discourse or ideas. It follows along Deleuzian lines, wherein artists create affects, pre-personal "intensities", and percepts, in Deleuze's words, "an aggregate of perceptions and sensations that outlive those who experience them".[23] Percepts are blocks of space-time independent of their perceivers, packets of sensations and relations, a way of expressing the intangibles that contemporary artists produce. Either of these may have material qualities, including that of language, but their power is in a kind of dematerialization.

At the core of these many artists's projects is an investigation of the transformation to a post-Fordist economy in which recombinant capital, ventures not specifically engaged in production but in hyper-accelerated financial flow, the extraction of money from capital, is in a kind of alliance or exploitive relation with cognitive and precarious labour. This "cognitariat" are workers whose main production is knowledge, such as artists, programmers, scientists, lawyers and teachers; Franco "Bifo" Berardi defines cognitive labour as "the kind of activity that generates semiotic flows and generates wealth, surplus value and capital in the semiotic field through a semiotic diffusion of merchandise and of goods".[24] Italian Marxist Antonio Negri argues that the originality of cognitive capitalism consists in capturing the innovative elements that produce value, and hence "capitalist development and the capitalist creation of value are based more and more on the concept of social capture of value itself".[25]

The recourse to immateriality in the work of this group of artists does not just simply parallel the transformations of capitalism but is often a strategic critical commentary on it. They examine a transformation of labour as it has been understood for the last 200 years gradually being displaced as the primary generator of value and capital. The "dematerialization" of the art object as traced by Lucy Lippard from 1966 to 1972 reckons with conceptual art, earthworks, minimalism, maintenance art, and early performance art, working between the two poles of art as idea and art as action. "In the first case, matter is denied, as sensation has been turned into concept; in the second case, matter has been transformed into energy and time-motion."[26] In other words, matter is either transformed (i.e. energized) into performance art or abstracted into a concept. Lippard strategically deploys the words of conceptual artist Sol LeWitt: "When an artist uses a conceptual form of art, it means that all the planning and decisions are made beforehand and the execution is a perfunctory affair. The idea becomes the machine that makes the art."[27] While many of these pieces were originally not for sale or conceived of to circumvent commodification, they were being bought and sold within five years of their creation, proving in a sense the determining power of the market.

Following up their highly influential analysis of late capitalism in *Empire*, Marxist theorists Hardt and Negri brilliantly trace the trend toward the prevalence of immaterial production in their 2009 work, *Commonwealth*. Intangibles such as information, knowledge, affects, codes, images, and social relationships, for example, are coming to outweigh material commodities or the material aspects of commodities in the capitalist valorization process. This does not mean that the production of material goods, such as automobiles and steel, is disappearing or even declining, but rather that their value is increasingly dependent on and subordinated to immaterial factors and goods. "The forms of labor that produce these immaterial goods (or the immaterial aspects of material goods) can be called colloquially the labor of the head and heart, including forms of service work, affective labour, and cognitive labour, although we should not be misled by these conventional synecdoches: cognitive and affective labour is not isolated to specific organs but engages the entire body and mind together. Even when the products are immaterial, in other words, the act of producing remains both corporeal and intellectual. What is common to these different forms of labor, once we abstract from their concrete differences, is best expressed by their biopolitical character."[28] Hardt and Negri develop the concept of biopolitics to describe forms of resistance to capitalism, using life and bodies as weapons of escape from economic domination, from practical interventions such as barter economies to the tragic extremes of suicide terrorism.

***

Fallen Fruit, a collaboration founded in 2004 by artists David Burns, Austin Young and myself, began by working within our own Los Angeles neighbourhood to map and deploy the fruit found growing in or over its public space — often overlooked and gone to waste, a form of urban trash. The first maps were a way to interrogate land use in Los Angeles, with an urban ecology devoted primarily to ornamentation rather than production. How could the vast amounts of fruit growing in public space be activated as a public resource, and indeed be deployed to create a new, utopian kinds of publics? In 2006 we began an ongoing series of *Public Fruit Jams* that invite the general public to join us in making jam together, mostly in an art space rather than a community space — the setting of an artists space allowed the event to take on a speculative and playful air. Fallen Fruit brings street-picked fruit and participants often bring home-grown fruit, but no one is turned away, nor is there ever an admission charge. Groups that arrive together are asked to separate and sit with strangers, and the collective jam making proceeds slightly anarchically, deprived of recipes.

Working along a general formula, the participants must negotiate which fruits to use and this negotiation provides the nucleus of a prolonged social interaction. If one participant brought figs, and another lemons and lavender, the outcome might be fig-lemon jam with lavender. As Fallen Fruit claims no expertise, communal knowledge-sharing initiates a set of social bonds that cross generations, races, and cultural differences. The talk often turns to the neighbourhoods where the fruit has been picked: what grows where, what once grew, and what might grow. "The subject of place is always related to migration and of course food: Americans move an average of every five years. The event becomes a forum on how we live, eat, and use space that is neither theoretical nor abstract: everyone is an expert on the taste of a banana."[29] Fruit becomes a neutral way to talk about ethnicity and also ecology, the conditions of heterogeneous and often gentrifying urban neighbourhoods.

The different jams produced at the event are often traded by the participants before they are taken home, and Fallen Fruit has spoken of the jams as the "by-product or even side effect of the basic social experiment this work engages in". While the collaboration has produced many images, graphics, videos, sculptural objects and installations, Fallen Fruit cites the *Public Fruit Jam* as "a key template of [their] collaboration".[30] The emphasis on social relations displaces the market economy

PUBLIC FRUIT JAM (DOCUMENTATION), FALLEN FRUIT, 2008

through barter and shared labour, with echoes of premodern and pre-mercantile communitarianism. While there is no exchange of money (the events are funded either through grants or art institutions), there is an exchange of labour — both physical (the making of jam) and affective (the building of community). Money is hidden, concealed within the greater apparatus of the art world economy, in which affective labour is transformed into immaterial commodities; the system of grants (a genial form of venture capital), and even more importantly the way artists build their "portfolios" to increase their future investment value.

Food and gardening form the basis of a great many social practices, with diverse examples such as the Bitter Melon Council, Fritz Haeg's *Edible Estates*, and Amy Franceschini's *Futurefarmers*. Chicago-based artist Michael Rakowitz,[31] who couples ethnic cuisine with political awareness, says "Cooking is like building".[32] His project *Enemy Kitchen* began in 2004 by preparing and eating shared meals based on the recipes of his Iraqi-Jewish mother. The conversations that occur over the course of preparing the foods are a core of Rakowitz's practice, but getting to that moment can be "really stressful". Chicago has one of the largest Iraqi expatriate communities in the United States, and the Enemy Kitchen was deployed on a food truck, with local Iraqis as cooks and Iraq war veterans as their assistance and servers. The project creates a forum for Americans to engage with both Iraqis and Iraq war veterans, who they might otherwise never meet, and the food truck's mobility brings the conversation to the street.

Amy Franceschini's *Victory Garden* project[33] in San Francisco provides a striking contrast, enlisting residents to plant back- and front-yard edible landscapes and providing workshops and tours of participating gardens. Franceschini, a founder of the collaborative group *Futurefarmers*, created a demonstration Victory Garden in front of City Hall in 2006 in conjunction with San Francisco's Museum of Modern Art. The highly successful programme has since become an ongoing, city-funded initiative and a model for other urban agriculture projects around the United States. Franceschini declared it "a victory of self-reliance, independence from the industrial food system, and community involvement", and describes the impact of the project

PUBLIC FRUIT JAM JAR. **FALLEN FRUIT**

in even broader terms. "It addresses the disconnection we have with everything we consume," she explains. "It's a point of initiation to a deeper connection with food. As soon as people started farming and realizing how difficult it was, a lot of other questions unfolded."[34]

Rirkrit Tiravanija's famous food installations of the 1990s often took the form of stages or rooms for sharing meals, cooking, reading or playing music; architecture or structures for living and socializing are a core element in his work. In his best-known series, begun with *Pad Thai* (1990) at the Paula Allen Gallery in New York, he rejected traditional art objects altogether and instead cooked and served food for exhibition visitors, asking nothing more of them but their engagement. Tiravanija's work forms one of the core examples of what curator Nicholas Bourriaud called relational aesthetics, "a set of artistic practices which take as their theoretical and practical point of departure the whole of human relations and their social context, rather than an independent and private space".[35]

The artist is viewed as a kind of "catalyst" in relational art, and Bourriaud appropriates the language of the 1990s Internet boom to describe the work's operations, deploying terms such as interactivity, user-friendliness, and DIY (do-it-yourself); in later statements, he defines relational aesthetics as addressing work that originate in the changing mental space opened by the Internet. But "if relational art produces human relations," asks Claire Bishop, Bourriaud's most prominent critic, "the next logical question to ask is what types of relations are being produced, for whom, and why?"[36] She argues that "the relations set up by relational aesthetics are not intrinsically democratic, as Bourriaud suggests, since they rest too comfortably within an ideal of subjectivity as whole and of community as immanent togetherness".[37] They often erase the antagonisms and contradictions inherent in the modern world, creating simple and palatable solutions to intractable problems.

How do artists such as Tiravanija make money? Like many artists whose work resists immediate commodification, his work is supported primarily through museum and gallery commissions as well as a secondary "line" of multiples and ephemera connected with exhibitions. Since the early 1990s, Tiravanija has published multiples in the form of backpacks, cooking utensils, and maps. These commonplace objects serve as tokens or signifiers of the artist's earlier projects and might also stimulate new interactions, whether actual or conceptual. Similarly, Fallen Fruit has issued editioned wallpapers, videos and prints and un-editioned "Everyday Objects" such as cutting boards, knives and wooden spoons emblazoned with quotations from their work. The invisible aspect of social practice art making is the accrual of cultural capital, a concept originated by sociologist Pierre Bourdieu: valorized forms of knowledge or fluency, and especially forms of institutional validation, of which the most abstracted is reputation or fame. This has little concrete value but can be monetized in terms of high paying positions and opportunities, or simply derivatives, the way bloggers or YouTube celebrities sell advertising space or generate publicity for others: an attention economy in which page hits are often monetized into income streams.

***

The work I have discussed here has been part of a paradigmatic shift over the last 50 years in both the art world and the broader world as reflected in how people live their everyday late capitalism. My penultimate example is the most recent one, artist Oscar Murillo's seven week participatory installation, *A Mercantile Novel,* recreating a candy assembly line from a factory in his family's hometown in La Paila, Colombia in late spring of 2014. Murillo brought 13 Colombian factory workers to work an eight-hour assembly line making chocolate-covered marshmallows in a blue-chip New York gallery. The space was divided roughly in half by industrial shelves housing palettes of candy-making supplies, and through the cracks the workers and the visitors can spy each other "at work". Visitors were encouraged to participate by eating the Chocmelos®, packaged three in a silver foil bag designed by Murillo with a stylized Colombina logo and a yellow smiley face. They were urged to take extra bags, share them with friends around the city and elsewhere, and to post pictures of themselves eating the candies on Twitter, Instagram, and the show's own website, *mercantilenovel.com*.

The exhibition's press release stresses how Murillo frequently invokes his cultural heritage in his practice and "broader issues of migration, sub-localities, and displacement inform many of his works. By turning the gallery into an operational production site, he opens up considerations not merely about trade and globalization, but also about individual relationships and communities, roots and immigration." But contact between the producers and consumers of the candy were minimum, and the only time visitors could enter the "factory" section was when the workers were on break; the separation was for hygiene and sanitation, but added to the mysterious quality of the installation.

The work's true participants might better said to be the 13 workers, most of whom had never left Colombia before and all of whom were visiting the United States for the first time. Murillo asked the workers to video-record their trip, as if to signify that they were the ones investigating New York and not the other way around. They were housed in comfort in Crown Heights, given special tours through the city, paid equitably for their labour, taught English two days a week, and ate lunch every Friday with the very fashionable New York gallery employees. Their presence seems to exalt labour and offer us analogies to art making itself, a celebration of disappearing Fordist labour tailor made to fit some of Claire Bishop's stinging critiques: contradictions are erased in the name of universalism and reconciliation. The press release reads as a near-parody of social practice statements: "As such, the Colombina factory becomes a catalyst for a consideration of socio-economic conditions in the United States, Colombia, and beyond, while also inviting visitors to reflect on the nature of societies, both personal and universal."

Despite the uncritical tone of the exhibition, we might take at face value Murillo's statements that the generations of his family who had worked at Colombina's factory in La Paila, including his parents, were treated fairly and were grateful for the security of their employment. The work rings with optimism, from the sparkling assembly line to the twinkling candies, a faithful reproduction of the originals, made with equipment imported from Colombia along with the workers. Visitors hear and smell their labour, but have no sense of the labourers since they are allowed into the production area only when the workers are on break. Likewise, the artist is mostly absent, almost occupying the space of a factory owner or a representative of benign corporate power such as Colombina, a multinational corporation doing business in 49 countries, which supported Murillo's exhibition and promoted it on their website.

Murillo himself embodies a triumph of class mobility, the son of two working class Colombians who immigrated to London when he was ten years old. He was barely finished with his masters from the Royal College of Art before his paintings started to sell; now at age 28 and dubbed "the next Basquiat", his record sale is already at US$400,000. Murillo is primarily known for his large, scribbly, minimalist graffiti-like canvases, often painted with a broomstick, mixing dirt into the paint, and containing enigmatic single words in English or Spanish like "yoga" and "bingo," with many of them foods such as "milk", "burrito", or "mango". Lest we think participatory pieces such as *A Mercantile Novel* are a ploy for some kind of street credibility, Murillo points out that installations and performances have always been present in his work, from yoga-based events to parties in Paris at which Colombian foods were served. The summer of 2012 at the Serpentine Gallery in London saw *The Cleaners' Late Summer Party with Comme des Garçons*, in which the artist (who himself had worked as a janitor in commercial galleries) invited all the janitors to dance with the art world, with dance competitions and raffles. The designer brand, as Murillo says, "which is usually very exclusive, became a democratized item".[38]

Rising in sixteenth century Europe through geographic exploration of foreign lands by merchant traders, mercantilism was a system of trade for profit, although commodities were still largely produced by pre-industrial production methods. Most scholars consider the era of mercantilism as the origin of modern capitalism, having paved the way for imperialism, and nation states. The title of *A Mercantile Novel* is misfit, since what is essentially celebrated here is an idealized version of Fordism, with its flexible joining of capitalist and socialist paradigms.

A MERCANTILE NOVEL, OSCAR MURILLO, 2014

This nostalgia is also countered by a raw display of art marketing: collectors could buy one of the gleaming crates stocked with one shift's worth of the candies for US$50,000. On one wall was a huge blown-up photo of Murillo's mother in her Colombina work uniform, head down, seemingly exhausted from her labour — losing her job in the mid-1990s prompted the family's move to London. On a stainless-steel shelf below the photo were a row of boxes of Jeff Koons–branded Dom Pérignon, with different sketches by Murillo of the Venus of Willendorf, an ancient fertility totem, each one hand drawn on copies of his mother's employment file. These are strangely broken up glass vases filled with melted Chocmelos, a seeming tribute to labour, candies, luxury, and fertility.

The aesthetic chaos (or at best eclecticism) here might turn us back to my original question of the role of social practice in relation to both commercial art making and to the activism at the heart of its origins. Murillo's work demonstrates how easily this kind of work can enter into the commercial gallery system, and how any form of resistance, such as simply giving things away, can be co-opted to simply sell a product. David Zwirner's gallery has been a pioneer in this sense; already in 2007 Rirkrit Tiravanija recreated his 1990 *Pad Thai* for the delectation of the New York blue-chip art scene. Both artists' "social" work is available to collectors in limited editions, much like the seemingly uncommodifiable conceptual art of the 1960s. Lawrence Weiner originally claimed that "Once you know about a work of mine you own it. There's no way I can climb inside somebody's head and remove it."[39] Now his works are bought and sold through certificates of ownership that permit the owner to re-create the physical work; that instantiation would have to be destroyed if its certificate is sold — rather like a financial security represents a share of a corporation. Collectors accrue social capital in showing how non-materialistic their taste is, refined to the purity of an idea. They can buy an idea that subverts buying and selling.

MERCANTILE NOVEL (PREVIEW), OSCAR MURILLO, 2014

***

My final counter-example is the Superflex collective's work, *Guaraná Power* (2003–ongoing), a soft drink created in collaboration with guaraná farmers cooperatives from Maués in the Brazilian Amazon. The farmers had begun to organize themselves in response to a cartel of multinational corporations, PepsiCo and AmBev (owned by Anheuser-Busch), whose monopoly had driven the price paid to farmers for the rich-in-caffeine guaraná seeds down by 80 per cent, while the cost of their finished guaraná sodas to the consumer has risen. As local guaraná sodas, once a regional specialty, were bought out one-by-one by PepsiCo or Ambev, the farmers in the Brazilian Amazon were obstructed from starting small competing guaraná soda brands by the multinationals. In collaboration with Superflex, they created a new brand and marketing campaign, which among other means promoted itself through the facilities of the art field — galleries, exhibitions and biennials.

The intention of *Guaraná Power* is to use global brands and their strategies as raw material for a counter-economy, reclaiming the original use of Maués guaraná as a local drink, not just a symbol of multinational economic domination. *Guaraná Power*'s original packaging pirates and *détourns* that of Guaraná Antarctica, a formerly regional brand of guaraná soda since bought by AmBev, with "for energy and empowerment" written on the neck. Superflex calls work such as *Guaraná Power* "projects for tools" which are not the fixed property of the artists, a museum or an art buyer: they only come into existence when they are used by people. As participatory practices become increasingly institutionalized and marketed, Superflex's work stands foremost in the arena of activism. Their practice is grounded in the faith of a counter-economy against neoliberal capitalism, and has always had an uneasy relationship with the superstructure of the art world. *Guaraná Power* was pulled from the São Paolo biennial by its president, who cited it as possibly upsetting "third parties". After the multinationals started legal proceedings against the artists and farmers for trademark infringement, Superflex had to redesign the brand, but it remains on the market today.

GUARANÁ POWER, SUPERFLEX

The tools that Superflex designs are adaptable, nomadic and slippery, resisting capital, rather than cohabiting with it, as does Oscar Murillo. They are pirated "supercopies". The brand name is a raw material that is culture jammed, much like Stephanie Syjuco's counterfeits, or even Fallen Fruit's *Public Fruit Jam*. Rosler's use of cast-offs, Ukeles' deployment of garbage and Institute for Figuring's *Crochet Coral Reef détourn* abjected materials into social commentary. It is noteworthy that the social practice work I have discussed here takes as its subject things which are generally marginalized from the commercial art world, such as food, rubbish, knit work, money, and luxury goods. While these subjects are addressed, they are more rightly appropriated as social forms that place art in the service of the social. All of them convert forms of potential financial exchange, or its derivatives, such as waste, into social exchanges that turn consumers of art into participants and collaborators in the work.

After facing resistance and now acceptance in the art world, social practice is currently at a crossroads. Though it doesn't claim autonomy in the modernist sense, the critical autonomy it has achieved seems easily erodible. Not only is it increasingly entering the commercial gallery system, it has also relied extensively on social media, without which it could arguably have never developed. It relies heavily on volunteers (termed "participants") and unpaid affective labour, such as Facebook, bloggers, Pinterest, Twitter, etc., where the attention economy of both posters and readers is monetized as their labour is peppered with ads to generate income streams. Artists must address not just issues such as labour that is temporary, nomadic and precarious, but the turn from industrial or Fordist capitalism to what many commentators call cognitive capitalism. Here, "the accumulation process is centered on immaterial assets utilizing immaterial or digital labor processes and production of symbolic goods and experiences".[40] These socio-economic changes have ushered in through the Internet as platform and new web 2.0 technologies that have impacted the mode of production and the nature of labour. If indeed artists aim to practice an emancipatory politics that places human freedom at its centre, they need to re-examine their practices along three axes. The first is that of pleasure vs. labour, in which most forms of pleasure are monetized and many forms of labour unpaid. The second axis is the commodity vs. service, in which artists increasingly create services and experiences rather than commodities, services that often create value for institutions rather than artists. And finally, we come to the contest between neoliberalism and the forms of social democracy that it seems to be vanquishing globally. Much of this work idealizes utopian forms of social democracy without coming to terms with its imminent disappearance: a future in which no one is paid enough, if at all, and money accumulates ever more disproportionately in the hands of the 1%. Peddling fantastic and unattainable utopias will do nothing to stop it.

***

1   Michel De Certeau, *The Practice of Everyday Life*, translated by Steven Rendall (Berkeley, CA: University of California Press, 1984).

2   Stephanie Syjuco, www.stephaniesyjuco.com.

3   The Institute for Figuring, www.theiff.org.

4   Martha Rosler, www.moma.org/interactives/exhibitions/2012/garagesale/.

5   e-flux, "Time/Bank," http://e-flux.com/timebank/about.

6   Fallen Fruit, www.fallenfruit.org.

7   Oscar Murillo, "A Mercantile Novel," press release, http://www.davidzwirner.com/exhibition/a-mercantile-novel/?view=-press-release.

8   Superflex, www.superflex.net/tools/guarana_power.

9   Immanuel Kant, *Critique of Judgement*, translated by James Creed Meredith (Oxford: Oxford University Press, 2009).

10 Casey Haskins, "Kant and the Autonomy of Art," *The Journal of Aesthetics and Art Criticism* 47, no. 1 (Winter 1989): 43.

11 Antonio Gramsci, *Selections from the Prison Notebooks*, edited and translated by Quinton Hoare & Geoffrey Nowell Smith (New York: New International Publishers, 1971), 279.

12 Ibid., 280.

13 Naomi Klein, *No Logo: No Space, No Choice, No Jobs* (New York: Picador, 2001), 81.

14 Adbusters, www.adbusters.org.

15 Stephanie Syjuco, "Tactical Refashionings: The Counterfeit Crochet Project (Critique of a Political Economy)," (unpublished text, 2013, emailed to author, 2 July 2014), 3.

16 Gillian Whitely, *Junk: Art and Politics of Trash* (London: I.B. Tauris, 2011).

17 Gramsci, *Selections from the Prison Notebooks*, 309.

18 Martha Rosler and Michael Arcega, "Martha Rosler and Michael Arcega in Conversation at the ISCP," *Musee Magazine*, New York, 15 October 2012, http://museemagazine.com/culture/reviews/review-martha-rosler-and-michael-arcega-in-conversation-at-the-iscp/.

19 Martha Rosler with Sabine Breitwieser, "In Conversation," MOMA, 2012, http://www.moma.org/interactives/exhibitions/2012/garagesale/qa.

20 Echo Park Time Bank, http://www.asntb.com.

21 Julieta Aranda, Liz Linden and Anton Vidokle, "Pawnshop," 25 September 2007, http://www.e-flux.com/announcements/pawnshop/.

22 Julieta Aranda and Anton Vidokle, "About time banking," nd, http://e-flux.com/timebank/about.

23 Pierre-Andre Boutang, dir., "I as in Idea," in *Deleuze from A to Z*, DVD (Los Angeles, CA: Semiotext(e), 2011).

24 Franco Berardi, "Market-Ideology, Semiocapitalism and the Digital Cognitariat," in *Public Netbase: Non Stop Future, New Practices in Art and Media*, ed. Branka Ćurčić & Zoran Pantelić (Frankfurt am Main: Revolver — Archiv für aktuelle Kunst, 2008), http://nonstop-future.org/txt?tid=57c26a6cc2bae24a2e-71c3f8a3da5ca4.

25 Antonio Negri, *Reflections on Empire* (Cambridge: Polity Press, 2008), 64.

26 Lucy Lippard, *Six Years: The Dematerialization of the Art Object from 1966 to 1972* (Berkeley and Los Angeles, CA: University of California Press, reprint edition, 1997), 43.

27 Sol LeWitt, "Paragraphs on Conceptual Art," re-printed from *Artforum* 5, no. 10 (June 1967), in *Sol LeWitt: Critical Texts*, ed. Adachiara Zevi (Rome: I Libri di Aeluo, 1994), 78.

28 Michael Hardt and Antonio Negri, *Commonwealth* (Cambridge, MA: Belknap Press, Harvard University, 2009), 132.

29 Fallen Fruit, "How to Have a Public Fruit Jam," in *A Guidebook to Alternative Nows*, ed. Amber Hickey (Los Angeles, CA: Journal of Aesthetics and Politics Press, 2012), 35.

30 Ibid.

31 Michael Rakowitz, http://michaelrakowitz.com/projects/enemy-kitchen/.

32 Nicole Carruth, "Food Hazards: Artists Dish on Working With Food," *Public Art Review* 23, no. 2, #46 (July 2012): 1, http://forecastpublicart.org/public-art-review/2012/08/food-hazards/.

33 Amy Franceschini (Futurefarmers), "Victory Gardens 2007+," http://www.futurefarmers.com/victorygardens/people.html.

34 Joseph Hart, "Art for Eat's Sake," *Public Art Review* 23, no. 2, #46 (July 2012): 3, http://forecastpublicart.org/public-art-review/2012/08/art-for-eats-sake/.

35 Nicolas Bourriaud, *Relational Aesthetics* (Dijon: Les presses du réel, 1998), 113.

36 Claire Bishop, "Antagonism and Relational Aesthetics," *October* 110 (2004): 65.

37 Ibid., 67.

38 Ermanno Rivetti, "Interview with Oscar Murillo: At Home with the Rubells," *The Art Newspaper*, 6 December 2012, http://theartnewspaper.com/articles/Interview-with-Oscar-Murillo-at-home-with-the-Rubells/28110.

39 Corinne Robins, *The Pluralist Era: American Art, 1968–81* (New York: Harper & Collins (Icon Editions), 1984), 29.

40 Michael A. Peters and Ergin Bulut, *Cognitive Capitalism, Education and the Question of Digital Labor* (New York: Peter Lang, 2011), xxv.

PART III CHANGING PRACTICES

CHANGING PRACTICES: ENGAGING INFORMAL PUBLIC DEMANDS

Teddy Cruz and Fonna Forman[1]

Zones of Conflict: Laboratories for Changing Practices

Border Zones as Sites of Intervention

In the last years, we have been investigating critical issues of urbanization and citizenship that emerge from observing the many communities that flank the U.S.-Mexico border. The Tijuana-San Diego border has served as our laboratory from which to rethink current politics of surveillance, immigration and labour, the polarization of informal and formal systems of urbanization and the widening gap between wealth and poverty.

The political specificity of this bi-national region has been our point of entry into other radical localities, distributed across the continents, arguing that some of the most relevant projects and new practices of urban intervention, forwarding socio-economic inclusion and artistic experimentation will not emerge from sites of economic power but from sites of poverty, in the midst of conflicts between geopolitical borders, natural resources and marginalized communities — sites where the collision between top-down and bottom-up urban development is most dramatic. We have been proposing a paradigm shift to rethink the role of architecture and political theory in geographies of conflict. New conceptual frameworks are needed, as well as new procedures of engagement, to straddle two radically different ways of constructing the city.

We live and work in a zone of conflict and poverty that divides two cities, two countries, two continents, two hemispheres. In fact, the border cities of San Diego and Tijuana, together comprise the largest bi-national metropolitan region in the world, with 100,000 border crossings every day. Our region is paradigmatic of the uneven urban growth of the last decades that has polarized centres of wealth and poverty across the world. Urban asymmetry is physicalized in our region, as some of the poorest, most marginalized informal settlements in Latin America sit just minutes away from San Diego's mega-wealthy suburban paradise, crashing against the gates of what is often called "America's finest city". This border region where we live and work is a microcosm of all of the conflicts and deprivations that globalization has inflicted on the world's poorest people, intensified by two geo-political institutions: first: the NAFTA treaty — the North American Free Trade Agreement — that enables multi-national corporations to set up maquiladoras on the peripheries of Tijuana, where they generate massive profits freed from any restriction on labour practices, environmental protection and urban zoning regulation; and second, an aggressively militarized political border that cuts across and radically disrupts the social, economic and environmental ecologies that situate and give meaning to people's lives in this region.

THE NEIGHBOURHOOD AS SITE OF PRODUCTION: INFORMAL SOCIO-ECONOMIC ACTIVITY IS TRANSLATED INTO NEW FORMS OF LOCAL URBAN POLICY: ESTUDIO TEDDY CRUZ, 2010

Both of our practices — in social and political theory; and in art, architecture and urbanization — are held together by a thread that we would like to explore further here. In our work together, we have been interested in exploring the convergence of informal flows in twenty-first-century cities (social, moral, economic, spatial, urban), and the way formal institutions have been compelled to invest resources in enabling and scaling up these bottom-up dynamics. One aspect of our work focuses on the sociological effects of bottom-up development, how the circulation of norms and beliefs in shared spaces construct patterns of group life endogenously — essentially how reciprocal expectations among the co-habitants of space informally generate patterns of collective behaviour. We have learned from the visionary Mayor of Bogotá, Colombia, Antanas Mockus that engaging the city at this informal, normative level is essential to rethinking strategies of urbanization. In tandem, we are investigating the physical implications or consequences of social informality, particularly among people navigating conditions of scarcity, and the emergence of informal settlements, economic flows and general strategies of collective survival.

These bottom-up phenomena have exploded in the last years of global economic boom, with the rapid urbanization of the world's population, and the proliferation of slums on the peripheries of global cities everywhere. We have witnessed how the different kinds of exclusionary power operating across the San Diego-Tijuana border have provoked the small border neighbourhoods that surround it to construct practices of adaptation and resiliency in order to transgress imposed political and economic forces, pointing to other ways of constructing city, other ways of constructing citizenship. We have been investigating how these bottom-up forms of local socio-economic production — operating outside of formal institutions — can help us formulate alternative economies of development and urbanization.

While our attention has focused on these emergent forms of bottom-up urbanization, however, the ultimate goal of our practical work together in San Diego/Tijuana and other cities is to seek ways by which this knowledge can trickle upwards to transform top-down urban policy. We are not developing theories of informality that let formal institutions off the hook, in terms of social welfare and inclusive governance. In fact, most of our research and practical work explores the way exemplary municipalities like Medellín, Colombia have committed to "co-producing" the city, investing top-down resources and capacities to support, and give full integrity to, the intelligent efficacy of bottom-up processes. We are seeking new models to facilitate interfaces between the top-down and the bottom-up.

Shifting Practices

For these reasons, one primary site of intervention today is the widening gap between institutions of knowledge and the public: How to mobilize new interfaces between the specialized knowledge of institutions and the community-based knowledge embedded in marginalized neighbourhoods. We insist that it is only through a meeting of knowledges that we can instigate a new civic imagination. This entails a critical intervention into our own practices and research protocols — cultivating epistemic and professional fallibility, learning to speak in languages that communicate beyond our own professional knowledge silos, and learning to listen and recognize the value of alternative ways of seeing and doing.

On one hand, we must question the role of architecture and urban planning, art and the humanities in engaging the major problems of urban development today, as well as the social and political sciences, and their obsession with quantified data as the only way to measure social inequity without giving us any qualitative way out of the problem. In other words, it is not enough only to reveal the socio-economic histories and injustices that have produced these crises, but it is essential that theory and practice become instruments to construct specific strategies for transcending them; it is not enough for architecture and urban planning to camouflage, with hyper-aesthetics and forms of beautification, the exclusionary politics and economics of urban development; at this moment, it is not buildings but the fundamental reorganization of socio-economic relations that must ground the expansion of democratization and urbanization. In the same manner, it is not enough for social and political sciences to simply "measure" and expose the institutional mechanisms that have produced current socio-economic inequality — important though that element is — but it is essential that they communicate these measurements to those who can make use of them, and work with communities to develop policy proposals and counter-urban development strategies to re-imagine how the surplus value of urbanization can be redirected to sites of marginalization.

What this suggests is a double project, one that exposes the institutional mechanisms that have systematically and through often overtly racist and nationalist policies, produced social stigmas, and the political and economic forces that perpetuate marginalization; but also one that simultaneously intervenes in the gap between top-down resources and bottom-up agency, avoiding the trap of static victimization that sometimes undermines capacity within marginalized communities for political agency. But the formation of new platforms of engagement in our creative fields can only be made possible with a sense of urgency, pushing us to rethink our very procedures. The need for expanded modes of artistic practice, pedagogy and research, which, connected to new sites of investigation and collaboration, can generate new conceptions of cultural and economic production, as well as the reorganization of social relations seem more urgent than ever.

This dual project of research and action must dwell within the specificity of these urban conflicts, exposing the particularity of hidden institutional histories, revealing the missing information that can enable us to think politically and piece together a more accurate, anticipatory urban research and design intervention. It is in fact at the collision between the top-down and the bottom-up where a new urban political economy can emerge. What is needed is a more critical role for design to encroach into the fragmented and discriminatory policies and economics that have produced these collisions in the first place. Artists and architects have a role in conceptualizing such new protocols. In other words, it is the construction of the political itself that is at stake here: not just political art or architecture. This opens up the idea that architects and artists, besides being researchers and designers of form, buildings and objects, can be designers of political processes, urban pedagogy, alternative economic models and collaborations across institutions and jurisdictions to assure accessibility and socio-economic justice. This means we need to expand forms of practice, through which design takes a less protagonist role, via small, incremental acts of alteration of existing urban fabrics and regulation to mobilize counter-propositions to the privatization of public domain and infrastructure. The most radical intervention in our time can emerge from specific, bottom-up urban and regulatory alterations, modest in nature, but with enough resolution and assurance to trickle up to transform top-down institutional structures. And this is the reason, we maintain, that the project of rethinking urban inequality today is not primarily an architectural or artistic project but a political one, a project that architects and artists can mobilize.

This new political project also demands cross-sector institutions to confront socio-economic inequality, seeking to elevate marginalized communities not only as sites of stigmatization, alienation and control, but primarily as sites of activism and praxis, where citizens themselves, pressed by the urgencies of socio-economic injustice, are pushed to imagine alternative spatial and socio-economic protocols. It is in the periphery, where conditions of social emergency are transforming our ways of thinking about urban matters, and the matters of concern about the city.

From Binary to Dialectic: Revisiting the Formal/Informal Question
Many practitioners and academics have been uncertain about the distinction between formal and informal urban dynamics. In fact, the *informal* is a dangerous word for many scholars who suggest that formal and informal categories do not exist, that they are mutually inclusive and that this polarization has not been fruitful in the construction of a more emancipatory consensus-democratic agenda for the city and the thinking of new models of infrastructure. But we believe that as long as socio-economic urban inequality and conflict exist in the city, we will continue experiencing bottom-up resistance and resilience in the shape of counter-urban tactics of adaptation of, and in some cases transgression to imposed urban, economic and political agendas that

negate the local and contingent particularities of everyday life in many marginalized communities around the globe.

How to rethink top-down institutions of development while acknowledging emergent, temporal and socio-economic urban conditions by engaging more agile management systems to facilitate differential dynamics in the contemporary city, negotiating large and small scales, public and private gradations and incremental adaptive growth? This eruption of informal urbanization has provoked these fundamental questions for us, as well as our desire to recalibrate the totalizing abstraction of certain fit-all urban recipes to enable a more socially and economically inclusive political economy of urban development. But just like democracy itself, the project of urbanization is always in flux; and just when we think we have accomplished the consensus agenda of a "melting-pot" cosmopolitanism, we realize we have only arrived to urban homogenization, where

INFOSITE: INFORMAL, NOMADIC RESEARCH LIBRARY FOR CROSS-BORDER CULTURAL PROJECT
INSITE: ESTUDIO TEDDY CRUZ, 2005

conflict is camouflaged, the neoliberal paradigm of gentrification ascends beneath a veneer of "creative class" innovation and multicultural inclusion, while the city is divided between enclaves of wealth and poverty.

Therefore our position here about the informal and its effects in shifting practices pertains first and foremost to the issue of socio-economic inequality. To confront poverty today we need first to intervene into our own fields of specialization, recalibrating our own practices, re-tooling ourselves in order to understand and engage the reorganization of formal institutions and their protocols. This also requires new spaces for collaboration across sectors that can link top-down and bottom-up interests to mobilize an unprecedented project of redistribution of both resources and knowledges across metropolitan, regional and continental scales.

While we understand the risk of perpetuating an oppositional relationship between formal and informal categories, we want to begin by acknowledging their difference. There has been a tendency across specialized creative fields to evade binary relations as a point of departure in the construction of new conceptual paradigms; probably still driven by the heritage of a cultural ideology that elevated concepts such as cultural relativism, hybrid identities, and the blurring of differential categories. While much of this "postmodern" scholarship and practice presented us with these new procedures to negotiate the established hierarchical and rational structures of modern thinking, it also exerted damage in our recognition of difference and conflict in the advancement of exclusionary neoliberal political economies since the early 1980s to now. We think it is time to reformulate the "politics of difference" as a tool that can penetrate the mechanisms that have produced today's socio-economic crisis, and it is here where the dialectic between formal and informal systems becomes a device to visualize conflict, enabling new strategies to mediate the top-down and the bottom-up.

In other words, any debate about the relation between the formal and the informal in the contemporary city today must begin with the question of inequality, and as such, this question must focus on confronting the institutional processes responsible for producing urban poverty. So, the formal/informal opposition we are advancing here is a point of entry into urban crisis, but we are not advancing a binary relation, as this would only perpetuate the polarization of such categories. We are proposing a dialectical understanding of their relation that enables us to "enter into" and negotiate the interface between them. The goal is to transcend binary stasis through dialectical tension and creativity, in search of a new Hegelian synthesis, new zones of research, and a new language. We are seeking new mediating practices to facilitate modes of intervention into the space of collision between visible, exclusionary top-down institutional policy and invisible, bottom-up socio-economic agency.

In addition, skepticism towards the formal/informal binary has produced, primarily in the fields of architecture, an indifference to the socio-economic and political conditions that can in fact "complicate" architectural form today. This denigration of the "bottom-up" has been the DNA of "*autonomy*" in architecture, whose recurring avant-garde utopian dream throughout history has always been to give formal order to the chaos of social difference by imposing structural and compositional strategies that somehow will bring political, cultural and aesthetic unity to a society gone amok. While we agree with recent political stances in architecture to return to a notion of "*autonomy*" in order to resist the aesthetic relativism behind the speculative commercial logic of hyper-capitalism, we are critical of the nostalgic return to a top-down autonomous and self-referential language as the only way out of this continued "post-modern nightmare". And while we also agree with how *autonomy*'s critique has been oriented to the bottom-up consumerist politics of neoliberalism, we equally condemn its abandonment of bottom-up social movements and the contested space between the public and the private, whose antagonism is at the centre of the "political" in urbanization today. After all, without a progressive welfare state to support the reinstating of an architectural public and social agenda at a massive scale, the void will be filled by anti-democratic governments, autocratic dictatorships and the corporate neoliberal economic power of privatization to build these top-down architectural dreams of the future.

For these reasons, the misunderstanding of formal/informal relations can only lead to urban paradigms that unify and materialize the universalist, consensus politics of neoliberal global capital, into an apolitical formalist project of beautification, whose relentless homogeneity and parametric veneer hide any vestige of difference, and the conflicts that drive today's urban crisis and negate the multiplicity of socio-economic relations that should inspire new, more experimental architectural paradigms today.

The Informal as Praxis: New Urban Processes to Challenge Neoliberal Hegemony
The neoliberal political economy of urban growth has widened the gap between rich and poor, and has produced dramatic marginalization and an expansion of slums surrounding major urban centres. This uneven urbanization is at the heart of today's socio-economic crises and urban conflicts, and has resulted in the incremental

erosion of a public imagination, as many governments around the world welcomed the encroachment of the private into the public.

Since the early 1980s, with the ascendance of neoliberal economic policies based on the deregulation and privatization of public resources, we have witnessed how an unchecked culture of individual and corporate greed has deepened income inequality and social disparity. This new period of institutional unaccountability and illegality has been framed politically by the erroneous idea that democracy is the "right to be left alone", a private dream devoid of social responsibility. The shift of resources from the many to the very few has exerted great violence to our public institutions and our social economy. This polarization of wealth and poverty mirrors the polarization of public and private resources — they are causally linked — and this has had profound implications for the evolution of the contemporary city and the uneven growth that has radically expanded peripheral territories of poverty.

While it is undeniable that these slums have erupted as the underbelly of exclusionary global neoliberal economic policies that have turned cities like Tijuana into tax-free factory-cities, where multinationals set up shop to take advantage of cheap labour and benefit from these zones of exception to avoid any sort of regulation against human exploitation and environmental degradation, they are also intensive urbanizations of juxtaposition, emblematic of how Tijuana's informal communities are growing faster than the urban cores they surround, creating a different set of rules for development, and blurring the distinctions between the urban, the suburban and the rural. How do we intervene into these environments? Beyond the institutions of charity that engage vertically with momentary and often condescending humanitarian pity, muddling the difference between resistance and complicity; beyond applied academic research that, again vertically, treats these communities as subjects to be "randomized" and "assessed"; and beyond the indifference of corrupt governments that in the name of austerity have allied themselves with greedy corporate interests, further marginalizing these neighbourhoods?

This hijacking of the *public* by the private has been mobilized by a powerful elite of individuals and corporations who, under a banner of free-market economic freedom, has enjoyed the endorsement of federal and municipal governments who continue to deregulate and privatize public resources and spaces of the city. This has prompted many planning and economic development offices to "unplug" from communities and neighbourhoods at the margins of predictable zones of economic investment, resulting in the uneven urban development that has characterized many cities across the world, from Shanghai to New York City. This retreat of the institutions of governance from public investment has resulted also in the erosion of public participation in the urban political process, as many communities affected by this public withdrawal have not been meaningfully involved in the planning processes behind these urban transformations, nor benefited from the municipal and private profits they engendered.

In this context, one of the most important aims of our research has been to produce new conceptions and interpretations of the informal. Instead of a fixed category or style, we see the informal as a set of urban practices that transgress imposed political boundaries and top-down economic models. Recall how Christopher Alexander's theories of "pattern language" in the 1960s were hijacked by the field of architecture and reduced to a stylistic sense of regionalism, and a folkloric idea of the vernacular. A more critical reading of Alexander would recognize that language is less a fixed category, than a performative system capable of reorganizing the political economy of building. Likewise, we are interested in translating the actual operative processes behind informal practices into new tactics of urban intervention to challenge existing, formal protocols of economic development.

In essence, neoliberal hegemony has turned the city into a site of consumption and display. At the same time, informal neighbourhoods at the margins of these centres of economic power were growing, and sustaining themselves with their own resources and the logics of local productivity. In these peripheral communities, we find economic configurations that emerge and thrive through the tactical adaptation and retrofit of existing discriminating zoning and exclusionary economic development, producing a different notion of the "political" and of the "economic". These stealth practices reside at the intersection between formal and informal urbanizations and the conflicts between top-down policy and bottom-up social contingency and survival. It is from these informal settlements worldwide that a new politics of urban growth for the contemporary city is being shaped, often off the radar of those who formally define the categories of urban development.

Through this lens, we see the informal not as a noun but as a verb, which detonates traditional notions of site specificity and context into a more complex system of hidden socio-economic exchanges. We see the informal as the urban unwanted, that which is left over after the pristine presence of architecture with capital "A" has been usurped and transformed into the tenuous scaffold for social encounters. Primarily, because of our work in marginal border neighbourhoods in San Diego and Tijuana, we see the informal as the site of a new interpretation of community and citizenship, understanding the informal not as an aesthetic category but as praxis. This is the reason we are interested in the emergent urban configurations produced out of social emergency, and the performative role of individuals constructing their own spaces, and their economic relations.

A community is always in dialogue with its immediate social and ecological environment; this is what defines its political nature. But when this relationship is disrupted and its productive capacity splintered by the very way in which jurisdictional power is instituted, it is necessary to find a means of recuperating its agency. This agency and activism can be found in informal urbanization, which we see not only as an image of institutional alienation and poverty exploitation but as a set of everyday practices that enable communities to negotiate time, space, boundaries and resources in conditions of emergency. We can learn from these urban processes in order to reimagine the meaning of public infrastructure in the official city and to mobilize new forms of accountability in institutions of planning and private industry, as well as to recognize these communities as agents capable of political action.

But as we return to these informal dynamics for clues, their stealth urban praxis also needs artistic interpretation and political representation and this should be one of the spaces of intervention for contemporary architectural practice, engaging the specificity of the political within the performativity of the informal as the main creative tool to expand notions of design. Beyond architectural form, designers can also design forms of socio-economic exchange that can frame a more inclusive urbanization.

Moreover, while it is compelling to witness the creative intelligence and entrepreneurship embedded in these informal communities, we must ensure that by elevating this creativity, we do not unwittingly send a message to governments and other sources of economic support, that because these communities are so "entrepreneurial", they are capable of sustaining themselves without public support and that institutions, across sectors, can ethically unplug from these precarious environments. There is a tendency to think of informality in formal terms, referring primarily to whether or not economic activity is encapsulated within formal market processes and thus whether its practitioners participate in and avail themselves of the resources of the welfare state. This is certainly one way of thinking about informality, a view propagated by the Peruvian economist Hernando De Soto and others. There is obviously great importance to these issues, particularly their relation to the maintenance of a healthy welfare state, so this debate is important from the perspective of social equity.

But it is not enough simply to give property titles to slum dwellers to incorporate them into the official economy without the social protection mechanisms that can guarantee environmental and social justice. Otherwise, we risk perpetuating these environments as laboratories of neoliberal economic tinkering, based on individuals improving and selling their own parcels as commodities, without any social protection mechanisms that can avoid exploitation by the neoliberal machine that neglects local communities and their social and economic well-being.

It is with these complexities in mind, that we have been researching the dynamics of resilience and adaptation in informal urbanization. We maintain that learning from these bottom-up forms of local socio-economic production is essential to rethinking urban sustainability, focusing on neighbourhoods as sites of environmental, cultural, and economic productivity. We realize that when these two topics — neighbourhood marginalization and economic productivity — are brought together, some academics and practitioners from the left get nervous, since this might suggest a complicity with the logics of top-down privatization and disinvestment, or that the language of entrepreneurship, resilience and sustainability resonates with neoliberal urban rhetoric. We want to retake those terms and give them meaning through a more robust community-based engagement. What we mean here is that one of the most fundamental questions today is how to mobilize other economic pro-formas of development that are neighbourhood-led and whose profits benefit the community and not private developers only.

Ultimately, these bottom-up urban transformations demand that we expand existing categories of zoning, producing alternative densities and transitional uses that can directly respond to the emergent political and economic informalities at play in the contemporary city. It is, in fact, the political and cultural dimension of informal housing and density as tools for social integration in the city that can be the conceptual armature for urbanism today. How to enable these micro-urbanisms to alter the rigidity of the discriminatory public policies of the contemporary city?

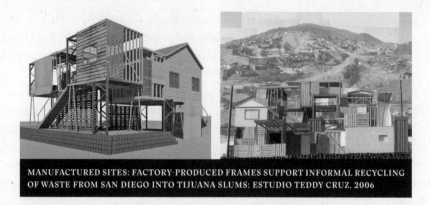

MANUFACTURED SITES: FACTORY-PRODUCED FRAMES SUPPORT INFORMAL RECYCLING OF WASTE FROM SAN DIEGO INTO TIJUANA SLUMS: ESTUDIO TEDDY CRUZ, 2006

How can the human capacity and creative intelligence embedded in informal urbanization be amplified as the main armature for challenging the hegemony of the neoliberal city?

Mediating the Top-down and the Bottom-up: Latin America and the Search for a New Civic Imagination

In recent years, our research has focused on the most compelling cases of informal urbanization across Latin America, and how to translate them into a new political language with particular spatial consequences, from which to produce new paradigms of housing, infrastructure, property and citizenship, inspiring "other" modes of intervention into the contemporary city.

Making urban development more democratic today is an urgent matter, because it has been controlled by a few urban actors — namely, the alliance of private developers, housing authorities and municipal governments. The question ought to be how to open alternative points of access into urbanization, expanding the horizon of opportunity for others (i.e., artists and architects as developers, communities as developers, etc.) so that other forms of economic development can emerge, supported by more inclusive and collaborative forms of governance. This might seem unattainable today, but examples of more democratic forms of urbanization, and a commitment to social justice in the city, have already happened throughout Latin America. It is there where many cities across the continent have begun to rethink public infrastructure by enabling inclusive political and civic processes, whose main function is to negotiate interfaces between the top-down and bottom-up, tapping into diverse social networks, informal economies, and imaginative forms of public participation.

The evidence of such developments is found in a lineage of progressive institutional transformations across the continent. Some date back to São Paulo's SESCs (Social Service of Commerce/Serviço Social do Comércio), privately-run, non-profit institutions that promote culture and healthy living in urban communities. Founded in 1946, these engines for "rethinking citizenship through cultural action" have spread throughout Brazil, and the city of São Paulo alone has 15 operating today. They are organized and run by social and cultural entrepreneurs, and focus on education, health and culture at the neighbourhood scale. In the 1970s, Curitiba Mayor, Jaimye Lerner re-imagined the notion of infrastructure as a mediating system to manage urban complexity, through low-tech and economic strategies of adaptation of existing spaces in the city, which paved the way for the renowned Bus Rapid Transit system, which became emblematic of intelligent mass transportation in the next decades.

Also significant was the idea of community-based cultural dissemination from Porto Alegre, Brazil, where in 1989 participatory budgeting began to link urban policy and public participation. The transformations of Favela-Bairro in Rio da Janeiro, Brazil, that began to take place in 1993 under the leadership of Sérgio Magalhães, engaged slums as new laboratories to rethink community-based, anti-gentrification development.

Antanas Mockus, a mathematician, philosopher, and former university rector, was twice elected Mayor of Bogotá in the mid-1990s and early 2000s. He came into office in a period of intense violence and urban chaos, and has become legendary for the ways he intervened into the behavioural patterns of the city. The election of Mockus in 1995 initiated a project of constructing a civic culture mediated by urban pedagogy — an urban educational model deployed as a generative tool for rethinking public infrastructure and social norms.

Mockus insisted that before transforming the physical city, we need to transform social behaviour; and maintained that infrastructural intervention and the deepening of social service commitments were only half the story. Top-down intervention was key, but a corresponding transformation of social norms, changing hearts from the bottom-up, was the key to sustainable urban transformation.

These creative urban policies and projects, aimed at re-imagining the relations between social norms and the city — from the sescs to Antanas Mockus — all converge in the case of Medellín, Colombia, where confronting urban conflict became a catalyst for dramatic urban transformation.

Medellín was the most violent city in the world in the late 1980s and early 1990s. A series of visionary mayors were determined to design new rights to the city, and construct a more radical and democratic urbanization. Medellín's determination to reduce poverty and violence was activated through experiments in collaborative municipal governance and planning, the coordination of massive cross-sector investments in public infrastructure and social services in the poorest and most violent *comunas* in the city, and the cultivation of a vibrant, participatory civic culture. Medellín was remarkable not only for its renowned public architecture and infrastructural interventions, but primarily for the egalitarian vision that inspired them, and the innovative political and civic processes that enabled them.

Among the most salient ideas behind the Medellín project were the rethinking and validation of transparent public management, a new role of government in curating cross-institutional collaborations to transform public spaces as places of education. This project was emblematized by the famous Library Parks, which were built in the most marginalized zones of the city, as a way to fight the root of violence — poverty — through education and public investment.

While these amazing urban transformations were made possible by rethinking municipal bureaucracy, public management and reorienting surplus value toward the poorest zones in the city, all these examples are characterized by a commitment to what we might call a "civic imagination", a way of thinking collectively about urban life that we have lost, not only in the United States but also incrementally across Europe during the recent years of decline in public spending, and the demonization of the welfare state. For these reasons, the case of Medellín is one of the most compelling stories because it gives us a powerful example of how a new political project can emerge that prioritizes equality and is generative of new forms of collaborative governance. As Medellín's former mayor Sergio Fajardo frequently points out, what transformed this city was not architectural or urban intervention; it was first a political project. In other words, the foundational agenda was to rethink the role of government, by coordinating cross-sector alliances capable of mediating formal and informal dynamics in the city. In essence, Medellín has taught us that progressive municipalities still exist. That the question today is not about eliminating government but reinventing it, reorganizing it in more efficient, inclusive ways. It is not a question of distrusting the top-down but recalibrating it with bottom-up sensibilities and knowledges.

Translating Process: The Medellín Diagram and the Cross-Border Citizen
It is from Latin America that we have learned most about local municipal and civic processes designed to produce more equitable forms of urbanization. In the last years, we have been interested in carrying these Latin American lessons to the San Diego-Tijuana border region, where we are investigating informal urban dynamics and citizenship culture as tools to transform urban and environmental policy. We have been developing, what we might call, "translation" projects in the last years, to appropriate these Latin American models and adapt their engagement with the informal to our own distinctive cross-border context. Medellín and Bogotá have been of particular importance to us — Medellín for its collaborative model of governance and intervention; and Bogotá for its strategies of infiltrating the behavioural patterns of civic dysfunction with performative gestures designed to change social norms and belief systems from the bottom up. To advance these translations, and adaptations, we have been partnering in the last years with former Mayor of Medellín Sergio Fajardo and his director of urban projects, Alejandro Echeverri, who was responsible for many of the city's most important interventions; as well as former Mayor of Bogotá, Antanas Mockus and his research team at Corpovisionarios. The catalyst for our own partnership, in fact, was our long connections with these Colombian cities. Translating and appropriating the models of Medellín and Bogotá, particularly the informal dimensions of these models, has been essential in rethinking our research and practice. Our two main projects pertaining to these cases are the *Medellín Diagram* in partnership with Echeverri and the *Binational Citizenship Culture Survey* in partnership with Mockus and Corpovisionarios:

Diagramming Process in Medellín
Medellín has gained global attention in recent years for the transformations that took place there, with frequent stories in the major global newspapers, as well as global prizes like the Urban Land Institute's "Most Innovative City" award in 2013, funded by Citibank with the Wall Street Journal. Medellín was also the site of the UN-Habitat's World Urban Forum in April 2014. For those of us interested in facilitating converges between bottom-up and top-down in pursuit of a more equitable urban development, the attention Medellín has received has been a double-edged sword. On the

one hand, yes: it is gratifying that institutions have acknowledged the excellence of the architectural and infrastructural interventions, situated in the most vulnerable sites across the city. Medellín has captured rightful attention for this egalitarian architectural gesture, and for the positive impact these interventions have had on poverty, crime and public health. But on the other hand, there are also problems with the narrative that has evolved. There is a tendency to miss the radical tactics of the mayors who effected these major shifts, by characterizing the transformations in a smooth neoliberal language of economic development that was stewarded by public-private partnerships that expanded public transport, opened markets and attracted foreign investment.

What the conventional narrative misses is the role of the bottom-up in the long history of urbanization in Medellín. The historically marginalized informal *comunas* of the city were not simply the needy recipients of top-down planning and charitable intervention, but were agents in an inclusive process of co-production, where shared responsibility and the mediation of institutions and communities produced very different ideas of local governance and urbanization.

Medellín is a story about how a public, unified across socio-economic divides, reclaimed the future of its own city. Ultimately, it is not by emulating buildings and transport systems that cities across the globe can begin to approximate the inclusive urbanization that transformed Medellín, and improved quality of life for the most vulnerable demographics over the last two decades. The key is to understand *process*, and that process must be responsive to the specificities of time and place, and how embedded socio-economic relations and conflicts can be the foundations for a new political reality.

But to elevate Medellín as a political and civic model that might be translated and adapted to other contexts, it is essential to understand just *how* the city managed to reorient resources on such a massive scale toward sites of greatest need. What must a city do, become, to pull off such an unprecedented accomplishment? How did government need to transform? What kinds of institutional intersections were necessary? How were these interventions funded? What was the role of the bottom-up in enabling these interventions to succeed and sustain themselves over time?

These are the questions we wanted to pursue. These are the processes we wanted to translate, so that Medellín might become intelligible, not only as a set of buildings, structures and spaces but primarily as an imaginative set of political and civic processes that organized themselves around what we ended up calling the "informal public demands", which we elaborate in the next section. Piecing these fragments together, translating and adapting them to the particularities of other contexts was essential, we thought, since the global media outlets were focusing on the final architectural and urban products but very seldom on the institutional reform that took place before physical interventions happened.

We began to work closely with Echeverri, in collaboration with his URBAM think tank, based at EAFIT University, to lead a project called *Visualizing Citizenship*. This project takes the shape of a relational physical map that visualizes and makes accessible the complexity of Medellín's political and civic processes, including unorthodox cross-institutional collaborations and processes of urban public management

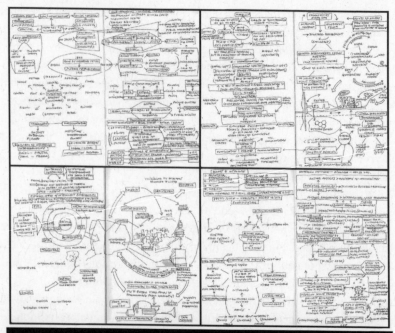

THE MEDELLÍN DIAGRAM: TRANSLATION OF CROSS-SECTOR INTERVIEWS FROM SOCIAL WORKERS TO THE MAYOR: TEDDY CRUZ AND FONNA FORMAN. 2013

that synergized community-based agencies, university research and the municipal government, as well as civic philanthropy. The "translation" of the "procedural complexity" behind these institutional transformations and their physical effects manifested in inclusive public infrastructure is essential because they represent critical alternatives to the way cities today tend to organize themselves, as well as the unsustainable metropolitan growth they promote.

To substantiate this effort, we conducted interviews with dozens of individuals involved in Medellín's political and civic processes, from the Mayor to social workers, from artists and academics to civic philanthropists, since what happened there was a complex process of negotiation and collaboration across institutions and publics. This exercise produced a new political language structured by a complex network of institutional relationships and dialogical processes with communities. We translated these stories and anecdotes, mapped them out and identified connections, tracing the ideas and tendencies across time and through diverse geographies, incrementally stitching them together and visualizing their complexity in the *Medellín Diagram*.

The *Medellín Diagram* demonstrates that the most effective urban interventions in the city today are not achieved by top-down logics of urban renewal, but by engaging the complexity of the existing real, mobilizing strategies of alteration and adaptation that benefit layered as opposed to tabula rasa approaches. This also involves intervening into critical proximities, exposing urban and community borders as sites of engagement, and operating at various scales simultaneously, while infiltrating existing institutional protocols, negotiating modest alterations, and being compelling enough to transform top-down urban policy and economy. A particular lesson here is the advancement of new forms of public communication, urban pedagogical processes that use art and

PRIORITIES			PROCESSES			INTERVENTIONS		
1. Constructing the Political Medellín confronted urban inequality			**2.** Designing Governance Medellín transformed municipal bureaucracy			**3.** Spatializing Citizenship Medellín built performative infrastructures of inclusion		
1.A Taking a position: Inequality is the Root of Urban Violence	1.B Mediating Urban Conflict	1.C Provoking a New Civic Imagination	2.A Assembling New Protocols of Public Management	2.B Integrating Fragmented Institutions and Communities	2.C Redistributing Knowledges and Resources	3.A Intervening into Urban Borders	3.B Transforming Public Spaces into sites for knowledge-exchange	3.C Curating the convergence of spaces, programs and institutional collaborations
		"There is much to be done: How do we assure the transfer of urban knowledge and who are the translators of institutional memory?"			"There is much to be done: How do we assure continuity of successful urban policies and approaches through political transition?"			"There is much to be done: How do we advance models of community inclusion to avoid the over-institutionalization of civic programming?"

THE MEDELLIN DIAGRAM: TRANSLATION OF POLITICAL AND CIVIC PROCESSES. TABLE OF CONTENTS: TEDDY CRUZ AND FONNA FORMAN. WITH ALEJANDRO ECHEVERRI AND MATTHIAS GOERLICH. 2014

culture as cognitive systems to enable communities to access the complexity of urban policy, activating the capacities of the bottom-up for political action.

We believe that among the most pressing crises today is the crisis of knowledge transfer between institutions, fields of specialization and publics. For this reason, our current work has engaged the complexity of transferring urban knowledge, from informal communities of practice to formal institutions and back, in the construction of the new *political* today. In this context, the story of Medellín helped us to clarify something essential to our own urban and political research: that an informal act in the city, whether through stealth spatial alterations, jurisdictional encroachment, or social behaviour, does not have to stop at the small and symbolic gestural scale, but it can trickle upwards with enough self-assurance to construct a political process that can ultimately transform top-down policy. This journey from the bottom-up to the top-down is urgent today, and it necessitates a new political leadership. But these procedures need translation and facilitation, what we call "tactics of translation": a deliberate effort to expose and visualize urban conflict as an operational and creative tool capable of re-appropriating the broken pieces of urbanization that have manifested in the space of the metropolis, the by-products of imposed, exclusionary political and economic urban recipes of privatization.

Strategies of Co-existence: Informal Flows and the Cross-border Citizen

Informality is conventionally understood as an economic concept, referring primarily to whether or not economic activity takes place within formal market processes. But Antanas Mockus, legendary former mayor of Bogotá, approaches informality in anthropological and sociological terms, helping us to think about the informal dimensions of social coordination and governance in the city. He insists that urban reform begins not with infrastructural intervention, but behavioural intervention at the level of norms. For Mockus, urban transformation is as much about changing patterns of public trust and social cooperation from the bottom up as it is about changing urban and environmental policy from the top down.

In collaboration with Mockus and his NGO, Corpovisionarios, the municipalities of San Diego and Tijuana and stakeholders from across the cross-border region, we have produced the *Binational Citizenship Culture Survey*. It is an instrument that measures what Mockus calls "citizenship culture" in San Diego and Tijuana.

Corpovisionarios has applied the survey in 30 cities across Latin America, and recently in Europe, and has developed a database of comparative research. In our case, the survey is not a study of just one city but two, and not simply parallel surveys to compare their similarities and differences, but a survey of two cities intimately intertwined across a militarized wall that has been fortified over time as a Federal bulwark against porosity. Our claim has always been that the wall ultimately cannot disrupt the bottom-up normative, social, economic and environmental flows that define our region; and the purpose of the survey was to identify these informal flows to compel a new era of top-down cross-border municipal collaboration.

The survey ultimately provokes the idea of the "cross-border citizen", whose conception of citizenship is organized around the shared values and social norms, the common interests and sense of mutual responsibility around which a new bi-national citizenship culture can be cultivated — beyond the arbitrary and formal jurisdictional boundaries that too rigidly define both cityhood and the politics of citizenship in the United States.

One of the most important lessons of Antanas Mockus' administration in Bogotá is that it makes no sense to sign formal agreements among factions if citizens themselves don't "interiorize" a new civic consciousness. This is precisely how we see our work. We are working with the mayors to build new relations of trust and cooperation from the top down, but we are primarily interested in identifying the informal dynamics that bind these two cities together, from the bottom up, through which a new regional, cross-border collective consciousness can emerge.

On Public Goods and Social Norms: Mockus and the Legacy of Adam Smith
It has been central to our research that Mockus takes his place in a long tradition of social theory that focuses on the informal dynamics of social coordination, notably eighteenth century Scottish social theory and and its greatest voice, Adam Smith. Most people think of Smith as the father of free-market capitalism, and this interpretation is obviously not without good reason. Smith's book *The Wealth of Nations*, published in 1776, is a manifesto of open markets and minimal states, where human beings are motivated primarily by self-interest — and that the social bonds among them are the product of cost-benefit calculation and nothing more.

The truth is that this conventional neoliberal interpretation of Smith neglects what he really said or why he said it. Smith in fact was a vicious critic of greedy capitalism, the commodification of human relationships, and the degradation of the working poor in early industrial capitalism. He was among the century's most vocal critics of European slavery and empire — indeed, his fear of the state was rooted primarily in this, since state policy in the eighteenth century was too easily hijacked by the agendas of corrupt international trading companies like the East India Company. And most astonishing to the contemporary mind, Adam Smith devoted an entire section of his *Wealth of Nations*, indeed the longest section, to elaborating the state's provision of public goods and the necessity of cultivating a vibrant public culture, producing citizens who are civically engaged with one another, and aware enough to collectively constrain the vices and corruptions of their leaders.

These are dimensions of classical economic thought — the primacy of the ethical, the limits on accumulation, the degradations of labouring poor, the virtues of an engaged citizenry, the importance of public goods, and public space, and public education and public health — all the provisions that private entities do not have proper incentives to carry out well. These elements of Smith's thinking have lost currency in the last two centuries, as neoliberals have effectively severed capitalism from its classical roots.

Here, we are interested in teasing out a particular strand of Smith's thinking about social norms and informal social coordination. An intellectual history of Antanas Mockus and his approach to social norms and urban transformation must begin in the eighteenth century with Adam Smith.

In brief, Smith insisted that modern societies cohered after the dissolution of traditional forms of formal authority (kings, churches, static feudal hierarchy) because our relations with one another are regulated by the conventions and habits that emerge through informal social interface. His richly detailed empirical account of informal social coordination was contained in his book *The Theory of Moral Sentiments* of 1759, the book he wrote as a young man which nobody reads anymore. There Smith offered a brilliant theory about emergent sources of human cooperation and culture formation, a view that cognitive scientists and neuro-researchers today have confirmed with increasingly sophisticated diagnostic technologies in the lab.

We are interested in Smith's theory of the informal social processes through which societies cohere, without the formal institutions of state coercion, how people in shared spaces discipline and regulate each other collectively through ordinary daily interaction and produce social norms; and how these norms are then transmitted, passed from each generation to the next through the infinite repetition of informal interfaces.

The relevant insight here is that "social" — or "acceptable" — behaviour for Smith, and for Mockus, is essentially an internalization of one's experiences moving through the world, a cultural artefact, that some have compared to a Freudian superego. As such, if you live in a society where violence is the norm, where racism and the degradation of human dignity are the norm, where criminality and gang violence is the norm, where violence against women is tolerated, where paying one's taxes is perceived as optional, and natural resources like water are expendable, and so forth, then social interaction will not constrain the behaviour but will actually reinforce it.

It is here that an external normative vantage is required. This is precisely where formal, top-down norms became important for Smith — to provide an external and formal vantage and correction. In other words, Smith sought to bring social norms into harmony with what he called "moral" norms or standards. This distinction lies at the heart of Mockus's method as well, and is the basis of so much of Corpovisionarios' success. The greatest lesson of Mockus' leadership is this: Social norms that degrade the integrity of human life need to be changed and replaced with moral norms that honour and respect human life. Meeting urban violence with stricter penalties will not work. Law and order solutions don't interiorize new values, but community processes do.

SECOND-HAND URBANIZATION: TIJUANA SLUMS
BUILD THEMSELVES WITH THE WASTE OF SAN
DIEGO; ESTUDIO TEDDY CRUZ, 2006

A New Civic Imagination

What Antanas' work demonstrates is that informal social norms, which emerge from the bottom up, can be reoriented at the urban scale through formal, top-down municipal intervention — political leadership with a new civic imagination to declare and perform emphatically the moral norms that should regulate our relations: that human life is sacred, that radical inequality is unjust, that adequate education and health are basic human rights, that gender violence is intolerable, and so forth — and in the case of our region, that human beings regardless of formal legal citizenship, and regardless of race and class, have dignity, deserve equal respect and basic quality of life.

The Political Economy of the Bottom-up:
Informal Public Demands

An urgent challenge in our time, as the paradigm of private property has proven itself unsustainable in conditions of poverty, is to rethink existing norms of ownership: This means redefining urban development by amplifying the value of community participation: More than "owning" units of housing, residents, in collaboration with community based agencies, can also co-own and co-manage the economic and social infrastructure around them. In other words, we must amplify the value of people's participation in urban development, enhancing the role of communities in producing housing. We must envision housing configurations that elevate emergent local economies and new forms of sociability, allowing neighbourhoods to generate new markets "from the bottom up" (i.e., informal economies and densities that are usually off the radar of conventional top down economic recipes), as well as to promote new models of affordability, with financing schemes that allow unconventional mixed uses. This has led our research in San Diego to focus on social and economic informality in marginalized immigrant neighbourhoods.

Take the example of two women responding to the child care scarcity in one of these border neighbourhoods, who rent a three-bedroom apartment and transform it into a day-care facility, which in turn is recognized by a community-based organization that camouflages that activity, while supporting it with knowledge and economic resources, channelling and redirecting subsidies and other cash flows. Some will dismiss this sort of activity as "illegal", but we would like to pause and think about the ubiquity and potential of scaling up these informal acts into new legal frameworks that elevate local-scale economic and social creativity. Let's frame this agency and stealth knowledge as an operative tool to rethink economic development at local and small scales, and ultimately to help us reimagine typologies of housing and public space. For instance, how many of these informal neighbourhood-based practices, such as local food production, day care, elder care, arts production and informal education, etc. can be translated, evaluated, and ultimately politically represented?

THE MEDELLIN DIAGRAM, SECOND PHASE INSTALLATION, SANTA MONICA MUSEUM OF ART: TEDDY CRUZ AND FONNA FORMAN, WITH ALEJANDRO ECHEVERRI AND MATTHIAS GOERLICH, 2014

A recurring theme in our work at the U.S.-Mexico border has been, in fact, to investigate other modalities of economy, other policy frameworks that can transcend urbanisms of global consumption towards urbanizations of local production. The key issues here are how to mobilize the redistribution of resources, and mediate top-down and bottom-up dynamics; how to enable local communities to benefit from their own modes of production. Can a neighbourhood-based urbanization yield new typologies of public housing as the catalytic infrastructure for urban development today? In this respect, we have argued that surplus value is not necessarily evil; what is appalling is the way it has been hoarded by the very few at the expense of the many. We believe that the task of any urban and political practice today is to reorganize, redistribute, and redirect that surplus, so that it acquires a social mandate and takes on value that is not only economic but also social. We also believe that to address issues of social justice today, we must enable the redistribution of resources but also the redistribution of knowledges.

For instance, can the knowledge of the developer be appropriated as an instrument to construct community? In essence: Can the developer's pro forma be framed as a site of experimentation today, where we can aggregate the hidden value of informal economy, of sweat equity, of collaboration, and of new political representation framed by social protection systems? How to intervene in its organizational logics of financing and resources, elevating the social and economic contingencies found in informal urbanization? We believe that a new political economy of urbanization will be found not in the formal systems of architecture or urban planning, but in the construction of new socio-economic and political frameworks, within which the "informal public" can have not only a symbolic but an operational role, and where new aesthetic paradigms of building can be generated.

Informal Public Demands

We maintain that urban transformation begins at the social and behavioural level, and requires intervening into the dysfunctional and hierarchical social norms that situate relations in civil society. Only then can governance and physical intervention produce meaningful and sustainable change. As such, our call for an informal public begins with a set of normative demands, followed by demands for more democratic and collaborative forms of governance, culminating in a set of policy demands focused on the equitable physical transformation of the city.

— To transform cultural practices of social exclusion and the corresponding denigration of public goods by cultivating new urban norms of human dignity and equality, and to shame their violation.

— To advance a language of "a right to the city" to stimulate a new sense of possibility in communities long marginalized from the planning agendas of today's cities.

— To enable more inclusive and meaningful systems of political representation and civic engagement at the scale of neighbourhoods, tactically re-calibrating individual and collective interests.

— To produce new forms of local governance, along with the social protection systems that provide guarantees for marginalized communities, and to protect their right to control their own modes of production and share the profits of urbanization to prevent gentrification.

— To rethink existing models of property by redefining affordability and the value of social participation, augmenting the role of communities in co-producing housing, and enabling a more inclusive idea of ownership.

— To mobilize social networks into new spatial and economic infrastructures that benefit local communities in the long term, beyond the short-term problem solving of private developers or institutions of charity.

— To sponsor mediating agencies that can curate the interface between top-down, government-led infrastructural support and the creative bottom-up intelligence and sweat equity of communities and activists.

— To close the gap between the abstraction of large-scale planning logics and the specificity of everyday practices.

— To challenge the autonomy of buildings, often conceived as self-referential systems, benefiting the one-dimensionality of the object and indifferent to socio-economic temporalities embedded in the city. How to engage instead the complex temporalization of space found in informal urbanization's management of time, people, spaces, and resources?

— To question exclusionary recipes of *land use*, understanding zoning not as the punitive tool that prevents socialization but instead as a generative tool that organizes and anticipates local social and economic activity at the scale of neighbourhoods.

— To politicize *density*, no longer measured as an abstract amount of objects per acre but as an amount of socio-economic exchanges per acre.

— To retrofit the large with the small. The micro-social and economic contingencies of the informal will transform the homogeneous largeness of official urbanization into more sustainable, plural, and complex environments.

— To elevate the incremental low-cost layering of urban development found in informal urbanization in order to generate new paradigms of public infrastructure, beyond the dominance of private development alone and its exorbitant budgets.

— To reimagine exclusionary logics that shape jurisdiction. Conventional government protocols give primacy to the abstraction of administrative boundaries over the social and environmental boundaries that informality negotiates as devices to construct community.

— To challenge the idea of public space as an ambiguous and neutral place of beautification. We must move the discussion from the neutrality of the institutional public to the specificity of urban rights.

— To layer public space with protocols, designing not only physical systems but also the collaborative socio-economic and cultural programming and management to assure accessibility and sustainability in the long term.

The *Informal Public* is the site from which to generate "other" ways of constructing the city; and its role today is to mediate a two-way journey, between top-down and bottom-up dynamics: in one direction, how specific, bottom-up urban alterations by creative acts of citizenship can have enough resolution and political agency to trickle upward to transform top-down institutional structures; and, in the other direction, how top-down resources can reach sites of marginalization, transforming normative ideas of infrastructure by absorbing the creative intelligence embedded in informal dynamics. This critical interface between top-down and bottom-up resources and knowledges is essential at a time when the extreme left and the extreme right, bottom-up activism and top-down pro-development, neoliberal urban agendas, all join forces and converge in their mistrust of government. A fundamental role of the informal public in shaping the agenda for the future of the city is to press for new forms of governance, seeking a new role for progressive policy, a more efficient, transparent, inclusive, and collaborative form of government. For these reasons, one of the most important sites of intervention in our time is the opaque, exclusionary, and dysfunctional bureaucracy that characterizes many cities in the world, and the restoration of the linkages between government, social networks, and cultural institutions to reorient the surplus value of urbanization to benefit not merely the private but primarily a public imagination.

1 Our great thanks to Helge Mooshammer and Peter Mörtenböck for their partnership and support; to Alejandro Echeverri, Jean-Philippe Vassal and our 24 respondents for their enthusiastic participation; and to our editorial assistant and project manager, Aaron Cotkin, for his hard work and patient dedication to this project. Thanks also to Ximena Covaleda and Natalia Castaño Cardenas in Medellín and Marcos Garcia Rojo in Paris for helping to coordinate our exchanges with Echeverri and Vassal; and to Jose Escamilla who assisted with translation.

2 Some of the ideas presented here are refinements, summaries and convergences of earlier ideas that have appeared in: Fonna Forman and Teddy Cruz, "Municipal cosmopolitanism," in *Social Philosophy & Policy* (2016); Fonna Forman and Teddy Cruz, "Global Justice at the Municipal Scale: The Case of Medellín, Colombia," in *Institutional Cosmopolitanism*, ed. Thomas Pogge and Luis Cabrera (New York: Oxford University Press, 2016); Teddy Cruz, "The Architecture of Neoliberalism," in *The Politics of Parametricism*, ed. Matthew Poole and Manuel Shvartzberg (London: Bloomsbury, 2016); Teddy Cruz, "Where is Our Civic Imagination?" in *Concurrent Urbanities*, ed. Miodrag Mitrasinovic (London and New York: Routledge, 2015); "Spatializing Citizenship: Marginal Neighbourhoods as Sites of Production," in *Territories of Poverty* (Athens, GA: University of Georgia Press, 2015); Teddy Cruz, "The Informal Public," in *Istanbul Art Biennial 2013*, catalogue (Istanbul, 2014); "Uneven Growth: It's About Inequality, Stupid," in *Uneven Growth: Tactical Urbanisms for Expanding Megacities* ed. Pedro Gadanho (New York: MoMA, 2014); and Fonna Forman, *Adam Smith and the Circles of Sympathy: Cosmopolitanism and Moral Theory* (Cambridge: Cambridge University Press, 2010).

3 The Diagram was first presented in April 2014 in the Medellín Museum of Modern Art on the occasion of the 7th UN-Habitat World Urban Forum, which was hosted in Medellín to showcase the remarkable urban transformations that had occurred there. It was co-produced in collaboration with Echeverri and graphic designer Matthias Goerlich of Studio Matthias Goerlich, Frankfurt. See http://medellin-diagram.com/en/

A VIRTUAL ROUNDTABLE: THE INFORMAL PUBLIC DEMANDS A NEW CONVERSATION

Provocateurs: Teddy Cruz and Fonna Forman

Interlocutors: Jean Philippe Vassal and Alejandro Echeverri

Respondents: Martha Chen, Mauricio Corbalan, Ana Džokić, Emiliano Gandolfi, Laurent Gutierrez, Hou Hanru, Rahul Mehrotra, Alejandro Meitin, William Morrish, Henry Murraín, Marc Neelen, Robert Neuwirth, Kyong Park, Constantin Petcou, Doina Petrescu, Alessandro Petti, Valérie Portefaix, Marjetica Potrč, Lorenzo Romito, Lloyd Rudolph, Susanne Hoeber Rudolph, Saskia Sassen, Richard Sennett, and Jeanne van Heeswijk.

The critical reflections on the informal articulated in the beginning of this section served as provocations for a dialogue with two interlocutors, Alejandro Echeverri and Jean-Philippe Vassal, whose work on urbanism and architecture have opened new perspectives on informality.

Echeverri is co-founder and director of URBAM, the Center for Urban and Environmental Studies at EAFIT University. He was Director of Urban Projects for Medellín, Colombia in the administration of Mayor Sergio Fajardo, where he led a project of "Social Urbanism" and coordinated many interventions into informal settlements. His work within informal urban contexts has influenced architects and urban planners across the world. Jean Philippe Vassal is a Paris-based architect whose renowned work with partner Anne Lacaton on public space, housing and urban planning, as well as new bottom-up approaches to rethink the economy of building, is, to our mind, among the most powerful architectural expressions of informal spatial dynamics today, opening new aesthetic paradigms that embrace everyday practices.

What follows is a set of conversations with Echeverri and Vassal about the relation between their research-based practices and informal urbanization, centred around seven provocations which are critical to our own understanding of the informal. The conversations with Vassal and Echeverri were transcribed, and distributed to a diverse set of respondents, renowned practitioners and thinkers who represent a variety of practical and theoretical disciplines — architecture, art and curation, urban studies, social and political theory, economics, journalism and activism. We asked all respondents to react to the essential first provocation, locating "the informal". We then distributed the remaining provocations among the respondents.

The respondents included architects Constantin Petcou and Doina Petrescu of atelier d'architecture autogérée, Harvard-based development practitioner and scholar Martha (Marty) Chen, architect Mauricio Corbalan of m7red, urbanist and curator Emiliano Gandolfi of Cohabitation Strategies, curator of MAXXI Rome Hou Hanru, architects Laurent Gutierrez and Valérie Portefaix of MAP Office, Harvard architect and urbanist Rahul Mehrotra, environmental activist and artist Alejandro Meitin of Ala Plástica, New School urbanist and architect William Morrish, social scientist Henry Murraín of Corpovisionarios, journalist and writer Robert Neuwirth, urban curator Kyong Park, architect Alessandro Petti of Decolonizing Architecture, Ljubljana-based artist Marjetica Potrč, architect Lorenzo Romito of Primaveraromana, University of Chicago emeritus political economists Lloyd Rudolph and Susanne Hoeber Rudolph, social thinkers Saskia Sassen and Richard Sennett, architects and curators Ana Džokić and Marc Neelen of STEALTH, and Dutch artist Jeanne van Heeswijk.

The following seven provocations framed the conversation:

Provocations

1 Operating definition

What does the informal consist of for you (in the context of urbanization and otherwise)? What would be an operating definition for you?

2 Relation to the top-down

How do formal and informal dynamics interact, converge, diverge, etc. and how do you feel about the formal/informal dialectic (keeping in mind that these terms are often relative to context and that they often blur)?

3 Impact on practice

What operative role has the informal played in your own practice? And can you recall a moment or set of conditions that prompted a shift in your practice in order to address the informal?

4 Informal as praxis and procedure

In our introduction, we emphasize that the informal is not just an aesthetic category but primarily a set of procedures — a praxis. Can you comment on the informal as praxis and its procedures?

5 The informal aesthetic

Nevertheless, are there aesthetic potentialities that can be addressed?

6 Transformative urban impact

How can informal dynamics (i.e., informal economies, spatial organization and social networks) transform our thinking about infrastructure, democracy and inclusive urbanization?

7 Scaling up

In what ways can the contingent role of the informal at small scales can be scaled up?

1 OPERATING DEFINITION

What does the informal consist of for you? (In the context of urbanization and otherwise) what would be an operating definition?

Teddy Cruz and Fonna Forman (San Diego, usa) in conversation with architects Alejandro Echeverri (Medellín, Colombia) and Jean-Philippe Vassal (Paris, France)

Alejandro Echeverri

Teddy Cruz / Fonna Forman: *Even though many of us resist static definitions, what does the informal mean to you from an operational standpoint? What is the relationship of the informal to urbanization?*

Alejandro Echeverri: In the context of Medellín, our city's most interesting story has been written already, and it has been written by informal processes. For the most part, the informal dictates our reality. In Medellín and other Latin American cities, 50 per cent of society does not follow the norm. And it is not optional. It is a concrete reality. It is a response to urgency. These peripheral processes are what we call "informal". But this is a very general and vast definition. We would need to analyze it and dissect it further in order to really come up with a definition for the informal.

NEW INFRASTRUCTURE SUPPORTS PROCESSES OF CONSOLIDATION IN THE SANTO DOMINGO NEIGHBOURHOOD, MEDELLÍN

TC / FF: *What you are suggesting is that the informal is a notion that is being constantly redefined and that one of the goals today is to articulate it, investigate it, and create a more accurate perspective in relation to what it means to urbanization.*

AE: That which exists outside of our reality lies within the norm of formal economic processes. And I think that there is a second issue that is related to this. The difficulty behind defining "the informal" comes from the preconceptions and stigmas that many of us have of the term. The answers to these questions will vary depending on whom you ask or under what circumstances you ask them. For a lot of people and social groups with whom we collaborate, their "everyday" universe is the one they live in. For them, there is no differentiation or stigmatization between the formal and informal. The space where they carry out their everyday lives is their real world. I think that we need to have a more "transparent" perspective and forego many preconceptions in order to be able to define what informal processes are.

HATMAKER, NIGER

Jean-Philippe Vassal

<u>Jean-Philippe Vassal</u>: We are curious and interested in the informal. A long time ago, after graduating, I stayed in Nigeria for five years. It was the first time I came upon the question of the informal economy and the informal city. Ninety per cent of the city I was in, north of the Sahara, for example, was informal, so it was at this time that I began asking how the informal could transform our way of thinking about architecture, and perhaps other fields as well, such as urbanism as we know it today, which is, for me, problematic in the way it is currently practiced.

<u>TC / FF</u>: *Do you have a working definition of the informal and what you mean when you come upon it?*

<u>JPV</u>: To me, the informal is unpredictable. We cannot control it but we can partake in it. Its outcome is unpredictable yet often surprising. It is not defined by rules, regulations or systems. It heavily relies on improvisation, which is about "being alive". It is a difficult concept to define.

Respondents

<u>Marty Chen</u>: The "informal" can be found in multiple domains: transactions, relationships and institutions; economic, social and political. My work, and that of the WIEGO network I coordinate, focuses on the informal in the economic realm and, more specifically, in labour and product markets. One of the core functions of the WIEGO network is to improve the measurement of informality in labour force and in other economic statistics. To do this, we needed a clear and comprehensive concept and definition of informality.

With the International Labour Organization, the International Conference of Labour Statisticians, and the International Expert Group on Informal Sector Statistics;

WIEGO has developed an official international statistical definition of informal employment that includes the self-employed in *informal enterprises* (i.e., unincorporated small or unregistered enterprises) and the wage-employed in *informal jobs* (i.e., jobs without employer contributions to social protection). So defined, informal wage workers may be hired by informal enterprises, formal firms or households. So defined, the informal workforce represents between half and 80 per cent of the non-agricultural workforce in developing countries.

In brief, there are three related official definitions of economic informality which are often used imprecisely and interchangeably: the *informal sector* refers to the production and employment that takes place in unincorporated, small, or unregistered enterprises; *informal employment* refers to employment without legal and social protection — both inside and outside the informal sector; and the *informal economy* refers to all units, activities, and workers so defined and the output from them. Together, they form the broad base of the workforce and the economy, both nationally and globally.

In cities across the developing world, the informal workforce tends to be concentrated in the following sectors: construction, domestic work, manufacturing (including home-based production), personal services, trade, transport, and waste collection and recycling.

R AS IN REPUBLIC, COHABITATION STRATEGIES, MILAN, 2014

Mauricio Corbalan: Our practice is to describe complex scenarios and the agency this description implies for those engaged in them. Who informs the territory? How should data from unchartered territories be categorized? Is any territory unchartered unless it is contested by those who inhabit it? While researching a polluted river basin in the outskirts of Buenos Aires, we encountered the invisibility of citizen claims and at the same time the difficulties of gaining access to public information. This gap between the perceptions of those inhabiting a territory and those in government agencies monitoring that territory led us to develop a platform to equalize these two ways of producing information. By disclosing public information and by amplifying citizens' voices, we seek to avoid the hierarchization between the formal and the informal.

Emiliano Gandolfi:
in·for·mal adjective \(ˌ)in-ˈfoʳ-məl\

: having a friendly and relaxed quality
: suited for ordinary use when you are relaxing
of language : relaxed in tone : not suited for serious or official speech and writing [Merriam-Webster Dictionary]

Over the past decades, we have been looking at cities in terms of dichotomies. We have directed our sensibility to an understanding of urban, economic, and mental structures that are presented as the *correct* ways of organizing our societies. Beyond these ideas of *order*, there is *dis-order* — life that doesn't fit into these schemes. Yet things can be easily turned upside-down when looking at basic rights, such as the right to housing. If it is true that people on this planet should have the right to exist, they should equally have the right to sleep, eat, and make love somewhere.

We conventionally think of informal economies, or informal quarters, as illegal entities. In this perspective, any form of thought that doesn't correspond to the maximizing norm will inevitably be rendered informal, and therefore illegal. I prefer to look at cities beyond this typically Modernist dichotomy. We should go back to the basics, to human rights. Once it is accepted that housing is a right, we should look at urban forms in which people can have the space to build their dwellings based on a set of shared values. Therefore, the problem is not one of defining what is formal, or informal, but rather one of understanding how we can conceive of an urban form that can grow organically with the needs of all its inhabitants.

Hou Hanru: We often tend to romanticize informality because we are getting fed up with our formal lives — with formalized life in our specific spaces, that is, in the "West", where everything seems to be regulated and formalized by textual laws. By calling the "other" "informal", Western "theories" eventually reveal how Western modernity has turned into a formal system through invading other spaces and by means of an Orientalist observation of the "other".

Why this other? There is a need to consolidate the rightness of what we are doing here by framing it as a formal activity. Then, the discussion about the informal serves to further justify what we are doing here. It is a highly romanticized and exotic view of the other which excludes the possibility of accepting the influence of the other or changing what we have established here. Thus, the other, the informal, is defined as a purely aesthetic object.

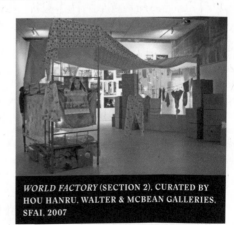

WORLD FACTORY (SECTION 2), CURATED BY HOU HANRU, WALTER & MCBEAN GALLERIES, SFAI, 2007

In the context of contemporary art, institutions have for some time been trying to be open to this so-called non-Western world — the other. Very often, samples of the informal are transported from remote places into our formalized space. This emphasizes certain aspects of those so-called informal things while taking away the actual vitality of those activities. However, there is one little aspect that we may have overlooked. Informality is not a thing that can easily be separated from the formal. Indeed, we are not looking at an overlapping of different systems but an interesting hybridization of those systems. And over time, because every situation and space has interpreted modernity in its own way through this process of hybridization, this has somehow challenged the definition of the formal and the informal.

MAP Office: The word informal does not stand for a lack of formality. Rather, it proposes, in the urbanization processes, a different condition of formality. As such, the informal plays an important role in offering spaces where "laissez-faire" can happen. It provides possible places outside the limits of regulation and opens up many possibilities for communities to settle, exist and develop. The informal as a new regulatory system exists within the specificity of the community, with its codes, and serves as a fertilizer for a new social construction. As with any processes, the definition and limits of the informal evolve and metamorphose according to a temporal dimension of four different stages:

(1) The birth of the informal is usually the result of an encounter between the needs of a specific community (often marginalized) and a strategic location (often at the margin or in-between). The result of this encounter is commonly articulated around a system of exchange — an economy, a market.

(2) The childhood and teenage life of the informal explores the limits of this encounter by stretching the spatial boundaries and by establishing a social contract in which the system of exchange can evolve. This age can venture beyond the informal toward the limits of the illegal.

(3) The adult life of the informal is characterized by an expansion of the community as well as its system of exchange. More and more exchanges are taking place due to growing demands from the community. It often reaches a sort of equilibrium between people leaving the community and others joining the system.

(4) Ageing and death of the informal occurs when a distinctive form is achieved and the informal begins to be absorbed by sets of regulations, leaving the members of the community spaceless. Then, a new platform of exchange is needed, with new specificities and a new social contract.

Rahul Mehrotra: Clearly, the most obvious definition of the "informal" takes us back to the origins of the popular use of this word in economics — which is the informal economy: the part of the economy that is outside the formal purview of the state and, thus, evades taxation and legislative oversight, etc. In my understanding, the use of this term was expanded in many disciplines to imply actions outside legal sanction and other legal transgressions. In design and urbanization, this naturally came to mean self-built, *laissez-faire*, without sanction and often on illegally occupied land. Sometime in the 1980s, perhaps even later, the rubric of the "informal city" emerged and gained traction in the profession of design and planning. Naturally, an aesthetic came to be associated with it — one of the "ultimate collage". An aesthetic and physical form that is not based on formal scriptures or predetermined rules; instead a visual culture where human ingenuity breaches the boundaries between the local and the global, the historic and contemporary, conveying the hybrid urgencies of contemporary architecture and urbanism in that context.

For me, a critical notion in relation to informality is that of time or the temporal. I say this, because it is eventually time, the uncertainty of existence and the incrementalism in attitudes of making and operating which give the informal its essential spirit and, perhaps, its intelligence. The formal is always arrogant about time, about its assumption to persist! The informal is tentative, accretive and uncertain. The implication of this in urbanistic terms is that it is an urbanism created by those outside the elite domains of the formal modernity of the state. It is a "pirate" modernity that slips under the laws of the city to simply survive, without any conscious attempt at constructing a counter-culture. Incomprehensible as a two-dimensional entity, it is perceived as a city in motion — a three-dimensional construct of incremental development that is not perceived by architecture, but by spaces which hold associative values and supportive lives. Patterns of occupation determine its form and perception. It is an indigenous urbanism that has its particular "local" logic. It is not necessarily the city of the poor, as most images might suggest; rather it is a temporal articulation and occupation of space, which not only creates a richer sensibility of spatial occupation, but also suggests how spatial limits are expanded to include formally unimagined uses in, often, dense urban conditions.

Alejandro Meitin: The informal summarizes creativity and self-organization, but most of all, it represents a position towards survival. Because of the pressures that surround it, the informal has to confront not only the challenges and limitations of extreme situations but also, most fundamentally, the imposition of a formalist authority of the factual. This comes both from the state and from corporate power, whose organizational agendas, whether for the environment or culture, always benefit homogenization, instead of capitalizing on the value of difference.

Communities identify themselves with the totality of the environmental systems that surround them, understood as the vocation of place. This integration of the symbolic role of place with the constructed form of the natural landscape has been represented by art across the majority of cultures. Advanced studies on immunodeficiency recognize that the human body is connected to a network of neurochemical communications found in our environment, which determine our health and wellbeing. For this, we do not need to develop sentimentalism or mysticism, nor an intense connection with nature. What is necessary is to understand the vocation of place, enabling the recognition that the environment, in its natural and cultural manifestations, is simply an extension of ourselves.

In the context of this relational recognition of the natural, many interventions into the environment can be read as an "occupation" that divides territorial zones based on economic interests and an imaginary that is led by the communicational media of commercial and financial institutions and their spaces of magnificent modernity, all of which we can define as an "Ego-system". These Ego-systems generate socio-environmental situations of toxicity that have a dramatic negative effect on the quality of life and health of the environment.

William Morrish: The authors of this publication rightly direct our attention to the critical work of "the people", deepening their civic imaginations in response to being expelled into the "informal" city. Once "the poor", this informal class is expanding through growing poverty and widening economic class segregation into "the 99%". This is the big group of people who struggle every day to fulfil their desire to be a contributing member of their city. I would like to reframe their collective desire outside the confines of the "formal and informal" rubric.

To seek this truly democratic urban society and city, "we" have to jettison the term "formal and informal". It has become an optical illusion — an aggressive political trope whose dark shadows hide the collective intelligence and churning creativity of the 99% in favour of what Andy Merrifield calls the "parasitic city". To me, the answer to this dilemma is to dig deeper and reveal what I see has been hidden behind the illusion.

In his book *For the City Yet to Come: Changing African Life in Four Cities*, AbdouMaliq Simone proposes that the "binary opposition" of the term "formal and informal" casts our urban society and especially our youth into a turbulent present, into an everyday environment that Henry A. Giroux describes as "a condition of liminal drift, with no way of knowing whether it is transitory or permanent". Maliq's work on African cities states that it is time to recognize the terms of engagement: "formal and informal" leads us to an outdated reading

of cities and perpetuates a state of eternal uncertainty for everyday people.

Another way to look at this dynamic [of the formal and informal] is to consider the ambiguity that ensues in the relationship between how cities are ruled and the responses to this rule in part of the majority of urban residents. For many urban residents, life is reduced to a state of emergency. What this means is that there is a rupture in the organization of the present. Normal approaches are insufficient.

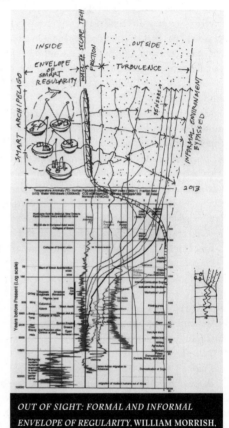

OUT OF SIGHT: FORMAL AND INFORMAL
ENVELOPE OF REGULARITY, WILLIAM MORRISH,
2013

Travelling through different countries, sharing notations with others at street tables as well as reading deeply across fields and places — piecing together a rich global library of texts and blogs and viral social narrative, I found a common thread. I found a collective desire to break free from the weight of our outdated urban terminology. These collective works reflect hives of ordinary people (Andy Merrifield's "shadow citizens") who have rediscovered the power of true citizenship in the face of oppressive austerity. In response, they have turned to soft power and become public scholars, edge providers and ground-truthers. I see my work as to give them a map of their collective urban work.

Henry Murraín I believe we are currently moving from an old understanding of "the informal" as anomaly and transgression to a more anthropological view of informality as the world of daily interactions inhabited by people. From a sociological or anthropological perspective, informality comprises the sphere of informal rules and informal institutions where most of the citizens' behaviours are displayed.

As Antanas Mockus' Bogotá mayorship showed, the key to solving many of the problems in Latin American cities depends on the transformation of informal rules of behaviour. From a public policy point of view, this approach has growing pertinence because the biggest challenges for cities around the world involve deep changes in cultural practices and behaviours, therefore in the informal rules. This applies to very diverse urban challenges like reducing the so-called ecological footprint, improving road safety or controlling adolescent pregnancy.

From the point of view of Citizenship Culture, formal institutions and legal norms are better understood as complementary to informal rules. Provided that citizens' behaviour is not only influenced by formal rules (the law) but also by moral and social rules, "informality" can be defined as the set of moral and social rules that influences behaviour. Moral rules are those internal principles that determine what is "right" or "wrong" for oneself while social rules are principles that determine what is "right" or "wrong" for one's social group or reference group.

Robert Neuwirth: Informal sector. Underground economy. Shadow economy. Black market. We have been imprisoned by the terminology. These phrases shackle spontaneous, creative action to the profit motive and the dark side of human motivations.

I have played my part in this festival of misdirection. I named my 2011 book on the informal *Stealth of Nations* — playing on the tongue-in-cheek implications that Adam Smith's invisible hand is the rule in the street markets of the developing world and that every transaction in these places is in some way suspect.

But being informal is not essentially about economics. It's not primarily about rational action and individual profit and loss. In fact, it's not really a market phenomenon at all. And it's certainly not criminal or out of the ordinary.

An unlicensed street market is at root a collective — a group of merchants figuring out how to grow their businesses together, cooperating and competing at the same time. Similarly, a squatter community (or as some NGOs say, an "informal settlement" or "slum") is, at least at its inception, a cooperative — a group of families determined to work together to house themselves in a world that otherwise denies them the possibility of having a home. A supply chain that, at every link, avoids customs duties and taxes is, in essence, a mutual aid network — a group of people who, through relationships and friendships

nurtured across national boundaries, find a way to achieve trust outside the law.

What we call informality is an upsurge of spontaneous joint action. This arena of human affairs is not dangerous and disorganized. Rather, it is governed by shared customs and the work is, in the main, done with honour.

So the merchants in Alaba International Market in Lagos may ask you for a bribe (they might call it "showing appreciation"), but will never simply rip you off. And the street DVD dealers of Brazil and Paraguay are upfront about selling knock-offs, though they may insist that they are super high quality "real copies". And the electronics wholesalers in Guangzhou might sell you a thousand useless fake-brand-name flash drives if they don't know you — but if you come recommended by someone they trust then the rules of the game are different.

Our system has difficulty acknowledging this primacy of camaraderie and shared purpose. The rich don't need these things. They can get everything they desire with their money. Those in the global majority, however, don't have that luxury. Community is their launching pad, solidarity their potential equalizer, the commons their shared stomping ground — and this is what informality is.

Kyong Park: In urbanization, the informal has been touted as a bottom-up movement that could counter the top-down dictate of "master plans", which have dominated the globe since the beginning of modernity. Extending into, or influenced by, difficult economic plights, the informal also symbolizes the revival of participatory democracy under the omnipresence of neoliberal policies (which are a marriage of convenience between governments and corporations that merges austerity politics with an unregulated capitalist economy). Here, the informal is associated with the identity-based power of localism within formalizing globalization, with the former representing the interests of self-sustaining communities and the latter insisting on a totalizing network system that is orchestrated globally. A specific example of this is the international food industry that ships agricultural products across the globe, forcing all of us to consume imported food, thereby diminishing the diversity of local production and distribution as well as extinguishing indigenous cuisine practices that historically reflected our environments.

But, is the informal really the opposite of the formal? And do informal activities only occur in the informal sector and never in the formal sector? Furthermore, is the informal a true remedy for all the ills of the formal, or is the informal just another master narrative of the formal? Can the two co-exist, and should they? Or, is the informal ultimately destined to be incorporated by the formal? Not only would my answers to these questions be premature and incompetent, I also think that these questions should remain unanswered for a while, as they, in their unanswered state, may have far more meaningful repercussions than if the answers were quickly revealed.

But for those who are impatient, I could mention that the rising level of the informal may be directly correlated to the rising division between those who "have" and those who "have not", within nations, societies and communities all around the globe. Here, the informal signifies the pervasive erosion of political states. People and communities of "have-nots" are reconstructing civic states, while those who "have" are perfectly content with the way things are heading. And, I hope that the informal is not the same master narrative disguised by new agencies of the old ruling class, but rather that the informal is beginning to master a new democratic narrative that will eventually incorporate the formal. Yes, the informal and the formal can, and indeed should, co-exist, but only within the spheres of the informal.

So what are your answers to these questions? And I am asking you very informally.

Alesandro Petti: Formal and informal should not be understood as necessarily oppositional definitions, but rather as two different yet complementary concepts, because one cannot exists without the other. Palestine refugee camps are formal *and* informal. When they first appeared after the 1948 Nakba, they were conceived as an emergency assistance to the massive expulsion of almost the entire Palestinian population of that time. Today, there are some 60 refugee camps located in Syria, Lebanon, Jordan, and the occupied Palestinian territories, with some five million refugees. These camps have been set up by state bodies following rather schematic and formalized layouts, much like military camps. The grid is a guiding principle for the establishment of most of the refugee camps, with a clear separation between the United Nations compounds with its humanitarian services and the rest divided into plots with tents assigned to refugee families. A short-term form of architecture, they are not built to last.

However, more than 65 years have passed, and the camps are no longer made of tents. Over the military formal grid laid out to control and manage the camp, refugees have built an informal architecture that constitutes the DNA of a new city. Today, it is hardly possible to recognize the old military grid, on top of which refugees have built new structures and spaces that follow a completely different logic.

Paradoxically, the prolonged exceptional temporality of the refugee camps has created a new spatial condition in which formal and informal are strictly related: on one side, the United Nations with its top down bureaucratic and static structure and, on the other side, the exiled communities of refugees with their transformative everyday spatial practices.

Instead of trying to oppose the formal with the informal, we should rather see them as operating at the same time, always co-present. In this delicate equilibrium resides the future of our cities.

Marjetica Potrč: The informal means accepting difference and otherness — in people, architecture, economic structures, etc. It is a form of tolerance. If formality is a box with defined sides, then the informal is the openings in the box. It means experiencing something you never encountered before, maybe never even thought about before. Something unexpected can happen — so it is full of hope, but also scary and foreign for politicians, economists and anyone accustomed to a more stable society. The informal thrives in dynamic instability. Is this chaos? Not at all.

When I worked on the Dry Toilet project in a Caracas barrio in 2003, we soon realized the barrio was a well-regulated structure. It was just regulated differently from the formal city. Instead of written rules, the barrio had oral rules. Community meetings were regularly scheduled, and issues were discussed and decisions made. The barrio had libraries and hospitals, only I couldn't recognize them at first; nothing told me this was a hospital. Here was public space in the making, not something given, which is how I understood public space before I came to Caracas. Most importantly, the barrios were built by the residents themselves. They speak of the urgency of the people who settle there, but they also reveal a life energy, the drive to build a life of dignity. I do not want to romanticize the often hard and inhuman living conditions there, but we have stigmatized the informal city for too long. The informal should be accepted as a workable system, which it clearly is, and as a system of values.

We befriended a family who had moved into a small one-room house at the top of the hill. By adding room after room, they ended up with a large two-storey house with an electrical pole in the middle, which used to be across the street. We asked the lady of the house to explain how the house evolved. She showed us around and when she came to the pole, she said that, unfortunately, it will be hard to build another floor, since it would reach up to the electrical wires. I love this story; the growing house shows how a never-ending intuition reacts to life's needs.

Intuition is the cousin of informality: we use it to make things, to imagine how we can do things differently, how we can live differently. We always want to make a better world.

Lorenzo Romito: The informal forces us to interrogate the limits of our cultural, political, religious and scientific preconceptions. It is about the often clandestine and spontaneous reappearing of what we do not want or are not capable of understanding or accepting. The formal and the informal should not be considered as two conflicting environments but rather as different phases of the same continuous process of transformation, deconstruction and reuse.

The informal has to do with processes and relationships that deconstruct or generate forms, before or after the moments in which forms become evident and accepted. It is a transitional dimension, both decadent and insurgent. We can conceive of it as the spontaneous feedback to abstract forms imposed on living environments, but also as the spontaneous emergence of new paradigmatic social forms beyond the control and reach of global power.

The impetus to refuse the reciprocity of formal and informal stems from a contemporary ideology which is focused on fending off any spontaneous, "risky" changes to the present. This makes our system fragile in respect of the future, incapable of learning how to adapt to what is happening. It is crucial to investigate the informal, to perceive in it possible emerging strategies for the future. It is important to give informality time and space to happen, to give it the possibility to shape new forms that can respond better to today's problems. Segregating, criminalizing and refusing the informal leaves us with less hope for the future.

Lloyd and Susanne Rudolph: German sociologists spoke of the differences between *Gemeinschaft* and *Gesellschaft*. Tocqueville contrasted France and America by finding in America the art of associating together. When a slate fell off the church steeple in France, he said, the parishioners wrote to Paris asking the state to do the repair. In America, the congregation got together to repair it themselves. When we first went to India, we were looking for whether and how Indians at the grassroots engaged in collective action. Myron Weiner, slightly before us, found that India had few formal organizations or interest groups. We found the country replete with the means for collective action in caste associations — to provide legal services, hostels near schools, etc., but most importantly, to participate in politics. The overwhelmingly more numerous lower castes brought about a social revolution in India via caste associations — by winning elections that put their people in power and using that power to gain respect, resources and benefits. (We described this at length in our first book *The Modernity of Tradition, Part I.*)

Saskia Sassen: We need to expand the familiar definition. The city itself generates informal knowledge because it tells us when something does not work (see my essay "Does the City Have Speech?" in *Public Culture* 25, no. 2 (2013): 209–221). But we do not listen or no longer understand its language.

Richard Sennett: For me, the "informal" is a structured process. By that, I mean it is a way of loosening the functional relations between people, making it possible for people to benefit from surprises and accidents, or in another form,

appreciating the differences between people which cannot be codified. The structural part of this definition means setting up architectural systems or social relations so that there is a loose fit between form and function. Nothing new is going to happen if the building or the social relationship is tightly defined.

I say all this because I do not think "informality" should be pinned only to the way poor people live, as a label for how they make do lacking the resources for a more defined, established way of life. The virtues of informality apply to everyone, or should apply. What is true, in terms of hierarchy and class, is that privileged people can take refuge in formalization, excluding a group below because it does not fit neatly into a fixed picture of how people should live. No homeboys are hanging out in the gated community; in this formula, "hanging out" is equated with lower-class. But informal knowledge is something any human being can and should acquire by loosening up. This is why I reject the equation, particularly strong in the urban domain, that informal = poor.

STEALTH.ultd: Informal is a charged term that we do not use with ease, as informality for many expresses a sense of betrayal of an expected order. It is mainly applied to acts that are of a fine grain and which make an impact only when amassed. Once you realize that the given order in cities does not provide existential conditions for all citizens, the informal can suddenly be understood as a domain of negotiation and democratization of space, even if it is unsolicited and often short-lived.

Jeanne van Heeswijk: For us — working on the Freehouse project in the Afrikaanderwijk, a neighbourhood characterized by social and economic marginalization in the south of Rotterdam and the first neighbourhood in the Netherlands to have a majority of residents with a migratory background — informality is about constantly renegotiating different urgencies and finding ways to create urban unions so that different forms of livelihood can come into being. These cannot be found in the dichotomy between

THE VALUE OF NOTHING. JEANNE VAN HEESWIJK AND AFRIKAANDERWIJK COOPERATIVE. TENT. ROTTERDAM. 2014

the formal and informal but in constantly walking the fault line between these two terms, working with ruptures in order to form alliances that can create greater solidarity. New forms of commonality and cooperation come into being through setting up chains of production that can generate locality — a process of social, economic and cultural activities that can operate on various scale levels. This collective production is about supporting the emergence of everyday informal practices while at the same time rooting them in stronger networks.

This is what we call radicalizing the local, a sensitivity highlighting the local as a condition rather than just as a physical site. It also refers to the space in your heart, the space in your mind, a space for sharing or "lived space", a social product that alters through time. This condition embodies both global issues and local specificities. It means becoming aware of the conflicts that stop things from thriving. From the different ways in which these informal practices are connected, new forms of governance can be developed.

atelier d'architecture autogérée: Informal means not determined by the prescribed, official or customary manners and rules but negotiated on an ad-hoc basis, between those directly involved according to contingent conditions and individual or collective interests.

The informal is the manifestation of bottom-up dynamics. It is also the manifestation of a diversified multitude. On one side, in absence of horizontal cooperation and/or top-down regulation, the informal tends to be excessive, abusive and chaotic. On the other side, the informal is always in danger of being hijacked and formalized; someone has to continually care for its maintenance. In terms of spatial and social organization (particularly within the urban), the informal expresses the rich diversity of individualities and micro-communities. This diversity should be in continual renegotiation with bigger-scale social and political entities and their normative frameworks.

As atelier d'architecture autogérée, we understand the notion of the informal in direct relation with that of "tactics". Being tactical is a way to trespass the prescribed and the official and to maintain informality at work. We defined our work as "urban tactics", referring to our engaged activity in the urban realm that encourages inhabitants to re-appropriate vacant land in the city and transform it into self-managed space.

Tactics, according to De Certeau, work with time and are opportunistic in their method; they do not "plan", but use their own deviousness and the element of surprise to get things done. Atelier d'architecture autogérée's tactical urbanism is different and, perhaps, in conflict with traditional urban planning. We do not "plan" but "act", sometimes without permission and against the rules that we consider inappropriate or unfair. This subversion involves inventiveness, time and passion. Tactics survive through their mobility, says De Certeau, and from this point of view, all of our spatial devices involve forms of temporariness and mobility: temporary occupations, mobile architectures, dismantling constructions.

We have been working with a particular type of spaces that we have termed "urban interstices": urban wastelands, vacant plots, abandoned buildings, neglected public spaces — all spaces that have so far eluded or delayed, perhaps only for a short time, land development programmes. We have negotiated the temporary use of these interstices, proposing activities that were not inscribed in urban regulations: gardening, recycling, cooking. Space is a high-value resource in big cities where land is expensive and scarce. Temporary use also implies that projects have a short lifespan and will disappear after a while. In the case of the ECobox project, in order to prevent this, we have produced mobile spatial devices to allow the project to move on to new locations whenever a site is no longer available. Many users have followed the project during its successive reinstallations. New users living nearby have also joined the project with each relocation. In this way, power structures have been continually questioned and revised: new assemblies of users have been formed, and new governance rules negotiated with each new location.

2 RELATION TO THE TOP-DOWN

How do you feel about the formal/informal dialectic? (Keeping in mind that these terms are often relative to context, and they often blur.)

Alejandro Echeverri

MEDELLÍN: PUBLIC ESCALATORS FACILITATE THE TWO-WAY COMMUTE FROM RESIDENTS' HOMES ON STEEP HILLSIDES TO WORK AND SCHOOL

TC / FF: *The next question deals with this "mystification" of the dialectic between formal and informal. A lot of people have argued that we must abandon this formal/informal binary, that this differentiation is not useful anymore since they interpenetrate each other. In a certain sense we agree with this but we feel that dissolving the binary entirely, and eliminating the categories from our thinking, we risk missing the essential difference here, between emergent and planned processes, and how often social and economic marginalization is connected with the emergent. Therefore, we need to be cognizant of the egalitarian clash between these two realms, and dissolving the distinction deprives us of a useful though obviously limited tool to describe the urban condition today.*

We need to resist an urge that has become prevalent in urban theory that borders do not exist, that they are dissolved by the "flows" of globalization. But for us, working in a border territory, while aspiring to a borderless reality, we are confronted daily with a concrete division materialized as formal jurisdictional power that disrupts the ordinary flows of human life, polarizing wealth and poverty. Of course, one need not consider extreme cases like ours, where divisions have been physicalized, to understand this point. Borders, like power itself, are often invisible and embedded within our norms and beliefs, our practices and our spaces.
So, in essence, we want to retain the distinction between the formal and the informal, but also be critical of it, which also has inherent value.

What are your thoughts on the relation between formal and informal?

AE: I think that one of the urgent spaces for innovation in the near future is the ability to build mediation — spaces of contact — where these dynamics, top-down and bottom-up, formal and informal, converge. But it has also been a tragic story. The obstacles to making these mediating spaces possible are the large distances resulting from preconceptions and stigmatization between one universe and the other, as well as the different paces at which they work, which call for different rates of flexibility. This has made it very difficult to construct these spaces, but there is no doubt that the key to approaching this question lies in dialogue as well as in the construction of potentially collaborative processes.

I think that one of the quintessential themes is the transparency of processes. It has to do with the concept of trust and the concept of humility. It is not easy to step down into a land where action is a collaborative effort and generates a conversation in a common language. Herein lies one of the most beautiful and difficult, yet exciting, tasks that exist in these convergent spaces — developing a new process of communication. The task that we all have — you, us — is to figure out how to build these spaces of collaboration between diametrically different dynamics that work at different paces and have different needs. However, in the end we all opt for a better place, a better city, and a common answer. But the ways in which these dynamics develop are completely different. The question consists in how to build that mediating space where different modes of collaboration and points of convergence can multiply. I would think that this is the challenge between the formal and the informal.

Jean-Philippe Vassal

TC/FF: *The reason we admire your work so much is that you might be one of the few, if not the only, architects who through design strategies involving space and the political economy of construction, have been able to frame the contingency of the "everyday" through a formal language. You accept informality and then frame and promote it architecturally, which is a fantastic way of speaking of the encounter between the top-down and bottom-up, and how they come together. Through our work with the informal at the San Diego-Tijuana border we have been researching urbanization as a phenomenon of top-down institutions and processes interacting with bottom-up dynamics. In your previous response, regarding definitions, you mentioned the limitations of the top-down approach to urbanization because it neglects a more improvisational, bottom-up agency and community participation in the shaping of cities. So, in fact you refer here to a collision between top-down urban planning and bottom-up social intelligence. Could you speak to this?*

JPV: There is a complementary question between the formal and informal and it is interesting to play with this situation because, contrary to the formal, the quality of the informal is reactive. It is adaptive. It is quick and intuitive. The formal, on the other hand, takes time to control and organize. There is a complementary game between these two situations that we can play as architects, which is exciting. We try to play with it in terms of economy, which is, today, perhaps the most interesting material. In today's urban situation and capacities, it is no longer about traditional materials, but the main material of architecture and urban planning today is economy. It is always a game to try to find the passage, your way. It is a difficult position for the architect to be in because these situations entail and redefine his or her relationship with the authorities. The architect is now interrelated with the formal but at the same time he or she is interested in working with the informal, which is exciting.

TC/FF: *While many argue that we need to transcend the distinction between formal and the informal, we have been trying to convey that they must be preserved as categories most often in conflict with each other. At the same time, we are interested in negotiating the coexistence of the formal and informal, as we seek solutions to persistent socio-economic inequality in our cities. How do you believe we can discover more constructive interfaces between these realms?*

JPV: When you work with the informal, you work with life. You work closely with people. At first we were interested in the question of housing, one of the most essential questions in architecture. Housing involves taking care of people living inside a space. Housing is not only about a house, flats, or villas. Housing involves the entire city. The city is your house. It is more than just museums, banks, or commercial centres (malls). We push the definition of housing because it places each inhabitant in the middle of the question. If you consider this, you can see that traditional urban planning is totally obsolete. If we consider democracy as the meeting point between architecture and society, then democracy is non-existent, because we are still producing urbanism like we are in the nineteenth century. In these last 30 years, urban planning has become more and more blocked and frozen. There were many more experiments that addressed these questions in the 1970s and the 1980s. We can look at the work of Yona Friedman, for instance, to revisit these questions of the formal/informal distinction and participatory urbanization. He argues, for instance, that participation is not the best word to describe this. Improvisation and using the energy and creativity of the people as a starting point are far more important.

Respondents

Mauricio Corbalan: In our context, "informal" does not provide a good description of the dynamics it pretends to address. We can say that there is an incorrect categorization process occurring when it shows up. This opposes the formal and the informal as separate worlds, when in fact there is a vast grey and contested area where many different collectives try to institute their own practices and languages amidst a state of uncertainty. Nowadays, urban ecologies are hybrid worlds where it is not easy to trace a clear bifurcation between state, society and nature, or between what is local and global; to describe these entanglements, we need to avoid the false conflicts that signify these practices in only one way.

So what do we need to catch up with these experiences on the ground? These processes, or modes of existence, produce their own set of rules according to which they are to be conceived, judged, expanded, and reproduced. We provisionally call them "paraformal" — a term with which we are trying to address these dynamics that are not against something (the formal) but cannot be described as an exception from the rule either. So we use the preposition *"para"*, which in Latin means both *through* and *towards*, to describe the iterations, trajectories and complex processes where the speed of organization and unexpected interconnection but also the steadiness of habits operate in a different way than they do in the case of the state and government agencies. This can take the form of inhabiting a site while making your own infrastructure, of squatting in order to gain access to citizenship rights, and so on.

Rahul Mehrotra: I think that rather than in relation to context, the blur between informal and formal happens, or does not happen, when you apply the lens of different disciplines. I think, in legal terms, the blur is probably more black and white than in terms of urban form where this blur is physical and often hard to differentiate. We often use the aesthetic bias and this is misleading — because what often looks like the informal city is not illegal but rather merely the landscape of poverty! I am personally more interested to extract from this what would be useful for us as designers and could be made operational to give design and planning agency. I think informality presents a compelling vision that potentially allows us to better understand the changing roles of people and spaces in urban society. The increasing concentration of global flows has exacerbated inequalities and the spatial division of social classes. In the context of this increasingly inequitable economic condition, an architecture (or urbanism) of equality requires looking deeper into a wide range of places to mark and commemorate the cultures of those excluded from the spaces of global flows. These places are not necessarily part of the formal production of architecture, but often challenge it. Here,

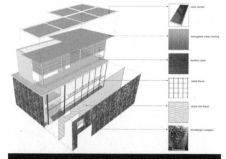

PROTOTYPE OF A COMMUNITY TOILET FOR THE SLUMS OF MUMBAI, WITH TOILETS FOR MEN ON THE GROUND FLOOR AND FOR WOMEN AND CHILDREN ON THE FIRST FLOOR. A COMMUNITY CENTRE ON TOP IS EQUIPPED WITH SOLAR PANELS, SO THAT THE TOILETS CAN ALSO BE USED AT NIGHT. (RMA ARCHITECTS, 2012)

the idea of a city is an elastic urban condition, not a grand vision, but a "grand adjustment". In design terms, a few characteristics are useful in extracting its intelligence in order to intervene in both the formal as well as informal landscapes of our cities.

The first is incrementalism — which is obvious and provides clear pointers for design imagination. The second is the ability of informal strategies to appropriate space on a temporal scale. The third is the notion of elasticity — the elastic nature by which form adapts to various conditions and its ability to create through its physical organization a sense of porosity — or what I refer to as the softening of thresholds in urban space. For me, this is the embedded intelligence of the informal, and if one recognizes these characteristics as being useful, the difference between the formal and informal begins to blur completely. This is not to say that this happens across disciplines. In some cases, it might be more productive to see this as a polarized binary, and that might be the product of disciplinary cultures. But not in design. Architecture and planning are synthetic by nature; they have the ability to create hybrids and blur this difference in space!

3 IMPACT ON PRACTICE

What operative role has the informal played in your own work? And can you recall a moment or a set of conditions that prompted a shift in your practice in order to address the informal?

PART OF PUI (URBAN HOLISTIC PROJECT), A NEW CABLE-CAR MAKES THE STEEPEST HILLS OF MEDELLÍN ACCESSIBLE

Alejandro Echeverri

TC / FF: *Let us talk about how the role of the informal has impacted your practice. Do you recall any particular moment in which certain conditions of urban informality produced a change in your thinking and procedures in relation to your own practice? A major topic for us in this chapter of a book on informality is how a variety of practices, from architecture to art, to theory and activism, redefine themselves in contexts of informality.*

Can you say more about the transformative impact that the informal has had on your architectural practice?

AE: Yes. It might not sound quite right in the translation but in my case, I have been "screwed" from the moment I was born. What I am trying to say is that I was born in Medellín in the middle of such a historic yet tragic moment, where the city was presented to us in such a violent way. There is segregation and other harsh problems to deal with in the terrains of informality in our city. So, I have experienced this in different ways throughout my entire life. What happens, though, is that sometimes we cannot see this or do not want to see it. In my case, I came to slowly understand what this city was about through literary works, such as those by Victor Gaviria, or the book *No Nacimos Pa' Semilla* by Antonio Salazar, which exposed this other reality and "language" to me. It was through this immersion, from having an intellectual perspective in trying to understand this other world, that I started working in the

HOUSE LATAPIE IN BORDEAUX-FLORIAC, LACATON & VASSAL, 1993

university, attempting to deal with the problems found in the north of Medellín — problems from which I have learned immensely and that have allowed me to build a more hybrid practice. I have gone from being an architect with a classic architectural training, call it more impermeable or narrow from an architectural perspective, to an architect that understands that the key to working with the city and its people has to do with building and generating more permeable, malleable, and porous processes and spatial systems that are able to incorporate a more trans-disciplinary work in its own process. To me, this is one of the great lessons that has allowed us to recognize and work with the whole spectrum of the informal in Medellín, where there must be a foundation in process and collaborative spaces in order to come up with answers and where the architect's tools become valuable.

Jean-Philippe Vassal

TC / FF: *Do you remember when the informal began to inform your practice? Was there a turning point or shift away from your formal education where you came into contact with something that made you realize your practice needed to shift?*

JPV: It was a while back, although I do not recall a particular moment. However, a good example is when a client, for instance, is pressuring you to finish a project. You finally have a botanical garden or green house in your mind, but in the end your client comes up with something that is ten or twenty times much better because it just uses space in a way that you would never imagine. There have been plenty of little moments like these. As an architect, It is really interesting to leave some possibilities open and be surprised by the outcome. This was the case in Maison Latapie, the first house we ever designed, but also in Palais de Tokyo. I do not know if it is exactly formal/informal but it is not so far from that.

Marty Chen: Throughout my career, I have focused on the working poor, especially women: as a field worker and organizer in rural Bangladesh in the 1970s, as an activist-practitioner in India during the 1980s, as a researcher and teacher at Harvard University since 1987, and as a researcher and practitioner with the WIEGO network since 1997. When I joined Harvard University, I realized that I needed to frame my experience and knowledge under an academic rubric: the obvious choice was the "informal economy" as most of the working poor in developing countries are informally employed. But I soon discovered that the informal economy was stigmatized in mainstream economic theory and policy as illegal or even criminal. Yet I knew that most of the working poor in the informal economy are trying to earn an honest living against great odds.

So, in 1997, I co-founded the WIEGO (Women in Informal Employment: Globalizing and Organizing) network with activists, researchers, and development professionals who shared my concern that the working poor in the informal economy, especially women, are not understood, valued, or supported in policy circles or by the international development community. The WIEGO network seeks to improve the status of the working poor in the informal economy through stronger organizations, improved statistics and research, informed understanding of informal workers and their contributions to society and the economy, and by creating an enabling environment. We seek most fundamentally to increase the voice of informal workers, to put a human face on the informal workforce, and to bridge the ground reality of informal workers and mainstream debates and policies.

To secure their livelihoods, the urban working poor need to be free from harassment by the police and other local authorities, from confiscations of their goods and equipment, and from evictions or demolitions of their homes and work places. To improve their livelihoods, the urban working poor need adequate housing, basic infrastructure services, and affordable, accessible public transportation. But as cities around the world begin to modernize, to invest in large infrastructure projects, and to privatize public land and services, urban informal livelihoods are often undermined or destroyed.

To address this urban challenge, the WIEGO network and our partners began a global initiative to promote urban planning and policies that are more inclusive of the urban working poor. What do urban informal workers need from cities? Some of their needs are sector-specific: home-based producers need basic infrastructure services for their homes-cum-workplaces, street vendors need a secure place to vend in a good location, and waste pickers need access to waste and the right to bid for solid waste management contracts. Other needs are common across sectors: all urban informal workers want to live and work

HOME-BASED WORKER IN THAILAND, 2014

in central locations, not on the periphery of cities; and they need affordable services, including health and education services; water, sanitation, and electricity services at their homes and workplaces; and transport between their homes and workplaces. They also want to be recognized for their contributions to cities and the local economy and to be integrated into urban planning and local economic development. Most fundamentally, the urban working poor want to have a voice in decisions that affect their lives and livelihoods.

MAP Office: We encountered the informal when researching the newly built infrastructure of the Pearl River Delta (PRD), and especially the superhighway between Guangzhou and

UNDERNEATH - THE SUPERHIGHWAY MARKET,
MAP OFFICE, 2003

Shenzhen, for the first Rotterdam Architecture Biennale, *Mobility*, held at the Netherlands Architecture Institute in 2003. Serving as a primary link between the factories and the port of Hong Kong, the highway is an efficient piece of urban planning in a booming region. Underneath this superhighway, we came across a massive open market that stood in stark contrast to the planned environment. Located in Songgan, halfway between Shenzhen and Guangzhou, this market was used by a multitude of workers to develop new social networks and was a perfect example of informal urbanism—a place for commodities to be sold, services to be offered, and food and entertainment to be consumed (see our chapter "Underneath—The Superhighway Market" in the sister volume of this publication, *Informal Market Worlds Atlas* (2015), 280–285).

STEALTH.ultd: During the end of the 1990s and the beginning of the 2000s, when we carried out the long-term research project "Wild City" on non-planned urban developments in Belgrade, the informal urban interventions that dotted the city (officially about 100,000 "wild" constructions, unofficially the number was closer to 200,000) looked to many like a massive chaotic attack on the urban landscape as we knew it. The sheer scale and messiness of the situation made it seem impossible to grasp this informal urbanism. Working together with Milica Topalović and Ivan Kucina, we soon understood that we had to go beyond how things appeared. Instead, we had to look into how things work. At that moment, we also came across Kevin Kelly's *Out of Control,* in which he explains the basic principles behind seemingly chaotic organizations and events in the natural world. We experimented with moving these principles from the natural to the urban world and, suddenly, we caught a glimpse of how to read this urban "chaos" in a much more profound way. This helped us to understand how a mass of dispersed, small actors could form unusual coalitions with larger institutional forces and have a powerful impact on the city. This has formed and informed our practice ever since.

atelier d'architecture autogérée: The informal is constitutive for our practice. It guarantees, through sequences of non-spatial and programmatic indetermination, the adaptation of architecture to mid- and long-term changes and to new usages and contexts.

All our projects start informally. They do not have a plan in the beginning but rather propose a vision: we know where we want to go, but we do not know how exactly to do it and how long it will take. The implementation is negotiated informally with all those participating in the project. From this informal instance, little by little, elements are gradually formalized: a programme and a group are formed, spatial devices are conceived and built. The project starts to take shape as it happens. At ECOBOX, for example, a series of pallet modules were built because people gradually claimed them: in the beginning, they needed a garden; after a few months, we realized that they needed a water collector; a kitchen was soon needed for processing the products of the garden; a mobile library and a media lab were desired by a different group of users who were not content with only gardening and wanted

ECOBOX GARDEN AND MOBILE KITCHEN, HALLE PAJOL, PARIS, ATELIER D'ARCHITECTURE AUTOGÉRÉE, 2004

other cultural assets. Our collection of architectural devices has grown informally in time, in direct relation to these emerging needs and desires.

We can say that many of our projects started with informal occupations of space and emerging uses, and incrementally, these tactics led to the creation of architectural programmes and spatial devices. This was a lesson to learn: how not to plan and try to design and fix a project from the beginning, but rather try to encourage some kind of use that may eventually induce its own kind of architecture. Not only the uses were important in our projects but also the users. They were important and influential in the decisions about how something that had started informally should evolve. We have also supported them in tactical appropriations. While the informal beginnings of our projects forced us to take the risk of losing control, they also guaranteed a very active and continuous participation of users in processes of decision-making, which eventually contributed to the sustainability of the projects. It guaranteed the self-managed dimension of our architecture and prevented us from occupying the arrogant position of the grand master architect.

4 INFORMAL AS PRAXIS

*In our introduction, we emphasize that the informal is less an aesthetic category,
and more a set of everyday practices. Can you comment on the informal as praxis?*

Alejandro Echeverri

TC/FF: *You mentioned earlier that you are interested in spatial configurations that are more permeable, different from the autonomy of architectural object, and that this sense of permeability has been emerging in your practice. What are some procedures or processes that characterize the temporalization of space and the flexibility, permeability, and porosity of the informal systems you referred to?*

We believe that everyday practices are the DNA that must reconfigure conventional architectural process. And this lies within the social and the informal. So, could we talk briefly about your interpretation of the informal as praxis and any related thoughts that come to mind?

AE: I think that there are some concepts that are essential to the discussion of praxis as a theme in my previous answer. But I am going to mention a few of them to elaborate. These are related to the concept of the "dynamic adaptable", which I think is absolutely necessary. As we say, you cannot show up with an already built toy. In other words, you cannot show up with a project that is already built, 100 per cent, because there is a need for a dynamic, two-way collaborative process. The construction of these projects, or answers, does not rest with a single author. And, surely, the author acts more as a curator in this case. Similarly, those who lead or can support these processes end up acting mostly as curators or co-authors of the resulting project. So, in a way, whatever gets built must have a great degree of constant innovation. In other words, it must be possible for it to be constantly innovative. It must be porous and adaptable in that sense. And I think there is one element that is fundamental to this, and it is quite simple. It has to do with learning to observe and listen. I think that, without a doubt, one of the keys to building processes lies in these two words, "observe" and "listen". We could define this as a transparent way of speaking and looking. We need to come up with a workspace that is transparent.

In our experience, many of the most interesting and effective answers (because this area of work is not theoretical but rather, it is through actions and hard facts that one builds processes) are found in local processes and logistics as well as in informal processes. We need to strip ourselves down and be open-minded, but be smart about it, and use our intelligence and knowledge to solidify and come up with new logistics and ways of working. We need to build logistics that can adapt to existing dynamics and needs. In that way, we really need to work with what we have — the existing footprints and fabric — and with the people who are already there. There is another element that is also very important: being firmly willing to change normative, legislative, and technical paradigms after being re-evaluated in processes.

TC / FF: *One of the main lessons we have learned from Medellín is how urban processes can be facilitated by what you have called the "meeting of knowledges". Could you talk a bit more about this encounter between the specialized knowledge of architects and the knowledge embedded in the informal? How a community's collective intelligence and social processes, sometimes mediated by activism and grassroots leadership, can inform the architect and vice versa?*

Does that encounter suggest the building of new procedures that can alter our practices, and prompt alternative spatial conditions and socio-economic organization?

AE: Yes. I think one of the most beautiful, or interesting, elements is building a space of common understanding between two very different contexts. One is part of an intellectual refinement of a more academic universe — let us call it "formal" in terms of practice. For the other, life experiences and the emergent are what form a basis for knowledge and reality, as well as a number of extraordinary solutions that diverge from the formal. As I said, one of the main themes is the ability to build a space for trust and a language that enables respect throughout the process, all in a collaborative manner. This is easier said than done. Language and vocabulary stigmatize. So I think that we need to begin by creating a language where we use the right words. When we sit down with someone else, we have to be convinced we can work with them because we believe in mutual process. And, again, this is easier said than done.

This only comes after acknowledging the "other". So, from my so-called more "academic" position, I must know and acknowledge that these local management processes play a structural role in many other things. If I do not know or acknowledge this with certainty, it becomes very difficult for me to partake in a collaborative effort where both parties bring something to the table. Same goes for them. I think that my university (EAFIT) built a very interesting space that has allowed us to navigate through works of real collaboration in the slums, just like when we were working under Mayor Fajardo. Today we no longer work for him but we keep leading these processes and have built a denser collaborative space with various local management communities and some local cultural groups. But that comes only after acknowledging "the other", building this space for communication with "the other", and really understanding the value of process.

Jean-Philippe Vassal

TC / FF: *The next question is central for us in this chapter. It comes down to advancing the discussion about informal urbanization by emphasizing the informal as a set of practices. Some of us have taken the role of interpreting the praxis embedded in the informal into new creative processes that can enable us to reimagine space, material, and economy. What procedures do you see embedded in the informal that have been useful in the transformation of your language as an architect and the way you conceptualize space, economy, and so on?*

JPV: Things start from a very small situation and grow, multiplying by ten or a hundred. I try to understand this growing movement. What I like about this, which I do not know if is good or not, is that I see no architectural form when I hear the word "informal". I only see procedures. They are procedures that move, develop, and extend. We do not know when they will stop. They can stop after 60 steps or much later and develop into something much bigger. There is no form. We do not know what it will be. One year it is something, another one it could be different. In the winter it could be different than in the summer. It is this idea of constant change. It is alive. It is in movement.

I also refer to the work of Friedman since we are in constant conversation. We always tell students the first step is the most important. Just make that first step and perhaps the second one will be different. You do not know. It is a system of improvisation. It is then that you will see all these things develop, but first you must take that first step. In the end, there is no façade. It is just something growing. The façade will be something one day and another thing another day. This is how the informal works. It is a movement. It is just space that develops, grows, and offers capacities and potentialities. Life takes place in it and social relations are made possible. As architects or urban planners we can take part in this, actively opening

ÖKOHÄUSER (FREI OTTO), BERLIN, 1987

up possibilities rather than passively staring at the process. Why is this possible? In many cases, the result comes from "sharing the minimum", which is not an interesting solution. What is interesting is to "share the maximum" — to open up people's imagination to other systems, platforms, and possibilities. I think this is the direction we need to take. We can help make the situation easier and friendlier, rather than trying to figure out all the problems at once. There is this fantastic building by Frei Otto in Berlin called Ökohäuser (Eco-Houses) where he developed some very big platforms, seven metres from the ground, sitting on stilts. These platforms opened up possibilities for streets and roads and for people to insert their houses into this framework. It is about leaving room for possibility.

When I was in Nigeria, I wondered, "What can I do here as an architect? This is much better than what I can offer." Perhaps the solution here was to just help open up possibilities, like building structures that are open to expansion through self-construction/owner intervention. We often forget some very simple facts in architecture. Take Corbusier's Maison Domino, for instance, as the first step. As a system, it is very simple. It is light and economic. It is "basic". It consists of four columns, two platforms, and one set of stairs that offer a range of possibilities as a single set. While this can be the starting element of a house, it can also be the starting element for a city. If we look at the city of Athens, for examples, it is a set of thousands and thousands of Maison Dominos on top of each other. So, there is an interest in modern architecture to open up these possibilities, and what is important is this possibility of "sharing the maximum", and with it, ambition and pleasure.

TC / FF: *When you gave a talk here at* UCSD *a while back, you mentioned that the major procedures that are important to your practice had to do with ideas of retrofit, alteration, and adaptation of environments. You mentioned that, for California, it was important not to build new buildings but to begin retrofitting one building at a time. We agree that this idea of adaptation is essential to the future of urbanization. It is not about "the new" or the typical tabula rasa — the top-down formal project that is driven by architects and developers at this moment — but rather, it is based on strategies of alteration of the existing city. So this question has to do more specifically with your work and your interest in enabling what you have called a "shared maximum", how to achieve a double economy of construction where you choreograph how formal spatial systems can interact with lighter extended environments that are achievable within the economy of construction, but that produce spaces where these extensions can accommodate the kinds of quotidian practices that we have been talking about. There is a variety of very specific procedures in the way you approach space, such as the Domino frame you already mentioned. Many of these architectural paradigms that want to accommodate informality focus on the "frame" and the production of spatial qualities that enable alteration and transformation, and in so doing are not preoccupied with the preciousness of form. Your architecture is great evidence that architecture does not have to be such a protagonist in an iconic way. It might even be considered "non-architecture" in that sense. There is a modesty and capacity to produce a space that incites and invites the social and economic activities that we are talking about. Can you share some of these very specific procedures that you use in your work?*

JPV: For me, it goes back to Africa where I saw people using very simple materials that were gathered from anywhere. There were both simple and more sophisticated ones but, for them, it was not a problem to use/mix them together. After I came back to Europe, I saw that materials were about particular situations, responding to a particular economy, and other related matters. So the question became whether it was more useful to transform an existing building or to make a new one. We had to work with what we had. This was what was happening in Africa. People were in the middle of nowhere and had to find the minimum of materials needed to produce something. And it is also like that in other countries. There is always this question of economy and efficiency but also the question of comfort and pleasure. It is important to develop places where life can be pleasant, accommodating the evolution of life styles, and where people can exercise their creativity freely. And we can do that through very simple gestures. We can do that with the fresh air outside, we can do that with sun or shadow, we can do that with light, and with the minimum elements to establish a pattern, in which people can run, jump, or lie, and if this pattern is already there, then it is unnecessary to make a new one. You would keep what you have. We try always to work with these very simple things and the question of economy but always keeping in mind the quality of space, shadow, and light, or the possibility to be close to the sun.

We offer possibilities of choice.

When we built the first house, we knew the client very well. It was very nice to have meetings with him and know precisely what he wanted. But when we had to make social housing in other places, we did not know yet who the clients would be. And you cannot build for someone you do not know. So at times like this, what kind of architecture can you try to do? For us, it is about the kind of architecture in which people have all sorts of possibilities. We try to make large spaces because we think they offer more available possibilities than smaller ones. We try to increase the relationship with the outside, with the sun and the climate, so that people can feel the air. We try to provide inhabitants with a sense of ease.

Respondents

Marjetica Potrč: I like to say it is inspiring and productive to share knowledge with people who think differently. So I was surprised that by working and sharing knowledge with construction workers in Soweto, South Africa — where I spent two months with my students in 2014 — I was taken out of my comfort zone. I was forced into an exchange between two different practices, between linear thinking and thinking in outliers — which is how I explain the rerouting of the working process.

The two kinds of thinking are fundamentally different. The Sowetans were thinking in outliers. We, however, were linear thinkers. When we built the platform in Ubuntu Park, we wanted to be efficient and not waste time. This was a concern, since we needed to complete the platform in time for the Soweto Street Festival. Themba Skosana, the construction worker we collaborated with, had the habit of "rerouting" the workday by trying out ideas we thought were unnecessary. For instance, we lost half a day when he planned the construction of walls on the platform, even though we all knew there would be no walls. I kept saying to him, "This doesn't make sense." Eventually, we realized that Themba's experimenting created a gap, a disruption, in the straight line of working, and this benefited the project.

NOTES ON PARTICIPATORY DESIGN, NO.18.
MARJETICA POTRČ. 2014

Let me explain these two thinking processes: Linear thinkers proceed from point A to point B directly, in a straight line. They plan things in advance and try to be objective in order to be more efficient. The goal is to save time. Thinking in outliers follows a curvy line, a winding path. It is subjective and involves rerouting, which takes more time than the straight path. When linear thinkers plan ahead, their grasp of the future allows them to move steadily towards the final result. People who think in outliers are more interested in the present. They create subjective gaps that reroute the path of their thought. They may eventually reach the same goal as linear thinkers, only it takes more time. The results may be different as well.

Maybe the most important lesson we learned from working with the Sowetans was to think in outliers: rerouting takes more time and can bring a different result from what was planned. We learned that both ways of working — linear thinking and thinking in outliers — are equally important. Ours was not better. For their part, our Sowetan collaborators told us that they learned from us the importance of the future — the method of linear thinking, which is based on planning ahead.

Jeanne van Heeswijk: In neighbourhoods that are undergoing rapid changes and are under huge pressure from the forces of globalization, everyday informal practices are often the only manner in which an engagement in these processes can take place. This is why we have to learn from these informal practices and look at the various forms of interventionist tactics they invent in relation to the "invisible design" of legislation and formal policies applied to the built environment. So it is essential for my practice to become part of the whole process of change in a neighbourhood and to embed myself with my skill set in the dynamics of the everyday. How can practices of the everyday foster a critical reading of one's own surroundings and an involvement in the changes that take place? This is a process of learning how to take responsibility for the creative potential of collective action offered by informal practices. It involves finding ways to reset the public value of urban space, to create an understanding of cities as a lived space, a shared space that everyone can change and contribute to.

5 THE INFORMAL AESTHETIC

Nevertheless, are there aesthetic potentialities that can be addressed?

Alejandro Echeverri

TC/FF: *This question has to do with aesthetics. Obviously, even though the previous question challenged the reduction of the informal to an aesthetic category, still, there is an undeniable aesthetic quality inherent in these dynamics. So, in relation to the ever-changing definitions of the aesthetic, can we reflect upon how the informal alters conventional categories?*

AE: I am not sure if I would call it "the informal aesthetic", but the aesthetic expressions (or at least some of them) that come from informal contexts are the result of a particular confluence. I would say they are more honest in a way since they are the result of a combination of the emerging need to respond to immediate situations and urgencies but also to the theme of cultural expressions and affection. At least in the case of Medellín and many other Colombian cities, informal realities respond to more than a single culture. Our country is vastly diverse due to the displacement and movement of people. People come from different places and cultures. And this has a lot to do with the combination of the city's pluralistic answer to the emergent. People will build the stage for a neighbourhood party with whatever they can find. People are wily enough to use what is available to them but they also tie their affection and memories into it. So, the nicest thing is exactly the amplitude of this very diverse aesthetic space that originates from what is essential and sincere.

It seems to me that there are codes, ways of building, and ways of representation that we can learn from more than we can teach them. I think that the main idea here is that we can learn from these expressions in order to build a new aesthetic if we want to pitch in. But we must have more of an open-minded attitude to come up with a new response to these processes. To me, more than a home, what we get is wonderful information that can be adapted or rewired in different ways. But I think the words that can best explain this are "the aesthetic of the essential". These words carry with them the nudity that one can find in the informal but also the beauty that one can find in these forms.

TC/FF: *Yes. That is wonderful as a concept. Which, just thinking about it, would be an interesting way to demystify functionalism, less with regard to an* Existenzminimum *(minimum subsistence level, Hans Meyer) but as maximum accommodation of social behaviour. What you are calling an "aesthetic of the essential" resonates with the way Chilean poet, founder of Open City, Godofredo Iommi referred to architecture as "the skin of human activity"? How to understand certain everyday behaviours that are related to use and function in relation to norms and the use of space, and their place in the construction of a process-based aesthetics.*

TC / FF: *Where do you see that aesthetic dimensions in your work?*

JPV: We do not focus on the aesthetic because we know and are confident that it will appear in the end. It will be there. So the question is not to look or search for it because at the end of the process it will be there, because the processes develop the aesthetic; and there is no reason for it to fail in the end. It is like that for everything. During the first years, we would sometimes get anxious because what we learned at architecture school said otherwise. But today, more and more, we are confident in the fact that if we just let the conditions grow, in the end we will have something that is clear, intelligent, and surprising — something that is unexpected and will be fantastic because of that. It is this kind of aesthetic that I am interested in. This aesthetic is never finished. It is no longer about producing masterpieces or buildings that will never be altered after completion. It is a living system. It is always alive. The inhabitants change and so does the system. It can grow, develop, and expand. It is this constant state of movement that interests me.

TC / FF: *This is the kind of thing that we are excited to generate from these dialogues: new concepts that help us to advance new paradigms of practice. The aesthetic as process is such an advance. In a way we can think of three interpretations of the aesthetic, when it comes to architecture. First, the aesthetic as an a priori set of moves that are imposed on reality and negate process. This is perhaps the more generic role of aesthetics for architects. Take Frank Gehry's napkin sketches, which are then deployed into the world, as an example. Second, there is process as the generator of aesthetic language. Take Rem Koolhaas in his understanding of the grit of the metropolitan and the programmatic juxtapositions embedded in it as the DNA of the aesthetic. But you are really talking about a third category, which is exciting, where the aesthetic is process itself: the encounter of form and the contingency of the everyday.*

JPV: I am totally convinced of this. And the processes do not have to be perturbed at any moment in the search for beauty. No. Just leave it intact and see what happens in the end.

TC / FF: *And actually, process is also embedded in what you observe. So, the beauty is not in looking at the finished product but looking at life as lived within the space and understanding the processes that enabled it. There is a beauty in observing the activity and life that the process has enabled.*

JPV: It is totally open. It is not "content" or "form" at that moment. Nor is it an idea that closes the system and refuses to open it to some new things. No! I think it is good to keep this system open and to keep the possibility of having the system be perturbed by something else. It always becomes richer this way. However, it is risky. It is not as safe as an idea carried out from beginning to end. No. It is more adventurous but also more interesting.

6 TRANSFORMATIVE URBAN IMPACT

How can informal dynamics (i.e., informal economies, spatial organization and social networks) transform our thinking about infrastructure, housing, economy and citizenship?

Alejandro Echeverri

TC/FF: *This question deals with the impact of bottom up processes, such as informal densities, economies and social networks, in the contemporary city. In other words, informality and its spatial consequences; how these systemic informal conditions can influence our way of thinking about infrastructure, housing and the political economy of growth in the city, and even our notions of democracy and citizenship.*

AE: There is a known element that has been around for a while that I think is essential to the informal. This element pertains to *incrementalism*. In reality, the building of a city, everything related to infrastructure, etc., is composed of "frozen" moments — more finite processes, which define the formal world. In the formal world, everything related to the building of infrastructure, urban transformation, etc., has codes and predefined timelines. The informal, on the other hand, deals with layers and the simultaneity of processes. The informal deals with the idea of reality as a progressive notion. You cannot point to a beginning or end. Informal space is really a living process to which different elements are constantly being added or subtracted. And I think this can redefine many themes and concepts if we start thinking in terms of urbanism and infrastructure.

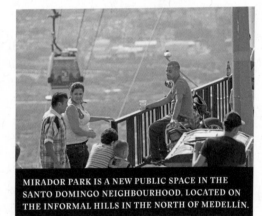

MIRADOR PARK IS A NEW PUBLIC SPACE IN THE SANTO DOMINGO NEIGHBOURHOOD, LOCATED ON THE INFORMAL HILLS IN THE NORTH OF MEDELLÍN.

I would also like to talk about the fragility of the urban fabric. I think that the informal has the ability to host multiple small situations and actions simultaneously. You could build a city or an urban system through repetition and viral actions. There is this concept of addition, a process formed by the aggregation of a number of small actions, which contrasts heavily with conventional formal infrastructural thinking. And it is this reality inherent in process that makes the mediating ground much easier to achieve. So, for this reason we find that it is in high-risk geographical conditions of the urban fabric, such as the hills of Medellín, where the layering of the informal thrives in negotiation with the topography.

NANTES SCHOOL OF ARCHITECTURE (ROOF), LACATON & VASSAL, 2009

Jean-Philippe Vassal

TC/FF: *How can these informal dynamics all over the world enable us to rethink the very meanings of the "political" itself and of democracy as conceptual systems that engage complex plural social relations? Mainly, when in recent decades they have been framed by the private paradigm of neoliberal economic policies and political constructs? What is the transformative impact of the informal on the city and its institutions, and new forms of economic development? Previously, we had a conversation about architects as developers, for example. We talked about the possibility of architects being more proactive in producing the new economic pro-formas that can enable more inclusive and democratic forms of urban development. A major focus of this book has to do, in fact, with the impact of the informal economy in the city, while much of the conversation in architecture circles continues to be about aesthetics for aesthetics sake. What your work has suggested is that, as architects, we can be the ones generating new economic frameworks to develop the city differently, and from which to reimagine infrastructure itself. Can you tell us more about how the informal can enable us to rethink the political economy of infrastructure? We are interested in thinking of infrastructure less as a totalizing, top-down intervention but rather as flexible system that supports the temporal dynamics embedded in the city. Can infrastructure be conceived differently?*

The other question is: Can we rethink public housing? At a moment when the benevolent top-down public institution of the welfare state, committed to the construction of social housing in many countries of the world has come to an end (hopefully temporarily), what is the role of public institutions today? The relevant role of public spending to generate more intelligent public infrastructure and housing is in hiding. So, we need to rethink the public. Through your work you might be suggesting that we can think of public housing through small scale interventions, as communities and architects become the developers of a new housing agenda that is inclusive, economic and democratic. Maybe we can argue that public housing today can be thought of as the aggregation of additive processes that need to evolve incrementally.

JPV: France has a very important organization that focuses on developing social housing but it is not very successful at it. They are not considering these questions. While there are many problems regarding the suburbs in big cities, I think the main question here deals with the people already living there. We cannot just build a project and say, "this is for you". No. Urbanism is actually a cultural question. It is a question of how we want to live together (and it is also interesting to see how artists partake in these situations).

There are many similarities between this way of thinking and the topics we have been discussing. These situations have to be democratically taken up by the population as a cultural question. We are not just helping people. It is a question of how we can build housing flats together. It is exciting and interesting to talk about creating democratic space and communicating this to people. It is a big challenge. It is also necessary to show them examples to make this network work. We need to show them what happens in workshops from Berlin to Tijuana. We need to look at these places simultaneously. It is knowledge for everyone.

TC/FF: *That particular question of how to democratize knowledge has been central for us here at UCSD, the university where we both teach. We have begun a series of efforts to connect the university with communities. We are interested in this notion of "knowledge transfer" that you imply. We believe, in fact, that one approach to the informal must focus not in defining it but on translating its knowledges.*

JPV: With the School of Architecture in Nantes, what we were trying to do is not a building just for architecture but a platform for discussion, debate, and information that could be open to artists and communities. This is why the building area is three times bigger. Inside, you have the school of architecture and the students and professors looking at what happens in these spaces of debate. And the total amount of work in there is three or four times greater because the inhabitants are invited to come in and read a book or look at the students' diploma projects or professors' research. It is this mixing of information that makes up this knowledge about space, and the city.

TC/FF: *It seems that movements and networks of young architects understand their practice and their engagement with the city very differently. But the transformative effect on communities on the ground seems to be equally dramatic. People want to understand their spaces and how they work. They want to understand the role of the city and their own role, their own capacity, as citizens. There is an amazing eruption of agency in communities when they begin to reclaim their own spaces. Have you witnessed this transformation over time working with community engagement and activism, and its impact on democracy in the city?*

JPV: The main questions remain. The question of democracy is so far away from the traditional institutions. We are ready to come up with something completely different. This is why the question of housing is so important. It is equally as important to be precise and work with these questions filtered by what we already have in front of us. We need to be extremely delicate and kind with the environment.

There is no reason to take away what is already there. It is more complicated in other situations but it is also more interesting and exciting and even more possible to be efficient. We need to forget the notion of the "master plan" and instead focus on small interventions in the city.

Respondents

Alejandro Meitin: Informal dynamics are experiments *in extremis*, produced by heterogeneous and multiple subjects whose actions benefit from the immediate resource and dialogue of knowledges. They combine different languages framed by a plurality of bodies to construct a powerful inter-subjectivity that enables, through radical and alternative approaches, instances of strategic resistance.

In order to transform our thinking through these dynamics, we first have to understand these types of challenges, daring to expand the limits of what we consider possible without falling prey to romanticisms and paralyzing interferences. Disinheriting the forms that condition our understanding of reality, we need to realize that beyond the world designed by the experts we have another vital reality in front of us, one that is disobedient and transforming. How can we express something fundamentally new within a known structure?

What is important is to cultivate the right to find new meanings and subjectivities in order to discover other forms of life, to be transformed by desire and action. This is not simply about a change in scale or perspective; it is about the possibility to develop another objectivity. In this way, we can integrate emergent movements in the collective experience of life.

Alesandro Petti: Citizenship is the political relation between the citizen and the city. Public space is the physical and symbolic manifestation of this relation. It is the site where political rights are inscribed and where they find their formal and figurative representation. Today however, this political link exacerbates and neglects the condition of the refugee camp, where enemy populations are detained or simply "taken care of". The "camp form" has complicated and transformed the very idea of the city as an organized and functional political community. The birth of the camp thus has the capacity to call into question the very idea of the city as a democratic space. And despite the fact that the "camp form" in its origin has been used as a tool for regulating the "excess of its political dimension", the camp as an exceptional space could also be seen as a counter-site for emerging political practices and a new form of urbanism.

Palestinian refugee camps are not only sites of poverty and political subjugation. Paradoxically, their prolonged political, spatial and social exceptionality has provided a context for the emergence of a different form of life as well as a culture of exile. Categorically refusing to normalize

DHEISHEH REFUGEE CAMP, ESTABLISHED IN 1949 SOUTH OF BETHLEHEM TO HOST REFUGEES FROM 45 VILLAGES WEST OF JERUSALEM

their condition of exile, refugees have opened up ways that make it possible to re-articulate the sacred relation between territory, state, and population. The extraterritorial condition of the camp, its new form of urbanity and social relations suggest political configurations beyond the idea of the nation state. Their subversive practices of being inside, but also outside, nation states problematize the very foundation of our contemporary political organizations.

The future of the refugee camps and their associated spatial, social, and political regime force us to re-think the very idea of the city as a space of political representation and to consider the camp as a counter-laboratory for new spatial and social practices.

7 SCALING UP

In what ways can the intelligence of the informal (at small scales) be scaled up?

Alejandro Echeverri

TC / FF: *Can we elaborate on this "aggregation" of local activities and small gestures, you mentioned before? How can these small gestures scale up? These are often the questions that emerge from thinkers who dwell on the macro scale of the city and are sceptical of the role of the micro, the local. We are asking: How do we problematize the interface between large and small, the planned and the unplanned, formal and informal? Is the informal merely a physical phenomenon, or does the possibility of scaling up also have to do with enabling us to rethink the institutional logics and protocols of governance, for example, or of civic participation processes, or economic flows?*

AE: I think it is a mistake to reduce the true value of small scales. I think that, at least from our experience here in Medellín, many of the city's greatest transformations really come from the systematization or construction of models or processes at local scales within local realities. At least, this is the case with the politically fragile environments of many Latin American cities, where government stability is not guaranteed and where the lack of follow-up to big projects is perhaps their greatest weakness. In this atmosphere, there is a need for replicability and the generalization of certain positive attributes that are built locally to enable elevating these transformations. I am a firm believer that the answer coming from these emerging contexts lies much more in the multiplication of small actions in local processes — emergent or not, formal or not.

MIRADOR PARK, MEDELLÍN

And I am certainly convinced that, in any type of urban action or process, sustainability results from the inclusion of local dynamics and participants. It is that level of support and its relational density that can generate projects, make them grow, allow them to be used, make them generate feedback, and guarantee permanence: that is what makes up the local.

I think that this is the question we need to ask ourselves: How to generate a series of processes that can be replicated and have an impact at a general scale on different fields. This is where the political can have a role — or top-down support in that sense. Unfortunately, there is a big void when it comes to understanding this. But I think that if we think past the physical, if we think about the value of processes, then there is a great lesson to be learned from local processes. We can justify recycling some of these concepts and using them in formal conditions. There are many formal processes that the city needs. We need to start incorporating spaces that allow for a dialogical way of building and that are more collaborative and dynamic. Today, the representation of the political has changed and the space of political power is now represented in some very strong ways by the micro. The local makes its presence felt more and more every day.

TC/FF: *This is where the question of evolving practices becomes even more relevant, as many of these new spaces of operation in the construction of the city need to be facilitated. Some of us become interlocutors between these scales, to produce new inter-dependencies, and collaborations. There is a space of operation for many kinds of practitioners to become mediators in the translation and transfer of knowledges, and to curate interfaces through which people and institutions at varying scales come to understand how these small actions can conceptually and operationally elevate themselves to transform the conventions of urbanization today, particularly the tendency to see the local as an obstacle.*

Jean-Philippe Vassal

TC/FF: *Let us turn to the last couple of questions, which relate to the impact that informal dynamics have had on the evolution of cities and how these small-scale dynamics are inevitably scaling up.*

JPV: It starts small. It is just one bedroom and then another bedroom, and another living room, and a kitchen, and a flat, and another flat, and another flat, and it

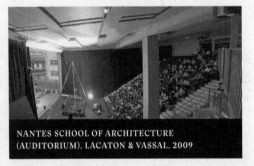

NANTES SCHOOL OF ARCHITECTURE
(AUDITORIUM), LACATON & VASSAL, 2009

becomes bigger and bigger. It starts in this precision/position, in this proximity to a human being, housing, and inhabiting. This precision/position is absolutely necessary in all situations — past and existing, countryside or in the cities, everywhere. We need this extreme precision at the beginning. And after that it is just the multiplication of these little things. In the end, the multiplication of these very small things can become much bigger than a single big thing that you try to control from the beginning. And it is always expanding. It is growing. To me, the city that grows and the possibility to develop what already exists can be much more ambitious than a huge project.

TC/FF: *To carry on from an earlier theme, about how bottom-up processes need direction or guidance from the expertise of the architect or the resources from a municipality, can we discuss how that convergence of top-down and bottom-up actually works, how scaling up happens, how the small scale begins to infect or infuse? What is the role of the architect in this? What is the role of the planner in enabling these dynamics to find their scale?*

JPV: It is also about information and being curious to all of these experiences, such as what is happening in South America. But it interesting to look at Berlin for example, where groups of architects are also working like developers but in much more interesting ways, making their own projects, buying parcels, working with banks, etc. In the end, the result is an extremely cheap, but quality housing system that is ten times better than what the traditional developers are doing. And these "experiments" are happening everywhere — in Johannesburg, in Berlin, in Europe. You have new movements where people and architects clearly want to create change, which is very powerful. And the resulting network is very efficient, and this is exciting because urban planning is absolutely obsolete today. We need to challenge it and change it. We need to think differently. Sadly, the quality of housing today is extremely low, at least in Europe, while in the 1950s really interesting social housing projects were being developed. Now, we just think about insulation, which results in flats that are starting to look more and more like jails due to a lower number of windows. Everything is defined not by the cost of construction but by the price in the market. The market says that you need to have small bedrooms because the more there are, the higher the price will be. The cost of construction is not the problem. The problem is adapting to standards defined by the market, which is worsening living standards. But we are willing to be ambitious and work differently. We are willing to propose better forms for life, movement, comfort, resulting in more affordable situations.

TC / FF: *Our final question is about this relationship between space and programme. When you talk about the Nantes School of Architecture, in the way you designed it to be such a democratic space that is transparent and enables that kind of fluidity but that is, at the same time, a space of debate. To what degree, as architects, should we be designing protocols and the kinds of curatorial programmes that can, without dominating, anticipate and guide social encounter in more intentional ways?*

JPV: The School of Architecture in Nantes is just a bigger Maison Latapie, a house we designed earlier. The question of housing, or living, is everywhere: living in museums, living in the city, living in libraries, living in restaurants, living on the border of the river. During the past 30 years, architects have been placed in situations where they lack freedom. Urban planning, programmes, economy, politicians, all define parcels and blocks, and on these blocks architects are asked to partake in competitions for buildings, forms, objects, iconic situations. There is no relation between this collection of economic objects and predefined plots and buildings. When we designed the School of Architecture in Nantes, we wanted to create relations with the exterior — between the inhabitants and the street and the rest of the city. In other words, we wanted to represent urban planning as a building. We drew inspiration from Cedric Price's Fun Palace, for example, and its intersection of programmes but also of seasons, times, and movements. Its vertical and horizontal systems allowed crossing people to debate, discuss, and observe. It transformed visitors into spectators. It was open 24/7. There was also an exhibition at the Palais de Tokyo that took these huge installations with more than 20,000 tiles to visualize nonstop debates, discussions, and meetings with people. It became a space where we could rethink the development of space and cities.

Respondents

<u>Saskia Sassen:</u> One key step is "open-sourcing" the neigh-
bourhood, the slum (see my essay "Open Source Urbanism,"
New City Reader 25 (Local), 14 January 2011, 2). Open-sourc-
ing resonates with what cities are at ground level. Every
neighbourhood has knowledge about the city that differs
from the codified knowledge of the centre-governments
and experts. The result? An *urban* wiki*leaks*.

<u>Richard Sennett:</u> This is the wrong question. We should
instead ask, how can the formal be informalized? It is a
question we should ask about fixed-function buildings
that tightly join shape and programme. We should want
to loosen this connection, so that buildings can evolve in
time. The same is true of people. Rigidly defining someone
as Latino or Black, or defining yourself that way, means
that the box of identity always contains the self. The glory
of cities is that people can acquire multiple identities, due
to the variety of things they do in a complex environment.
Their identities become loose in a city.

   Today, however, the city is becoming more and more
rigid, people boxed in by the effects of capitalism on the
city, segregating and isolating people into neatly-defined,
saleable pieces of turf. Misuses of smart technology also
tighten the city into a rigidly defined set of functions.
So to me, the question is not so much how to "scale up"
the informal, but how to "break up" the processes of
formalization.

Editors

Peter Mörtenböck is Professor of Visual Culture at the Vienna University of Technology and visiting researcher at Goldsmiths College, University of London, where he has initiated the Networked Cultures project (www. networkedcultures.org), a platform for global research on collaborative art and architecture practices. His current work explores the interaction of such practices with resource politics, global economies and urban transformation.

Helge Mooshammer is director of the international research projects Relational Architecture and Other Markets (www. othermarkets.org) at the School of Architecture and Urban Planning, Vienna University of Technology. He is currently a Research Fellow in the Department of Visual Cultures at Goldsmiths College, University of London. His research is concerned with changing forms of urban sociality arising from processes of transnationalization, capital movements, informal economies, and newly emerging regimes of governance.

Mörtenböck and Mooshammer have published numerous essays on contemporary art, bottom-up urbanism and collaborative forms of spatial production, including in Grey Room, Architectural Research Quarterly and Third Text. Venues where their research and curatorial work has been presented include the Whitechapel Gallery London, the Netherlands Architecture Institute Rotterdam, Storefront for Art and Architecture New York, Proekt Fabrika Moscow, Santral Istanbul, Ellen Gallery Montreal, and the Venice Architecture Biennale. Their recent books include Visual Cultures as Opportunity (2015), Occupy: Räume des Protests (2012), Space (Re) Solutions: Intervention and Research in Visual Culture (2011), and Networked Cultures: Parallel Architectures and the Politics of Space (2008). www.thinkarchitecture.net

Teddy Cruz is Professor of Public Culture and Urbanization in the Department of Visual Arts at the University of California, San Diego, where he is founding Co-Director of the Center for Urban Ecologies and the Blum Cross-Border Initiative. He is known internationally for his urban research on the Tijuana/San Diego border, advancing border neighbourhoods as sites of cultural production from which to rethink urban policy, affordable housing, and civic infrastructure. Recipient of the Rome Prize in Architecture in 1991, his honours include representing the United States in the 2008 Venice Architecture Biennale, the Ford Foundation Visionaries Award in 2011, and the 2013 Architecture Award from the U.S. Academy of Arts and Letters. From 2012–2013 Cruz was special advisor on Civic and Urban Initiatives for the City of San Diego, and with Fonna Forman led the development of its Civic Innovation Lab.

Fonna Forman is Associate Professor of Political Science at the University of California, San Diego. She is founding Co-Director of the Center on Global Justice and the Blum Cross-Border Initiative. She is a political theorist best known for her revisionist work on Adam Smith, recuperating the ethical, social, spatial and public dimensions of his thought. Current work focuses on theories and practices of global justice as they manifest at local and regional scales, with an emphasis on participatory urbanization and equitable economic development. She is presently leading (with Teddy Cruz) a Ford Foundation-funded study of "citizenship culture" in the San Diego-Tijuana border region, in collaboration with Antanas Mockus and the Bogotá-based NGO Corpovisionarios. From 2012–13 she was Special Advisor on Civic and Urban initiatives for the City of San Diego. She is Editor of The Adam Smith Review.

Authors

atelier d'architecture autogérée (aaa) is a collective platform founded in 2001 by Constantin Petcou and Doina Petrescu which includes architects, artists, urban planners, landscape designers, sociologists, students, and residents. aaa's practice enables the collective appropriation of temporarily available spaces by city dwellers and their transformation into a series of self-managed urban commons. This micro-political project has been carried out through different instances and locations: ECOBOX and Passage 56 in Paris, and more recently R-Urban, which started in the suburban town of Colombes, France. aaa has received a number of international prizes, including the Zumtobel Foundation prize for research and initiative 2012, Curry Stone Design Prize 2011, 2nd place at the Prix Grand Public des Architectures Contemporaines de la Métropole Parisienne 2010 and the special mention of the European Public Space Prize 2010. www.urbantactics.org

Martha (Marty) Chen is a Lecturer in Public Policy at the Harvard Kennedy School, an Affiliated Professor at the Harvard Graduate School of Design, and the International Coordinator of the global research-policy-action network Women in Informal Employment: Globalizing and Organizing (WIEGO). An experienced development practitioner and scholar, her areas of specialization are employment, gender, and poverty with a focus on the working poor in the informal economy. Before joining Harvard in 1987, she had two decades of resident experience in Bangladesh, working with BRAC, and in India, where she served as field representative of Oxfam America. Dr. Chen received a Ph.D. in South Asia Regional Studies from the University of Pennsylvania. She was awarded a high civilian award, the Padma Shri, by the Government of India in April 2011; and a Friends of Bangladesh Liberation War award by the Government of Bangladesh in December 2012.

Mauricio Corbalan founded m7red, an independent research platform based in Buenos Aires, with architect Pio

Torroja in 2005. m7red's focus lies on formatting complex scenarios and the "performativity" of regional networks by building up strategic associations with activists, "grass-roots communities", and experts from several domains. Since 2008, Corbalan and Torrojo have been actively involved in the clean-up of the Matanzas Riachuelo, the most polluted watershed in South America. In 2013, they launched "Que pasa, riachuelo?", an online platform to encourage stakeholders to monitor the restoration plan.

Vineet Diwadkar is an urbanist working at the intersection of spatial planning, environmental anthropology and critical cartography. Co-founder of the Spatial Ethnography Lab, he was previously a faculty member at the National Institute of Design (NID) in Ahmedabad, India, where his activities supported community-based advocacy efforts. Prior to joining NID, he worked with slum rehabilitation initiatives at the Centre for Development Studies & Activities in Pune, India, and with architecture studios in the United States. Diwadkar is currently a researcher with the Urban South Asia Project and Urban Theory Lab at Harvard University's Graduate School of Design.

Alejandro Echeverri is co-founder and director of URBAM, the Center for Urban and Environmental Studies at EAFIT University in Medellín, Colombia. His work has earned, among other awards, the National Architectural Award in 1996, the National Urban Planning Award in 2008, the Curry Stone Design Prize in 2009, and the 10th Veronica Rudge Green Prize in Urban Design from Harvard. As The General Manager of the Empresa de Desarrollo Urbano (EDU) from 2004 to 2005, and the City's Director of Urban Projects for the Municipality of Medellín from 2005 to 2008, Echeverri has played a crucial role in the rejuvenation of Medellín. With the mayor, Sergio Fajardo, Echeverri established public works programmes and initiated building a series of visually striking libraries, schools, parks, and community centres in Medellín's most impoverished areas. Because of these efforts, Medellín is now considered a blueprint for the future of other cities in the developing world.

Rika Febriyani is a researcher who focuses on urban development and change. She studied urban planning and has worked for several private consultancies and government agencies. For the past five years, she has observed resident interactions in daily life across various facets of the built environment, such as sidewalks, public lavatories, and bus stops. She has also designed a wide range of artistic interventions as a means of generating knowledge about spatial transformations underway in Jakarta, specializing in public art and interactive and documentary video.

Emiliano Gandolfi is an urbanist and independent curator. He is co-founder of Cohabitation Strategies, a non-profit cooperative for socio-spatial development based in New York City and Rotterdam. The cooperative's mission is to facilitate transformative urban intervention projects that bring together theoretical and community approaches to urban development around the desire for social, spatial, and environmental justice. Gandolfi is also the Director of the Curry Stone Design Prize, one of the most recognized social impact design awards, established to support design as a critical force to create positive social transformations and empower local communities.

Hou Hanru is a prolific writer and curator based in Rome, Paris, and San Francisco. He is currently the Artistic Director of MAXXI (National Museum for 21st Century Art and National Museum of Architecture) in Rome, Italy. He received degrees from the Central Academy of Fine Arts in Beijing in the 1980s. He was Director of Exhibitions and Public Program as well as Chair of Exhibition and Museum Studies at San Francisco Art Institute from 2006 to 2012. In the past two decades, Hou Hanru has curated and co-curated around 100 exhibitions across the world. He is a consultant for numerous cultural institutions internationally and frequently contributes to various journals on contemporary art and culture. He has also served as jury member for prestigious art prizes, including the recent "Hugo Boss Prize Asia Art" and Venice Biennale of Architecture (2014).

Keith Hart lives with his family in Paris. He is Centennial Professor of Economic Anthropology at the London School of Economics and International Director of the Human Economy research programme at the University of Pretoria, South Africa. He has taught in a dozen universities on both sides of the Atlantic, for the longest time at Cambridge, where he was Director of the African Studies Centre. He contributed the idea of an informal economy to development studies and has written extensively on money. He has also worked as a journalist, publisher, consultant and gambler. His recent books include (co-edited) *The Human Economy: A Citizen's Guide* (2010), *People, Money and Power in the Economic Crisis: Perspectives from the Global South* (2014) and (with Chris Hann) *Economic Anthropology: History, Ethnography, Critique* (2011). His website is http://thememorybank.co.uk

Jun Jiang is a research architect, archive editor and freelance-writer. He was the founding editor-in-chief of *Urban China* Magazine (2005–2010) and has worked as a project director at the Strelka School of Architecture, Design and Media in Moscow (2010–2011), a visiting fellow at the ESRC Centre on Migration Policy and Society of Oxford University (2011–2012) and an associate professor at Guangzhou Academy of Fine Arts. He has undertaken urban research and experimental studies to explore the interrelationship between design phenomena and urban dynamics, covering more than 200 Chinese cities and around 50 countries worldwide. He has been the editor-in-chief of books such as *Urban China: Work in Progress* (co-edited with Brendan McGetrick, 2009) and *A Village by the SEZ* (2010) for the Shenzhen Pavilion at the 2010 Shanghai EXPO. He was also curator of the China Pavilion at the Venice Architecture Biennale 2014.

Lawrence Liang is a co-founder of the Alternative Law Forum, where he is a lawyer and researcher. He has been working on the intersection of law, culture and technology and has also worked on issues relating to media piracy and the democratization of technology and culture. He is currently finishing a book on law, justice and cinema in India.

MAP Office is a multidisciplinary platform devised by Laurent Gutierrez and Valérie Portefaix, whose projects have been exhibited at major international art, design and architecture events, including their most recent project *Hong Kong is Land*, which was presented at the Museum of Modern Art in New York. Since 1996, the artist/architect duo has been based in Hong Kong, working on physical and imaginary territories using different means of expression, which include drawing, photography, video, installations, performance, and literary and theoretical texts. Gutierrez and Portefaix both teach at the School of Design at the Hong Kong Polytechnic University.

Rahul Mehrotra is a practising architect and educator. He works in Mumbai and teaches at Harvard University's Graduate School of Design, where he is Professor of Urban Design and Planning, and Chair of the Department of Urban Planning and Design as well as a member of the steering committee of Harvard's South Asia Initiative. His practice, RMA Architects, was founded in 1990 and has executed a range of projects across India. Mehrotra has written, co-authored and edited a vast repertoire of books on Mumbai, its urban history, its historic buildings, public spaces and planning processes. He is a member of the steering committee of the Aga Khan Awards for Architecture.

Alejandro Meitin is an artist, lawyer, social innovator, and co-founder of the art collective Ala Plástica (1991), which is based in La Plata, Argentina. He has been a member of an independent network of artists, critics, curators, and scholars interested in new ways of thinking about contemporary artistic practice and critical theory. Meitin has been involved in researching and developing collaborative artistic practices and has a number of exhibitions, residencies, and publications to his credit. He has also taught courses and given lectures in Latin America, North America, and Europe.

William Rees Morrish is an urban activist, architect, and Professor of Urban Ecologies at Parsons The New School of Design in New York City. His extensive urban research and professional design and policy work in numerous cities recognizes that infrastructure means much more than the highways, bridges, water systems, and power lines. It stands for the connective social and ecological tissue that loops people, places, and natural systems into a coherent set of urban relationships. It is a short hand for the structural underpinnings of civil society's public realm upon which a city's human and ecological resilience is defined. He received a Bachelor of Architecture from University of California, Berkeley (1971), and a Master of Architecture in Urban Design from the Harvard Graduate School of Design (1978).

Henry Murraín is Executive Director of Corporación Visionarios por Colombia (Corpovisionarios). Currently, he is completing his doctoral studies in the Human and Social Sciences Program of the Universidad Nacional de Colombia. Since 2002, he has coordinated the International Seminar of Research on Social Sciences and Political Studies at the Universidad Nacional de Colombia. His investigation is focused on the construction of cultural identity and the construction of social norms.

Robert Neuwirth has spent most of the past four years hanging out with street hawkers, smugglers, and sub-rosa import/export firms to write *Stealth of Nations*, a book that chronicles the global growth of System D — the parallel economic arena that today accounts for half the jobs on the planet. Prior to that, he lived in squatter communities across four continents to write *Shadow Cities*, a book that attempts to humanize these vibrant, energetic, and horribly misunderstood communities. His articles on cities, politics, and economic issues have appeared in many publications, including *Harper's*, *Scientific American*, *Forbes*, *Fortune*, *The Nation*, *The New York Times*, *The Washington Post*, *Metropolis*, and *City Limits*. Before becoming a reporter, Neuwirth worked as a community organizer and studied philosophy. He lives in New York City and does most of his writing on manual typewriters.

Kyong Park is Professor of Public Culture at the University of California, San Diego. He was the founding director of StoreFront for Art and Architecture in New York (1982–1998), of the International Center for Urban Ecology in Detroit (1998–2001), and of Centrala Foundation for Future Cities in Rotterdam (2005–2006). Park was also a curator of the Gwangju Biennale (1997) and Artistic Director/Chief Curator of the Anyang Public Art Project 2010 in South Korea. His work has been shown at the Museo de Arte Contemporaneo de Castilla y León, Kunsthalle Graz, Deichtorhallen Hamburg, Kunst-Werke Berlin and the Nam June Paik Art Center Seoul. Park is the editor of *Urban Ecology: Detroit and Beyond* (2005).

Alessandro Petti is an architect and researcher in urbanism and co-director of DAAR (Decolonizing Architecture Art Residency), an architectural office and an artistic residency programme that combines conceptual speculations and architectural interventions. DAAR was awarded the Prince Claus Prize for Architecture, the Foundation for Arts Initiative Grant, shortlisted for the Iakov Chernikhov Prize, and was shown in various biennales and museums around the world (www.decolonizing.ps). Alongside research and practice, Petti is engaged in critical pedagogy. He is founding member of *Campus in Camps*, an experimental educational programme of Al Quds University hosted by the Phoenix Center in Dheisheh refugee camp Bethlehem (www.campusincamps.ps). More recently, he co-authored the book *Architecture after Revolution* (2014), an invitation to rethink today's struggles for justice and equality not only from the historical perspective of revolution, but also from that of a continued struggle for decolonization.

Marjetica Potrč is an artist and architect who has been a professor at the University of Fine Arts/HFBK in Hamburg, Germany, since 2011. Students of her course "Design for the Living World" develop participatory design projects. Potrč's artworks have been exhibited extensively throughout Europe and the Americas, including at the Venice Biennial (1993, 2003, 2009) and the São Paulo Biennial (1996, 2006), and are shown regularly at the Galerie Nordenhake in Berlin. Her many community-based on-site projects include *Dry Toilet* (Caracas, 2003) and *The Cook, the Farmer, His Wife and Their Neighbour* (Stedelijk Goes West, Amsterdam, 2009). She has received numerous prestigious awards, including the Vera List Center for Arts and Politics Fellowship at The New School in New York (2007).
www.potrc.org / www.designforthelivingworld.com

Vyjayanthi Rao is Assistant Professor of Anthropology at The New School for Social Research in New York and has previously held positions at Yale University and at the University of Chicago. From 2003 to 2005, she served as a co-director of PUKAR (Partners for Urban Knowledge, Action and Research), an innovative urban think-tank based in Mumbai. Her work focuses on the intersections of urban planning, violence and speculation in the articulation of the contemporary global city. Her publications include *Speculation, Now: Essays and Artworks* (2014), edited with Carin Kuoni and Prem Krishnamurthi, and the forthcoming monograph *Speculative City: Infrastructure and Complexity in Global Mumbai.*

Lorenzo Romito is an Italy-based founding member of Stalker (since 1995, http://www.stalkerlab.org), ON/ OsservatorioNomade (since 2001 http://www.osservatorionomade.net) and Primaveraromana (since 2009, primaveraromana.wordpress.com). He is a graduate in Architecture at La Sapienza University, Rome (1997) and received the "Prix de Rome, architecte" at the Accademia di Francia VillaMedici, Rome. Stalker is a collective of architects and researchers connected to the Roma Tre University who came together in the mid-1990s. In 2002, Stalker founded the research network OsservatorioNomade (ON), which consists of architects, artists, activists, and researchers working experimentally and engaging in actions to create self-organized spaces and situations.

Ananya Roy is Professor of City and Regional Planning and Distinguished Chair in Global Poverty and Practice at the University of California, Berkeley. Her research and scholarship are concerned with global urbanisms, urban poverty and inequality, and the politics of international development. Her books include *Poverty Capital: Microfinance and the Making of Development* (2010) and the forthcoming co-edited volume, *Territories of Poverty* (2015). Roy is also committed to developing new genres of public scholarship. One recent endeavour is The #Globalpov Project: http://blumcenter.berkeley.edu/globalpov/

Lloyd Rudolph is Emeritus Professor of the University of Chicago, Department of Political Science, renowned for his scholarship on Indian society and politics, and the writings of Mohandas Gandhi. He received his Ph.D. in 1956 from Harvard University. He has co-authored eight books with Susanne Hoeber Rudolph, including *The Modernity of Tradition: Political Development in India* (1967), *In Pursuit of Lakshmi: The Political Economy of the Indian State* (1987), and *Postmodern Gandhi and Other Essays: Gandhi in the World and at Home* (2006). In 2014, the Government of India honoured Lloyd Rudolph and Susanne Hoeber Rudolph for their services to literature and education by bestowing on them the third highest civilian award, the Padma Bhushan.

Susanne Hoeber Rudolph is the William Benton Distinguished Service Professor of Political Science Emerita and took her Ph.D. from Harvard in 1955. She has served as president of the Association of Asian Studies and of the American Political Science Association (2003–2004). She studies comparative politics with special interest in the political economy and political sociology of South Asia, state formation, Max Weber, and the politics of category and culture. Her books include *Transnational Religion and Fading States*; *Education and Politics in India*; *In Pursuit of Lakshmi: the Political Economy of the Indian State*; and *Essays on Rajputana*. Rudolph also edited *Agrarian Power and Agricultural Productivity in South Asia*.

Saskia Sassen is the Robert S. Lynd Professor of Sociology and Chair of The Committee on Global Thought, Columbia University (www.saskiasassen.com). Her new book is

Expulsions: Brutality and Complexity in the Global Economy (2014). Recent books are *Territory, Authority, Rights: From Medieval to Global Assemblages* (2008), *A Sociology of Globalization* (2007), and the 4th fully updated edition of *Cities in a World Economy* (2012). Among her older books is *The Global City* (1991/2001). Her books have been translated into over 20 languages. Sassen is the recipient of diverse awards and mentions, ranging from multiple doctor honoris causa to named lectures and being selected for various honours lists. Most recently, she was awarded the Principe de Asturias 2013 Prize in the Social Sciences.

Richard Sennett explores how individuals and groups make social and cultural sense of material facts — about the cities in which they live and about the labour they do. He focuses on how people can become competent interpreters of their own experience, despite the obstacles society may put in their way. His research entails ethnography, history, and social theory. As a social analyst, he continues the pragmatist tradition begun by William James and John Dewey. In the mid-1990s, he began a multi-study project charting modern capitalism's personal consequences for workers. These studies include *The Corrosion of Character* (1998), *Respect in a World of Inequality* (2002), and *The Culture of the New Capitalism* (2006). Most recently, Sennett has explored more positive aspects of labour in *The Craftsman* (2008), and in *Together: The Rituals, Pleasures and Politics of Cooperation* (2012). The third volume in this trilogy, *The Open City*, will appear in 2016.

AbdouMaliq Simone is an urbanist with particular interest in emerging forms of collective life across cities of the so-called Global South. Simone is presently Research Professor at the University of South Australia, Visiting Professor of Sociology, Goldsmiths College, University of London and Visiting Professor of Urban Studies at the African Centre for Cities, University of Cape Town. Key publications include *In Whose Image: Political Islam and Urban Practices in Sudan* (1994), *For the City Yet to Come: Urban Change in Four African Cities* (2004), *City Life from Jakarta to Dakar: Movements at the Crossroads* (2009), and *Jakarta: Drawing the City Near* (2014).

Gayatri Chakravorty Spivak is University Professor at Columbia University, the first woman of colour to receive this highest award, not to be confused with the rank of full professor, which she attained at the University of Iowa in 1975. Latest books: *Other Asias* (2007) and *An Aesthetic Education in An Era of Globalization* (2012). 2012 Kyoto laureate in Art and Philosophy. 2013 Padma Bhushan. Trains teachers and guides ecological agriculture in western Birbhum, West Bengal, India. Current projects: consortial initiatives, continental Africa; Himalayan Studies, Kathmandu-Kolk-ata- Kunming; thinking globality together, French India

and Senegambia; re-translating *Of Grammatology*, doing a book on W.E.B. Du Bois. Member, Council on Values, World Economic Forum. Daughter of a feminist mother and gender sensitive father, entrenched in feminism across the spectrum and beyond single issue.

STEALTH.ultd [Ana Džokić and Marc Neelen] is a practice that spans urban research, spatial intervention, curation, and cultural activism. Based between Rotterdam and Belgrade, STEALTH investigates urban developments in South East Europe, starting with their research on the massive unplanned transformation of the city of Belgrade that began in the 1990s ("The Wild City"). STEALTH co-curated, among others, the Dutch Pavilion at the 2008 Venice Architecture Biennale and the 2009 International Contemporary Art Biennial in Tirana. In 2010, they co-initiated the platform "Who Builds the City" in Belgrade and in 2013 the association "City in The Making" in Rotterdam. Ana Džokić is a practice-based Ph.D. candidate at the Royal Institute of Art (KKH) in Stockholm. Marc Neelen is Visiting Professor at the University of Sheffield, School of Architecture.

Ignacio Valero is Associate Professor of Humanities and Sciences at CCA, San Francisco. He has also taught at the University of Madrid, University of the Andes, and Xavier University of Colombia. Valero was formerly with the International Center for Environmental Education, CIFCA/UNEP, and UNDP. He was a senior associate with the Colombian Science Foundation, Deputy Director of Colombi's Environmental Protection Agency, and a member of the presidential environmental advisory council for the writing of the new Colombian constitution. Valero's current interests include: affective capitalism, design thinking, and the society of the spectacle; biopolitics, neoliberalism, the commons, social movements, and post-growth globalization; the aesthetic, philosophical, and socio-cultural dimensions of "archaic modernity" in science fiction, anime, gender and sexual difference, mass media, and the economy; and critical and creative pedagogies. He is also working on a poetry manuscript, and developing a book based on his concepts of *ecoDomics*, the *emotariat*, and the *aesthetic(s) of the common(s)*.

Jeanne van Heeswijk is a visual artist who facilitates the creation of dynamic and diversified public spaces in order to "radicalize the local". Van Heeswijk embeds herself as an active citizen in communities, often working for years at a time. These long-scale projects, which have occurred in many different countries, transcend the traditional boundaries of art in duration, space, and media and questions art's autonomy by combining performative actions, meetings, discussions, seminars and other forms of organizing and pedagogy. Inspired by a particular current event, cultural context, or intractable social problem, she dynamically involves neighbours and community members in the planning and realization of a given project. As an "urban curator", van Heeswijk's work often unravels invisible legislation, governmental codes and social institutions in order to enable communities to take control over their own futures.

Jean Philippe Vassal was born in Casablanca in 1954. He graduated from the school of architecture of Bordeaux in 1980 and worked as an urban planner in Niger from 1980 to 1985. Vassal has been Professor at the UDK in Berlin since 2012. In partnership with Anne Lacaton, the office Lacaton & Vassal works on various programmes of public buildings, housing, and urban planning. Works by the office include a contemporary art centre in Dunkerque; the Palais de Tokyo, Paris; and the "Cité Manifeste" in Mulhouse. Current projects include transforming social housing blocks in Bordeaux Grand Parc (530 apartments) and a five-star hotel in Dakar, Senegal. Amongst other awards, Lacaton & Vassal have received the Grand Prix National d'Architecture, France, 2008; Rolf Schock Prize, Stockholm 2014; and were twice finalist for the Mies Van der Rohe Award. www.lacatonvassal.com

Matias Viegener is a writer, artist and critic who lives in Los Angeles and teaches at CalArts. His critical focus ranges from drones and surveillance, to public space, food, participatory art, gender and text. His work has been exhibited at LACMA, Yerba Buena Center, Ars Electronica, ARCO Madrid, the Whitney, Los Angeles Contemporary Exhibitions, Machine Project, MOCA Los Angeles, MOCA San Diego, and internationally in Mexico, Colombia, Germany, and Austria. He is the author of *2500 Random Things About Me Too,* and editor of forthcoming *I'm Very Into You*, the correspondence of Kathy Acker and McKenzie Wark. His work has been written about in *The New Yorker, salon.com, The New York Times, Art in America, Frieze, Art:21, The Los Angeles Times, Hyperallergic,* and *The Huffington Post,* and he is a 2013 Creative Capital award recipient.

The *Informal Market Worlds Reader* is part of a two-volume publication. Together with the *Informal Market Worlds Atlas*, it presents the outcomes of a multi-year and multi-sited research project based at the Institute of Art and Design at the Vienna University of Technology and conducted in collaboration with the Visual Cultures Department at Goldsmiths College, University of London as well as the Center for Urban Ecologies and the Center on Global Justice at the University of California San Diego (UCSD) and Hong Kong University's Shanghai Study Centre.

ACKNOWLEDGEMENTS

This publication has been made possible by the generous support of the following institutions:
Austrian Science Fund (FWF): P 22809-G17
Goldsmiths College, University of London
University of California San Diego, Center for Urban Ecology
    and Center on Global Justice
University of Hong Kong, Shanghai Study Centre
Vienna University of Technology, School of Architecture
    and Planning

PUBLICATION

Editors
    Peter Mörtenböck and Helge Mooshammer
    with Teddy Cruz and Fonna Forman
Translations and copy editing
    Joseph O'Donnell
Editorial assistance
    Aaron Cotkin, Jose Escamilla
Cover image
    Peter Vlam
Design
    Studio Joost Grootens / Joost Grootens,
    Tine van Wel, Silke Koeck
Printing and lithography
    NPN Drukkers, Breda
Paper
    Cyclus Offset, 90 grs
Typeface
    Stanley by Ludovic Balland (www.optimo.ch)
Publisher
    Eelco van Welie, nai010 publishers, Rotterdam

nai010 publishers is an internationally orientated publisher specialized in developing, producing and distributing books on architecture, visual arts and related disciplines. www.nai010.com

nai010 books are available internationally at selected bookstores and from the following distribution partners:
North, Central and South America – Artbook | D.A.P., New York, USA, dap@dapinc.com
Rest of the world – Idea Books, Amsterdam, the Netherlands, idea@ideabooks.nl

For general questions, please contact nai010 publishers directly at sales@nai010.com or visit our website www.nai010.com for further information.

Printed and bound in the Netherlands

ISBN 978-94-6208-195-6